SMOKING
Individual Differences, Psychopathology, and Emotion

David G. Gilbert
Department of Psychology
Southern Illinois University
Carbondale, Illinois

Taylor & Francis
Publishers since 1798

USA	Publishing Office:	Taylor & Francis
		1101 Vermont Avenue, N.W., Suite 200
		Washington, DC 20005-3521
		Tel: (202) 289-2174
		Fax: (202) 289-3665
	Distribution Center:	Taylor & Francis
		1900 Frost Road, Suite 101
		Bristol, PA 19007-1598
		Tel: (215) 785-5800
		Fax: (215) 785-5515
UK		Taylor & Francis Ltd.
		4 John St.
		London WC1N 2ET
		Tel: 071 405 2237
		Fax: 071 831 2035

SMOKING: Individual Differences, Psychopathology, and Emotion

1 2 3 4 5 6 7 8 9 0   B R B R   9 8 7 6 5

This book was set in Times Roman by Harlowe Typography, Inc. The editors were Kathleen P. Baker and Holly Seltzer. Cover design by Michelle M. Fleitz. Prepress supervisor was Miriam Gonzalez. Printing and binding by Braun-Brumfield, Inc.

A CIP catalog record for this book is available from the British Library.
♾ The paper in this publication meets the requirements of the ANSI Standard Z39.48-1984 (Permanence of Paper)

Library of Congress Cataloging-in-Publication Data
Gilbert, David G., date
   Smoking: individual difference, psychopathology, and emotion / by
David G. Gilbert
      p. cm. — (The Series in health psychology and behavioral
medicine)
   Includes bibliographical references.

   1. Smoking—Psychological aspects.   2. Individual differences.
3. Nicotine—Physiological effect.   4. Tobacco—Psychological
aspects.   5. Psychopathology.   6. Emotions.   I. Title   II. Series.
   [DNLM: 1. Smoking—psychology.   2. Individuality.
3. Psychopathology.   4. Emotions.   WM 176 G464s 1995]
BF789.S6G55   1995
616.86'5'001—dc20
DNLM/DLC
for Library of Congress

94-46759
CIP

ISBN 1-56032-171-7✓
ISSN 8756-467X

Dedicated to my family

With love to
Brenda
Aline
Elizabeth
Naomi and Wyn
Sandra Stephen

and to others who have helped me grow and grow this book: HJE, RLH, WB,

RAJ, TK, JER, JHR, WP, VJK, RW, CDS, KOC, MW, MM, MK, JWF, RP,

SF, LCP, AR, SH, NR, SE, TS, KC, JM, HD, JG, HB, SC, JMG,

RO, PP, OFP, CJM, SM, CLM, SM, SS, DM, HD, HB, DM, MR,

MG, MK, SW, SS, JAG, GW, SD, WPG, BBG, CG, SIIG, JG, FG,

MG, SG, JG, DG, GG, DJKB.

Contents

                Characterization of Affective Processes   39
                Biological Bases of Affect   49
                Conclusions   58

CHAPTER 4   Personality, Temperament, and Psychopathology   61

                Personality   62
                A Person × Situation Evolutionary Model of Personality
                Development and Psychopathology   76
                Psychopathology   76
                Summary and Integration   82

CHAPTER 5   Evidence of Affect Modulation, Performance
                Enhancement, and Reinforcement by Nicotine   85

                Self-Reported (Smoker-Attributed) Smoking Affect
                Modulation and Performance Enhancement   86
                Affect During Tobacco Abstinence and Nicotine
                Replacement   88
                Laboratory Studies of Affect Modulation by Smoking
                and Nicotine   100
                Cognition and Performance Modulation and
                Enhancement   117
                Conclusions and Recommendations   121

CHAPTER 6   Mechanisms Underlying Nicotine's Reinforcing
                and Affect-Modulating Effects   123

                CNS Hedonic and Reinforcement Systems Models   124
                Mechanisms Underlying Negative-Affect-Reducing
                Effects   130
                Summary and Conclusions   147

CHAPTER 7   Personality, Psychopathology, Tobacco Use, and
                Individual Differences in Effects of Nicotine   149

                Individual Differences and Tobacco Use   149
                Mechanisms and Causal Pathways Underlying Tobacco's

Foreword

There is a huge literature on smoking; having battled with the flood I know how difficult it is to keep it at bay. One problem is the multiplicity of disciplines (and journals!) involved. Chemistry, biology, psychology, psychophysiology, personality study, emotion, psychopathology—the list is endless. Yet no proper understanding is possible unless all these avenues are explored. They are not independent, but hang together and mutually influence, affect, and determine each other. Only a polymath could have written a book that judiciously combines these specialities, and David Gilbert has succeeded admirably in a task that many might have considered impossible of achievement.

Advances in scientific understanding often depend on learning what are the right questions to ask. Investigators started out asking impossible questions like, "Why do people smoke?" As Gilbert documents, we have learned since to ask more meaningful questions such as, "In whom, after what dose history, in what circumstances, does what dose of nicotine result in what type of affect-modulating and reinforcing effect?" An unanswerable "why" question is changed into a "how" question that can in principle be answered, and which, as Gilbert states, has already received at least partial answers that begin to hang together. There is still much noise in the system, but at least we are beginning to realize what aspects of the experimental situations have to be included, controlled, or modulated. We are in the process to realize the interdependence of personality, situation, genetics, personal history, psychophysiological make-up, and motivational-emotional factors; this should enable us to produce better experiments and more trustworthy replicable results.

The practical results could be spectacular. Attempts to stop smoking are one of the disaster areas of psychology, together with sexual impotence and other complex psychophysiological problems. Success is dependent on a better understanding of what is going on when a person lights up a cigarette, and smokes it. Simple univariate studies will never give us a proper answer; however difficult it may be, a multivariate process of investigation is indispensable.

Gilbert's STAR model of smoking (Situation × Trait Adaptive Response) lays down the essential features such a model requires. He cleverly uses the vast literature to help in putting flesh on the skeleton of the model, and there can be no doubt that at present this is the best overall model available. It is thus useful in bringing together the unruly mass of thousands of empirical studies in a meaningful, coordinated way; it is potentially even more useful in giving directions to future research efforts. On both grounds, this is a milestone in the history of smoking research, and no one engaged in research in this field, or generally concerned with the effects of smoking, can afford to ignore it.

H. J. Eysenck, Ph.D., D.Sc.
Professor Emeritus of Psychology
Institute of Psychiatry
University of London

Preface

The editors of a special issue of the *British Journal of Addiction* on future directions in tobacco research (West & Grunberg, 1991) concluded that a more sophisticated multidimensional view of dependence and smoking behavior than that presented in the Surgeon General's 1988 Report (USDHHS, 1988) and other current theoretical articles needs to be developed. There is growing consensus that such an account should include individual differences in personality traits and personal needs, as well as environmental factors. This book is an attempt to develop an empirically based model that reflects the multidimensional, individual-difference-related, causal paths associated with smoking and its reinforcing and affect-modulating effects. Personality, psychopathology, and emotional factors are intimately related to each other and to smoking, yet there are few efforts to integrate relevant findings in these areas. A body of work by H. J. Eysenck (1965; 1980) stands out as the major effort to integrate smoking, personality, and stress. However, the explosion of new information in recent years is yet to be incorporated into an integrative model. Relative to Eysenck's personality-model-driven approach, this text takes a more comprehensive, current, and detailed view of mechanisms mediating relations between smoking and individual differences. This book stands on the shoulders of the hundreds of scientists who have made major contributions to the fields of smoking, psychopharmacology, personality, psychopathology, and behavior.

Who cannot be interested in emotion, personality, and psychopathology? Emotions and affective processes are related to those things we value. Personality is related to the uniqueness and individual differences that set each of us apart. Psychopathology is something we hope to avoid, yet most of us can relate to it one way or another. Moreover, the exploration of smoking's relationships to these pervasive, essential factors draws attention to common influential mechanisms, innovative new hypotheses, and potential treatments. This exploration has greatly enriched my thinking and provided direction for future research and clinical interventions.

This book is written with the conviction that smoking, like most human behaviors, is multiply determined and best understood from an integrated biopsychosocial perspective. My adoption of a biopsychosocial situation by trait-profile model is based on the view that such a comprehensive and integrative view is required for anything approximating a complete understanding of individual differences in smoking behavior. The fields of smoking research and intervention have grown dramatically during the last two decades, and professionals from a wide spectrum of disciplines have contributed to our knowledge of smoking. Nonetheless, few scientists have comprehensively addressed the major questions of: (a) why some individuals smoke while others do not; (b) why some individuals experience great difficulty in abstaining from smoking while others quit with relative ease; and (c) what mechanisms mediate situational and individual differences in psychological and behavioral responses to nicotine and smoking.

The book starts with a review of models of smoking motivation, then sets the foundation for subsequent integrative discussions with two chapters: one reviewing affect and emotion, and the other reviewing the nature, biological basis, and relationships among personality, temperament, and psychopathology. The last few decades have seen many important new developments in the fields of emotion and affect, personality, and psychopathology. Thus, it is no surprise that few have been able to keep abreast of the progress in each of these areas. It is expected that for a vast majority of readers, the early chapters will facilitate an understanding of concepts provided in later chapters that deal more exclusively with smoking. By juxtaposing smoking motivation with personality, psychopathology, and emotional theory, common mechanisms as well as new questions and syntheses arise.

The middle set of four chapters addresses: evidence of affect modulation, performance enhancement, and reinforcement by smoking and nicotine (Chapter 5); biological and psychological mechanisms underlying affect-modulating, performance-enhancing, and reinforcing effects of nicotine and smoking (Chapter 6); personality, psychopathology, tobacco use and the effects of nicotine (Chapter 7); and gender differences in smoking and effects of nicotine (Chapter 8). These chapters focus attention on questions of when, in whom, and what mechanisms promote and reinforce smoking and tobacco use.

Chapter 9 presents an integrative biopsychosocial Situation × Trait Adaptive Response (STAR) model of smoking effects and motivation. The mechanisms and findings articulated in preceding chapters are synthesized into a set of propositions and corollaries that relate individual differences to mechanisms which mediate smoking reinforcement and affect modulation.

This book concludes with a chapter titled "Implications of the Biopsychosocial Situation × Trait Adaptive Response Model for Smoking Interventions." It is argued that the relative ineffectiveness of contemporary smoking cessation interventions is due in significant part to their ignoring individual differences in situations and traits. To correct this shortcoming, an individualized cognitive-behavioral approach is proposed. This approach includes careful assessment of individual differences in temperament-based personality and educational and intellectual dimensions, as well as more proximal and recent-learning-based, middle-level, cognitive and behavioral traits. Great value is seen in combining traditional-trait and syndromal approaches with more cognitive-behavioral, idiographic approaches in smoking assessment and intervention.

As the percentage of smokers in the general population decreases, a growing percentage of those continuing to smoke will be high in psychopathology, social alienation, and related factors associated with treatment failure. A theory of smoking that neglects the roles of individual differences in personality, psychopathology, and middle-level traits such as expectations, goals, and learning and conditioning is neither complete nor adequate. It is argued that smoking cessation interventions that ignore such differences are doomed to poor long-term outcomes, especially among the growing hard-core smokers. Individualized interventions may cost more initially, but the greater efficacy of such interventions is likely to more than offset this cost. Furthermore, individualized interventions are designed to be beneficial to the individual not only by promoting abstinence, but by enhancing quality of life by increasing psychological coping efficacy and reducing negative affect and psychopathology.

Although public health campaigns have cut the prevalence of smoking substantially in the general U.S. population, interventions have generally failed with a number of groups, especially those high in psychopathology, alienation, impulsivity, and related personality traits. Such individuals appear to require more individualized and intensive interventions, some of which are suggested in the book's concluding chapter.

David G. Gilbert

Acknowledgments

I am grateful above all to my wife, Brenda Gilbert, for her support over the years in this effort. Her nurturance, love, and helpful comments were essential to the completion of the manuscript. She did these things and many more while carrying on her own career, attending multiple weekly music lessons, sporting events, and related functions to support our family. I love and thank you! My appreciation also goes to my daughters, Aline Marie and Elizabeth Ann, whose company I so enjoy. You helped me with this book by teaching me about personality and temperament, by having such good temperaments and person-alities, and by being the so many good things that each of you are.

I also appreciate the valuable comments from two faculty members at South-ern Illinois University at Carbondale: Dr. David DiLalla and Dr. Susan Labott, for their comments on Chapters 4, and 3, respectively. Also, I thank the research assistants working in my smoking and psychophysiology laboratory at SIUC who received less of my attention than I would have liked or they deserved while I wrote the manuscript. Moreover, they helped in numerous ways to put the book together, from proofreading to tracking down references.

I thank Professor Charles D. Spielberger, who has facilitated my career in a number of important ways over the years. Finally, I thank the editors who helped me polish, further integrate, and publish this volume.

Chapter 1

Introduction and Overview: Smoking's Relationship to Individual Differences, Psychopathology, and Emotion

WHY INDIVIDUAL DIFFERENCES, PSYCHOPATHOLOGY, AND EMOTION NOW?

The 1988 Surgeon General's report (or SGR, U.S. Department of Health and Human Services [USDHHS], 1988) proclaiming smoking to be an addiction "similar to heroin and cocaine" (p. 9) was followed by an explosion of research on the individual differences, the psychopathology, and emotional processes associated with smoking. The 1988 SGR assessed relationships of smoking with stress, coping, and affect but gave little attention to individual differences in personality and psychopathology associated with smoking and devoted only a few sentences to genetic factors associated with smoking. U. S. congressional hearings on whether smoking is addictive and whether cigarettes should be further regulated received a great deal of press during April 1994. The front cover of the April 18, 1994, *Time* magazine depicted a smoker with a dozen guns aimed at his head and the caption *"Is It All Over for Smokers? The Battle Against Tobacco Is Turning Into a Rout"* (Farley, 1994). Members of the House of Representatives attacked tobacco, saying that it was spiked with added nicotine so as to ensure that smokers became hooked. In contrast, tobacco industry executives countered by saying that tobacco can be considered addictive only under a very liberal definition of addiction that includes things such as coffee. James W. Johnson, chairman and CEO of R. J. Reynolds Tobacco Company, told a House subcommittee that nicotine is not addictive and that "the allegation that smoking cigarettes is addictive is part of a growing and disturbing trend that has destroyed the meaning of the term, by characterizing virtually any enjoyable activity as addictive, whether it is eating sweets, drinking coffee, playing video games or watching TV" (Shapiro, 1994, p. A4). These debates have rarely included discussion of individual differences in predisposition to smoke or the mechanisms involved in becoming a highly dependent smoker. Empirical evidence makes it clear that almost all smokers smoke primarily to obtain nicotine; however, many individuals do not become highly dependent on nicotine, and many others exhibit strong dependence on smoking. This book explores these and many other individual differences that make the study of smoking far more interesting than the casual observer might expect.

This book presents evidence indicating that both sides of the tobacco battle are in some respects correct, but they miss the complex nature of the causal processes associated with smoking behavior. Smoking is neither just a habit nor just an addiction. It is both and much more. The reinforcing and dependence-producing effects of smoking result primarily from nicotine, but simple exposure to nicotine does not account for the the large individual differences in smoking effects and prevalence observed across situations and individuals.

The half-dozen years subsequent to the SGR (USDHHS, 1988) were characterized by both a wide acceptance of the addictive nature of smoking and a rediscovery of the importance of individual differences in personality, psychopathology, genetics, and environment in determining who becomes a smoker and who quits for how long. Numerous genetic studies have shown high heritability for smoking and common genetic components for smoking, personality, and psychopathology.

The major purpose of this book is to summarize and synthesize the literature on the relationship of smoking and smoking dependence and addiction to individual differences and affective processes. Although it has long been noted that personality and emotional factors are intimately related to each other and to smoking, there is no model or book that integrates relevant findings and models in a comprehensive fashion. This lack of an integrative model stems from the fact that research in this area is scattered across a wide variety of disciplines so as to make integration a formidable challenge. This book reviews and attempts to integrate the numerous complex and interesting biological, psychological, and social mechanisms by which personality, psychopathology, emotion, and smoking influence each other and relate to smoking.

INTO AND BEYOND THE ADDICTION QUESTION

At the same time as the U.S. Surgeon General published his 1988 report (USDHHS, 1988) concluding that smoking is an addiction just like cocaine, others were saying that cocaine use was just like gambling addiction, food addiction, and excessive dependence on members of the opposite sex (Peele,

1988). Yet some were noting that simply labeling smoking as a form of nicotine addiction did very little to explain the smoking process (Ashton & Golding, 1989; O. F. Pomerleau & Pomerleau, 1984, 1989; Warburton, 1989). Almost immediately after the 1988 SGR, a number of well-respected and influential researchers (e.g., Jaffe, 1990; Warburton, 1990) began to question the degree to which smoking and the effects of nicotine are in fact similar to those of cocaine, heroin, and other "harder" drugs.

These and other motivation-related issues are reviewed in Chapter 2. Chapters 3 and 4 address emotional processes and individual differences in personality and psychopathology. The juxtaposition of smoking motivation, personality, and emotional processes draws attention to common mechanisms underlying these constructs and suggests new syntheses and questions related to individual differences in smoking prevalence, effects, and quitting. These become important in later chapters that address smoking's relationship to and differential effects on emotional and motivational processes as a function of personality, psychopathology, gender, and situation.

At the same time as the importance of differentiation among drugs has been underscored, other investigators have argued that the psychobiological and psychosocial mechanisms underlying addiction to drugs do not differ from those underlying other forms of compulsive behavior (Bozarth, 1990; Peele, 1985, 1988). The paradoxical result of this conceptual focus is that yes, nicotine is like cocaine, which is like heroin and alcohol, which are all like mother's milk—or at least like compulsive jogging or adolescents' compulsive crushes (Peele, 1985). To some extent, brain and psychological mechanisms are common across a wide range of reinforcing activities. There are certainly things to be learned by focusing on similarities, just as there are by studying differences. Thus, one of this book's focuses is this similarity–difference dimension. The similarity–difference dimension is important not only when characterizing different drugs and compulsive or habitual behaviors, but also when characterizing conditions under which users and nonusers differ. To what degree are users and nonusers similar or different, on what variables, in what situations, and why?

What motivates smokers to smoke in spite of continuous health warnings and the belief of the vast majority of smokers that smoking causes cancer and a variety of other serious diseases? Do smokers possess a psychological or psychobiological predisposition to smoke? If so, what might the specific nature of this disposition be? Do some individuals find smoking and nicotine more inherently rewarding than do others? A great deal of progress has been made in understanding the smoking habit during the past 2 decades, especially in the understanding of nicotine's effects on biological and psychobiological processes. It is now well established that nicotine reinforces the smoking habit (see Chapters 2 and 5). Furthermore, the view that it does so by a number of mechanisms is receiving growing acceptance (Ashton & Golding, 1989; O. F. Pomerleau & Pomerleau, 1989). The complexities of smoking and of nicotine's effects are demonstrated by evidence indicating that the effects of smoking-sized doses of nicotine are dependent on (a) environmental demands and stress level (see Chapter 5), (b) personality and psychopathology (see Chapter 7), (c) dose and rate of administration (Armitage, Hall, & Sellers, 1969; Gilbert, Meliska, Williams, & Jensen, 1992), and (d) time since previous dose (Goldstein, Beck, & Mundschenk, 1967; Guha & Pradhan, 1976).

The biopsychosocial Situation × Trait adaptive response (STAR) model proposed in Chapter 9 summarizes recent insights and provides a broad structure from which one can obtain fundamental new insights. The model draws attention to the unique Person × Situation transactional nature of smoking motivation and abstinence responses. I propose that each smoker must be viewed as a complex system of multiple traits: interrelated subsystems (temperament, personality, nicotine history, goals, and cognition and affect). The adaptations and transactions of this ever-changing set of subsystems with the environment determines overall systemic behavior, including whether the individual smokes. Evidence presented in Chapters 6, 7 and 8 has indicated that a consideration of biological, psychological, and social and environmental systems and subsystems across time as they influence each other is a necessary requirement and a foundation for any future adequate characterization and theory of smoking and its effects. Evidence provided in these chapters has suggested that interactive perspectives, such as that provided by the STAR model, are more accurate depictions of smoking-related processes and mechanisms than those found in previous models. Thus, I predict that the STAR model will be useful in leading to improvements in intervention approaches designed to achieve long-term abstinence, as well as in prevention efforts.

The question of what cessation interventions are most effective in given subgroups of smokers is drawing increasing attention. This increased focus on treatment matching for particular smoking subgroups is motivated in part by high relapse rates in general smoker populations and in particular by the very high relapse rates in special groups (see Chapter 7) that are constituting an ever-higher percentage of the smoking population (Coambs, Kozlowski, & Ferrence, 1989). Another reason for developing specific interventions for specific subgroups is that empirical evidence has supported the view that the relative balance of mechanisms maintaining smoking and promoting relapse vary systematically as a function of individual traits, including one's typical work and interpersonal environment. Special high-risk populations include individuals high in characteristics that have always differentiated smokers from nonsmokers: neuroticism and emotional disorders, impulsivity, and antisocial behavior. Personality-, psychopathology-, and situation-specific mechanisms are identified in Chapters 7 and 9 as contributing to the difficulty these groups have in achieving smoking cessation success. These individual differences point to a need for the development, refinement, and efficacy testing of theoretically driven psychosocial interventions for smoking dependence that take into account individual differences.

New cessation and prevention interventions need to be based on the current understanding of the joint and interactive influence of situational and trait factors.

Chapter 10 considers potential interventions based on the STAR model reviewed in Chapter 9. Characterization of individual differences in those who are and those who are not successful in quitting permanently is an important first step toward eventually providing smoker-focused individualized interventions with a higher probability of success. More generally, successful interventions must build on empirically based knowledge of the psychological and biological mechanisms mediating the development of smoking initiation and maintenance if trial and treatment error are to be avoided (Leventhal & Cleary, 1980).

Shiffman (1993b) concluded that the lack of clinical innovation during the past decade has resulted in part from the near universal use of multicomponent programs that has ended in all programs looking alike. He suggested that the field is now focused on "tinkering with details of existing programs. . . . [and that it] has stopped producing innovative approaches to smoking cessation" (p. 719).

Shiffman's (1993b) articulate observations should be supplemented with the observation that (contrary to superficial appearance) most current interventions are focused on technique rather than on individual smokers and smoking theory. For example, nicotine replacement therapies (nicotine gum and patch) are generally prescribed with minimal or no individualized smoking, situational, or trait-based counseling or therapy. Acupuncture, hypnosis, relaxation training, and coping skill development are also technique-driven interventions that fail to adequately address complex situational, motivational, trait, biological, and learning factors involved at various stages of the cessation process. In addition, minimal or no consideration is given to the very long-term impact of relapsing after using what many smokers believe will be a "magic bullet."

Finally, Leventhal and Cleary (1980) hypothesized that all effective interventions, regardless of specific technique, must deal with motivation to quit smoking and coping skills to sustain avoidance. Evidence provided in Chapters 9 and 10 shows that situational and trait factors influence and are correlated both with motivation to quit and with coping skills and should be added to the list of important causal factors.

In summary, this book draws together the very large body of basic theory and data into the development of a sound, adequately complex model of smoking behavior. Furthermore, I hope that this model is productive in directing future research, theory development, and effective cessation interventions. The model proposed is in no way intended to be taken as a definitive theory of smoking. It is intended to stand as a general theoretical framework that can guide the observation and analysis of smoking-related processes. I assume that specific aspects of this framework will change as a result of empirical findings. The value of the theoretical framework as a whole is evaluated with reference to its utility for generating productive research and more efficient treatment interventions.

Chapter 2

Smoking Motivation: Models and Issues

The brain systems are so interlinked that their functions cannot be meaningfully separated, and . . . nicotine and smoking affect simultaneously all the major functional systems governing behavior. . . .Viewed from this perspective, older models of smoking, such as the addiction model and the arousal modulating model, appear somewhat naive. (Ashton & Golding, 1989, p. 42)

The scientific process is an uneven path of evolution toward more powerful heuristic, predictive, and explanatory formulations. Some aspects of smoking have received more attention at different points along this evolutionary path. There is an ever-present danger that researchers will forget the experiences of earlier generations as they become enamored with the latest Zeitgeist, the new construction of explanatory and theoretical truth. Thus, this chapter provides an overview of past and current thinking and research that is designed to prepare the reader for more critical and in-depth discussions in subsequent chapters. There is a need for examination of why some smokers are more dependent than others and how such differences can be characterized (West & Grunberg, 1991). Related questions include "Are all smokers to some extent dependent?" "What is meant by dependent or addicted?" and "Do similarities of heroin and cocaine reflect common mechanisms of reinforcement and equivalent reinforcement strength?"

The literature reviewed in the following pages is voluminous, and more questions than answers exist. Still, much more is known about smoking, individual differences, and emotion today than was known a decade ago. This new knowledge has implications concerning processes as divergent as individual differences in genetic reward and punishment sensitivities and free will and self-control. The flow of this chapter largely reflects the historical progression from models that viewed smoking as motivated by psychological behavior not involving nicotine, to monolithic nicotine addiction models, and finally to more complex causal models that recognize the importance of both nicotine and nonpharmacological factors.

MODELS OF SMOKING NOT INVOLVING NICOTINE

Nervous Habit Models

Although it is now widely recognized that nicotine plays an essential role in reinforcing smoking behavior, as recently as the 1970s many leading scientists argued that smoking had little to do with nicotine ingestion. Instead, it was viewed as a habit influenced by learning mechanisms no different from those reinforcing non-drug-related behaviors. Smoking was seen in the same way as fingernail biting, pencil or gum chewing, and numerous other habits, many of which appear to be habits of nervous tension. Smoking's putative relaxing effects were seen as resulting from a planned siesta legitimizing relaxation and disengagement from activity (Ferster, 1970) or as displacement activity associated with conflict (D. Morris, 1977). Consistent with this view of smoking as a nervous habit or as reducing negative affect is the finding that smoking is correlated with habits of nervous tension, including oral habits such as nail biting (Jacobs & Spilken, 1971; Jacobs et al., 1965, 1966). Furthermore, empirical evidence has suggested that habits associated with nervous tension may in fact be tension reducing (e.g., chewing gum promotes relaxation; Hollingworth, 1939). Smoking may also have nonpharmacological reinforcing effects from the avoidance of aversive social patterns. Smoking to fill conversational silences and pace social interactions may provide a comfortable structure for the smoker, especially during stressful interactions (Ferster, 1970). Similarly, smoking may provide a diversion or self-condoned break from an aversive situation.

Psychodynamic Theory

There is relatively little rigorous empirical support for the psychoanalytic hypothesis that smoking is rewarding because of its oral gratifying attributes that are especially rewarding to oral personalities (Kline, 1972; Stepney, 1980). Nail biting, thumb sucking, and other oral habits correlate both with smoking (Jacobs et al., 1965, 1966; Jacobs & Spilken, 1971) and with neuroticism, which in turn correlates with smoking (see Chapter 7). However, these correlations do not provide any direct support for the psychodynamic hypothesis that the covariation of these traits is a result of oral fixation.

Sensory Gratification

There is a strong case for the view that nonpharmacological factors such as smell, taste, and throat and lung sensation play important reinforcing roles in smoking (Rose, 1988). Rose (1988) has argued that "the desire for a cigarette is not fully satisfied by nicotine alone" (p. 95) and that smoking reinforcement may have a great deal of similarity to food reinforcement. He suggested that tracheal and other smoking ingestion cues are strong conditioned reinforcers because they are quickly followed by the reinforcing effects of nicotine subsequent to inhalation. He also hypothesized that taste cues associated with consummatory behavior act as unconditional stimuli or goal objects that the smoker, like the eater, seeks.

A number of lines of evidence have supported the view that sensory factors play important roles in tobacco use. For example, intravenous administration of nicotine has less of an effect on desire to smoke than does smoking (Henningfield, Miyasato, & Jasinski, 1985). Other evidence comes from a study by Rose (1988). Smokers either inhaled smoke deeply into their lungs, where nicotine was absorbed, or shallowly after their lungs were already filled with air so that nicotine resided in the throat and upper airways and was only minimally absorbed, but where tracheal impact was maximal. Deep inhalations produced large increases in heart rate and carbon monoxide changes approximating those of normal smoking. Although the shallow inhalation procedure resulted in minimal changes in these two measures, it produced more sensory impact. Smoking satisfaction paralleled the sensory effects more closely than physiological indexes of nicotine's pharmacologic effects. These and related studies led Rose to conclude that maximal smoking satisfaction and reinforcement is produced when peripheral, nonpharmacologic factors are combined with nicotine's central effects.

The use of a citric acid aerosol inhaler during a 3–week cessation trial whenever the urge to smoke occurred resulted in enhanced rates of smoking abstinence, reduced craving, and alleviated negative affect in smokers (Behm, Schur, Levin, Tashkin, & Rose, 1993). Similarly, in another study regenerated cigarette smoke condensate with minimal nicotine significantly reduced craving (Behm, Levin, Lee, & Rose, 1990).

NICOTINE ADDICTION AND DEPENDENCE MODELS

Although a small number of investigators in the first half of the century likened tobacco use to the use of hard drugs, with nicotine being responsible for its routine use (Armstrong-Jones, 1927; Dorsey, 1936; Johnston, 1942), most scientific and other discussions of tobacco viewed it in a more benign light. As late as 1964, the Advisory Committee of the U. S. Surgeon General on Smoking and Health (U.S. Public Health Service, 1964) concluded that tobacco use was a habit rather than an addiction. The reasons for viewing heavy smoking as a compulsive habit rather than as an addiction were these: (a) [lack of a] "characteristic abstinence syndrome" (p. 354); (b) the variable duration of cessation symptoms; (c) the belief that symptoms observed when smokers stop tobacco use were "secondary to the deprivation of a desired object or habitual experience" (p. 352; and not a specific nicotine syndrome); (d) the nonfatal nature of sudden cessation of tobacco use; (e) the tolerance of smokers for nicotine is low grade and of a distinct variety as excessive doses can still elicit toxic effects in habitual users; (f) the variety of interventions that seemed to be equally efficacious (or nonefficacious) in helping motivated smokers give up the behavior; and (g) "dependence and emotional disturbances caused by smoking . . . , like coffee . . . are not comparable to those of morphine, alcohol, barbiturates, and many other potent addicting drugs" (U.S. Public Health Service, 1964, p. 350).

In contrast to the U.S. Public Health Service (1964) report's differentiation of tobacco use from addictive drugs, in 1980 the *Diagnostic and Statistical Manual of Mental Disorders* (3rd ed., or DSM–III, American Psychiatric Association [APA], 1980) included nicotine dependence (not addiction) as one of its diagnostic categories. Eight years later the SGR (USDHHS 1988, p. 9), titled *Nicotine Addiction*, came to three major conclusions: (a) cigarettes and other forms of tobacco are addictive, (b) nicotine is the drug in tobacco that causes addiction, and (c) the pharmacologic and behavioral processes that determine tobacco addiction are similar to those that determine addiction to drugs such as heroin and cocaine.

Thus, in contrast to the 1964 SGR (U.S. Public Health Service, 1964), which focused on differentiation of nicotine and tobacco use from traditional drugs of abuse, the 1988 SGR (USDHHS, 1988) emphasized similarities and minimized differences. Reasons for this change in focus reflected in part a large number of new studies during the past 3 decades indicating that (a) tobacco use is associated with a mild withdrawal syndrome; (b) nicotine reinforces behavior; and (c) nicotine influences brain mechanisms involved in the mediation of reinforcement. A broadening of the concept of addiction and public health concerns may also have played an important role.

There are no universally accepted definitions of addiction, dependence, or habituation. Although the 1988 SGR (USDHHS, 1988) recognized that the term *drug dependence* is now seen as a more technical term, it used the term *addiction* in its major conclusions. The stated reason (p. 7) was that drug addiction continues to be used by the National Institute on Drug Abuse and other organizations when it is important to provide information at a more general level. Apparently the authors of the 1988 SGR felt that the term addiction more accurately conveys to the public what is meant by the more precise term drug dependence. It also seems clear that the term addiction has many negative connotations that the term drug dependence may not have (Peele, 1985; Warburton, 1989, 1990). Generally the terms *addiction* and *addict* imply an underlying medical disease over which the individual has little or no control (Warburton, 1989). The use of the term addiction implies that the public, as well as the scientific community, has in fact a clear understanding of what other addictions are like and that there are important biological and behavioral similarities between nicotine and tobacco use and the use of drugs such as cocaine and heroin.

The empirical and conceptual bases on which the 1988 (USDHHS, 1988) SGR came to its conclusions regarding addiction and the equality of nicotine with other drugs of abuse are discussed and evaluated below.

Primary Criteria for Drug Dependence and Addiction

The 1964 SGR (U.S. Public Health Service, 1964) defined *habituation* as "a condition resulting from the repeated consumption of a drug" (p. 351). Its characteristics include the following: (a) a desire (but not a compulsion) to continue taking the drug for the sense of improved well-being that it engenders, (b) little or no tendency to increase the dose, (c) some degree of psychic dependence on the effect of the drug but absence of physical dependence and hence of an abstinence syndrome, and (d) detrimental effects, if any, affect primarily the individual.

The 1964 SGR (U.S. Public Health Service, 1964, p. 351) based its distinction between addiction and habituation on then-current World Health Organization definitions. Addiction was defined as a state characterized by (a) an overpowering desire or need (compulsion) to continue taking the drug and to obtain it by any means, (b) a tendency to increase the dose, (c) a psychic (psychological) and generally a physical dependence on the effects of the drug, and (d) detrimental effects on the individual and society.

The 1964 SGR (U.S. Public Health Service, 1964) differentiated between addiction and habituation because it concluded that smoking "should be labeled habituation to distinguish it clearly from addiction, since the biological effects of tobacco, like coffee and other caffeine-containing beverages, . . . are not comparable to those produced by morphine, alcohol, barbiturates, and many other potent addicting drugs" (p. 350).

The 1988 SGR (USDHHS, 1988) recognized the importance of its change in characterization of tobacco use from habituation to addiction and based its change on two grounds. First, the World Health Organization no longer used the terms addiction and habituation but rather adopted a single concept of drug dependence. Second, empirical findings since the 1964 SGR (U.S. Public Health Service, 1964) were seen as demonstrating that nicotine shares numerous characteristics of prototypic drugs of abuse and meets the three criteria used by the 1988 SGR that characterize a drug as addicting: (a) highly controlled or compulsive use, (b) psychoactive effects, and (c) drug-reinforced behavior.

The 1988 SGR (USDHHS, 1988) stated that the primary criteria are "sufficient to define drug dependence" (p. 7). In addition, it described the following additional criteria as useful in characterizing a drug as addictive: (a) stereotypic patterns of use, (b) relapse following abstinence, (c) recurrent drug cravings, (d) tolerance, (e) physical dependence, and (f) pleasant (euphoriant) effects.

Highly Controlled or Compulsive Use   Highly controlled or compulsive use is defined by the 1988 SGR (USDHHS, 1988) as drug-related behavior "driven by strong, often irresistible" (p. 250) urges. Such drug-related habitual behavior is differentiated from non-drug-related habitual behavior by the second two primary criteria: demonstration that the drug produces psychoactive effects and that the drug acts as a reinforcer. Most definitions of addiction and dependence have used the concept of compulsive use (Peele, 1985), and there is little disagreement with the fact that many, if not most, smokers experience a strong urge to smoke. However, a number of investigators have argued that there are major problems with conceptualizing smoking as a compulsive behavior.

Criticisms of Compulsive Use Evidence   J. H. Robinson and Pritchard (1992) noted that in a recent Gallup Poll 61% of smokers said "yes" in response to the question "Do you consider yourself addicted to cigarettes or not?" Yet even more (78%) answered yes to the question "Do you feel you would be able to quit smoking if you made the decision to do so or not?" (Gallup Poll National Survey, 1990; Public Opinion On-Line Database, as cited in J. H. Robinson & Pritchard, 1992). They noted that with current restrictive environmental smoking regulations smokers routinely abstain from smoking on planes, at work, and in public places without disruptive effects on behavior or performance. Warburton (1990) made similar observations. Even one of the early addiction model proponents, Schachter (1979), observed that many smokers smoke only at work or at parties and others regularly abstain on religious holidays without apparent strain. In fact, many regular smokers go on extended vacations and report minimal or no compulsion to smoke.

In short, some smokers do not fit the category of compulsive smoker. Very light smokers clearly do not fall into the addicted category, as they have no compulsion to smoke and rarely experience withdrawal symptoms when abstaining (Shiffman, 1989). Individual differences in difficulty abstaining from smoking are related to habitual nicotine intake, as well as to personality and environmental factors discussed later in this book. One might consider compulsive smoking to be a characterization of a subgroup of smokers who have an especially difficult time refraining from smoking even when given clear incentive to quit.

Alternatively, although compulsive use does not characterize all smokers, neither does it characterize the behavior of many regular users of cocaine, heroin, and other more potent drugs (Peele, 1985). When soldiers who were heavy daily users of heroin in Vietnam returned to the United States, the vast majority quit their habit cold turkey without a continued compulsion for heroin (Robins, Helzer, Hesselbrock, & Wish, 1980). This fact emphasizes several things. First, drug use, like most problem behaviors, is highly situation specific (S. Epstein,

1979, 1983). Second, the general public (and possibly a large portion of the medical and scientific communities) has misperceptions as to the nature of drug use. It is interesting to note that the Robins et al. study was titled "Vietnam Veterans Three Years After Vietnam: How Our Study Changed Our View of Heroin."

The situations during which smoking and many other drugs are likely to be used are those associated with some perceived benefit from the drug. Thus, during stressful Vietnam War combat situations U.S. soldiers used heroin to cope with fear and depression (Robins et al., 1980). Similarly, nicotine may be used especially frequently in situations in which the user desires to enhance concentration or reduce a variety of negative affects, but may not be used during a relaxing vacation where there are few performance or emotional demands.

J. H. Robinson and Pritchard (1992) suggested that the 1988 SGR's (USDHHS, 1988) definition of compulsive use is so broad that anything an individual ingests and enjoys and therefore ingests again on a regular basis fulfills this criterion of addiction. For example, the regular use of coffee, sweets, and aspirin to relieve arthritic pain all result in psychoactive effects and alteration of neurotransmitters, thus meeting the criteria for compulsive use. The 1988 SGR noted that "to distinguish drug dependence from habitual behaviors not involving drugs, it must be demonstrated that a drug with psychoactive (mood-altering) effects in the brain enters the blood stream" (p. 8). However, this definition has been questioned on two grounds. First, gambling, foods, exciting sports events, jogging, and other activities have clear biological bases that influence brain processes and may have much in common with drug dependence (Peele, 1985, 1988). Second, using a different term (dependent vs. habitual) simply on the basis of whether a drug enters the bloodstream may be of little theoretical value.

Psychoactive Effects   The 1988 SGR's (USDHHS, 1988) criterion of psychoactive effects is clearly met by nicotine, yet the magnitude and nature of these effects is dramatically different from those of prototypic drugs of abuse. Henningfield and colleagues (Henningfield, 1984; Jasinski, Johnson, & Henningfield, 1984) interpreted the results of two of their studies as indicating that nicotine has euphoriant and other psychoactive effects similar to and equivalent in magnitude to those of morphine, alcohol, d-amphetamine, and other drugs of abuse. Intravenous nicotine was shown to result in increases in liking that approximated those associated with subcutaneous morphine and d-amphetamine in a small number of drug abusers (Jasinski et al., 1984). However, the mean liking for all of these drugs was only approximately 2 on a scale ranging from 0 to 4, indicating only a moderate liking of the drug. Thus, not only was the liking or effect of iv nicotine only moderate, but that produced by the other drugs was of similar magnitude. Whereas nicotine was administered intravenously at a maximally rewarding dose, the other drugs were administered subcutaneously and in doses lower than those associated with maximal liking. Thus, the finding of equality of liking across drugs is unlikely to be representative of liking in the natural environment where ideal doses and means of administration are generally used. In a related study, Henningfield (1984) found tobacco smoking and iv nicotine to result in much smaller increases above placebo (1.0 and 1.7 units, respectively) than pentobarbital (3.5), *d*-amphetamine (5.5), morphine (6.2), ethanol (3.0), and gambling (3.8).

Careful examination of the effects of nicotine on self-administration, affect, and performance indicates complex and highly situationally specific effects (see Chapter 5). Jaffe (1990) accurately concluded that "the subjective effects produced by inhaled tobacco, or nicotine by any route, are far less dramatic than those . . . [of] other dependence-producing drugs" (p. 20). Others (e.g., Kozlowski et al., 1989; Warburton, 1990) have made similar conclusions.

Criticisms of Psychoactivity Criterion   Warburton (1989) stated that the use of psychoactive effects as a criterion is novel and trivial. He noted that although nicotine, like heroin and cocaine, is psychoactive, these drugs are very different in their effects. In comparison with cocaine and heroin, nicotine's psychoactive effects are of very small magnitude and are not easily measured. J. H. Robinson and Pritchard (1992) suggested that those factors that determine classification as addicting should be specific effects and magnitudes of these effects. They concluded that the research findings indicate that nicotine's psychoactive effects are subtle and clearly distinct from the psychological and behavioral disturbances observed with traditional addicting drugs. In contrast to the euphoria and impaired performance observed with morphine and cocaine, nicotine results in improved performance, increased alertness, and reduced negative affect. On the basis of these observations, O. F. Pomerleau and Pomerleau (1984) stated that

> Nicotine has a pharmacological profile that accords ideally with its use as a "coping response" in diverse situations. . . . For example, in contrast to drugs of abuse, nicotine from smoking is not only compatible with work but actually facilitates performance of certain kinds of tasks. (p. 509)

Although intoxication was a criterion for dependence and addiction in most previous characterizations, the 1988 SGR (USDHHS, 1988) dropped it. J. H. Robinson and Pritchard (1992, p. 8) noted that the World Health Organization maintained intoxication, a key element in its original differentiation of addiction from habituation, in its new construct of dependence. The term *intoxication* refers to a state of impaired cognitive functioning and performance with associated adverse behavioral effects on self and others.

Summary of Psychoactivity Criterion for Nicotine   A review of the literature (see Chapter 5) indicates that nicotine does not exhibit euphoriant properties equivalent to those associated with classic drugs of abuse. Furthermore, in contrast to most classic drugs of abuse, the psychoactive effects it does have are related to the enhancement of normal alert and competent, nonemotional functioning.

Drug-Reinforced Behavior   A number of lines of evidence converge to strongly support the view that nicotine is the primary reinforcer in smoking and other forms of tobacco use. Smoking, chewing, and snuffing all have a common denominator—comparable concentrations of blood nicotine (Benowitz, Porchet, Scheiner, & Jacob, 1988). Although the various forms of tobacco use include stimulation of peripheral receptors in the mouth, nose, or throat, these sensations are very different. The fact that people are more likely to use tobacco than to snort or chew hot pepper-laced lettuce or other nonpsychoactive substances is consistent with the hypothesis that nicotine is the most important reinforcer of tobacco use. Neither tobacco-free (e.g., lettuce leaf) nor denicotinized tobacco cigarettes (e.g., Next$_®$) has been a commercial success. Because nicotine is the only substance in tobacco with substantial pharmacological effects, it is difficult to argue that another common denominator is responsible for its reinforcing effects.

The pattern and range of dose and dosing over which nicotine is reinforcing is relatively narrow compared with other substances (Corrigall, 1991; Koslowski & Herman, 1984). Just doubling one's typical plasma nicotine concentration results in nausea and other forms of subjective distress (D. G. Gilbert, Meliska, Williams, & Jensen, 1992).

Self-administration in animals   Many species of mammals can be taught to self-administer nicotine under certain restricted conditions (Corrigall, 1991; S. R. Goldberg, Spealman, & Goldberg, 1981; USDHHS, 1988). Early attempts to generate self-administration used adjunctive behavior paradigms (providing concomitant food and nicotine delivery) and chronic nicotine administration because nicotine was considered a weak reinforcer. However, a better appreciation of the sensitivity of animals to overdose aversion (Etscorn, 1980; Jensen, Gilbert, Meliska, Landrum, & Szary, 1990; Kumar, Pratt, & Stolerman, 1983) led investigators during the past decade to use schedules providing only limited access to nicotine (Corrigall, 1991). Nonetheless, on the basis of self-administration rates in subhuman species, nicotine is a weak reinforcer even in maximally effective situations compared with cocaine and other drugs of abuse (USDHHS, 1988). More precise characterization of the strength of nicotine's reinforcing effects could be made by studies providing animals with alternative behaviors that could lead to other reinforcers such as food, cocaine, sex, and glucose injections (Dworkin, Broadbent, Guarino, & Robinson, 1991).

Although it is now clear that animals can be taught to self-administer nicotine in certain conditions, it is not clear why and by what mechanisms nicotine operates as a reinforcer. Self-administration of nicotine and other drugs has frequently been presumed to be an example of positive reinforcement as positive reinforcement is defined as the process whereby a behavior (e.g., lever pressing) is increased when it is contingently increased by a subsequent change in stimuli (e.g., provision of drug or food). However, it is possible that the self-administration of nicotine eliminates an aversive internal state. If the reinforcement of nicotine is a function of the removal of an aversive state through self-administration, then the process can be characterized as negative reinforcement. This point is important because many, if not all, of the paradigms demonstrating self-administration include aversive components (e.g., indwelling catheters or sitting for substantial periods of time on a hard seat). Furthermore, it is important to note that electric shock has been demonstrated to act as a positive reinforcer in certain conditions (McKearney, 1968; Morse, Mead, & Kelleher, 1967). Fixed-interval schedules used by McKearney resulted in monkeys lever pressing to self-administer painful electric shocks. Fixed-interval schedules are one of the few conditions in which animals will self-administer nicotine (Corrigall, 1991).

Conditioned preference in animals   If a drug is serving as a reinforcer, then the stimuli associated with drug administration should also come to serve as conditioned reinforcers. The importance of conditioning may be especially important in the case of nicotine because nicotine is paired with other stimuli numerous times each day. Some studies have demonstrated conditioned place preference in rodents (e.g., Fudala & Iwamoto, 1986; Fudala, Teoh, & Iwamoto, 1985; Shoaib, Stolerman, & Kumar, 1994), and others have failed to do so (Clarke & Fibiger, 1987; Jorenby, Steinpreis, Sherman, & Baker, 1990; Mucha et al., 1982, as cited in O. F. Pomerleau & Rosecrans, 1989). Jorenby et al. suggested that their failure to demonstrate conditioned place preference was because, in contrast to other studies, they habituated their rats to handling and injection stress before the conditioning or pre-exposure phases. Thus, the habituation-induced attenuation of stress in their paradigm may have prevented nicotine from producing preference-conditioning negative reinforcement (stress reduction). Consistent with the stress reduction interpretation, Iwamoto (1989) found that intracerebral administration of nicotine resulted in antinociceptive effects, as well as conditioned place preference (Iwamoto, 1990).

Conditioned aversion in animals   Conditioned taste aversions have been consistently found in nicotine-naive rodents with high doses of nicotine (Etscorn, 1980; Jensen et al., 1990) and in some cases with doses as small as 0.046 mg/kg (Jensen et al., 1990) and 0.08 mg/kg (Kumar et al., 1983). Fudala et al. demonstrated conditioned place preferences (1985) by using 0.8 mg/kg in certain conditions, but aversion occurred with doses between 0.2 and 0.8 mg/kg when drug administration followed exposure by 5 minutes or less. Jorenby et al. (1990) observed conditioned aversion in nicotine-naive rats with 0.8 mg/kg and 1.2 mg/kg doses, but no aversion or preference in animals given six nicotine exposures before conditioning.

In summary, nicotine can act as a reinforcer in some subhuman species. Under conditions used to date, nicotine acts as a much weaker reinforcer than substances such as cocaine and heroin. It seems likely that under certain conditions not studied in detail to date (e.g., stressful or vigilance performance-demanding tasks) nicotine may prove to be a more potent reinforcer. To the degree that situational, species, and genetic strain factors influence the reinforcing properties of nicotine, STAR models are required (see Chapter 9 for a detailed presentation of and rationale for such models).

Self-administration in humans   Intravenous self-administration of nicotine has been demonstrated in chronic drug users (Henningfield & Goldberg, 1983; Henningfield, Lukas, & Bigelow, 1986; Henningfield, Miyasato, & Jasinski, 1983). In these studies, nicotine was available on some days but not others or nicotine could be delivered by pressing one lever and saline solution by pressing the other. Substitution of saline for nicotine resulted in decreased lever pressing, and lever pressing for nicotine occurred more often than for saline. However, the interpretation of these studies is unclear because of subject expectancies (Sutton, 1991), experimental demand characteristics, and the subject population used (subjects had previous drug use histories). Sutton has noted that there are a number of problems with the traditional placebo-controlled experimental design when investigating the effects of nicotine in humans. For example, experimental instructions may result in a ''guessing set'' in which subjects try to guess which group they are in or which substance is the active drug versus the placebo. Furthermore, participant expectancies may result in threats to the internal validity of studies, as individuals may act in accordance with these expectancies. Experimentally manipulated expectancies can influence whether nicotine (in chewing gum) will act as a reinforcer (Hughes, Pickens, Spring, & Keenan, 1985), alleviate withdrawal symptoms (Gottlieb, Killen, Marlatt, & West, 1987; Hughes, Guilliver, Amori, Mireault, & Fenwick, 1989), and influence relapse (Gottlieb, Killen, Marlat, & Taylor, 1987).

In summary, although the iv self-administration studies in humans to date are of limited value because of methodological weaknesses (Collins, 1990; J. H. Robinson & Pritchard, 1992), the convergence of evidence provides substantial proof that individuals use tobacco products to self-administer nicotine.

Criticisms of drug-reinforced behavior   Virtually all serious smoking researchers agree that smoking and other forms of nicotine administration result from the reinforcing effects of nicotine. The evidence that nicotine can reinforce self-administration in many mammals is now established. However, the nature and biological mechanisms associated with this reinforcement are not clear (see Chapter 6). Furthermore, in spite of nicotine's strong habit-forming characteristic, a majority of researchers agree that it is a much weaker reinforcer than cocaine, morphine, and related classic drugs of abuse. The strength of the habit appears to be a function of minimal response cost and repeated self-administrations across a variety of environments.

Summary Evaluation of Primary Criteria   None of the primary criteria proposed by the 1988 SGR (USDHHS, 1988) as applying to addiction in general and smoking in particular has gone without criticism. The compulsive use concept is challenged by findings that not only do many smokers not smoke in a narrowly defined compulsive manner, but neither do many users of heroin or cocaine. The criterion of psychoactivity has been seen as weak because many substances, including caffeine and chocolate bars, have such effects. The final primary criterion, drug-reinforced behavior, may be the least controversial, yet the means by which nicotine reinforces behavior is far more subtle, unstable, and situation dependent than simplistic models of self-administration would suggest. Furthermore, the reinforcing effects of nicotine are far less potent than those of cocaine and morphine and are more akin to those associated with caffeine and normal waking behavior, as opposed to states of abnormal intoxication associated with the more potent drugs such as cocaine and heroin.

Additional Criteria

Additional criteria indicated in the 1988 SGR (USDHHS, 1988) that characterize drug dependence included

> (1) regular temporal and physical patterns of use (repetitive and stereotypic); (2) drug use persisting despite adverse physical, psychological, or social consequences; (3) quitting episodes often followed by resumption of drug use (relapse); (4) urges (cravings) to use the drug that are recurrent and persistent, especially during drug abstinence. (p. 8)

In addition, the SGR stated that

> several common effects of dependence-producing drugs can strengthen their control over behavior and increase the likelihood of harm by contributing to the regularity and overall level of drug intake: (1) diminished responsiveness (tolerance) to the effects of a drug occurs, and may be accompanied by increased intake over time; (2) abstinence-associated withdrawal reactions (due to physical dependence) can motivate further drug intake; and (3) effects that are considered pleasant (euphoriant) to the drug user can be provided by the drug itself. Dependence-producing drugs can also produce effects that individuals find useful. (p. 8)

Stereotypic Patterns of Use   Smoking patterns of many, if not most, smokers clearly tend to be stereotypic in nature. Individuals tend to smoke a similar number of cigarettes each day, to obtain similar day-to-day and cigarette-to-cigarette nicotine intakes, and to exhibit puff-to-puff volumes (Nil & Bättig, 1989). However, experimental and self-monitoring studies have indicated that the probability of smoking varies significantly as a function of environmental conditions (Paty & Shiffman, 1991; Shiffman, 1993a; see Chapter 5).

A review of studies assessing nicotine regulation shows that very low nicotine-delivery cigarettes are associated with reductions in nicotine intake (De-Grandpre, Bickel, Hughes, & Higgins, 1992). That is, smokers significantly reduce their nicotine intake when they have to smoke more to obtain a given nicotine intake. Thus, nicotine intake is elastic; it is highly dependent on the amount of work required.

Criticisms of stereotyped smoking   Some prominent tobacco researchers have disagreed with the characterization of smoking as highly stereotyped behavior (Collins, 1990; Warburton, 1989). Warburton noted that stereotypy implies drug-focused effects rather than environmentally influenced behavior. Thus, to the degree that smoking is under the influence of the environment, its use would not be stereotypic. Warburton further argued that heroin is clearly under the control of withdrawal symptoms, whereas nicotine use is generally more social in nature and under environmental control by factors such as stress. It is also noteworthy that environmental stimuli elicit use of a wide range of drugs, including alcohol and heroin by animals and humans (Peele, 1985; USDHHS, 1988).

Use Despite Harmful Effects   A vast majority of smokers believe that smoking is harmful to health and express the desire to quit (American Medical News, 1990). Nonetheless, they smoke in spite of the fact that 78% of them report that they feel able to quit smoking if they made the decision to do so (Gallup Poll National Survey, 1990; Public Opinion On-Line Database, as cited in J. H. Robinson & Pritchard, 1992). Examination of these apparently contradictory beliefs might provide insight into smoking motivation and the eventual decisions to quit.

Criticisms of the Harmful Effects Argument   Warburton (1989) has noted that people engage in many behaviors that present risks to themselves. Sex, sunbathing, eating fatty foods, skiing, bungee jumping, and a host of other common behaviors have high risks of serious injury or death. Starr (1969) compared some of these voluntary risky behaviors in terms of the probability of fatality per person-hour of activity exposure. He determined that the subjective acceptability of risk was the same for smoking as for other common risky behaviors. On the basis of Starr's findings, Warburton (1989) suggested that the choice to smoke and the choice to engage in other risky behaviors are determined by similar decision processes. Furthermore, he suggested that compared with other risky behavior, the choice to smoke is not associated with excessive risk. The risky behavior interpretation is consistent with the fact that as a group smokers tend to be risk takers and sensation seekers (Zuckerman, 1991).

Relapse Following Abstinence   Relapse is common for smokers attempting to stop smoking, and also for dieters and gamblers (Peele, 1985) and for many behaviors inhibited by fear of punishment (Bouton & Swartzentruber, 1991). Relapse to an inactive lifestyle, fingernail biting, and numerous other habits occur at a similarly high rate. Thus, figures comparing the relapse rate of cocaine and heroin with smoking (e.g., Hunt, Barnett, & Branch, 1971) should also consider other common habitual human behaviors if they are to make convincing arguments that these rates are unique and discriminable from relapse to all habitual behaviors. Nonetheless, the fact that nicotine replacement therapy (nicotine patch and gum) reduces smoking relapse, especially in those with high precessation nicotine intake (Fagerstrom, 1994; Transdermal Nicotine Study Group, 1991) supports the view that nicotine is the primary reinforcer in smoking motivation.

Schachter (1982) stated that the view of abstinence as hard to maintain "has been molded largely by that self-selected hard-core group of people who . . . go to therapists for help, thereby becoming the only easily available subjects for studies of recidivism" (p. 437). Individuals who find it easy to abstain from smoking by themselves have no need to seek outside help. Warburton (1989) concluded that the belief that nicotine is as hard to give up as classic drugs of dependence ignores self-selection processes in the research populations and ignores differential social controls deterring nicotine and hard-drug use. Warburton's criticisms of the 1988 SGR's (USDHHS, 1988) interpretation of recidivism, as well as Peele's (1985) more general criticisms of the addiction concept, challenge researchers to articulate more precise conceptualizations of smoking and relapse phenomena. A biopsychosocial view of smoking as a process with associated costs and benefits is consistent with the view that smoking behavior is indeed very difficult to change and that relapse is the norm. More specifically, the social and financial costs of smoking are relatively minimal and the health costs are delayed, whereas the rewarding effects are immediate, no matter how subtle.

Recurrent Drug Cravings   *Craving* is a term used to describe the urge to use a drug. However, there is a great deal of debate about its functional utility as its use has often impeded rather than facilitated understanding (Hughes, 1987; Kozlowski & Wilkinson, 1987). Kozlowski and Wilkinson (1987) suggested that smoking researchers tend to equate craving with thinking about or missing smoking, whereas alcohol researchers use the term to refer to a very different process. Thus, in spite of listing craving as one of the additional criteria used to characterize drug dependence, the 1988 SGR (USDHHS, 1988) acknowledged the term's ambiguity and generally replaced it with more descriptive phrases and terms. On the basis of these criticisms of the craving construct and the lack of craving-related subjective and physiological equivalence across drugs, Warburton (1989) concluded that "the evidence is not available to say 'craving for nicotine' is the same as 'craving for heroin' or 'craving for cocaine' and so this criterion is invalid" (p. 167).

Thoughts of smoking and the urge to smoke are a function of a variety of factors, including abstinence, environmental stimuli, and stress (Shiffman,

1986). The relationship between withdrawal symptoms and craving is tenuous. Urges to smoke are frequently not reduced by factors that alleviate withdrawal symptoms. For example, although tobacco withdrawal symptoms are diminished by nicotine replacement (nicotine gum and patch), the craving to smoke is not significantly reduced (Henningfield & Jasinski, 1988). Tiffany (1992) reviewed extensive evidence indicating that drug self-administration is a function of a different set of factors than is craving.

Tolerance The lack of evidence of tolerance for most of nicotine's rewarding effects may reflect minimal effects or minimal study of such processes. However, tolerance has been suggested for some effects. Evidence indicates moderate tolerance to nicotine-induced nausea and dizziness. Nonsmokers administered nicotine gum have developed nausea, whereas smokers rarely do (Srivastava, Russell, Feyerabend, Masterson, & Rhodes, 1991). However, an alternative to the tolerance interpretation of this finding is that smokers smoke because they are inherently insensitive to nicotine's aversive effects (Srivastava et al., 1991). Clearly more research on this interesting possibility is warranted. Although acute tolerance (occurring within a given day) to nicotine has been demonstrated in tobacco nonusers and users alike, with the exception to the aversive properties noted above, the development of chronic tolerance to nicotine has not been systematically demonstrated (M. A. H. Russell, Jarvis, Jones, & Feyerabend, 1990). The fact that smokers do not smoke progressively more cigarettes over their years of smoking suggests that any tolerance to nicotine is minimal (Warburton, 1989).

Physical Dependence The primary index of physical dependence is the existence of a withdrawal syndrome subsequent to cessation of chronic drug administration (Kalant, 1978). Withdrawal syndromes are composed of various physiological, subjective, and behavioral states associated with cessation of chronic drug use (APA, 1987). The severity of the withdrawal syndrome of a given drug is a function of the chronic drug-dosing pattern. Tolerance (decreased response to a given dose) may occur without other evidence of physical dependence (e.g., withdrawal subsequent to cessation). The pattern of group mean tobacco withdrawal symptoms is notably consistent across studies, but highly variable across individuals within a study. Withdrawal symptoms include craving for tobacco (nicotine), irritability, increased anger, restlessness, anxiety, depression, disturbed sleep, trouble concentrating, increased appetite, weight gain, decreased urine concentrations of adrenaline and noradrenaline, increased slow-wave electroencephalogram (EEG) activity, increased rapid-eye-movement sleep, and decreased vigilance (Hughes & Hatsukami, 1986; A. L. Murray & Lawrence, 1984; see Chapter 5).

The fact that there is a relatively consistent pattern of emotional, cognitive, and physiological processes subsequent to smoking cessation should be interpreted in light of other findings. Smoking withdrawal symptoms are very similar in nature and intensity to those observed with food deprivation, relationship breakup, loss of a loved one, and caffeine withdrawal (D. G. Gilbert, Gilbert, & Schultz, 1994). This commonality of symptoms subsequent to the loss of important reinforcers suggests that nicotine withdrawal may precipitate a general distress response that includes a common set of emotional, cognitive, and physiological processes.

Euphoriant (Pleasant) Effects   The euphoriant effects criterion is simply a further specification of the psychoactive effects criterion. The preceding discussion of psychoactive effects noted that although intravenous administration of nicotine has been found to increase scores on the Addiction Research Center morphine–benzedrine scale (Haertzen & Hickey, 1987) that is sometimes referred to as the "euphoriant" scale, numerous studies have failed to detect elevations of happiness, pleasure, or pleasantness subsequent to smoking (D. G. Gilbert, Meliska, Williams, & Jensen, 1992; Meliska & Gilbert, 1991; see Chapter 5).

The pleasant effects of smoking were found by Warburton (1988) to be of the same magnitude as those of coffee and chocolate and far less than the pleasurable stimulation associated with alcohol, amphetamines, amyl nitrite, cocaine, glue, heroin, marijuana, and sex. In terms of pleasurable relaxation, tobacco and chocolate were equivalent, but significantly less relaxation-inducing, than alcohol, sex, sleeping tablets, and tranquilizers. Consistent with Warburton's observations as noted above, Jaffe (1990) concluded that "the subjective effects produced by inhaled tobacco, or nicotine by any route, are far less dramatic than those provided . . . [by] other dependence-producing drugs" (p. 20).

Summary of Addiction–Dependence Models

The addiction model as presently formulated does not account for a number of important facts. A number of formal critiques of the addiction model of smoking have been published during the past decade (Collins, 1990; Peele, 1985; J. H. Robinson & Pritchard, 1992; Warburton, 1988, 1989, 1990). Major points made by these critiques include those listed below.

   1   Withdrawal symptoms vary more as a function of environment and person than as a function of plasma nicotine concentrations or time since last nicotine dose. A purely pharmacologic view of smoking as addiction does not take into account important individual difference variables such as differences in types of smokers, psychopathology, and personality and does not assess the effects of stress and other factors known to modulate smoking initiation, maintenance, and relapse.

2 Relapse to smoking frequently occurs after a period of prolonged abstinence, long after withdrawal symptoms have subsided.

3 A sizable number of smokers smoke only a few cigarettes per day over a period of years, do not increase the number of cigarettes smoked, and do not experience the compulsive craving and withdrawal symptoms found in many heavy smokers (Shiffman, 1989). These findings are contrary to most models of drug dependence, which assume that repeated exposure to an addictive drug necessarily results in dependence (Shiffman, Fischer, Zettler-Segal, & Benowitz, 1990). These very light smokers (1–5 cigarettes per day, 5 or more days per week) have been labeled by Shiffmann as *chippers*, a term used by Harding, Zinberg, Stelmack, and Barry (1980) to identify individuals who regularly use heroin without becoming addicted; that is, individuals whose heroin use is under environmental or self-control rather than a result of physiologic or pharmacologic stimuli. Plasma nicotine assays show that chippers absorb the same amount of nicotine from the smoking of a given cigarette as do heavier smokers, thus they are chronically exposed to nicotine, but do not become dependent and do not compensate for their reduced number of cigarettes by obtaining abnormally large amounts of nicotine from each cigarette (Shiffman et al., 1990). Because chippers are apparently not reinforced by relief from nicotine withdrawal symptoms, the examination of chippers and the reinforcement of smoking in them may play an important role in understanding nicotine's inherent reinforcing effects (Shiffman et al., 1990).

4 Withdrawal symptoms associated with nicotine are similar to those associated with loss of numerous other important nonpharmacological, as well as pharmacological, reinforcers (D. G. Gilbert, Gilbert, & Schultz 1994).

There are problems with the addiction model that are not enumerated above or in earlier portions of this chapter. These include the fact that a simple addiction model does not account for the associations of various dimensions of personality and psychopathology with smoking prevalence or individual differences in withdrawal symptoms, reported smoking motivations, or relapse rates and situations (discussed in Chapters 7 and 9).

If one chooses to label smoking as an addictive or dependence-related process, it is incumbent not only to draw commonalities across various addictive drugs and behaviors, but also to differentiate among such behaviors and to consider individual differences and environmental contributions and interactions. It is not enough to simply say that individuals smoke because they are addicted and that we know this because they smoke. Nicotine use can be called an addiction, but so can sex, running, "dependence" on abusive men, frequent consumption of chocolate, anger, and gambling. Labeling must not substitute for the equally important process of differentiation and growth in our models.

Identifying problems with the addiction model of smoking provides opportunities to develop more adequate formulations. The strengths and weaknesses of a number of alternative models are discussed in the remaining portions of this chapter.

AFFECT-REGULATION MODELS OF SMOKING MOTIVATION

Smoking is reinforced by a number of mechanisms. Smokers report that they smoke to enhance positive experiences, to help them concentrate, and to alleviate or cope with stress or negative affect (Frith, 1971; Ikard, Green, & Horn, 1969; Ikard & Tompkins, 1973; Spielberger, 1986; Tomkins, 1968). Numerous experimental investigations have shown that smoking is reinforced in part by the reduction of negative affect and possibly by the enhancement or facilitation of positive affect (see Chapter 5). The remainder of this chapter summarizes general models of smoking.

Tomkins's Model (1966, 1968)

Because the affect-regulation model of smoking proposed by Tomkins (1966, 1968) was one of the earliest most detailed and influential models of smoking motivation, it is described in detail below. This model is based on Tomkins' (1962) theory of affective processes, in which affects are defined as innate psychobiological mechanisms that motivate behavior. Any behavior resulting in positive affect or the reduction of negative affect is reinforced and more likely to be repeated. Thus, smoking is sustained because it increases positive affect or reduces negative affect.

Positive Affect Smoking   The positive affect smoker envisioned by Tomkins (1968) smokes for the love of smoking. Positive affect smokers may smoke a cigarette or cigar at the end of a meal or for a celebration. Tomkins (1968, p. 168) distinguished between enhancement of positive affect and induction of positive affect. He provided data indicating that smoking increases positive affect only in situations in which the smoker is already experiencing positive affect. He suggested that positive affect smokers are more in control of their lives than negative affect smokers and do not think of themselves as using tobacco as a coping tool. They would light up a cigarette after, but not before, solving a problem. In general, they are characterized by more healthy personality traits and typically do not rely on smoking for sedation when distressed. His observation led him to believe that such smokers can quit smoking with relative ease if given good reason to do so.

Negative-Affect Smoking   In contrast to his view of positive-affect smokers, Tompkins (1968) hypothesized a wide range of types of negative affect smokers. Some individuals were seen as having such high frequencies of negative affect that they smoke throughout the day, relatively independent of situational factors. In addition to differing in types and number of situations in which they smoke, negative-affect smokers were seen as varying in the types of negative affect that result in smoking. Some were seen as responding with smoking to any negative affect, whereas other smokers smoked only in response to a small number of specific negative affects.

Affect intensity was hypothesized by Tomkins (1968) to be an important variable influencing whether a given smoker would light up. Some individuals were seen as smoking only when negative affect is mild, but never when strong. It was speculated that such individuals would see smoking-induced sedation as appropriate for mild emotions, but that they would view extreme emotions as calling for direct confrontation of problems. Alternatively, it was suggested that others would deal with negative affect in the opposite direction, confronting minor problems but seeking sedation by means of smoking in situations where no alternative appeared available.

Tomkins (1968) also stated that there are variations in sedative smoking as a function of duration of negative affect. According to his studies, some smokers do not smoke unless their distress continues for some period of time. Whether one resorts to sedative smoking is also seen as a function of the degree to which the stressful situation can be solved. Some negative affect smokers smoke when the situation appears hopeless; others smoke only when they think they can solve the problem. Thus, the latter group uses smoking as a problem-solving tool rather than for sedative disengagement.

Tomkins (1968) noted that some negative affect smokers do not smoke until actual or anticipated affect density reaches a critical level. Thus, a person may anticipate becoming anxious during a conversation with a superior and light up before the conversation even though not anxious at that time. If such smoking in anticipation of negative affect occurs before the experience of negative affect, this occurrence would make it more difficult to study the varieties of negative affect smoking. Affect type, intensity, density, duration, and probability of successful coping are usually anticipated in advance of the stressor situation. Therefore, Tomkins noted that smoking observed before, during, and after stressors is generally smoking in response to one's perceptions of the situation, one's coping resources, and the probable outcome rather than to the situation's observable characteristics. Smokers may be unaware or have only a vague awareness of these anticipatory processes associated with smoking. Thus, when the smokers are asked why they smoke, they may find it difficult to conceptualize or articulate the process.

Finally, Tomkins (1968) addressed the question of the degree to which smoking helps the individual cope with the source of negative-affect. He found that smokers differed greatly in the degree to which negative-affect smoking helped them resolve the situations contributing to their negative affect. Some passive–helpless individuals are seen as using negative-affect smoking simply to self-medicate distress, whereas others find that smoking helps them to cope with their stressors in an active manner.

In conclusion, although Tomkins (1968) tentatively identified a number of different types of negative-affect smokers, he recognized that the actual number of types is an empirical question requiring additional research.

Addicted Smoking   Negative-affect smoking was seen by Tomkins (1968) as rational, instrumental, means–end behavior designed to reduce anticipated or actual negative affect. He hypothesized that for negative affect smoking to be transformed into addictive smoking, a number of criteria need to happen: (a) a desperate need to reduce negative affect, (b) a desperate need for a cigarette, and (c) suffering about not having a cigarette that increases and masks the original negative affect because the cigarette is viewed as the only means by which the original negative affect can be eliminated. According to Tomkins, the paradox of this addictive process is that the means (cigarette) has become much more important than the end (the resolution of negative affect). Attention is shifted away from the present stressor and distress to the missing of the cigarette and the rapidly escalating distress this missing produces.

Means–end transformations are essential to Tomkins's (1966, 1968) model of addictive smoking. There are two types of means–end relationships, the one–many relationship and the many–one relationship. In the former, there is only one means to many ends. In the latter, there are many means to a common end. If the negative affect smoker had alternative means of reducing negative affect, he or she would not become an addicted smoker. If there is no other perceived means of reducing negative affect, then the smoker will become obsessed with (addicted to) cigarettes.

The strength of addiction was seen by Tomkins (1968) to vary as a function of environmental stress, negative affect, and self-confidence and optimism. He noted that many apparently addicted smokers can go for long periods of time, even on protracted vacations, without missing their cigarettes. In support of his contention, he cited the work of Suedfeld, Suedfeld and Best (1977) and Suedfeld and Ikard (1974), who found that, contrary to their expectations, heavy smokers almost unanimously stated that they did not experience any negative feelings during prolonged periods of sensory deprivation.

Tomkins (1966, 1968) emphasized the importance of assessing individual differences between smokers. Tomkins and his associates (Ikard et al., 1969; Ikard & Tomkins, 1973) devised a smoking motivations questionnaire (generally referred to as the Horn-Waingrow Survey) to assess the four types of smokers hypothesized in Tomkins's model (1966, 1968). The 23-item questionnaire was factor analyzed, and six factors were identified: (a) Pleasurable Relaxation, (b) Negative Affect Reduction, (c) Dependence–Addiction, (d) Stimulation, (e) Sensorimotor–Manipulative Enjoyment, and (f) Habitual–nonconscious smoking. Almost all smokers reported finding cigarettes pleasurable and relaxing and as reducing negative affect, but relatively few indicated that they frequently used cigarettes as a stimulant or obtained sensorimotor gratification from smoking.

Experimental studies assessing behavioral correlates of Tomkins's (1966, 1968) self-report factors have provided some support for their validity (Leventhal & Avis, 1976; McFall, 1970; Shiffman et al., 1992a; Tate & Stanton, 1990). However, such investigations are few in number, variable in outcome, and of limited scope. Thus, it is not clear to what degree these factors reflect differences in actual smoking behavior, motivation, and reinforcement (see Chapter 5). In conclusion, Tomkins's appreciation of the subtle complexities of the interactions between cognition, coping, and affect has rarely been duplicated in the smoking literature. A number of studies have tested Tomkins's (1966, 1968) model of smoking by the administration of questionnaires designed to assess his typology of individual differences in smoking motivation. Factor-analytic evaluations of smokers' responses to such questions have generally supported his model by demonstrating individual differences in tendencies to smoke for positive affect, negative-affect reduction, and for smoking in an addictive-like manner. This model appears in many respects to be a more accurate characterization of smoking than are unifactorial addiction models.

Multiple Regulation Model

Leventhal and Cleary (1980) proposed a multiple regulation model that evolved in response to findings inconsistent with unifactorial addiction models of smoking. The model assumes that smokers regulate nicotine levels because certain emotional states have been conditioned to them, not because of pharmacologically induced dependency.

In this model (Leventhal & Cleary, 1980), it is assumed that emotional regulation is the variable of primary importance in smoking and that variances from emotional or hedonic homeostasis result in smoking. Heavy smokers are seen as dependent and thus smoke to regulate nicotine level because reductions in nicotine concentration result in a dysphoric subjective state typically experienced as craving. However, other stimuli can also cause such dysphoria. The distress associated with reductions in blood nicotine concentrations can combine with distress associated with a variety of other stressors. Thus, external and internal cues can influence emotional states.

The multiple regulation model posits that an adequate model of smoking motivation must explain how craving becomes associated with drops in nicotine concentrations. This model sees two possible means by which such an association comes about. One is based on the assumptions of the opponent-process theory of emotional motivation (Solomon & Corbit, 1973, 1974), in which it is hypothesized that nicotine initially gives rise to a hedonically positive reaction, which in turn results in a weaker opponent (homeostatic), negative subjective response. With repeated nicotine use, the opponent negative affective state (craving) becomes stronger. The secondary opponent state can be reduced by administration of nicotine. Thus, the more one smokes the stronger the negative affect associated with the opponent process, so that repeated smoking automatically causes its own craving.

The Leventhal and Cleary model also posits that external stimulation is an alternative cause of craving. Although initially, the novice smoker sees smoking as being mature and exciting, the new smoker begins to smoke in various stressful situations. These situations are seen as providing negative affective states that become conditioned to reductions in plasma nicotine concentrations. Smoking or nicotine is seen as reducing anxiety that will reappear (because of continuing environmental stressors and/or temperament) when the cigarette is withdrawn (as blood nicotine concentration begins to decline). This conditioning of cigarette abstinence with declines in nicotine and resulting increased negative affect (due to the loss of nicotine's tranquilizing effects) is seen as conditioning negative affect to the bodily sensations resulting from reductions in nicotine concentration. Thus, craving is seen not as the sensations resulting from drops in nicotine concentration, but as conditioned reactions to such sensations.

Leventhal and Cleary (1980) noted that although either of the two above mechanisms may account for the negative affect associated with the development of craving, these mechanisms do not account for the problems with the pharmacological model. They also addressed the fact that additional questions need to be addressed, including why changes in stress significantly influence craving, why abstinence increases inaccuracies in performance and changes in response to shock, and why craving can be so rapidly elicited by external cues.

The Leventhal and Cleary (1980) model assumes first that several emotional processes can operate simultaneously (e.g., environmental stress plus smoking-induced positive affect) or multiple opponent processes (e.g., those associated with simultaneous nicotine and caffeine abstinence). Second, it assumes that emotional or hedonic states from different sources combine algebraically at a given point in time. For example, the negative affect associated with craving will be amplified by the opponent process of smoking and the negative affect of social or other environmentally induced stress. The third major assumption made is that changes in blood nicotine result in a range of bodily sensations that can be conditioned to emotional states. Leventhal and Cleary used the term *sensations* to differentiate experiences resulting from increases or decreases in nicotine from well-formed emotional reactions. Fourth, the model assumes that smoking enhances adaptive responses to stressful situations. Smoking-induced increases in arousal are seen as enhancing the capacity to cope effectively with intellectual challenges. The social aspects of smoking reduce social anxiety, and its ability to reduce muscle tension produces relaxation and counteracts the distress associated with a variety of negative affects.

The model's final assumption is that if smoking can modulate arousal from external circumstances and thus facilitate coping, then smoking will be strongly associated with memories of such coping episodes and will form emotional memory schemas. These schematic emotional memories combine with representations of situations and with motoric and physiological reactions in those situations. They integrate external stimulus cues with internal ones. Elicitation of any of the components of a memory schema can elicit remaining components of the schema. Thus, the schema makes it possible for the smoker to crave smoking when any of a wide range of schema components (e.g., seeing a cigarette, lowered blood nicotine concentrations, and negative affect) are available as cues.

According to the multiple regulation model, individual differences between smokers result from differences in the vividness of elements in the schema. Negative affect smokers are sensitive to nicotine, but these sensations are conditioned to stressful situations. In contrast, social smokers are also nicotine sensitive, but their conditioning imagery is associated with social situations. Heavy smokers are seen as trying to maintain their blood nicotine concentrations within a narrow window because sensations associated with declines in nicotine have been conditioned to emotional schemas that elicit negative affect. The model suggests that such internal conditioning may take a substantial length of time because the cues are less noticeable or because a high rate of smoking across a wide range of conditions is required before internal cues are the primary cues in the emotional schema. An implication of this model is that sudden changes in the emotional schema associated with smoking would help break the addictive pattern. Consistent with this hypothesis, Robins et al. (1980) found that U.S. soldiers returning from Vietnam were surprisingly successful in quitting regular heroin use. That is, changing the environment changed the pattern of use even with an archetypal drug of addiction.

In summary, Leventhal and Cleary's (1980) multiple regulation model proposes that smoking initially regulates emotional responses elicited by environmental stimuli, later comes to regulate craving conditioned to external cues, and finally modulates craving and negative affect resulting from change in nicotine itself. The model hypothesizes that the association between decrements in blood nicotine and craving is not automatic, but instead depends on the smoker's history of smoking.

Affect Regulation Through Arousal Modulation

Another model emphasizing multiple reinforcement mechanisms was proposed by H. J. Eysenck (1973), who argued that the effects of nicotine on cortical and subjective arousal are a function of the degree of arousal in the cerebral cortex. When cortical arousal is high, as during emotional states, the effects on cortical arousal are seen as dearousing and thus tranquilizing. When cortical arousal is low, as when one is drowsy, however, the effects of nicotine on cortical arousal are seen as stimulating. Thus, in both conditions smoking nicotine moves the smoker's cortical and subjective arousal to a more ideal and hedonically pleasing level. Support for the hypothesis that the effects of nicotine are a function of cortical arousal level comes from several lines of evidence reviewed in Chapters 6 and 7.

H. J. Eysenck's (1973, 1980) model has been important not only because it hypothesizes multiple reinforcing effects and their associated neurobiological mechanisms, but also because it hypothesizes individual differences in motivations to smoke as a function of personality differences based on an individual's tendency to be cortically underaroused or overaroused. A small number of studies have supported Eysenck's hypothesis that the effects of nicotine vary as a function of central nervous system (CNS) arousal state, which in turn is a function of environmental stress potential and personality factors. The related hypothesis that small doses of nicotine increase cortical and subjective arousal and larger doses result in depressant effects has not been conclusively demonstrated with smoking-sized doses in humans (see Chapters 6 and 7). This model can be viewed as a psychological tool or resource model, in which smokers are seen as using tobacco to obtain a more desirable psychological state, whether that be increased alertness, performance or emotional tranquilization, or both. The concept of nicotine as a psychological tool is inherent not only in Eysenck's theorizing, but also in Leventhal and Cleary's (1980) multiple regulation model and the self-medication models discussed in Chapter 7. All of these models posit multiple mechanisms of reinforcement, a characteristic required to fully account for nicotine's affect-modulating and reinforcing effects.

SELF-REPORTED SMOKING MOTIVATIONS

Numerous studies have attempted to characterize individual differences in smoking motivations through the use of questionnaires. Contents of such questionnaires typically assess (a) situations in which individuals perceive themselves to be more or less likely to smoke, (b) desires to smoke in different settings, or (c) attributed motivations for smoking. In spite of the heterogeneity of items used, the factor structure of smoking motivation questionnaires have relatively consistently found two major factors (negative affect reduction and positive affect enhancement or pleasurable relaxation). In addition, such studies have frequently also found factors suggestive of habitual, addictive, sensorimotor, stimulation, social, and food substitution (for a review of smoking motivation questionnaires, see Shiffman, 1993a). McKennell (1970) found three strongly correlated negative-affect-related factors: Nervous Irritation Smoking, Smoking Alone, and Food Substitution. Factors frequently labelled as *Addictive* consist of items suggesting that the smoker is dependent on cigarettes in the sense that he or she finds the unavailability of smoking a distressing and intolerable condition. The Horn-Waingrow scale addictive items are "I am very much aware of the fact when I am not smoking a cigarette," "Between cigarettes I get a craving that only a cigarette can satisfy," "When I have run out of cigarettes I find it almost unbearable until I can get them," "I get a real gnawing hunger for a cigarette when I haven't smoked for a while," and "I am not contented for long unless I am smoking a cigarette" (Ikard et al., 1969, pp. 652–653). Only one third of the smokers in Ikard et al.'s study rated these two items with a mean score of 3.5 or above, in which a score of 4 is *frequently* and 3 is *occasionally*. In contrast, in excess of 80% of all smokers gave mean ratings of 3.5 or above to pleasurable relaxation items. Thus, as defined by the Horn-Waingrow scale, far more smokers are motivated by the desire for pleasurable relaxation than by addiction.

The fact that negative affect smoking generally correlates more highly with habitual and addictive subscales than with other factors (Coan, 1973; Ikard et al., 1969; Leventhal & Avis, 1976) may have theoretical implications. Correlations between negative affect factors and habitual or dependence factors typically range from .30 to .58 (Ikard et al., 1969; Shiffman, 1993a). Thus, they account at most for 9–35% of common variance, much of which may be methods variance. Thus, these correlations provide minimal support for the hypothesis that nicotine's negative-affect-modulating effects are simply a function of nicotine dependence.

Although many smokers report smoking to maintain a lower body weight (Charlton, 1984; Feldman, Hodgson, & Corber, 1985), none of the traditionally used measures of smoking motivation have included such items. What one gets out of a factor analysis is a function of what items are included. There is no assurance that all important motivations for smoking are measured by such questionnaires.

Perceived Smoking Motivation

Spielberger (1986) assessed reasons for continuing to smoke once started in a study of a large number of college student current, occasional, and former smokers. Table 2.1 presents his findings, showing that tranquilizing effects (i.e., "relaxes me" and "helps me forget my worries") were among the top four reasons given for continuing to smoke among regular female smokers. Contrary to a withdrawal-symptom-alleviation conception "relaxes me" and "helps me forget my worries" were ranked by occasional smokers as the most and third most important reasons, respectively, for continuing to smoke. Among current and occasional smokers, relaxation was rated by both men and women as the most or second most important reason for continuing to smoke. However, "helps me forget my worries" was ranked as more important by women than by men. "Because I enjoy it" is a highly general or summary term that lacks the specificity of the other items and thus may have acted as a cover-all item that included a combination of sensory, tranquilizing, and stimulation factors. From this perspective, tranquilizing effects would be ranked first among specific reasons for continuing to smoke.

Perceived Smoking Situations or Occasions

Questionnaires asking individuals about the occasions when they smoke or desire to smoke have frequently shown negative affective states as the primary occasions during which they are most likely to smoke. However, in one of the first studies in this area, Frith (1971) found that of 12 high-arousal and 10 low-arousal situations, individuals were more likely to report desiring to smoke in underarousing conditions than in overly arousing ones. The high-arousal situations assessed by Frith were biased in that it would be difficult or inappropriate to

Table 2.1 Means and Rank Order of the Ratings of Current, Occasional, and Exsmokers of the Reasons that Influenced Them to Continue to Smoke (Spielberger, 1986)

Variable	Women			Men		
	Current	Occasional	Exsmokers	Current	Occasional	Exsmokers
Because I enjoy it						
m	3.37	2.35	2.45	3.13	2.03	2.37
Rank	1	2	1	1	1	1
Relaxes me when I'm upset/nervous						
m	2.94	2.43	2.36	2.53	1.81	1.83
Rank	2	1	3	2	2	4
Helps me forget my worries						
m	2.26	2.03	2.01	1.70	1.54	1.54
Rank	4	3	5	7	4	7
Gives me something to do when alone						
m	2.44	1.79	1.97	2.00	1.35	1.78
Rank	3	5	6	4	6	5
Makes feel more comfortable around my friends						
m	1.99	1.88	2.41	1.98	1.59	1.89
Rank	6	4	2	5	3	3

Get bored when not smoke						
m	2.26	1.39	1.76	2.18	1.43	1.57
Rank	4	8	7	3	5	6
Because most of friends smoke						
m	1.55	1.75	2.30	1.48	1.32	2.18
Rank	9	6	4	9	7	2
Because is stimulating						
m	1.85	1.52	1.71	1.78	1.30	1.52
Rank	8	7	8	6	8	8
Facilitates thinking						
m	1.88	1.20	1.40	1.63	1.11	1.24
Rank	7	9	9	8	9	9
Media advertise						
m	1.11	1.12	1.30	1.20	1.05	1.15
Rank	10	10	10	10	10	10

Note. 1 = *not at all*; 2 = *some*; 3 = *moderate influence*; 4 = *strong influence on reason for continuing to smoke*. Ranks are within-group ranks. Adapted with the permission of Lexington Books, an imprint of Macmillan Publishing Company from SMOKING AND SOCIETY: Toward a More Balanced Assessment by Robert D. Tollison, editor. Copyright© 1986 by Lexington Books.

smoke in a number of them (e.g., while driving at high speed in heavy traffic or while sitting in a dentist's waiting room). Although Frith did instruct subjects that they should indicate desire rather than properness or possibility of smoking, high-arousal items still appear to suffer from the problem of mixed motivations or desires. Frith's low-arousal items do not depict situations in which there are social prohibitions or response competitions for smoking behavior. Interestingly, strong gender differences emerged such that women were much more likely to report smoking in high-arousal situations than were men, although men reported being more likely to smoke in low-arousal conditions.

In contrast to Frith's (1971) findings, McKennell (1970) found that smokers were more likely to smoke when in a negative affective state (e.g., irritable, anxious, worried, nervous, or bored) than during relaxing situations or positive affective states (e.g., watching TV). McKennell's items refer to affective-state-dependent smoking, whereas those in Frith's study were external situation dependent. Affective-state-specific questions have the advantage of being free of differential environmental inhibitions associated with environmental situation questionnaires.

Spielberger's (1986) Smoking Motivation Questionnaire includes a large subset of items assessing urge to smoke in a variety of different emotional states. In a large sample, anxiety was associated with the strongest urge, followed closely by anger and restful–relaxing. Scores on Automatic–Habitual, Social–Sensory, and Intellectual–Stimulation factors were significantly lower. As in earlier surveys, women, relative to men, reported greater urges to smoke when experiencing negative affect (anger and anxiety). Congruent with this, Best and Hakstian (1978) determined that mean intensity of smoking urge was higher during negative affective states than during a vast majority of other states.

In conclusion, individuals perceive themselves to smoke more often when experiencing negative affect than when experiencing positive or neutral affective states. As with all retrospective self-report measures, these beliefs may reflect actual behavior, or they may be biased by a number of attributional or other distortions. Findings from experimental studies designed to minimize such biases are discussed in subsequent portions of this chapter.

Validational Studies of Smoking Motivation or Situation Questionnaires

Individual differences in self-reported motivations may simply reflect individual differences in self-presentational style rather than actual differences in smoking motivations, situations, or responses. The validity of such questionnaires is established to the degree that they correlate with behavioral and physiological measures of the same constructs.

Attempts to establish the validity of smoking motivation questionnaires have met with mixed success. Several experimental studies have assessed the validity of addiction factors and have generally found that brief abstinence results in stronger craving and larger increases in negative affect in individuals scoring high on the addiction factor, relative to other motives (Ikard & Tomkins, 1973; Leventhal & Avis, 1976). Poor-tasting cigarettes produced greater reductions in smoking in high pleasure–taste smokers than in those scoring low on this dimension (Leventhal & Avis, 1976). Shiffman, Reynolds, Maurer and Quick (1992) found that individuals scoring high on the negative-affect-reduction factor reported larger increases in cigarette craving during stressful tasks.

Self-monitoring of reasons for smoking in one's natural environment has produced mixed and largely negative evidence for the validity of smoking motivation questionnaires. In a 7-day self-monitoring study in which the motivation for each cigarette was noted, Tate and Stanton (1990) found convergent validity coefficients ranging from .39 to .51 for the habit, pleasure, psychological addiction, and stimulation scales of the Reasons for Smoking scale (Horn & Waingrow, 1966). For example, individuals scoring high on the Smoking for Stimulation scale self-monitored more stimulation motives than those scoring low on the scale ($r = .51$). Validity coefficients for the Negative-Affect-Reduction and Sensorimotor Manipulation scales were not significant. To the degree that the self-monitoring procedure was a more valid sample of a participant's general motives, it can be concluded that the Reasons for Smoking scale has at best modest validity for some of its scales. Although the Negative-Affect-Reduction scale did not have a significant validity coefficient, negative affect reduction was the second most frequent of the six self-monitored motives.

Other self-monitoring studies have found small to modest validity coefficients for the Negative-Affect-Reduction factor of the Reasons for Smoking scale. Joffe, Lowe, and Fisher (1981) obtained validity coefficients of .46 and .51 for the negative-affect-reduction and sensorimotor-manipulation motives, respectively. Negative-affect-reduction validity coefficients in three studies by Shiffman and Prange (1988) were .19, .26, and .30.

Accurate modeling of smoking requires consideration of the above-noted individual differences in smoking motivation within and across individuals. Monolithic models are inadequate descriptions of the processes and individual differences involved in smoking motivation and affect modulation. Cigarette smoking appears to be motivated by a number of factors. Individuals differ in the importance of these factors in the maintenance of their smoking. However, smoking motivation questionnaires developed to date do not characterize differences in smoking motivation with enough precision to be of much utility.

Retrospectively Reported Motivations and Effects: What Can We Infer?

Although there is little doubt that smokers generally believe that smoking helps them to relax, concentrate, and cope with a variety of stressors, there remain the questions of why they believe these things. What specific experiences with smoking lead smokers to such conclusions? Are these conclusions valid? Findings from a number of sources suggest that one should be very cautious when making inferences from retrospectively reported motivations. For example, although conceptual and methodological limitations may have precluded their identifying negative-affect-induced smoking, two prospective studies have failed to find relationships between negative affect and smoking where retrospective assessment in the same subjects suggested such an association (S. M. Hall, Havassy, & Wasserman, 1990; Paty & Shiffman, 1991; see Chapter 5).

The question of what effects smoking has on the smoker's subjective and behavioral state is different from the question of self-attributed motives for smoking. Smokers may not accurately identify certain effects of smoking as influencing their smoking. Some effects may be so subtle that they are not reliably perceived as important to the smoking habit when they in fact are. For example, habitual smoking in response to cues predictive of stress or of decreased arousal may be ignored as discriminant stimuli for smoking. In contrast, highly salient stimuli such as intense emotional states or frustration at not having a cigarette available when one wants one may be especially strongly coded in long-term episodic memory.

In conclusion, the literature has indicated that smokers see smoking as involved in affect regulation. They report smoking more when in negative affective states, and they believe that smoking helps them feel better when in such states. In some conditions, some smokers believe that smoking increases positive affective states, but these situations have been less well characterized.

SUMMARY

Although it is clear that smoking and other forms of tobacco use are motivated primarily by nicotine's effects and that many who smoke become highly dependent on nicotine, many smokers do not become dependent on nicotine, and nicotine's reinforcing effects appear to be more situation and person specific than prototypic drugs of abuse. There are dangers in not recognizing the fact that smoking results in a very strong and difficult-to-break habit in a high percentage of individuals. However, there is also a potential danger in labeling smoking an addiction or a dependence. The danger is that smoking will be seen merely as a result of history of nicotine exposure, with little or no influence of individual differences in situational, psychological, or genetic or biological influences. It is important that this simplistic view of smoking not gain popularity because it is clearly erroneous and will not lead to an accurate understanding of smoking motivation or effective smoking interventions or substitutes. Simply labeling smoking as nicotine addiction or dependence explains very little. When, how, why, and in whom nicotine has what reinforcing effects are questions that will be much more informative than a simplistic answer to the question of whether smoking is addictive.

Chapter 5 extends the understanding of smoking motivation by characterizing the nature and situations in which nicotine has reinforcing and affect-modulating effects. Chapter 6 assesses the mechanisms underlying these effects, and Chapter 9 provides an integrated model of smoking reinforcement and affect regulation that includes individual differences in these causes and effects. Because a state-of-the-art understanding of smoking's relationship to emotion, personality, and psychopathology requires state-of-the-art models of each of these domains, the following two chapters (Chapters 3 and 4) provide a foundation in these areas.

Chapter 3

Affect and Emotion

This chapter reviews the nature, etiology, and assessment of affect and emotion, and Chapter 4 summarizes basic dimensions of personality and psychopathology and their relationship to affective processes. Fundamental dimensions and biological bases are emphasized because nicotine interacts directly with a number of biological mechanisms thought to underlie affect and emotion, psychopathology, and personality. This information provides a foundation for later discussions of mechanisms mediating the affect-modulating and reinforcing effects of smoking.

CHARACTERIZATION OF AFFECTIVE PROCESSES

Smoking research and clinical efforts have been impeded by a failure to differentiate between affective processes. Although it is rare to find affect-related processes differentiated in the smoking literature, in the nonsmoking literature affect-related processes that are traditionally differentiated include emotion, affect, feelings, moods, and sensations. Further distinctions are generally made between emotional states, reflexes, drives, and pleasure pain (Arnold, 1960; Lazarus, 1991; P. T. Young, 1975). Such differentiations among affective states and related processes may lead to important and more comprehensive questions; for example, to what degree are various forms of tobacco use similar to drive reduction and appetitive behavior, as opposed to affect regulation or withdrawal symptom alleviation.

Emotions

Primary Emotions Emotions are primary or basic to the degree that they are the products of evolution, occur across individuals, are found across diverse cultures, have reliable physiological patterns (Ekman & Friesen, 1975; Izard, 1971; Panksepp, 1992), appear early in life, and are associated with basic adaptational tasks of animals (Lazarus, 1991). Combinations or blends of primary emotions, like colors, have been proposed to account for the subtle and complex affective reactions frequently observed in nature (Plutchik, 1970). Emotions are largely genetically determined, patterned bodily responses designed by evolution to deal with social and other basic needs such as protection, rejection, reproduction, and goal obtainment. Widely researched, empirically derived lists of primary emotions include fear, surprise, sadness and distress, disgust, anger, anticipation, and happiness and joy (Ekman & Friesen, 1975; Izard, 1971; Plutchik, 1962). Others that have been identified are contempt (Ekman & Friesen, 1975; Izard, 1971), anticipation (Plutchik, 1962), acceptance (Plutchik, 1962), shame, guilt, and interest (Izard, 1971).

Functions of Emotions Rolls (1990) proposed eight functions of emotions. The first function is the elicitation of autonomic and endocrine responses. For example, increases in heart rate and blood pressure enhance both fight and flight responses. The second function is flexibility of behavioral responses to reinforcing stimuli. This flexibility is seen in the Miller–Mowrer two-process (Dollard & Miller, 1950) theory of avoidance conditioning, in which the first process is the classical conditioning of an emotional response and the second is instrumental learning to avoid the fear-eliciting stimulus.

The third function of emotion is motivation. Organisms work to obtain positive reinforcers and to avoid negative ones. Communication is the fourth function of emotion, which is related to social bonding, the fifth function. The attachment of parents to their young and of the young to their parents has genetic survival value because it increases the chances of gene transmission to the next generation.

The sixth function is a generalization of the first through fifth in that things that have survival value are experienced as pleasant and are reinforcing. Acting in a manner inconsistent with survival value results in unpleasant feelings. However, genetically based biological structures are misled at times, as when individuals self-administer non-nutritive sweetener or harmful drugs.

The seventh function of emotion is to influence cognitive evaluations of present conditions and memories. This cognitive–emotional interaction facilitates the interpretation of the environment in a reinforcing or punishing manner and thus enhances sensitivity to potential beneficial or dangerous aspects of the situation.

The final function of emotion is the facilitation of memory storage. Memory is enhanced by strong emotions so that individuals remember numerous details occurring at the time of the emotion. The storage of such details may be useful in helping the individual behave in a more effective manner the next time a similar situation arises. A related mechanism by which emotion can influence memory is through the storage of the current emotional state along with other current episodic facts. Such affect tagging provides a means for future emotional states to influence which memories are recalled.

Subjective Emotional Experience   There are adaptive advantages to awareness of one's own emotional state (Buck, 1984; Gray, 1990; Tucker & Williamson, 1984; Zillmann, 1979). For example, it would be dysfunctional for higher guidance systems to ignore or easily override input from affect systems indicative of danger or challenge to one's resources or social status. The most prominent theories of what constitutes subjective emotional experience follow.

Bodily and Visceral Feedback   James (James & Lange, 1884–1885/1922) proposed that the conscious experience of emotion results from the complex mosaic of sensations produced by emotional behaviors and associated muscular and visceral activity. That is, people experience anger because they clench their jaws, feel the urge to strike, and feel their blood pressure and heart activity increase. The perception of muscular activity, including the face, and visceral activity were seen by James as the totality of the emotional experience. Although there is evidence that visceral feedback frequently plays a role in emotional experience, it does not appear to be necessary or sufficient for all types of emotional experience.

The frequently reported finding across various emotions of an increase in sympathetic- nervous-system (SNS)-innervated visceral activity led many theoreticians (e.g., Mander, 1984; Schachter & Singer, 1962) to erroneously conclude that emotional states are characterized by undifferentiated autonomic arousal. However, contrary to this formulation, peripheral patterns of activity associated with different emotional states are complex, differentiated, and interactive processes across autonomic, endocrine, and motor systems (Henry, 1986; Levenson, Ekman, & Friesen, 1990). Overall, evidence suggests that feedback from subcervical bodily activity, including organs innervated by the autonomic nervous system (ANS) is not necessary for a subjective experience of emotion. However, findings do suggest that such peripheral activity may intensify and enrich subjective emotional experiences. The frequently reported finding of minimal correlations between verbal reports of emotional experience and physiological measures of muscular and SNS end-organ activity (B. O. Gilbert, 1991; Mandler, Mandler, Kremen, & Sholiton, 1961) and between perceived bodily activity and actual peripheral activation (Mandler & Kremen, 1960; Mandler, et al., 1961) has led some (e.g., Buck, 1984) to conclude that peripheral activity plays little if any role in subjective emotional experience. Most such studies have assessed only a limited number of physiological variables and have used between-subjects designs. Given the general view that peripheral feedback from most emotional states is a complex syndrome or mosaic of differentially patterned peripheral activity, there is little reason to believe that a single or small number of physiological measures will capture the peripheral input into subjective experience. H. J. Eysenck (1975) noted that the cortex can detect and integrate complex physiological patterning more adequately than a researcher with a limited number of physiological measures. On the basis of integrative capacity, he concluded that in many cases verbal report is the preferred method of measuring emotional arousal (H. J. Eysenck, 1975, p. 441).

Facial feedback hypothesis   Tomkins (1962) proposed that subjective emotion results largely from naturally occurring emotional expression, especially that associated with the face. Although it has been suggested that one cannot feel angry and smile a complete or genuine smile at the same time, the evidence supporting the influence of facial feedback on experienced emotion is open to alternative interpretations (Buck, 1984; Izard, 1990). Experimental studies designed to assess the importance of facial feedback in emotional experience have had mixed results (Buck, 1984; Izard, 1990). The frequent failure of posed emotions to influence experienced emotion is not surprising given that the voluntary simulation of emotional expressions is not the same as sensory feedback experienced during genuine emotions (Tomkins, 1981). On a final note, Lanzetta and McHugo (1989) concluded

> that the facial feedback hypothesis has been wrongly extracted from the larger context, where emotion is considered to result from the actions of several interacting subsystems. The expressive system is only one component in the complex process that determines emotional experience. (p. 115)

Summary of Peripheral Contributions   Evidence suggests that patterned feedback from peripheral somatic and facial musculature contributes to, but is not generally necessary for, most subjective experiences of emotion.

Direct Central Activity Hypothesis   Many neurobiologically oriented investigators have argued that peripheral feedback is neither sufficient nor necessary for emotional experience (Buck, 1984). Brain stimulation studies are relevant to the debate over the etiology of the subjective experience of emotion as such studies do not involve an external stimulus. However, brain stimulation not only results in subjective reports of emotional experience (R. G. Heath, 1954, 1986), but also elicits simultaneous bodily arousal, the feedback from which may cause or contribute to the subjective emotional experience (R. G. Heath,

1964; Valenstein, 1973). It is not clear whether these subjects experience affective states because stimulation of these subcortical regions leads directly to emotional experience or because the peripheral arousal elicited by such stimulation is experienced (possibly only after appropriate labeling) as emotion. Brain stimulation studies have failed to manipulate and control expectations, environmental factors, and the nature of peripherally induced arousal.

Consistent with the peripheral feedback view of brain stimulation-produced emotional experience are the observations of Sem-Jacobsen (1968, as cited in Valenstein, 1973). He reported that a patient who had been having her brain's "pleasure center" stimulated and who had been smiling and laughing on its electrical stimulation for a number of days one day became fed up and angry at being stimulated. She told the researchers that she did not enjoy the stimulations, but that they had been causing her muscles to contract and tingle in a manner that tickled and that she, in turn, was forced to smile and laugh. Valenstein's review of brain stimulation studies concluded that the effects of brain stimulation are greatly determined by the person's past experience, the present setting, and the individual's personality.

Summary of Direct Central Activity Hypothesis Demand characteristics and patient expectancies associated with electrical stimulation studies have not been systematically assessed. In addition, careful characterization of the full subjective nature and associated detailed multichannel, fine-grained peripheral activity associated with such stimulation has not been performed. Thus, little can be said conclusively regarding whether electrical brain stimulation studies demonstrate changes in subjective emotional or other affective tone independently of their effects on peripheral feedback.

Cognitive–Physiological Interactions and Affect Maranon (1924) and B. Russell (1927/1961) proposed that for a complete state of subjective emotional experience to occur, peripheral feedback from autonomic arousal must be combined with an emotional reason for feeling aroused. Schachter and Singer (1962) promoted and further articulated the Maranon-Russell two-factor model with their study that independently manipulated epinephrine and autonomic arousal and attributions for the arousal. Although Schachter and Singer found some evidence that tended to support this model, their findings were not convincing. Furthermore, subsequent attempts at replication (Marshall & Zimbardo, 1979; Maslach, 1979) showed increased sympathetic arousal to result in negative feelings in all situations, including those meant to induce euphoria. However, work by Erdmann (Erdmann & Janke, 1978) did find support that the sympathomimetic drug ephedrine (also a CNS stimulant) resulted in differential positive versus negative moods in different situations.

In summarizing work in this area, Erdmann (1983) concluded that the two-factor model of emotion has only limited value in the prediction of interactions between situational and autonomic states in the modulation of affective states.

Similarly, Reisenzein (1983) concluded that the role of arousal in emotion is overstated in the arousal-plus-attribution (two-factor) model, but that peripheral arousal feedback can intensify emotional states, in part as a result of causal attributions related to the source of arousal.

Moods

The significant degree of commonality between many of the processes involved in moods and those in emotions (biased information processing, negative or positive feelings, and altered arousal levels) indicates that moods are psychobiological states that have much in common with low-intensity emotions. In some cases, mood states are low-level biological and emotional response residuals or continued low-level emotional responses. They will result in overt expression only when additional stimulus configurations rise above threshold.

Moods may have much in common with low-intensity emotional states because they frequently have common elicitors, subjective experiences, and biological substrates. Consistent with this possibility, an intense emotion is frequently followed by a congruent change in one's mood. Bioinformational biases predispose an individual toward perceiving and reacting to the environment in affect-specific emotional and coping manners. In particular, ambiguous situations are perceived and responded to in a manner congruent with one's mood state (Bower, 1981; Dalgleish & Watts, 1990; Gilligan & Bower, 1984).

Factor-analytic studies of moods over long periods of time have consistently demonstrated two main orthogonal factors: (a) High Positive Affect–High Energy versus Low Positive Affect–Low Energy–Drowsy and (b) High Negative Affect–Distress versus Low Negative Affect–Calm (Thayer, 1989; Watson & Tellegen, 1985). One of the problems with the two-factor circumplex model is that the orthogonal nature of the mood factors implies that one may be in both a positive and a negative mood at the same time (Thayer, 1989). This apparent orthogonality may be the result of methodological and statistical artifacts (Cooper & McConville, 1993; Diener & Emmons, 1985; Thayer, 1989). Specifically, when individuals are asked to provide global evaluations of their mood over periods of a week or more, positive and negative moods appear to be independent and reflect the higher order personality dimensions of neuroticism and extraversion (Watson & Tellegen, 1985). However, when assessed on the same day and in highly emotional situations, positive and negative moods correlate negatively and form a bipolar dimension with positive affect at one end and negative affect at the other (Diener & Emmons, 1985; Diener & Iran-Nejad, 1986).

Thayer (1989) found that energetic and tense arousal were positively correlated at low intensities, but negatively correlated at high levels even though orthogonal when factor-analytic methods are used. Thus, factor-analytic models are not definitive and applicable in every case. Furthermore, the influences of psychotropic drugs on mood and psychiatric disorders suggest that the simple two-dimensional approach is not adequate to differentiate clinically important phenomena. Therefore, studies should report analyses of individual moods as well as higher order correlations among moods in each of the conditions (Thayer, 1989).

Mood Induction and Functions   Lazarus (1991) viewed both moods and acute emotions as reactions to one's appraisal of the environment, with moods being responses to overall issues of one's life and acute emotions resulting from specific adaptational encounters with the environment. It is clear that moods are influenced by many factors other than the immediate external environment. These factors include physical illness, diurnal and monthly hormonal variations, food, and psychoactive drugs.

Feelings

Feelings result from external or internal stimuli. Sense feelings are associated with sensory or perceptual processes originating from the external environment or from within the body. Pleasant feelings can come from hearing beautiful music. Unpleasant feelings are associated with foul odors and indigestion. Activity feelings are associated with interest and disinterest and include an impulse to action resulting from bodily states such as hunger, thirst, a full bladder, and sexual drives (P. T. Young, 1975). Feelings, thus, are pleasant or unpleasant reactions to something determined or appraised by the state of the organism to be good or bad (Arnold, 1960). This appraisal process frequently occurs at basic biological levels outside of conscious awareness or volition. These appraisals in some cases vary rapidly across time as a function of the individual's state. In other cases, appraisal of a stimulus will be relatively constantly positive or negative, depending on the nature of the stimulus and of the individual.

Functions of Feelings   Stimuli are generally experienced as pleasant or unpleasant depending on their usefulness in maintaining homeostasis. Cabanac (1971) demonstrated that the affective–motivational component of perception depends on prestimulus physiological state as exactly the same physical stimulus is perceived as pleasant or unpleasant depending on a departure from the constant body state. For example, when people are cold, they experience pleasant feelings when a hand is placed in hot water, whereas individuals who are warm experience the same hot water as unpleasant.

However, homeostatic explanations are inadequate to explain responses to some stimuli. For example, the aversive feelings elicited by hearing fingernails scratch a chalkboard (Halpen, Blake, & Hillenbrand, 1986) and the positive feelings induced by music are difficult to explain as a function of homeostasis.

Sensations

The definition of sensations as perceptions of bodily or external states that are not highly biologically prepared to contribute to affective states sets them apart from the three major affective processes: moods, emotions, and feelings. Nonetheless, sensations may contribute to all three affective classes. Intense stimuli may result not only in intense sensation, but in negative feelings as well. With less intense stimuli, whether the sensation is experienced as pleasant depends more on the organism's internal state than on the stimulus's pure sensory aspects. Certain peripheral emotion-related patterned bodily activity may be conditioned to elicit affect-related responses. Finally, bodily sensations may act as unconditioned stimuli that are interpreted by subcortical limbic structures in a manner that augments affective processes (Panksepp, 1986).

Functions of Sensations   Although the survival value of perceiving external stimuli is obvious and the value of proprioception associated with balance, movement, and pain is evident, the value of perceiving one's heartbeat and other forms of visceral feedback are less obvious. LeDoux (1989) suggested that although visceral feedback may not be essential for the subjective experience and response to affective processes, it may play two very important emotional roles. The first role is to "give the brain a second chance at emotional experience when the central mechanisms fail to produce such an experience" (p. 283). The second role is seen as an affect-amplifying effect in which the amplification may increase either the intensity or the duration of the emotional experience.

Stress

Stress responses are complex, multidimensional processes, the conceptualization of which has undergone an evolution from simple stimulus–response formulations to the current more transactional and process characterizations (Lazarus, 1991). During the past decade, interest has evolved from general stress responses to the recognition that although most negative affective states have the common denominator of frustration (Lazarus, 1991; Mander, 1984), there are diverse reactions to frustration—anger, fear, depression, and so on. Each emotion is characterized by a relatively unique pattern of physiological and behavioral activity (Henry, 1986), so that discussion of a unified stress response is of little value. Thus, Lazarus (1991) concluded that "once one has sampled the potential richness of the concept of emotions, psychological stress seems too restrictive as a basis of understanding the process of adaptation" (p. 11).

Affect–Cognition Interactions

Although it is clear that cognition and emotion are highly interactive and related, it is not clear whether they should be considered separate systems. Gray (1990) argued that the neurobiological systems underlying cognitions and emotional systems overlap to such an extent that it is "difficult, if not impossible, to maintain any clear distinction between them" (p. 269). In contrast, many other prominent emotion theorists (dualists) have argued that emotion and cognition are mediated by separate but interacting brain systems (Izard, 1992; LeDoux, 1989; Panksepp, 1990). If rapid, unconscious computations of stimulus survival-related significance is a cognitive process, then Le Doux (1989) and most other dualists would be willing to consider emotion to be a type of cognition. However, dualists have noted that it is important to distinguish such rapid, survival-related computations from rational, analytic processing not associated with basic survival functions.

Associational, memorial, and interpretive processes are strongly influenced by and generally congruent with one's mood state (Bower, 1981; Dalgleish & Watts, 1990; Gilligan & Bower, 1984). When one is in a good mood, one tends to view situations in a more positive manner; when one is in a negative mood, one tends to view situations in a more negative way. Limbic emotional systems physiologically bias neocortical cognitive guidance systems to selectively process and attend to emotionally appropriate internal and external stimuli. Thus, subconscious emotional systems can alter higher cognitive processes before the latter can "rationally" determine what the appropriate response is. Furthermore, rational neocortical processes are frequently rationalizations of more rapidly made subcortical appraisals.

Emotional Stimuli, Coping, and Reinforcement

Emotions and other affective states are activated in a number of different manners. Biologically prepared stimuli such as pain, loud noises, goal interference and frustration, and threatening facial patterns constitute direct, unconditioned pathways for emotion elicitation (Izard, 1971; Tomkins, 1962). Classical and other forms of limbic conditioning result in the formation of many conditioned stimuli capable of eliciting mood and emotional responses (H. J. Eysenck, 1979). Such prepared stimuli may play a role in the development of phobias and in the distribution of fears (Rachman, 1977; Seligman & Hager, 1972). For example, although few individuals have been harmed by a bug or spider, many have great fears of these stimuli.

Neocortically based higher cognitive processes can also result in emotions through a number of appraisal and attributional processes that imply potential benefit or threat to the individual's well-being (Lazarus, 1991). Neocortical affective activation can be instigated by transmission of information and instruction, as well as by vicarious exposures (Rachman, 1977). A complete characterization of affective responses requires consideration of these processes from a cognitive–motivational–relational perspective. That is, emotion is part of a larger motivational coping complex (Lazarus, 1991). Emotion and motivation can be seen as opposite sides of the same coin, two aspects of largely the same underlying processes (Buck, 1984). Motivation implies movement toward goals, movement that can be facilitated or impeded by environmental stimuli. Interruption of progress toward achieving one's goal has been hypothesized as the major cause of emotion (Berscheid, 1982; Mander, 1984). Lazarus (1991) stated that "though all negative emotions share the property of being a reaction to thwarting, each of these emotions—that is anger, fear, guilt, shame, and so on—is also a separate and distinct reaction to diverse forms of thwarting" (p. 11). Phylogenetically basic goals such as survival and avoidance of pain are largely unconscious organismic goals until their achievement is acutely threatened. Humans, however, are consciously aware of many other goals, ranging from various forms of academic achievement to getting to a show on time, for example

To the degree that emotion is a function of thwarted goals, one's emotional state should be a joint combination of one's environmental and personal characteristics conducive to goal generation and goal attainment. Personal characteristics conducive to failure in obtaining one's goals include a range of skill deficits in relevant domains: technical, social, motor, intellectual, and emotional competence (Buck, 1991).

Emotional and Reinforcing Stimuli

There is a close relationship between emotion and reinforcement; the stimuli that elicit emotional reactions are the same stimuli that serve as reinforcers in operant conditioning (Staats & Eifert, 1990). Furthermore, limbic and other brain mechanisms underlying reward and reinforcement are largely the same as those associated with affective processes.

Measurement of Affective and Motivational States

The Triple Response Mode Approach   It has long been recognized that simply assessing affect by using global self-report measures is plagued by a number of potentially invalidating problems. The tripartite, or triple response, mode approach promoted by Lang (1968) and subsequent affect researchers reminds one of the fact that affective states are constructs inferred from the use of three types of measures: behavioral, physiological, and self-report. The importance of considering affective states and responses as constructs can be seen in Buck's (1984) work showing extraverts to be more facially expressive than introverts in response to emotion-eliciting stimuli, but to exhibit smaller heart rate and skin conductance changes than introverts to the same stimuli. Those smoking studies simultaneously observing two or more response modes have produced theoretically important findings, including the paradoxical observation of nicotine's physiologically arousing yet affectively tranquilizing effects (D. G. Gilbert, 1979).

Temporal Resolution and Time Span of Measures It is not clear whether the increases in irritability and other forms of negative affect generally reported during the first days of smoking abstinence are chronic and constant subjective states or whether abstaining individuals are simply more affectively reactive to eliciting situations. This deficit stems from the pervasive use of mood ratings requesting the individual to provide mood averages for "today." Reported increases in negative affect thus represent an averaging across time that prevents an understanding of whether abstainers experience periods of calm, tranquility, and pleasure during abstinence.

More time-specific and frequent assessments of affect are also desirable because retrospective reports of how one felt on the average or how one typically feels before or after smoking are prone to various expectational and other attributional biases. For example, because individuals are more prone to recall events associated with emotional situations than with nonemotional ones, they may more often recall smoking during stressful situations. Questionnaires asking individuals how they currently feel or felt during the past few minutes are less likely to be influenced by these differential biases (Shiffman, 1993a).

BIOLOGICAL BASES OF AFFECT

The following section briefly outlines the current understanding of biological systems underlying affective processes. It begins by describing first the autonomic and endocrine portions of the adaptive and homeostatic affective functions and then the portion of the nervous system controlling the skeletal muscles. Biological mechanisms underlying peripheral physiological activity, facial and bodily expressions, and mood and other affective states are then presented. Finally, interactions between limbic processing and neocortical affective appraisal systems are discussed to provide a background for ecologically valid modeling of the complexity of human affective and reinforcement processes associated with smoking.

Affective Functions of the Brain Stem

Descending Brain Stem Circuits Brain stem projections modulate autonomic and endocrine activity. Peripheral organ systems are controlled by sympathetic and parasympathetic outputs from the medulla, which receives its input from other brain stem and cortical structures (Derryberry & Tucker, 1992). The ANS is frequently activated in a somewhat diffuse, nonspecific manner, typically increasing activity of many, if not most, end organs during many different types of intense emotional reactions. However, differential, emotion-specific patterns of autonomic end-organ activity have been reliably demonstrated (Ekman, Levenson, & Friesen, 1983; Levenson, Carstensen, Friesen, & Ekman, 1991; Levenson et al., 1990). Nicotine exerts some of its ANS-activating effects by stimulating descending brain stem circuits controlling heart rate, blood pressure, and other ANS end organs (S. M. Hall, 1984). Emotion-elicited brain stem control of endocrine system output occurs through a series of feedback loops that release and modulate peripheral hormones. Projections from higher (cortical) brain centers cause the hypothalamus and pituitary gland to release various hormones (e.g., adrenocorticotrophin, beta-endorphin, and vasopressin). These hormones in turn influence brain activity by means of receptors throughout the brain and thereby modulate various higher brain processes, including arousal, attentional, perception, memory, and affect. Most hormones have effects on numerous physiological and psychological processes (Astertia, 1985). For example, cortisol and beta-endorphin appear to have homeostatic and antistress restorative effects, helping to re-equilibrate stress-induced physiological arousal in a number of biological systems (Munck, Guyre, & Holbrook, 1984).

Ascending Brain Stem Projections   The reticular activating system consists of a number of ascending systems, each with different neurotransmitters, projection sites, and effects (J. R. Cooper, Bloom, & Roth, 1991; Saper, 1987). The cell bodies of these ascending projections are found in clusters in the brain stem; each cluster is devoted to one particular transmitter system. Although ascending projections from each of the major neurotransmitter groups innervate most of the cortex, the densities of these projections vary from region to region and as a function of cortical layer (Derryberry & Tucker, 1992). Significant dysfunctions of these ascending systems are associated with medical and psychological disorders (J. R. Cooper et al., 1991), whereas smaller differential activities in these systems are likely related to individual differences in temperament and personality (Zuckerman, 1991). The major ascending systems are especially sensitive to emotional, stimulating, and other survival-related stimuli, although they contribute to the modulation of virtually all behavior (J. R. Cooper et al., 1991).

Cholinergic projections consist of two major groups. Cell bodies in the brain stem cholinergic complex project to the entire neocortex. Cell bodies of the pontomesencephalotegmental cholinergic complex project upward to the thalamus and other diencephalic sites and downward to pontine and medullary reticular formations and cerebellar and vestibular nuclei and cranial nerve nuclei (J. R. Cooper et al., 1991). Cholinergic projections are essential to the functioning of a variety of cognitive processes (Becker & Giacobini, 1991). Consistent with the view that nicotine exerts many of its arousing effects by means of ascending cholinergic paths, human brain dissections suggest that nicotine binding in the brain is highest in the nucleus basalis of Meynert (Shimohama, Taniguchi, Fujiwara, & Kameyama, 1985). Cholinergic projections appear to be relatively more dense in the left than in the right hemiphere (Tucker & Williamson, 1984). Nicotine's numerous effects are initially instigated by its binding to nicotinic–cholinergic receptors throughout the CNS and the peripheral nervous system (Balfour, 1991b). Nicotine's effects on dopaminergic, noradrenergic, serotonergic, and other systems result from a combination of indirect, cholinergically modulated effects and cholinergic receptors on neurons related to these noncholinergic structures.

A majority of dopaminergic projections are associated with two systems. The nigrostriatal dopaminergic system originates in the substantia nigra, and its cell bodies send their projections to the striatum nuclei associated with extrapyramidal motor activity. The mesolimbic dopaminergic system cell bodies are in the brain stem ventral tegmental area and project to the nucleus accumbens, limbic areas, and forebrain areas including the lateral and medial prefrontal cortex (J. R. Cooper et al., 1991). Nicotine binds to dopaminergic neurons in the ventral tegmental area of rodents and thereby modulates their activity in certain circumstances (Balfour, 1991b). The mesolimbic system modulates arousal, affect, motivation, and reinforcement. Lesions of the ascending dopaminergic tracks, such as those traversing the lateral hypothalamus, result in a sensory neglect syndrome in which there is a massive loss of motivation to respond to anything (Thompson, 1985). Until recently, it was generally concluded that increased activity in the mesolimbic system was consistently reflective of positive reinforcement and reward system activity. However, there is growing recognition that mesolimbic activation occurs during aversive and stressful conditions. Dopaminergic systems appear to be relatively more dense in the left than in the right hemisphere (Tucker & Williamson, 1984).

Noradrenergic projections arise from two major clusters of cell bodies: the locus coeruleus and the lateral ventral tegmental fields. Mason (1984) proposed that a primary function of the noradrenergic system is the enhancement of attention to significant stimuli and the screening of irrelevant stimuli. Anxiety- and attention-related roles have been hypothesized for this system on the basis of its inhibitory effects and those of anxiety (Gray, 1992a; Zuckerman, 1991). Panksepp (1982), however, has argued that norepinepherine is associated with the general arousal of all emotive systems. Noradrenergic projections appear to be relatively more dense in the right hemiphere (Tucker & Williamson, 1984).

Evidence indicates that nicotine in moderately high doses can increase norepinephrine turnover in the hippocampus and other brain areas, including the locus coeruleus (Balfour, 1991b). However, because the locus coeruleus increases activity in response to novel and threatening stimuli, increased locus coeruleus activity subsequent to nicotine administration is not proof of a direct effect of nicotine on locus coeruleus activity (Balfour, 1991b). In fact, some findings suggest that the effects of nicotine on locus coeruleus activity is an indirect effect of peripheral release of excitatory amino acids that innervate the locus coeruleus (Engberg, 1989). Furthermore, toxically high doses or other effects of nicotine may be perceived by the organism as novel or threatening and thereby lead to norepineperine release. Serotonergic projections arise primarily from the dorsal and median raphe nuclei of the pons and upper brain stem (J. R. Cooper et al., 1991, p. 348). There is a general concensus that serotonin is involved in the inhibition of behavior and possibly in the experience of anxiety

(Zuckerman, 1991). Low CNS serotonin is associated with aggression and impulsivity (Pritchard, 1991b).

Nicotine can decrease serotonin release and turnover in the hippocampus and increase the density of serotonergic receptors in the hippocampus. In his review, Balfour (1991b) concluded that chronic nicotine acts primarily on the median raphe and that it is tempting to hypothesize that nicotine acts preferentially on serotonergic pathways involved in mood modulation, the same pathways influenced by antidepressant drugs. Many anxiolytic drugs inhibit serotonergic cells originating in the dorsal raphe, but nicotine appears to have less of an effect on these cells than it does on those in the median raphe.

Major histamine pathways arise from the posterior basal hypothalamus and mesencephalic reticular formation and project ipsilaterally to numerous brain areas (J. R. Cooper et al., 1991). Histamine is generally an excitatory neurotransmitter that results in subjective, behavioral, and electrocortical arousal. The effects of nicotine on histaminergic activity have not been characterized. However, the fact that both nicotine and the histaminergic pathways are associated with arousal suggests that these pathways may mediate some of nicotine's arousal and affect-modulating effects.

Affect-Influencing Effects of Brain Stem Systems   The affect-modulating effects of the ascending brain stem systems are potentially great given that these systems modulate all major psychological and behavioral functions. Because nicotine appears to influence directly or indirectly most, if not all, of these ascending systems, its potential effects are equally wide. Each system innervates the entire cortex; however, different systems are relatively more influential in different cortical regions and layers (Derryberry & Tucker, 1992). For example, dopaminergic and cholinergic systems appear to be relatively more dense in the left than in the right hemisphere, and noradrenergic and serotonergic systems are relatively more dense in the right hemisphere (Tucker & Williamson, 1984).

The ascending systems directly modulate responsivity of cortical neurons and thus help shape the nature of affect- and motivation-related bioinformation processing in such a manner that significant signals receive relatively higher priority and response (Derryberry & Tucker, 1992). Derryberry and Tucker (1992) suggested that enhanced dopaminergic activity may be especially important in object-based ventral cortical networks and left-hemisphere information processing, whereas noradrenergic enhancement of dorsal cortical and right-hemisphere processes may bias in favor of spatial information. Such modulation of attentional processes is the basis for the Tucker and Williamson (1984) hypothesis that the left-hemisphere specialization for sequential analytic processing is based on a brain stem dopaminergic focal attention system. Thus, in this model strong dopaminergic activation resulting from emotionally or motivationally significant stimuli would increase focal attention and the identification of specific parts at the cost of broad attention and spatial memory. Tucker and Williamson noted the relevance of these differences in lateralized attentional processes to a range of psychopathologies, as well as to personality dimensions and effects of drugs. The effects of nicotine on affect and performance have been hypothesized to be a function of its differential effects on these lateralized processes (D. G. Gilbert & Welser, 1989).

The affect-influencing effects of the descending brain stem systems are more indirect than the ascending ones. There are two major means by which these systems exert their influence over higher information-processing centers. The most direct is the sensory perception of brain-stem-controlled autonomic end-organ activity, such as the sensation of one's heart pounding. The second means involves brain-stem-produced increases in endocrine hormones that then modulate both central brain excitability, and peripheral processes. For example, cortisol appears to help differentially shape and bias various cortical regions in a manner akin to that resulting from ascending brain stem neurotransmitter systems (Wolkowitz et al., 1990).

Derryberry and Tucker (1992) noted that the modulation of bioinformation processing by the ascending brain stem projections are not easily conceptualized within the conventional constructs of cortical arousal. Different ascending systems modulate different processes; however, a common direct or indirect effect of most, if not all, of these ascending systems may be to modulate electrocortical activation and perceptual and affective states.

Limbic System

An overall view of the limbic system may be accomplished by conceptualizing it as composed of two divisions: the hippocampal system and the amygdalar system (Derryberry & Tucker, 1992; Gray, 1990). Gray's (1990) influential model of personality and emotion assumes the existence of three basic emotion systems: a behavioral approach system, a flight-or-fight system, and a behavioral inhibition system. He viewed the (septo)hippocampal system as the biological basis of the behavioral inhibition system, whereas the amygdaloid system is seen as the basis of the flight-or-fight system. The biological basis of the behavioral approach system includes both the amygdaloid and hippocampal systems, as well as brain stem, paralimbic structures, and neocortical systems.

The Hippocampal System   Like the brain stem sytems, the hippocampal system generally responds to important stimuli before their neocortical processing (Coburn, Ashford, & Fuster, 1990). The connections of the hippocampal system with numerous cortical and brain stem systems allow it to function as a primary cognitive network heavily involved in spatial memory (O'Keefe & Nadel, 1978) and working memory (Olton, Becker, & Handelmann, 1979) and in comparing sensory information with cognitive predictions (Gray, 1982). Forebrain projections to the hippocampal formation are implicated in various aspects of attention and memory (Bartus, Dean, Beer, & Lippa, 1982). Gray (1982, 1990) noted a remarkable similarity between the effects of antianxiety drugs and the behavioral effects of lesions to the septal area and the hippocampus. On the basis of his observations of the effects of antianxiety drugs on behavior, Gray (1990) developed a septohippocampal model of anxiety. He noted evidence indicating that the septohippocampal system is sensitive to signals predicting punishment, frustrative nonreward, and innate fear cues. Detection of such signals results in septohippocampal processes that inhibit behavior, activate autonomic processes, and modulate cortical activity, including those associated with focused attention. Increases in noradrenergic input into the hippocampus were seen by Gray as predisposing the organism toward anxiety by flagging certain stimuli as important, whereas the ascending serotonergic projection is seen as adding a flag indicating that the stimulus is associated with punishment and as biasing the organism toward motor inhibition. Gray viewed cholinergic inputs to the behavioral inhibition system as facilitating stimulus analysis. Evidence suggests that the amygdala is also tuned to detect both novel stimuli and stimuli with affective significance (LeDoux, 1987; Zuckerman, 1991).

The Amygdaloid System   The amygdala (located in the anterior temporal lobe) contributes to the attachment of emotional significance by classical conditioning to stimuli that predict the occurrence of reinforcement, both positive and negative (Gray, 1990). Thus, the amygdala is widely viewed as involved in almost all emotional behavior and experience (Kentridge & Aggleton, 1990; Rolls, 1990). LeDoux (1987) and Derryberry and Tucker (1992) have noted that the amygdala, like the hippocampus, receives projections from multimodal association areas of the cortex, but that it also receives information from earlier and unimodal processing states, thus possibly causing the immediate global emotional reactions to stimuli discussed by Zajonc (1984). This sensory convergence is an important requirement for the assigning of a stimulus complex's emotional significance.

Descending Limbic Effects   The septohippocampal and amygdaloid systems project to autonomic, endocrine, and emotion-related motor regions (Price & Amaral, 1981). Output from the central amygdaloid nucleus can stimulate specific brain stem nuclei whose activity results in emotional behavior including freezing, facial emotions, startle, and autonomic changes (Davis, Hitchcock, & Rosen, 1987; Kentridge & Aggleton, 1990).

Ascending Limbic Effects   The hippocampus and amygdala project to ascending brain stem neurotransmitter systems, which in turn tune brain activity to meet survival needs. The amygdala also projects to prefrontal, insular, temporal, and occipital cortex and thus influences both primary sensory and associative cortical areas (Aggleton & Mishkin, 1986; Derryberry & Tucker, 1992). Ascending limbic emotional priming and the generation of conditioned overt and covert (bioinformational) responses influence and bias higher neocortical information processing in a manner that is likely to generate a congruence between more immediate limbic subconscious appraisals and slower neocortical rationalizations and decisions.

Affect and the Paralimbic Cortices   The paralimbic cortex is an intermediate tissue between the limbic system and the neocortex. One of the two major divisions of the paralimbic cortex is highly interconnected with and influenced by the hippocampus, and the other is associated more closely with the amygdala (Derryberry & Tucker, 1992). The hippocampal division includes the cingulate, retrosplenial, and parahippocampal regions. The hippocampal division of paralimbic cortex, like the hippocampus, is sensitive to spatial processing, and the cingulate neurons respond to significance and novelty of stimuli (Derryberry & Tucker, 1992). It has been suggested that paralimbic circuits modulated by endorphin and enkephalin are involved in attachment and separation behavior (MacLean, 1990; Panksepp, 1982). Thus, the hippocampal division of the paralimbic cortex may be associated with social maps or propositional structures of bioinformation processing (Lang, 1979) and associated social bonding, attachment, and the inhibition of aggression.

The amygdaloid division of paralimbic cortex is a site of convergence for exteroceptive and interoceptive projections (LeDoux, 1987). Like the amygdala, the amygdaloid paralimbic cortex is involved in the ascribing of emotional or motivational importance to external stimuli (Rolls, 1990). Thus, the amygdala may be the biological basis of much of Pavlovian conditioning, and the paralimbic orbital cortex may be involved in more cognitive insight-oriented learning (Thorpe, Rolls, & Maddison, 1983). Gray (1990) viewed anxiety and his related behavioral inhibition system as being mediated by amygdaloid and septohippocampal subsystems.

Gorenstein and Newman (1980) considered the septum as part of a system composed of the hippocampus and orbitofrontal cortex. Both the septohippocampal and the amygdaloid paralimbic systems appear to interact in the control of impulsive and sensation-seeking behavior and in the generation of behavioral inhibition and anxiety. Gray (1982) has provided extensive evidence to support the view that there is a "remarkable parallel that exists between the behavioral effects of lesions to the septal area and hippocampal formation on the one hand, and those of the anti-anxiety drugs, on the other" (p. 50). The overall ability of the amygdaloid paralimbic system to integrate bioinformation from interoceptive and exteroceptive stimuli and to form complex, environmentally sensitive models may allow this system to contribute significantly to feeling tones and moods. Lesions to this system frequently result in dysfunctional emotional behavior, including an inability to integrate external context with internal stimuli. For example, frontally lesioned patients frequently fail to respond with appropriate affect to situations, even though they can accurately characterize the situation (Nauta, 1971).

Ascending Paralimbic Effects   The amygdaloid division of the paralimbic cortex projects to the occipital lobe, where it may modulate early visual information processing in an affective-state-dependent manner (Derryberry & Tucker, 1992). In addition, interoceptive information from this division may play an important role in modulating feeling tone and mood. The hippocampal division, by means of projections from the cingulate motivational map, appears to modulate parietal affective–spatial maps and thereby direct attention to important stimuli, whereas paralimbic projections to the prefrontal regions are likely to modulate the planning, impulse control, and goal-state processes that are known to be closely associated with prefrontal bioinformational processing (Derryberry & Tucker, 1992).

Affect-Related Interhemispheric (Lateralized) and Intrahemispheric Neocortical Processes

In addition to the limbic and paralimbic structures, neocortical structures contribute to perceptual, experiential, and expressive aspects of emotion and affect. Dominance of one hemisphere is generally relative rather than absolute. In right-handed persons, the left hemisphere is the primary biological basis of verbal, linguistic, analytic, sequential, and logical processes and reasoning, whereas the right hemisphere plays a relatively dominant role in nonverbal, affective, spatial, and melodic processes and uses a configurational, holistic, synthetic, and concrete perceptual style (Borod, 1992).

There are two general hypotheses concerning hemispheric specialization for affective processes: (a) The right hemisphere is dominant for both emotional perception and expression, independent of affective valence, and (b) the right hemisphere is specialized for negative affect, whereas the left hemisphere is specialized for positive affect. The perception of emotional expression would be expected to be especially suited for the right hemisphere, given its visuospatial and patterned perception specialization. Evidence is largely consistent with the view that the right hemisphere has more direct connections with subcortical and limbic structures than does the left (Gainotti, Caltagirone, & Zoccolotti, 1993; Heilman, Schwartz, & Watson, 1978). Although there appears to be no direct evidence of more connections between limbic structures in the right than the left hemisphere (Tucker, 1991), a higher ratio of white to gray matter in the right than the left hemisphere (Gur et al., 1980) and longer proximal dendritic fibers crossing more neocortical layers in the right than the left hemisphere (Scheibel, 1990) are consistent with the hypothesis that there are more regional interconnections between various right-hemisphere areas and functional systems (Gur et al., 1980).

There are also two versions of the valence hypothesis (for a review, see Borod, 1992). One version suggests that the right hemisphere is specialized for all modes of negative affect and the left for all modes of positive affect. The other version assumes that the expression and experience of positive affect is related to left-hemisphere-dominant processes, and the perception of positive affect processes as well as all negative affective processes are predominantly right-hemisphere processes. Negative affective processes are associated with immediate emergency survival needs such as escape from a threatening situation. Thus, the immediate holistic right-hemispheric mode of analysis and associated heightened arousal and vigilance to external stimuli are seen as more rapidly preparing the organism for active coping than are the more methodical, sequential, logical analyses of the left hemisphere (Borod, 1992; Davidson, 1984).

Consistent with both versions of the valence hypothesis, studies of right-hemisphere lesions show larger decrements in autonomic responses to stimuli than do studies of left-hemisphere lesions (Tucker & Williamson, 1984). Pribram and McGuinness (1975) and Tucker and Williamson (1984) have summarized evidence indicating that the right hemisphere is more associated with arousal (phasic changes in attention providing a rapid, broad, context-rich meaning analysis), whereas the left hemisphere is associated with more sustained discrete, object-focused analysis.

Approach-related behavior may be relatively more mediated by the left hemisphere (Davidson, 1984; Davidson, Ekman, Saron, Senulis, & Friesen, 1990; Fox, 1991). Left-hemisphere processing resulting in sequentially analyzed input and outputs including high-resolution, flexible fine motor behavior (speech and fine motor movement) is more appropriate for approach and predatory behavior than for avoidance and prey behavior. Davidson (1984) argued that these left–right differences in hemispheric specialization for affect-related approach and avoidance behaviors occur only in the frontal lobes, whereas the posterior regions are associated with relatively pure cognitive–perceptual processes.

Differences in findings across studies may be due to the specific nature of the affective processes being assessed (Borod, 1992). Levy (1990) noted that differential hemispheric specialization may vary as a function of valence only in the context of mood states. Empirical findings have recently been interpreted as tending to support the right-hemisphere hypothesis, especially in the case of emotional perception (Borod, 1992).

Overall, findings support the view that the right hemisphere is dominant for the emotional perception and expression of both negative and positive affect. However, evidence briefly outlined below suggests that mood states, psychopathology, and mood disorders may be differentially associated with frontal lobe states or dysfunctions.

A number of investigators (Davidson, 1993; Fox, 1991) have observed interhemispheric and intrahemispheric differences in EEG activity as a function of depressed mood states and withdrawal-prone personality dispositions in clinically depressed persons and in nonclinical samples. In contrast to the above-suggested overall importance of the right hemisphere in emotional perception and expression, these mood and personality studies have suggested that both the left and the right frontal lobes are of particular importance in determining and mediating mood (Davidson, 1993).

Lateralized and Localized Effects of Psychoactive Substances   Tucker and Williamson (1984) summarized the significant body of evidence indicating that different neurotransmitter systems are lateralized, such that dopamine and acetylcholine are relatively more dense in the left hemisphere and serotonin and norepinephrine are more dense in the right hemisphere. The neurotransmitter- and receptor-specific binding of drugs and most other psychoactive substances allows these substances to interact with relatively neuromodulator-specific localized and lateralized brain systems that are differentially related to various affective processes. Thus, different drugs can influence different cognitive and affective processes. A number of investigators have found smoking to be associated with relatively greater right-hemisphere changes than left-hemisphere changes in EEG activation (D. G. Gilbert, 1987; D. G. Gilbert, Robinson, Chamberlin, & Spielberger, 1989; Gilbert, Meliska, Welser, & Estes, 1994; Elbert & Birbaumer, 1987; Norton, Brown, & Howard, 1992; Pritchard, 1991a).

Arousal-State-Dependent Information Processing

Maximally effective cognitive efficiency and task performance generally occurs when individuals are at intermediate levels of arousal. High levels of arousal tend to potentiate certain affects, as well as rigid, overlearned, and overly constricted problem-solving strategies. Low levels of arousal are associated with inefficient problem solving that may also contribute to negative affect. High levels of physiological arousal bias information processing and environmental cue use in a manner that likely reduces task performance (Easterbrook, 1959). At extremely high and low levels of arousal, the individual is unable to process complex response alternatives and is preoccupied with avoiding or eliminating potential annoyances (Zillmann, 1979). At these extreme levels of arousal, behavioral responses are aimed at immediate relief, irrespective of long-term implications.

CONCLUSIONS

The complexity, functions, and biological basis of the multiple dimensions of affect (emotions, moods, feelings, arousal, and sensations) have received a great deal of empirical and theoretical articulation during the past decade. A sophisticated model of the reinforcing and affect-modulating properties of smoking and nicotine needs to address the complexity, functions, and biological bases of affect to a degree that current models of smoking have not achieved.

A few guidelines may be of use to researchers in this area. Empirical evidence has suggested that future investigations of the affect-modulating effects of smoking and nicotine would benefit from the following:

1 Characterization and differentiation of affective states should include careful measurement of moods, emotions, feelings, and arousal. Such characterization generally benefits from inclusion of self-report, physiological, and behavioral measures because emotional processes, like most other psychological processes, are composed of numerous parallel and frequently interacting bioinformational sequences, most of which occur out of conscious awareness.

2 Constructs such as *high* or *euphoria* should be defined and characterized within a matrix of established affective constructs and measures.

3 Characterization and functional analyses of affective processes generally benefit from recognition of the phylogenetic, as well as ontogenetic, adaptive and motivational roles of such processes.

4 Characterization of temporal summation and dissipation processes associated with a variety of interacting affect-related arousal and activation patterns is needed.

5 The interactions of affective processes with higher level cognitive, associative, behavioral, and reinforcement processes need further characterization in the smoking literature, as well as more general characterization.

The multiple functional relationships between cognitive, affective, and behavioral processes should sensitize the reader to the numerous indirect and direct actions that smoking and nicotine may exert on affective processes. Indirect affect modulation would be expected to occur when nicotine enhances arousal and the associated cognitive processes required to achieve performance goals. Similarly, negative affect and irritability may occur during nicotine withdrawal in large part because of the frustration of not being able to perform cognitively and behaviorally at the desired level. The likelihood of such indirect affect-modulatory mechanisms are discussed in subsequent chapters.

Chapter 4

Personality, Temperament, and Psychopathology

Building on the previous chapter's review of affective processes, this chapter describes current empirically derived models of the basic dimensions of personality and their putative biological bases as well as major forms of psychopathology, all of which are statistically associated with smoking. A basic question is the degree to which common mechanisms relate affective processes, personality traits, and psychopathologies. Emphasis is given to fundamental dimensions and biological bases, and a foundation is thus provided for discussions in later chapters of mechanisms that may mediate relationships between smoking, personality, affect, and psychopathology. For example, schizophrenia appears to be mediated by the neurotransmitter dopamine, the same substance that many have argued mediates nicotine's reinforcing effects as well as differences in personality traits associated with smoking. Parallels seen by such juxtaposition suggest that certain mechanisms important in one of the three domains may also be important in the other two. Finally, familiarity with current research in each of these three domains is expected to lead to new questions concerning mechanisms by which nicotine exerts its effects. For example, many emotional processes appear to be mediated by the amygdala, yet research and theories have not addressed the role that nicotine may play in modulating affective states through its direct or indirect modulation of amygdaloid functioning.

PERSONALITY

Although the structure of the table of personality traits is less well defined than that of the chemical elements, a large number of factor-analytic and other empirically based studies have demonstrated the importance of a small number of biologically based, fundamental, higher order dimensions that characterize individual differences between people (Costa & McCrae, 1992a; H. J. Eysenck, 1991). In contrast to this small number of basic traits, there may be as many primary personality traits as there are chemical elements. Like the elements, primary traits vary in their similarity to each other. Grouping of primary factor traits is statistically determined by factor analysis in such a manner that those traits that correlate significantly with each other form a higher order trait, or superfactor. For example, the superfactor Neuroticism (N) results from moderately high correlations consistently observed between trait anxiety, depression, psychological vulnerability, hostility, and related negative-affect-related measures (see Table 4.1). That is, individuals who score high on one of these measures also tend to score high on others, whereas individuals who score low on one of these measures tend to score low on the others. Similarly, the superfactor Extraversion (E) is based on the significant correlations among the primary traits of gregariousness, warmth, positive affect, assertiveness, and activity (see Table 4.1).

E and N are important, smoking-relevant, genetically influenced personality dimensions. These two dimensions are typically the first two higher order factors that emerge in virtually all personality questionnaires and generally account for substantially more common variance than other higher order factors (Costa & McCrae, 1992a; Kline & Barrett, 1983; Zuckerman, Kuhlman, Thornquist, & Kiers, 1991).

H. J. Eysenck and Eysenck (1985) argued that the best grouping of primary traits into "superfactors" is the three factor model: the Psychoticism, Extraversion, and Neuroticism, or PEN model. In support of the PEN grouping, several meta-analytic reviews of factor-analytic personality studies have concluded that a three-megafactor solution results in a more stable solution than a larger number of factors (H. J. Eysenck, 1992b; Royce & Powell, 1983; Tellegen & Waller, in press).

Other theoreticians have argued that it is more useful to aggregate the numerous primary traits into five superfactors rather than three. Zuckerman (1991, 1992) saw it as frequently useful to break P into two component superfactors (Impulsive–Unsocialized–Sensation Seeking and Aggressive–Sensation Seeking) and to separate the activity factor out of E (see Table 4.1). This five-factor grouping thus includes Impulsive–Unsocialized–Sensation–Seeking (IUSS), Aggression–Hostility (H), and Activity (A), in addition to N and E (NEIHA). In contrast, Costa and McCrae (1992a) added Openness, Agreeableness, and Conscientiousness to their five-factor (NEOAC) model.

Table 4.1 Hierarchical Table of Human Traits

3-Factor model (H. J. Eysenck, (1991))	5-Factor model		Primary factors
	Zuckerman et al. (1991)	Costa & McCrae (1992c)	
P-IUSS	P-IUSS	Openness	Rebellious Conservative (−) Intellectual (−) Impulsive
	Agg-SS	Agreeableness (−)	Aggressive Critical Distrustful Hostility (expressed or behavioral)
		Conscientiousness (−)	Responsible (−) Productive (−) Ethical (−) Self-indulgent Conforming (−) Unable to delay gratification
Neuroticism	Neuroticism	Neuroticism	Anxiety Depression Vulnerability Hostility (felt or subjective)
	Activity		Activity Lively Vigor
Extraversion	Sociability	Extraversion	Gregariousness Warmth Positive emotions Excitement seeking Assertiveness

Note. Data from Costa and McCrae (1992a,c); Zuckerman, Kuhlman, and Camac (1988); and Zuckerman et al. (1991). P = Psychoticism; IUSS = Impulsive–Unsocialized–Sensation Seeking; Agg-SS = Aggression–Sensation Seeking. (−) = Inverse association between the factor and the corresponding 3-factor model factor.

In spite of the disagreement as to how many and what superfactors beyond N and E are most theoretically useful and psychobiologically fundamental, there is wide consensus on the general nature of the superfactors. Zuckerman et al. (1991) argued that the IUSS dimension is essentially identical to Eysenck's P dimension. However, he concluded that H and A also have many of the characteristics of fundamental, biologically based superfactors (Zuckerman, 1991). H. J. Eysenck (1992a, 1992b, 1992c) in turn proposed that differences between the PEN and the NEOAC models is primarily whether agreeableness and conscientiousness, which both correlate negatively with P, should be considered as basic personality dimensions or as facets forming part of P. The traits of agreeableness and conscientiousness clearly exist (Costa & McCrae, 1992a); the question is how they should be grouped—as supertraits or as lower order traits. Zuckerman (1992) aptly noted that ''in the last analysis, the determination of what is a basic dimension of personality does not depend on factor loading but on predictive power of the dimension for behavior and its biological basis'' (p. 679). There are a number of advantages to the use of megafactors or superfactors, as opposed to primary factors. First, superfactors are frequently more predictive (H. J. Eysenck, 1991). Second, superfactors are more reliable within individuals and are more reliably demonstrated across time and cultures throughout the world (Connolly, 1991; H. J. Eysenck, 1991; Wilson & Doolabh, 1992). The third advantage is that superfactors have demonstrated genetic bases, biological correlates, and theoretical biological bases (H. J. Eysenck & Eysenck, 1985; Zuckerman, 1991). Finally, the megatraits and supertraits have been extensively assessed in hundreds of experimental and correlational studies. Given these advantages, this chapter and the rest of the book focuses significantly more on superfactors than on primary factors; however, several smoking-relevant primary factors and clinical disorders (e.g., depressive, anxiety, schizophrenic, and antisocial disorders) are also discussed in some detail in sections dealing with psychopathology.

Genetics of Personality

All of the personality superfactors have a large degree of heritability (Eaves, Eysenck, & Martin, 1989; Loehlin, 1992; Zuckerman, 1991). Dozens of twin studies have demonstrated a genetic basis to the higher order N and E factors as well as to their constituent primary factors (Eaves et al., 1989; N. Martin & Jardine, 1986; Vandenberg, Singer, & Pauls, 1986). These studies have suggested that nearly half of the variance of questionnaire-assessed N and E is genetically determined and that shared family environment accounts for little to none of the variance (Eaves et al., 1989). Although fewer studies have assessed heritabilities of P–impulsive–sensation seeking, aggressive–sensation seeking, activity, openness, agreeableness, and conscientiousness, there is clear evidence of a substantial amount (40% or more) of heritability for these dimensions (Loehlin, 1992).

The extensive evidence for genetic influence sets the stage for the more challenging task of understanding the processes by which genes influence personality (Plomin et al., 1992). People do not directly inherit personality traits or dispositions to drug use or other behaviors; instead, they inherit variations in structure and biochemistry of the nervous, endocrine, and other body systems. These variations result in individual differences in dispositions to certain types of behavioral, affective, and cognitive reactions to the environment (Zuckerman, 1992). Reactions to the environment in turn influence choice of one's environment, the environment's reaction to the individual, and the development of one's social skills, self-perceptions, and various personality components (Scarr & McCartney, 1983). It is typically assumed that numerous genes underlie each of the personality superfactors (Eaves et al., 1989; Loehlin, 1992; Zuckerman, 1991) and that a number of gene-determined biological differences contribute to individual differences in personality. This gene-based variability may be localized within single psychobiological systems or may be spread through a number of relatively independent systems that mediate different components of the supertraits.

It seems likely that a significant portion of the personality-related genes are the same genes that mediate individual differences in drug and stress responses. Loci of drug action (e.g., mesolimbic dopaminergic activity) correspond to the same biological mechanisms postulated to mediate individual differences in temperament and personality. To the degree that common mechanisms do in fact mediate individual differences in personality, psychopathology, and drug effects, it is likely that these differences are genetically determined. At the present time, the specific genes and gene combinations responsible for individual differences in personality and most drug responses have not been characterized. However, as noted in later chapters, there are strong genetic influences on individual differences in response to and preference for psychoactive drugs. I now turn to a more detailed discussion of the nature of the major personality dimensions.

Extraversion

The extraversion–introversion personality dimension (the E superfactor) has received a great deal of attention for at least three reasons (Graziano, Rahe, & Feldesman, 1985). First, the dimension is related to clearly evident, common behaviors that are inherently interesting to many people. These include degree of smoking, drug use, sociability, dominance, assertiveness, impulsivity, and activity (H. J. Eysenck & Eysenck, 1985). Extraverts (i.e., individuals scoring high on this factor) are sociable, assertive, active, and generally prefer high levels of environmental stimulation. Introverts, however, prefer nonsocial situations, tend not to like excitement, and prefer to avoid arousal and tension-producing conditions (H. J. Eysenck & Eysenck, 1985). Second, E is related to a wide variety of psychological and behavioral constructs ranging from individual differences in sensitivity to indications of rewards and punishments (Gray, 1981) to individual differences in psychophysiological responses to drugs (D. G. Gilbert, 1987; D. G. Gilbert, Meliska et al., 1994; B. D. Smith, Wilson, & Jones, 1983). Finally, E is associated with a biopsychological framework that relates biological factors to psychological and social processes, as well as to drug and stress effects.

Gray (1981) believes that E reflects the relative strength of an individual's brain-mediated reward and punishment systems. Consistent with his hypothesis that extraverts are relatively more sensitive to conditioned stimuli associated with reward and introverts are relatively sensitive to signs of punishment, extraverts have been found to remember rewarding and positive characteristics about interactions, whereas introverts remember more of the negative aspects (Graziano et al., 1985; Thorne, 1987). Evidence of a relative sensitivity to punishment in introverts is provided by studies showing introverts to anticipate more disagreement between themselves and others (J. Cooper & Scalise, 1974), to report such disagreements as more aversive (R. M. G. Norman & Waston, 1976), and to rate others more negatively than do extraverts (Lishman, 1972). Congruent with their greater sensitivity to reward or diminished sensitivity to punishment, extraverts tend to date frequently and to engage in sex at an earlier age and with more partners (H. J. Eysenck & Wilson, 1979), whereas those who date rarely are more often introverted (Himadi, Arkowitz, Hinton, & Pearl, 1980).

Also consistent with this model of disparity in sensitivity to reward and punishment are findings showing that extraverts are more assertive and dominant than introverts (Infante, 1987), talk more, talk first, and talk more rapidly and loudly than introverts; and are more persuasive and less persuadable than introverts (Carment & Miles, 1971; Markel, Phillis, Vargas, & Harvard, 1972). This active, assertive, and reward-oriented behavior is also seen in stressful situations, where extraverts are more likely to experience anger, whereas introverts are more likely to experience anxiety and communication apprehension (Bell & Daly, 1985; Sipprelle, Ascough, Detrio, & Horst, 1977).

The relative sensitivity of extraverts to potential rewards combined with their relative insensitivity to potential punishments appears to predispose them to impulsivity and low anxiety levels (Gray, 1981). Conversely, introverts are less impulsive and more anxious because they are sensitive to potential punishments and less influenced by potential rewards. U. Gupta (1984) found support for Gray's formulations in extraverts' and introverts' pattern of differential to sensitivity to reinforcement and punishment during a verbal conditioning paradigm.

Although Gray (1981) has hypothesized that the differences in extraverts' and introverts' sensitivity to signs of reward and punishment are genetically based, it may be that these negative cognitive assessments of introverts result in part from environmental factors such as a high rate of negative social feedback resulting from poor social skills. Extraverts tend to be rated by both introverts and extraverts as being more interesting at parties, having the ideal personality, and being the preferred leader (Hendrick & Brown, 1971). Although high rates of negative social feedback may contribute to the introvert's negative evaluation of social situations, introverts have a selective attentional bias and recall for negative aspects of social situations (Graziano et al., 1985). This selective recall could be based on biological dispositions, or a history of negative social experiences, or both. It may be that some introverts are introverted solely because of learning histories and poor social skills. Alternatively, it is likely that complex Temperament × Environment interactions produce differences both in sensitivity to punishment versus reward (Gray, 1981) and in social skills (Scarr & McCartney, 1983).

Biological Basis of Extraversion Biological mechanisms hypothesized to mediate genetic influences on temperament, affect, and behavior have received growing attention during the past few decades. H. J. Eysenck (1967) hypothesized that a genetically determined tendency of the CNS toward a relatively low level of arousal is the biological factor promoting extraversion, whereas a tendency toward high CNS arousal promotes introversion. That is, introverts have a more chronically aroused and arousable cerebral cortex and reticular activating system than do extraverts. Assuming that the optimal level of arousal is a moderate one, introverts would be expected to spend more energy trying to reduce their cortical arousal by reducing external stimulation. Extraverts, however, would be expected to spend more time trying to increase the intensity of external stimulation to elevate their CNS arousal. Although there is some support for these arousal-related hypotheses (for a review, see H. J. Eysenck & Eysenck, 1985, and Gale, 1983), arousal appears to be too general a concept to adequately account for all of the genetically based biological and behavioral differences between extraverts and introverts (Claridge, 1986; Gray, 1981; Zuckerman, 1991). Gray's (1981, 1990) view that E is related to the relative strength of response to cues associated with reward and punishment suggests that there are important individual differences in the relative tuning of mesolimbic dopaminergic reward circuits relative to periventricular gray punishment or negative reinforcement circuits. Dopaminergic agonists (e.g., amphetamines and cocaine) clearly increase mesolimbic dopaminergic physiologic activity and have behaviorally extraverting effects (e.g., increased activity and positive affect). Consistent with the view that extraverts are more sensitive to signs of reward and introverts are more sensitive to cues of punishment and frustrative nonreward, cortical event-related potentials to cues indicating positive outcomes (winning money) have been found to be higher in extraverts, whereas event-related potentials to cues indicating loss were larger in introverts (Bartussek, Diedrich, Naumann, & Collet, 1993). To the degree that left frontal neocortical and paralimbic cortices are relatively more associated with approach behavior and positive affect (Davidson, 1984), one would expect extraversion to be associated with tendencies toward increased left frontal activation and introversion to be associated with tendencies toward increased right frontal activation.

Environment, Learning and Conditioning and E   Not only do genes in part determine the environment to which one is exposed, but personality-related, gene-based, individual biological differences modulate a number of learning processes. Since Pavlov's time, individual differences in temperament and personality have been seen as related to differences in conditionability, learning, and other sensitivities to the environment. H. J. Eysenck (1967) argued that much of the difference in introverts' and extraverts' behavior is a function of differences in conditionability (both classical and operant). He proposed that introverts condition more efficiently than extraverts in situations in which environmental stimulation is minimal because they are more aroused by weak stimulation in such circumstances (H. J. Eysenck & Eysenck, 1985). The poorer classical conditionability of extraverts is viewed by Eysenck as resulting in poorer inhibitory socialization processes resulting in a tendency to be uninhibited. Although some evidence has supported Eysenck's hypothesized association between conditionability and E, findings suggest that introverts are conditioned more easily to aversive stimuli, but that extraverts may be more easily conditioned to rewarding stimuli (Gray, 1981; Zuckerman, 1991). Impulsivity appears to be the component of E that is most highly correlated (negatively) with conditionability and electrocortical activation (Zuckerman, 1991).

Neuroticism

Individuals high in N are characterized by high negative emotionality and diminished emotional control across all negative affective states, including depression, anxiety, and anger (H. J. Eysenck & Eysenck, 1985). The affective lability of neurotics is viewed by Gray (1981) as resulting from high susceptibility to both reward and punishment. This dual sensitivity predisposes high-N individuals to high emotional arousal and emotional conflict in many situations. However, a dual sensitivity view of N is not consistent with findings indicating that positive affect correlates with E and not with N, whereas N correlates solely with negative affect (Costa & McCrae, 1980). Recent findings have suggested that negative affect manipulations are more likely to influence the neurotics' moods, whereas positive mood manipulations have relatively stronger influences on extraverts (Larsen & Ketelaar, 1991). Individuals high in N, especially those high in depression, tend to induce negative affect in those with whom they interact, apparently because they display fewer friendly, pleasant, appropriate, and skilled behaviors and more negative ones (Graziano et al., 1985; for a review, see Hokanson & Rubert, 1991). Responsiveness and attentiveness are also inversely related to neuroticism (Cegala, Savage, Brunner, & Conrad, 1982). Consistent with these negative social traits, neurotic and depressed individuals and their spouses have more stressed marriages and lower marital satisfaction than more stable individuals (H. J. Eysenck & Wakefield, 1981; Lewinsohn, Steinmetz, Larson, & Franklin, 1981). These findings suggest that N is in part a function of a cognitive–affective–behavioral disposition to act in a socially unskilled or cognitively and emotionally defeating manner. Mounting evidence reviewed in later portions of this chapter has suggested that such performance and skills deficits may be more a function of cognitive–affective schemas and information-processing biases than of overtly expressed emotions and SNS lability (M. W. Eysenck, 1987).

Biological Basis of Neuroticism　The genetically determined biological foundations of the various neurotic processes have not been well characterized but are clearly in part located in affect-related brain systems. Significant deviations in a variety of the affect-related brain system components could contribute to enhanced emotionality. Specifically, individuals with low thresholds for limbic system activation are often assumed to be predisposed toward more frequent, prolonged, and intense emotional reactions, including overly intense and prolonged activation of the pituitary–adrenal cortical system and the SNS (H. J. Eysenck, 1967; H. S. Kaplan, 1987; Mander, 1984).

Pathologically anxious individuals seen during acute episodes of distress in clinical settings often are characterized by heightened levels of many indexes of SNS activation such as increased heart rate, blood pressure, and skin conductance (Naveteur & Baque, 1987). Clinically depressed individuals and those prone to depression, however, tend to have abnormally low levels of skin conductance (for a review, see N. G. Ward & Doerr, 1986) but tend to have elevated plasma cortisol concentrations (Henry, 1986). In contrast to clinical settings, in nonclinical settings individuals high in N and anxiety are typically characterized by abnormally low rather than high baseline SNS activation (B. O. Gilbert & Gilbert, 1991; Naveteur & Baque, 1987; Netter, 1985; Roessler, 1973). In addition, this paradoxical N-related hypoactivation occurs in the case of plasma catecholamine concentrations in nonstress conditions and low plasma epinephrine concentrations in certain stressful situations (Forsman, 1980; Netter, 1985) and in response to stressful movies (Hubert & de Jong-Meyer, 1992). Thus, while some clinically neurotic individuals exhibit exaggeration of SNS and pituitary–adrenal cortical overactivity, nonclinical high-N populations tend to be underreactive in terms of their peripheral activation. When the paradoxical underarousal associated with high N is not observed, findings are generally not significant (Stemmler & Meinhardt, 1990; Zuckerman, 1990).

This phenomenon is likely a function of the nature of the laboratory tasks used and possibly the physiological measures assessed (D. G. Gilbert, 1991). The SNS physiological measures typically used are processes generally maximally activated during active coping tasks and high levels of active engagement (Henry, 1986; Singer, 1974). In contrast, cortisol is generally most highly elevated during stressful conditions in which the individual experiences helplessness and copes passively (Henry, 1986). Thus, if one assumes that high-N individuals, like individuals with clinical depression, feel hopeless and cope passively in most situations, it is not surprising that blood cortisol concentrations are frequently elevated in both high-N clinical and nonclinical samples (Dabbs & Hopper, 1990; D. G. Gilbert, Meliska, et al., 1994; Henry, 1986).

I have suggested elsewhere (D. G. Gilbert, 1991) that whether individuals high in N show high peripheral activation is likely a function of several factors, including degree of setting pull for active versus passive coping and the degree to which threat is ambiguous. Such Person × Situation specificity is seen in interactions of Type A and Type B individuals, in which cardiovascular response magnitude is a function of task control as well as of the personalities of each of the interactants (Abbott, Sutherland, & Watt, 1987). Unfortunately, studies assessing physiological responses to stress as a function of N have generally not used potentially threatening ambiguous stressors or designs that allow individual differences in perceived control to manifest themselves. To the degree that N is a function of a disposition to interpret ambiguous stimuli as threatening (M. W. Eysenck, 1987), studies using clearly nonthreatening or threatening stimuli are unlikely to differentiate neurotic individuals from stable ones. Furthermore, laboratory and other situations are likely to observe increased peripheral activation in neurotic people only in situations promoting active coping.

In summary, N is not a simple function of lability of brain systems mediating peripheral arousal (Zuckerman, 1990) but is more likely a function of affect-related information-processing biases. The most viable alternatives to general arousal models of N are bioinformational explanations. Biased cognitive processes, including a low degree of perceived control, appear to make neurotic individuals vulnerable to clinical depression (Abramson, Seligman, & Teasdale, 1978; M. Martin, 1985). Cognitive biases associated with N also include a tendency to recall negative memories more frequently and rapidly than positive memories (M. Martin, 1985). The biological mechanisms underlying these information-processing biases appear to be associated with underactivation of the left frontal cortex, overactivation of the right frontal cortex, or both (Davidson, 1984; Lolas, 1987; Tomarken, Davidson, Wheeler, & Doss, 1992). As noted in Chapter 3, the left, relative to the right, hemisphere is more associated with approach behavior connected with active coping and is frequently associated with positive affect. In contrast, the right hemispheric processes appear to mediate bioinformational processes associated with withdrawal, negative affect, and passive coping (Davidson et al., 1990; Tucker & Williamson, 1984). Neurophysiological processing biases may increase the probability of seeing oneself as helpless in a given situation and thus promote a lack of coping, which in turn further promotes feelings of helplessness. It is not yet clear how biological and experiential factors combine to produce a disposition toward right-hemisphere-based depressive information processing. The genetic basis of N may in part be a relatively greater right- than left-hemisphere information-processing bias that when combined with a stressful environment results in clinical disorders.

As a number of different primary factors contribute to the higher order N megafactor, it is understandable that N is not consistently related to either over- or underactivation of the SNS or other biological processes. Component factors of N may be more closely aligned with specific biological mechanisms than is the higher order N factor. In this sense, N may be a final common pathway resulting from a number of biological factors, each of which influences, directly or indirectly, a number of negative affect mechanisms related to N.

An additional consideration is that there is no reason that all of N's components should have similar associations with physiological measures. As Claridge (1986) has noted, the existence of N as a descriptive factor does not necessarily imply that it must have a unitary biological basis. However, studies have demonstrated that N has a genetic basis and that environmental factors interact with genetic disposition toward N to generate specific clinical disorders (Kendler et al., 1992a).

Learning and Conditioning, and Environment In addition to the genetic contribution to N, various current and historical (learning and conditioning) factors are important. Direct environmental correlates of and probable contributors to N include sexual and physical abuse (Nash, Hulsey, Sexton, Harralson, & Lambert, 1993), distressed or deficient social-emotional environments (Buck, 1991), conflicting incompatible desires and motivations (Dollard & Miller, 1950; Horney, 1945), and cultural and family rules and expectations that exceed the individual's skills, temperament, and ability (Buck, 1991; McColloch & Gilbert, 1991). The possibility that different environmental factors promote different neurotic components is discussed later.

Eysenck (1979) proposed that the persistence of emotional responses in high-N individuals is due to the inability of an overly active limbic system to extinguish Pavlovian-conditioned emotional responses to a variety of stimuli. He stated that neurosis is primarily a result of Pavlovian conditioning and that the neurotic state is a function of a positive feedback process in which conditioned emotional stimuli result in such strong conditioned emotional responses that reinforcement, rather than extinction, of the conditioned stimulus–conditioned response association occurs. He viewed cognitive processes as a subclass of higher order conditioned stimuli. Thus, his model bridges traditional conditional models with currently popular cognitive ones.

Although there is some support for Eysenck's model of N (Diaz & Pickering, 1993; H. J. Eysenck, 1979; H. J. Eysenck & Eysenck, 1985), there is also some support for Gray's (1981) hypothesis that the N dimension reflects response magnitude to both cues of reward and of punishment (Zuckerman, 1991). The fact that high Harm Avoidance (HA) correlates highly with N suggests that HA is conceptually and empirically related to N (Heath, Cloninger, & Martin, 1994). Cloniger (1987) hypothesized that his HA personality dimension is associated with behavioral inhibition and avoidance of potentially aversive situations.

Evidence has been presented that many neurotic individuals are characterized by bimodal response dispositions that alternate between ineffective passive coping and chaotic, hyperemotional active coping (D. G. Gilbert, 1991). Neurotic individuals frequently do not express themselves adequately or otherwise try to actively cope with stressful situations (Hernandez & Mauger, 1980). Such individuals tend to be preoccupied with internal stimuli and disengaged from the environment in a manner that fails to provide opportunities for the development of effective social or other coping skills. To the degree that such individuals are disengaged from their surroundings, they are less aroused by external stimuli than most others (Roessler, 1973). However, when stimuli are highly personal, high-N individuals may no longer be able to cope by avoidance (Bernstein, Schneider, Juni, & Pope, 1980). In such situations, they are likely to become overly aroused. Thus, only when they become highly motivated or otherwise cannot avoid stressful engagements are neurotic individuals likely to become hyperaroused and thus conform to the characterization of neuroticism so common in the literature. Consistent with this bimodal model, Singer (1974) argued that engagement and involvement is the critical factor determining degree of psychophysiological responsivity.

Neurotic individuals probably fail to develop adequate social skills in part because their excessive and chaotic attempts at active coping are punished, a fact that promotes rapid retreat to passive avoidance coping and a failure to learn adequate problem-solving and coping skills (D. G. Gilbert, 1991). Consistent with the view that physiological correlates of N are not associated with uniformly elevated arousal to all sorts of stimuli, a number of large and well-controlled studies have observed no significant correlations between N and a variety of physiological response factors with a wide range of stimuli (Stemmler & Meinhardt, 1990). However, as noted in the preceding section, the stimuli used in these studies may not be of the ambiguous, distal, and moderate threat variety that are likely to differentiate neurotic from stable individuals.

Further support for a coping-strategy-specific model of neurotic arousal level is provided by the fact that cardiovascular arousal is a function of motor-related processes associated with active coping (Obrist, 1981), whereas elevated blood pituitary-adrenal hormones are related to passive coping, learned helplessness, and depression (Henry, 1986). Effects of perceived control on cardiovascular, hormonal, and emotional responses to stressful situations may be understood in terms of perceived control over a stressor and the strategy used to cope with the stressor (Henry, 1986).

Psychoticism/Impulsive–Unsocialized–Sensation Seeking

Although there is near universal agreement as to the nature, naming, and importance of the E and N dimensions, the use of the name *psychoticism* to characterize the third higher order factor is controversial. Zuckerman (1991) concluded that there is overwhelming evidence for a basic dimension that is assessed by Eysenck's P scale, but that its name is inappropriate because the relationship of this dimension to psychosis is weak. Instead, Zuckerman substituted *Psychopathy* or *Impulsive–Unsocialized–Sensation Seeking* (IUSS) as more reflective of the nature of this dimension. Consistent with this, Claridge (1987) noted that recent revisions of Eysenck's measures of P contain items more reflective of antisocial or psychopathic traits than of psychotic traits. Tellegen and Waller (in press) argued that P is more accurately characterized as reflecting constraint (impulsiveness vs. control, harm avoidance vs. thrill seeking, and traditionalism vs. nontraditionalism). Nonetheless, H. J. Eysenck (1992a) and some others (Berenbaum & Fujita, 1994) saw the P continuum as extending from functional psychoses to spectrum disorders, borderline traits, and schizoidy and finally as merging into normal personality.

Biological Basis of P-IUSS and Its Facets   To the degree that P-IUSS is linearly related to schizophrenia, one would expect both to have a common biological basis. Consistent with the commonality hypothesis, Meehl (1989, 1990) assumed that a single major gene predisposes individuals toward a CNS attention-related dysfunction (schizotaxia) that is required for most forms of schizophrenia. Schizotaxia, when combined with other genetic liabilities and learning history, can result in schizotypy, a tendency to exhibit cognitive slippage, interpersonal aversion, hypohedonia, and ambivalence. Highly predisposing genetic and environmental factors result in decompensation into clinical states of schizophrenia. Because converging lines of evidence have suggested that dopaminergic circuits and the temporal lobes are intimately involved in the genesis (and pharmacological treatment) of schizophrenia (Gray, 1991), H. J. Eysenck's (1992a) emphasis on the relationship of P to psychosis would implicate temporal lobe dopaminergic circuits as a biological substrate for P and the cognitive dysfunctions noted by Meehl's schizotypic individuals.

Reduced central serotonin function has generally been observed in impulsive, aggressive individuals (Coccaro, Astill, Szeeley, & Malkowicz, 1990). Thus, to the degree that P-IUSS is associated with aggressive and psychopathic behavior, as opposed to schizophrenia-prone processes, one would expect low serotonergic activity to characterize high-P individuals (Pritchard, 1991b). Consistent with this hypothesis and the antisocial and psychopathic interpretation of P-IUSS, studies have found P to be inversely correlated with spinal fluid serotonin concentrations (Zuckerman, 1991).

A biological synthesis or commonality of the psychopathy and psychoticism and schizophrenia interpretations of P-IUSS can be seen when one considers that both schizophrenia and psychopathy may be related to left-hemisphere disorders. Future genetic and experimental studies are required before it will be possible to determine to what extent psychopathy and schizophrenia are simply different points on the P-IUSS continuum, as opposed to psychobiologically different disorders. The frontal lobes are also involved in complex planning and monitoring of behavior, and frontal lobe dysfunction frequently results in impulsive, automatic, and overtly controlled behavior that is highly inappropriate (Stuss, Gow, & Hetherington, 1992). Thus, it seems reasonable to speculate that a variety of biological mechanisms contributing to relative degrees of left-hemisphere and frontal information-processing efficacy or dysfunction may contribute to the biological foundation of the P-IUSS dimension.

Learning and Conditioning and P-IUSS   Both psychopathy and extraversion have been related to relatively reduced passive avoidance learning. This passive avoidance deficit is especially evident in situations requiring inhibition of a rewarded response to avoid punishment (Newman, Widom, & Nathan, 1985). Such deficits in avoidance sensitivity may be related to highly primed mesolimbic dopaminergic psychomotor output systems in extraverts and psychopaths or to decreased inhibitory processes. Inadequate inhibitory processes are suggested by the relatively consistent finding of excessive slow-wave EEG activity (S. Snyder & Pitts, 1984) and other forms of physiological underresponsivity among individuals high in antisocial and schizoid tendencies (Raine, Venables, & Williams, 1990). Impulsive and sensation-seeking individuals have also frequently been reported to be event-related augmenters in response to increasing stimulus intensity (for a review, see Carillo-de-le Pena & Barratt, 1993).

Agreeableness and Conscientiousness

Characteristics associated with individuals scoring low in Agreeableness (A) and Conscientiousness (C) are similar in many respects to aggressive–sensation seeking and P. These traits may be considered facets of the higher order factor P-IUSS because they correlate negatively with P (Costa, McCrae, & Dye, 1992; H. J. Eysenck, 1992a). However, the correlations with P are only modest (for both, $r = -.33$; Costa et al., 1992) in normal population samples, indicating that these two dimensions characterize only certain aspects of P. Goldberg (1993) has noted that items on the P scale "are rather equally spaced over the 90 degree arc between the poles of the two orthogonal [A and C] factors" (p. 31).

The agreeableness factor of the Neuroticism Extraversion Openness Personality Inventory—Revised (NEO–PI–R, Costa et al., 1992) includes six facets: trust, straightforwardness, altruism, compliance, modesty, and tender-mindedness. These facets are clearly inversely related to characteristics typical of high P-IUSS individuals, as are the six facets of C: competence, order, dutifulness, achievement striving, self-discipline, and deliberation. Thus, A and C may be seen as elaborations of the inverse of P-IUSS; that is, they are indicative of competent, socialized, and deliberate information processing that is typically considered pro-social, as opposed to the antisocial traits characteristic of P-IUSS. Agreeableness and conscientiousness are probably biologically and psychologically based on the same mechanisms as those hypothesized to underlie P-IUSS. Thus, the biological integrity of the CNS and past and current environmental milieus of high A and C individuals would be expected to be qualitatively high.

Culture–Openness–Intellect

The Culture–Openness–Intellect (COI) factor of the Big Five personality dimensions includes interest in and openness to ideas, experiences, and actions, as well as wide interests, imagination, curiosity, and inventiveness (Loehlin, 1992). It is also associated with flexibility of thought, creative interests, and intelligence (Digman, 1990). The openness dimension of the NEO–PI–R includes six facets: openness to fantasy, aesthetics, feelings, actions, ideas, and values. However, it does not formally assess other components of the higher order COI factor. Costa and McCrae (1992b) have agreed that P, E, and N are important higher order factors but argued that they are not comprehensive and that an O dimension is also required to generate a minimally comprehensive higher order model.

COI is correlated moderately with education, cultural experiences, and intelligence (L. R. Goldberg, 1993), all of which result from an interaction of genetically based CNS capacity with environmental factors. Thus, it is not surprising that COI, like the other major personality dimensions, is substantially determined by genetics (Loehlin, 1992).

Intelligence and Socioeconomic Status

Because coping, drug use, smoking, and smoking cessation are related to intelligence and intelligence-related factors such as socio-economic status (reviewed in Chapter 7), it is important to consider this variable in any comprehensive model of individual differences in drug use, personality, affect, and coping. Although a substantial portion of psychometrically assessed intelligence is influenced by environmental factors, half or more of the individual differences in psychometrically assessed intelligence is a result of genetic factors (Plomin & DeFries, 1980). Furthermore, brain dysfunction resulting from perinatal and postnatal experiences also contributes to the individual differences in information-processing capacities commonly referred to as intelligence (Hendrickson & Hendrickson, 1980; Sternberg & Gardner, 1982).

Intelligence-related information processing can be broken down into three components: mental speed, accuracy and error checking, and persistence (White, 1981). Each of these components of intelligence appears to be influenced by nicotine (see Chapter 6). CNS cholinergic synapses have been hypothesized to be critical in the mediation of nicotine's effects (see Chapter 2), as well as to a number of intelligence-related information-processing functions, including memory, arousal, and vigilance and attention (Hendrickson & Hendrickson, 1980).

Consistency of Personality Traits across Time and Situations

The concept of personality and temperamental traits implies a degree of consistency across time and situations. The major personality factors reviewed in this chapter have been demonstrated to be relatively constant across time and situations when appropriately averaged or aggregated (S. Epstein, 1983; Zuckerman, 1991). However, given the situational specificity of behavior, behavior must be sampled across time and situations to demonstrate reliable and strong associations with personality traits (S. Epstein, 1983). Genetic factors are involved in maintaining personality consistency, whereas nonshared environmental effects are related to personality change (McGue, Bacon, & Lykken, 1993).

A PERSON × SITUATION EVOLUTIONARY MODEL OF PERSONALITY DEVELOPMENT AND PSYCHOPATHOLOGY

Relationships between personality, psychopathology, and genetically based temperamental factors develop from the first months of an infant's life and continue through adulthood. The smiling, active, and socially extraverted infant elicits a different environment than the quiet one (Lytton, 1980). Later in life, the individual with a genetically based social and active disposition is more likely to join social groups in which social skills will become more highly polished and differentiated (Scarr & McCartney, 1983). Unattractive and intellectually dull individuals who experience high rates of rejection from the earliest days of schooling may become not only socially unskilled, but socially anxious and withdrawn. Emotionally labile and irritable infants and children are more likely to elicit negative reactions from family and rejection by and isolation from peers. Isolation, in turn, precludes the learning of important social and emotional skills, including appropriate responses to emotions in others, as well as the modulation of one's own emotions (McColloch & Gilbert, 1991). Thus, although all complex behavior is influenced by the environment and learning, what is learned, how it is learned, environmental selection, and reactions to the environment all are in part a function of one's genetically based biological constitution (Buck, 1991; H. J. Eysenck & Eysenck, 1985; Scarr & McCartney, 1983; Zuckerman, 1991).

PSYCHOPATHOLOGY

Relationships of Personality to Psychopathology

Psychological disturbances can be classified as all-or-none discrete disorders or as one end of a continuous dimension, ranging in quantity but not in quality (H. J. Eysenck & Eysenck, 1985). A number of theorists have argued that personality factors and psychopathology are part of the same continuum and contribute to and therefore are predictive of the development of a wide range of clinical psychopathologies (Cloniger, 1987; H. J. Eysenck & Eysenck, 1985; Gray, 1981; Meehl, 1989; Watson, Clark, & Harkness, 1994). Thus, H. J. Eysenck and Eysenck (1976) predicted that high-N individuals would develop depressive and anxiety disorders, and those scoring very high in P would be predisposed toward schizophrenia. Although H. J. Eysenck saw N and P as determining the probability of disorder, he viewed E as influencing the nature of the disorder (H. J. Eysenck & Eysenck, 1985). Evidence described later in this section, although limited, is supportive of a genetic and predictive continuity between personality and psychopathology.

Few studies have assessed genetic relationships between personality and the development of psychopathology (G. Carey & DiLalla, 1994). Individuals very high in neuroticism have a high probability of developing clinical depression (Connolly, 1991; M. Martin, 1985). Similarly, the genetic analysis of twin data by G. Carey and DiLalla (1994) led them to conclude that "genes may account for over 50% of the observed correlation between neuroticism and state symptoms of anxiety and depression" (p. 32). The Person × Situation evolutionary model of personality development and psychopathology noted earlier may be a useful model for characterizing relationships between personality and psychopathology. To the degree that there is continuity between personality and psychopathology, one can assume that certain genetic and personality factors tend to generate stressful and predisposing environments that result in a positive feedback cycle of dysfunction that eventuates in clinical states of cognitive–affective distress and behavioral dysfunction.

Genetics of Psychopathology

Virtually all major forms of psychopathology are in part genetically based (Vandenberg, Singer, & Pauls, 1986). Strong genetic contributions have been demonstrated for schizophrenia, major affective disorders, alcohol abuse, and personality disorders (Vandenberg et al., 1986). Nonetheless, it is clear that none of the major psychopathological disorders is a direct result of a Mendelian dominant or recessive gene (G. Carey & DiLalla, 1994). Although it may be that some genes are major contributors to psychopathology, such strong genes probably operate in conjunction with other contributing genes and the environment (G. Carey & DiLalla, 1994).

Studies of subtypes of phobias (Kendler et al., 1992a) and of relationships between major depression and generalized anxiety disorder (Kendler, Neale, Kessler, Heath, & Eaves, 1992b) are consistent with the view that these disorders result from a combination of genetic and individual-specific environmental factors. Major depression and generalized anxiety disorder appear to result from a common set of neuroticism-related genes (Kendler et al., 1992b). Further evidence consistent with an underlying genetic-based N dimension comes from studies showing that a single genetic factor is the major reason why depression, anxiety, and N are correlated (Eaves et al., 1989; Jardine, Martin, & Henderson, 1984). Bipolar disorder, however, is genetically distinct from unipolar depression and anxiety disorders (Vandenberg et al., 1986). Consistent with the concept of a higher order N factor, a general common genetic propensity toward fears and phobias in general, as well as additional genetic propensities for each fear and phobia subtype, have been observed (Kendler et al., 1992a).

Antisocial personality and other disinhibitory disorders may have a varying pattern of genetic contribution. Cloniger and Gottesman (1987) concluded from their twin data that crimes against persons were genetically unrelated to crimes against property and that the latter were higher in heritability. Crimes against persons may reflect aggressiveness and excitatory functions, whereas those against property may reflect reduced inhibitory processes. It is unclear to what extent either of these two types of crime are in part related to intelligence, other forms of psychopathology, and drug or alcohol abuse. However, Cloniger and Gottesman found no support in their adoption data for the hypothesis that the high incidence of alcoholism in antisocial personality is due to a common genetically based disinhibitory tendency. Alcoholism in biological fathers predicted alcoholism but not criminality in adopted-away sons.

Although current evidence is inadequate to make a precise statement, it appears that different disorders are mediated in part by different genes and that genes and environment interact in complex manners in the development of such behavior (H. J. Eysenck, 1977; Vandenberg et al., 1986).

Schizophrenia has a very high degree of heritability, with estimates of polygenic factors accounting for something in the range of 70% of the phenotypic variability and 20% a result of environmental factors (Vandenberg et al., 1986). Although it is likely that some of the different types of schizophrenia differ from each other in their biological and genetic bases, most forms appear to involve dopaminergic systems associated with the temporal lobe (Gray, 1991). It may be, as Meehl (1989, 1990) has suggested, that a common gene (possibly mediating dopaminergic pathways or temporal lobe structures) mediates most forms of schizophrenia, whereas the specific type of schizophrenia and whether the disposition manifests itself is a function of other modulatory genes and the environment.

Mood Disorders

Neuroticism and a number of clinical disorders appear to result from the same genetic base. The genetic evidence (Kendler et al., 1992a) suggests that the same genes predispose individuals toward depressive and anxiety disorders and that environmental factors determine whether and which of the two disorders will evolve. Other studies have found that N predicts clinical depression (M. Martin, 1985) and that major depressive disorders, clinical anxiety, and neuroticism result from a common genetic base (Eaves et al., 1989; Jardine et al., 1984).

Convergent lines of evidence support the view that depressive disorders are mediated to a substantial extent by norepinephrine and serotonin at CNS synapses; however, this evidence does not preclude the possible participation of dopamine and other neuromodulators in depression-related processes (J. R.

Cooper et al., 1991). The supersensitivity model hypothesizes that depression results from excessive responses of norepinephrine, serotonin receptors, or both. The dysregulation model proposes that stress results in excessive transmitter release and that the regulation of norepinephrine, rather than too much or too little norepinephrine, is responsible for clinical depression (Lickey & Gordon, 1991).

Evidence indicates a probable decrement in left relative to right frontal and prefrontal cortical functioning in depressed individuals. EEG studies have observed this pattern in depressed individuals relative to controls (Henriques & Davidson, 1991). Positron emission tomography scans have also provided evidence of lowered metabolic left prefrontal cortical activity in depressed groups (Martinot et al., 1990). These frontal asymmetries and the tendency for decreased metabolic activity throughout the brain (especially in left frontal regions) even after a remission of depressive symptomatology (Martinot et al., 1990) are consistent with the view that depression and its predisposing traits (neuroticism) are characterized by decreased analytic, planning, and goal implementation functions.

Antidepressant medications have been observed to have lateralized effects, and when clinically depressed individuals improve clinically their right-hemisphere performance also improves (Tucker & Williamson, 1984). Antidepressants attenuate virtually all depressive symptoms, including guilt, mood, loss of interest or pleasure, and hopelessness, but their effects are more pronounced on vegetative symptoms (Lickey & Gordon, 1991).

It has been suggested that major affective disorder may reflect a dysregulation of ACTH or cortisol and the effects of these neuromodulators on cognitive and emotional functioning (E. A. Young, Haskett, Murphy-Weinberg, Watson, & Akil, 1991). E. A. Young et al. (1991) observed a defect in a rapid-feedback pathway that normally allows cortisol to suppress ACTH secretion from the pituitary gland and thus to inhibit further cortisol secretion. This defective feedback may be responsible for the elevated serum cortisol concentrations found in many individuals with major depressive disorder. Furthermore, E. A. Young et al. presented evidence that chronic elevations of cortisol may damage hippocampal cells. Changes in mood and cognition may result from such cortisol-induced changes as the hippocampus is involved in a number of limbic and memory processes. The finding that high-N individuals also frequently exhibit elevated serum cortisol (Dabbs & Hopper, 1990; D. G. Gilbert, Meliska, et al., 1994) is consistent with a continuous dimension from low to high neuroticism and depressive disorder.

Anxiety Disorders

Anxiety becomes a clinical disorder when it is significantly more intense than called for by actual threat. There are a number of types of anxiety disorders, for example, phobia, posttraumatic stress disorder, panic disorder, and agoraphobia. Phobias involve intense fear of a specific object or situation that the individual can avoid and thereby reduce his or her anxiety. Posttraumatic stress disorder follows an intensely stressful experience that is outside the normal range of most individuals. People with this disorder have repeated intrusive recollections of the event that interfere with their daily life, and they act or feel as though the event were recurring. Panic disorder is defined by the experiencing of panic attacks, which include a number of symptoms, most of which are physiological in nature (e.g., shortness of breath, dizziness, and palpitations), but also include fear of dying, going crazy, or doing something uncontrolled. Agoraphobia is defined as fear of being in places or situations from which escape might be difficult or embarrassing.

To the degree that neuroticism underlies the disposition toward both anxiety and depressive disorders, these disorders should be characterized by common psychobiological abnormalities and respond similarly to psychotropic medications. Evidence suggests that antidepressant medications are often effective in treating several anxiety disorders (e.g., panic and obsessive–compulsive disorder) but not others (e.g., phobias; Noyes, 1991). Similarly, anxiolytics are sometimes helpful in attenuation of clinical depression (Noyes, 1991).

Gray (1982) provided evidence that

> there is one kind of depression . . . found in neurotic introverts, which is closely related to anxiety, and which responds to the same kinds of therapy as anxiety; and another kind . . . found in stable extroverts, which is not so closely related to anxiety, and which responds to different types of therapy than does anxiety. A more parsimonious conclusion is that there exist only two states: anxiety, found especially in neurotic introverts, and depression, found especially in stable extroverts. . . . Anxiety is due in part to excessive activity in forebrain noradrenergic systems, and depression to underactivity in diencephalic noradrenergic systems. (pg. 408)

Serotonin is also implicated in the etiology of anxiety disorders. However, at present, neither the serotonergic nor the noradrenergic model appears capable of explaining all anxiety symptoms or their attenuation by various classes of drugs (Zuckerman, 1991).

Lateral asymmetry has been observed in some anxiety disorders. Reiman et al. (1986) found individuals prone to lactate-induced panic to exhibit higher parahippocampal blood flow in the right hemisphere than in the left hemisphere than did controls. Reiman et al. interpreted these findings as reflecting relatively more intense activation by limbic affect-related input into the parahippocampal region. Buchsbaum et al. (1987) found greater effects of benzodiazepine anxiolytics on regional glucose use in the right frontal and visual cortex. The relatively greater activity of the right than the left hemisphere in these studies is consistent with a relatively greater involvement of noradrenergic and serotonergic systems with the right hemisphere (Tucker & Williamson, 1984) and with a greater involvement of the right hemisphere than the left hemisphere with negative affect (Davidson, 1984; see Chapter 3).

Schizophrenic Disorders

Schizophrenic disorders (APA, 1987) are characterized by disturbances of reasoning, perception, emotional expression, and motivation. Whereas clear organic etiology is precluded in cases of schizophrenic disorders, convergent evidence indicates genetic determinants (Lickey & Gordon, 1991). Such determinants are clearly biological in nature. Biological models of schizophrenia universally assume malfunctioning of mesolimbic dopaminergic systems and the frontal and temporal lobes (Swerdlow & Koob, 1987). In addition, gross structural changes, including enlarged brain ventricles and abnormal folds in frontal and prefrontal brain regions (for a review, see Lickey & Gordon, 1991), may be functionally related to altered complex information processing in these disorders.

As noted earlier, Meehl (1989, 1990) believed that genetically based attentional dysfunction (schizotaxia) plus a predisposing environment are required for most forms of schizophrenia. The observation that only about 50% of identical twins are concordant for schizophrenia supports the contention that environmental factors contribute to the development of the disorder (Gottesman, 1991).

Converging lines of evidence suggest that dopaminergic circuits innervating the temporal lobes are intimately involved in the genesis (and pharmacological treatment) of schizophrenia (Gray, 1991). Gray's model emphasizes a failure in acute schizophrenia to integrate memories of previous regularities of perceptual input with current motor programs in the modulation of current perception. Neuroanatomically, the model emphasizes the interaction of ascending dopaminergic projections to the accumbens with projections from the septohippocampal system, by way of the subiculum and the amygdala to the nucleus accumbens.

The antipsychotic drugs used to treat schizophrenia significantly attenuate or eliminate hallucinations, delusions, and cognitive disorganization in a majority of patients and generally improve social appropriateness and self-care (for a review, see Lickey & Gordon, 1991). These drugs are thought to exert these beneficial effects by altering dopaminergic functioning. Clinical efficacy of drugs is generally a function of their ability to inhibit dopaminergic receptors (Lickey & Gordon, 1991). Amphetamine and other drugs that increase dopaminergic functioning have induced schizophrenia-like symptoms in nonschizophrenic persons (S. H. Snyder, 1973). To the degree that smoking and nicotine increase dopamine, one might expect smoking to worsen schizophrenic symptomatology; however, there is currently no evidence (but no rigorous tests of the possibility) that nicotine exacerbates symptomatology.

As in most forms of psychopathology, schizophrenia is characterized by minimal responses to long-term contingencies and therefore relatively greater responsivity to short-term cost-benefit relationships.

Antisocial and Disinhibitory Disorders

Antisocial disorder (APD) is characterized by ''a pattern of irresponsible and antisocial behavior beginning in childhood or early adolescence and continuing into adulthood (APA, 1987, p. 342).'' Arrests for unlawful behavior, fighting, spouse and child abuse, impulsivity, lying, reckless or drunken driving, and inability to maintain a monogamous relationship for more than a year are examples of behavior considered irresponsible and antisocial. The focus of diagnosis is on behavior rather than on affect and preference. Empirical evidence (see Zuckerman, 1991) indicates that APD is associated with Eysenck's (1992a) P scale, as well as with measures of impulsivity and sensation seeking (the P-IUSS personality dimension noted earlier). Extraversion and neuroticism appear to be relatively uncorrelated with APD diagnosis (Zuckerman, 1991), although it appears that incarcerated populations are higher in E and N, as well as P (H. J. Eysenck, 1977). However, elevated anxiety and other neurotic traits appear to be associated with what has been identified as a secondary type of neurotic psychopath, as opposed to the lower than normal neuroticism associated with the primary psychopath (Harpur, Hare, & Hakstian, 1989).

The extremely high prevalence of alcohol abuse in APD seems to be more a function of impulsive tendencies in APD rather than of a genetic linkage. Cloniger and Gottesman (1987) found that criminality of biological parents increased prevalence of crime, but not alcoholism, in adopted-away sons and that biological fathers' alcoholism increased alcoholism, but not criminal behavior, in adopted-away sons.

Hyperactivity and attention deficit disorder are related to APD. APD parents are more likely to have hyperactive children (J. Morrison, 1980), and hyperactive boys with conduct or oppositional disorder have relatives with higher prevalences of APD (Biederman, Munir, & Knee, 1987). The high impulsivity of attention deficit hyperactivity disorder seems in many respects to reflect traits associated with APD.

The inability or unwillingness of people with APD to behave within societal rules and expectations may be related to any of a combination of possibilities enumerated by Zuckerman (1991): (a) failure to learn norms, (b) failure to apply norms, (c) lack of ability to anticipate consequences of their actions, (d) failure to plan ahead or to integrate actions with long-term goals, and (e) failure to learn from negative consequences. To this list one might add a greater sensitivity to rewards than to potential punishments (Gray, 1981). As in most forms of psychopathology, APD is characterized by minimal responses to potential long-term costs associated with short-term gains. Risky or impulsive behavior engaged in by APD individuals includes smoking and other legal and illegal drug use and abuse.

SUMMARY AND INTEGRATION

Commonalities among affect, personality, and psychopathology are so great as to make consideration of one without the others questionable in many cases. The relationship of affect to personality is perhaps clearest when one considers the N and E factors of the NEO–PI–R, the most commonly used measure of the Big

Five factor model. The six facets of NEO–PI–R neuroticism are all negative affects or directly affect related: anxiety, angry hostility, depression, self-consciousness, impulsiveness, and vulnerability. NEO–PI–R extraversion, however, is characterized by positive affect and positive-affect-related behavior: warmth, gregariousness, assertiveness, activity, excitement seeking, and positive emotions. Several of the facets of the remaining three of the Big Five factors (openness, agreeableness, and conscientiousness) are also directly related to affect. Openness includes openness to feelings, aesthetics, and fantasy, as well as to actions, ideas, and values. Agreeableness implies an affective component, and all of its facets refer directly to or can be seen as a function of affect: trust, straightforwardness, altruism, compliance, modesty and tender-mindedness. Although the final Big Five factor, conscientiousness, does not directly assess affect, its components are clearly affect and motivation related and can be viewed as cognitive–affective goal motivation complexes: competence, order, dutifulness, achievement striving, self-discipline, and deliberation. Evidence reviewed in this chapter suggests that in many cases psychopathology can be seen as an extreme position on a personality dimension or as personality and temperamental dispositions interacting with pathology promoting past and current environmental factors.

The hypothesized biological bases of personality and psychopathology are essentially identical to those suggested by others to mediate affective processes (Chapter 3 reviews these affective mechanisms). Mesolimbic dopaminergic systems are implicated in positive affect, approach behavior, and reward systems as well as in schizophrenia, psychopathy, extraversion, and possibly depression. High activity in serotonin systems is thought to mediate inhibitory processes and restraint associated with introversion and socialization, and low activity is thought to lead to impulsivity and sensation seeking. Norepinephrine appears to be associated with anxiety and punishment expectancies, which in turn are associated with neuroticism, anxiety disorders, depression, and introversion.

Because motivation and reinforcement processes are closely associated with affect, it is not surprising that the same psychobiological mechanisms hypothesized to mediate affect, personality, and psychopathology are also hypothesized by others to mediate the reinforcing and affect-modulating effects of smoking and nicotine (reviewed in Chapter 6). Thus, the mesolimbic dopaminergic system hypothesized to underlie approach behavior, reward, and individual differences in extraversion has also been hypothesized to be involved in the reinforcement of nicotine self-administration. Similarly, it has been proposed that nicotine self-administration is reinforced by negative affect reduction mediated by modulation of serotonin, or norepinephrine, or both, both of which are neuromodulators associated with anxiety, depression, and impulse disorders.

The parallels between personality, psychopathology, and affect reviewed in this chapter provide a conceptual foundation for exploring smoking's relationships with personality, psychopathology, affect, and reinforcement in subsequent chapters.

Evidence of Affect Modulation, Performance Enhancement, and Reinforcement by Nicotine

For most individuals, nicotine appears to be the most important component of the affect-modulating properties of tobacco use. Because there is a great similarity between tobacco withdrawal symptoms and the negative affective states that nicotine and tobacco use alleviate (Hughes, Hatsukami, Pickens, Krahn, Malin, & Luknic, 1984), a fundamental question is whether nicotine has mood and performance-enhancing effects above and beyond those associated with withdrawal symptom alleviation. It is necessary to determine whether these effects arise from withdrawal alleviation, from inherent properties of nicotine, or from various interactions and combinations of environmental, conditioning, pharmacological, and sensory parameters.

A second fundamental question addressed in this chapter is that of individual differences. Many individuals report experiencing few, if any, withdrawal symptoms when they quit smoking (A. L. Murray & Lawrence, 1984; Schachter, 1979; Shiffman, 1989). Do such withdrawal-symptom-free individuals experience tranquilizing and cognition and performance-enhancing effects when they smoke? Are such individuals so well psychobiologically balanced that they cope with stress, including nicotine withdrawal, with relative impunity? If so, withdrawal symptom severity should correlate significantly with acute negative-affect-reducing effects of nicotine and with personality and psychopathology.

An important related question is whether symptoms associated with smoking cessation are a function of one's general disposition to emotional distress and psychopathology, that is, do some individuals smoke to self-medicate psycho-pathology? The broader question of whether individuals typically respond to abstinence with their predominant stress response has not yet been adequately assessed. If response to abstinence is largely a function of the individual's typical stress response, one would expect to see an exacerbation of anxiety in anxiety-prone individuals, increased hostility in hostility-prone people, and so forth.

SELF-REPORTED (SMOKER-ATTRIBUTED) SMOKING AFFECT MODULATION AND PERFORMANCE ENHANCEMENT

Recalled Effects of Smoking

Most smokers say that for them cigarettes are pleasurable and relaxing and reduce negative affect. In fact, these are the primary two or three reasons given for continuing to smoke. Consistent with these perceived effects and motivations for smoking, findings have suggested that smokers may be more likely to smoke during stressful situations than nonstressful situations (Dobbs, Strickler, & Maxwell, 1981; Perkins & Grobe, 1992; C. S. Pomerleau & Pomerleau, 1987; Rose, Ananda, & Jarvik, 1983; Schachter, 1978). Other reasons reported for smoking include positive affect enhancement, concentration enhancement, stimulation, and habit. Spielberger (1986) found that the tranquilizing effects experienced by smokers were the most important reasons for continuing to smoke among regular as well as occasional smokers. Similarly, feeling calmer was the most frequently recalled effect of smoking in both daily and occasional smoking adolescents in a study by McNeill, Jarvis, and West (1987). Such expectations likely result from recalled experiences, but could result from misattributions (Hall, Havassey, & Wasserman, 1990; Shiffman, 1993a).

In a comparison of the subjective effects of smoking with those of other substances and activities, Warburton (1988) evaluated the recalled experiences of persons who had used a variety of substances. Alcohol, amphetamines, amyl nitrite, cocaine, glue, heroin, marijuana, and sex produced significantly more pleasurable stimulation than smoking, whereas sleeping tablets and tranquilizers were significantly less stimulating than smoking. There were no differences between the pleasurable stimulation produced by coffee, chocolate, and smoking. Smoking's relaxing effects were similar to those of chocolate; significantly less than those of tranquilizers, sleeping tablets, alcohol, heroin, and sex; but significantly more than those of amphetamines, amyl nitrite, cocaine, coffee, and glue. In a related study, cigarettes were rated by habitual users as less pleasurable than alcohol or other drugs (Kozlowski et al., 1989).

In conclusion, smokers attribute very modest psychoactive effects to smoking. The affect modulation and pleasure associated with smoking are similar to those obtained from foods and sweets and are significantly less intense than prototypic drugs of abuse. Smokers report experiencing decreases in negative affect and, in some cases, slight increases in arousal, pleasurable relaxation, and ability to concentrate.

Retrospectively Reported Calming Effects: What Can Be Inferred?

Although smokers generally believe that smoking helps them relax, concentrate, and cope with a variety of stressors, there remains the question of why they believe these things. One possibility noted by Shiffman (1993a) was that anxiety will become a cue for smoking if nicotine reduces anxiety. Moreover, what cues a person to smoke is closely related to the person's motives for smoking.

However, one should be cautious in making inferences from retrospectively reported motivations. For example, two prospective studies failed to find a relationship between negative affect and smoking, where retrospective assessment of the same subjects found one. S. M. Hall et al. (1990) found that retrospectively reported negative affect and withdrawal symptoms were correlated with relapse after relapse had occurred. However, when these authors examined their data prospectively, this relationship disappeared. Similarly, Paty and Shiffman (1991) found that although most smokers report smoking more during times of negative affect, the relationship between affect and smoking as they actually occurred failed to demonstrate that acute increases in negative affect are predictive of immediate subsequent smoking. Thus, although negative affect predicts relapse to smoking (Shiffman, 1986), smokers may not be more likely to light up a cigarette when in a negative affective state than when not. Shiffman (1991) suggested that the beliefs that smoking attenuates stress and that smoking increases when one is under stress are misattributions. These misattributions stem from the fact that smokers attempting to quit experience negative affect and thereby erroneously develop the belief that smoking has inherent tranquilizing effects, when in fact it only alleviates nicotine withdrawal.

It is not clear why these prospective studies failed to observe increased smoking in response to negative affect. One possibility is that smokers accurately anticipate experiencing negative affect in most real-world situations and thus smoke before its onset as a form of anticipatory coping. A second factor contributing to the failure to identify stress-smoking links is the point at which affect is assessed. The study by S. M. Hall et al. (1990) assessed stress at weekly intervals that would not detect acute fluctuations in stress that may have promoted relapse. A final possibility is that negative affect is not generally predictive of smoking. However, contrary to this view, experimental manipulations of stress have reliably demonstrated that stress increased the probability of smoking. As experimental designs are generally the best means of assessing causation, it seems most probable that anticipatory smoking and methodological weakness are responsible for the failure of prospective studies to find correlations between stress and smoking.

The question of what effects smoking has on subjective and behavioral states is different than the question of self-attributed motives for smoking. Smokers may not accurately identify certain effects of smoking as influencing their smoking. For example, habitual smoking in response to cues predictive of stress or of decreased arousal associated with decreased blood nicotine concentrations may be significantly discounted or even ignored as discriminant stimuli for smoking. In contrast, highly salient stimuli such as intense emotional states or frustration at not having cigarettes available when wanted may be especially strongly coded in memory.

In conclusion, smokers report that they smoke more when in negative affective states and that smoking attenuates such states. In some conditions, smokers believe that smoking increases positive affective states. However, nicotine's affect-modulating properties appear to consist primarily of negative affect reduction and attention enhancement.

AFFECT DURING TOBACCO ABSTINENCE AND NICOTINE REPLACEMENT

Affective Responses to Abstinence

Individuals vary from one another and a given individual varies from one occasion to another in response to abstinence from tobacco. Some individuals report severe affective distress when abstaining from smoking for a few hours or days, whereas other, equally as heavy smokers experience minimal or no distress. This abstinence response variability is not surprising given that response to abstinence from a wide range of substances varies widely across individuals and within individuals over time (Peele, 1985). This variability demonstrates that abstinence responses are not a simple function of drug history and length of abstinence. Rather, a number of factors interact to determine the response. Similarities and differences across response classes, substances, individuals, and situations provide important clues about individual differences in smoking motivation and the affect-modulating properties of nicotine. Such characterization facilitates understanding of the affect-modulating effects of smoking and allows more effective smoking interventions.

Abstinence from drugs—as well as from food, love objects, important relationships, and goal attainment—frequently results in extreme subjective distress and dramatic physiological changes. To the extent that different substances or objects produce different effects, abstinence symptoms can be considered substance or object specific. In contrast to such differential responsivity, there is much commonality in the negative-affect-response-class patterns associated with abstinence or loss across a wide range of drugs, love objects, and other desired goals (Gilbert, Gilbert, & Schultz, 1994; Peele, 1985). For example, Gilbert and associates (Gilbert, Gilbert, & Schultz, 1994) found that college students reported that irritation, restlessness, impatience, anxiety, poor concentration, sleep disturbances, lack of energy, and depression (ranked in this order) were the most intense affective responses to abstinence or frustration associated with relationship breakup, loss of a loved one, dieting, and abstinence from caffeine, alcohol, and smoking. Much of this commonality is a generalized distress factor resulting from abstinence from a reinforcing object.

The first few days of abstinence from tobacco are associated with group mean increases in negative affect and changes in a number of other psychological and physiological state domains. The withdrawal symptoms listed in the fourth edition of the *DSM* (or *DSM–IV*; APA, 1994) are (a) dysphoric or depressed mood; (b) insomnia; (c) irritability, frustration, or anger; (d) difficulty concentrating; (e) restlessness; (f) decreased heart rate; and (g) increased appetite or weight gain. With the exception of the decrease in heart rate and increased appetite, all of the *DSM–IV* withdrawal symptoms are identical to those listed in the proceding paragraph as being most frequently associated with abstinence from or a loss of any cherished substance or person. The understanding of these commonalities, as well as variations in response to abstinence, are facilitated by the concurrent assessment of a wide range of responses to a range of stimuli, rather than by a small number of traditional measures.

Types of Abstinence Effects

Subtypes of abstinence effects can be identified, including offset, transient, rebound, and novel effects (Hughes, Higgins, & Hatsukami, 1990). Subtypes are distinguished by time patterns of effects, as well as by the amount of data and follow-up required to characterize a subtype. All effects assume an assessment of dependent variables during a preabstinence smoking baseline.

Offset or permanent effects occur when two or more points in time postabstinence indicate a change opposite in direction to those of nicotine. Thus, offset effects result in a return to predrug baseline values. Although many researchers do not consider offset effects important, they may be aversive (e.g., weight gain) and may lead to relapse (Hughes et al., 1990).

Transient effects are biphasic and are not a simple function of offset of drug effects. The limited duration of these effects differentiates them from offset effects. Definitions of withdrawal are based on transient subjective and physiological effects.

Rebound effects are a subtype of transient effects in which the transient effects are opposite to those of the drug and exceed the predrug baseline. Because predrug values are rarely obtained in studies with humans, they can generally only be observed in animal studies.

Novel effects are those that are not directly opposite to effects of the drugs (e.g., tremors and seizures). Hughes et al. (1990) found no instances of novel effects in their comprehensive review of the effects of tobacco and nicotine abstinence.

Difficulty in Differentiation of Transient from Offset Effects

At first glance, the apparently transient nature of cessation on negative affect suggests that the negative-affect-reducing effects of nicotine are withdrawal-symptom-alleviating effects. However, there are several alternative interpretations. For example, individuals may seek smoking cessation treatment when more distressed than is typical or they may experience increases in negative affect as they anticipate quitting. Either of these possibilities would lead to an artificially high baseline immediately before quitting, which would mask residual negative affect resulting from giving up smoking. Thus, what appears to be a return to baseline level may in fact reflect stabilization at a level of subjective distress higher than the typical preabstinence level. Consistent with this possibility, Cinciripini et al. (1994) found that anxiety increased during the 2 weeks immediately before quitting.

The quitting process for many is a lifestyle change effort that may coincide with a number of similar efforts, all of which are designed to decrease stress, improve physical and mental health, and promote subjective feelings of well-being. These positive lifestyle enhancements may artificially lower negative affect so that what in fact was a combination of an offset effect and transient effect appears solely to be a transient effect.

Other explanations include the following: On cessation, individuals and their spouses may change their reference levels for reporting negative affect because of psychological, behavioral, or pharmacological adaptation; or quitters may develop new pharmacological or nonpharmacological coping techniques. Furthermore, only a select subgroup of those individuals who attempt to abstain do so for the required period. The response curve of those who achieve abstinence cannot be assumed to parallel that for those who did not. Finally, individuals who maintain abstinence may do so because environmental and other factors change in a positive direction. Individuals whose environment or psychobiological disposition change for the worse would be expected to be more likely to relapse. It appears that abstainers return to a psychobiological state equivalent to the preabstinence level when in fact positive environmental and lifestyle changes, rather than neurobiological adaptation, lower their level of negative affect.

An appropriately long period of drug deprivation is required to demonstrate the psychoactive effects of any drug. Ceiling effects and therapeutic windows of maximal rewarding effect occur with virtually all drugs. Thus, smokers must be deprived of nicotine for some period before a nicotine boost will result in substantial alteration of mood. The minimal deprivation period may be as short as an hour (O. F. Pomerleau, Turk, & Fertig, 1984), but a period of one half-life or more of nicotine (2 hours) should result in more robust effects.

This need to ensure some degree of abstinence must be balanced by the fact that depriving users for too long may result in significant abstinence responses.

Several approaches can be followed in differentiating inherent negative-affect-reducing effects from withdrawal symptoms. If one can demonstrate that the level of negative affect associated with withdrawal symptomatology during short-term deprivation is similar to that of nondeprived states, then it is arguable that nicotine has negative-affect-reducing effects independent of any withdrawal-alleviating effects (O. F. Pomerleau et al., 1984). Several studies have supported the view that minimal deprivation in a laboratory setting does not result in increased negative affect and that nicotine can influence negative affect after as little as 1 hour of deprivation (Fertig, Pomerleau, & Sanders, 1986; Meliska & Gilbert, 1991; C. S. Pomerleau & Pomerleau, 1987; O. F. Pomerleau et al., 1984). However, confidence in these findings is limited by the small number of subjects used. The finding that 38% of nondaily smokers report feeling calmer as a result of smoking (McNeill et al., 1987) is also consistent with the occurrence of withdrawal-symptom independent tranquilization.

Response-Class-Dependent Abstinence Response Time Courses

Different abstinence response classes exhibit different group-mean time courses subsequent to cessation. For example, most abstinence-induced negative affect increments and concentration decrements resolve within 4 weeks of successful abstinence, whereas hunger, weight gain, and craving continue throughout 6-month follow-ups (Hughes, 1992; Hughes, Gust, Skoog, Keenan, & Fenwick, 1991; West, Hajek, & McNeill, 1991). Individual differences are nonetheless clear, with 20–25% of quitters exhibiting elevated negative affect throughout 6-month follow-ups (Hughes, 1992; Hughes et al., 1991; West et al., 1991).

It is important to recognize that abstinence curves only characterize the responses of the select group of successful abstainers. Those who fail to abstain for a month are more neurotic, depression-prone, impulsive, and otherwise prone to negative affect (Cohen & Lichtenstein, 1990; Glassman et al., 1990; S. M. Hall, Bachman, Henderson, Barstow, & Jones, 1983; Hughes, 1992; O. F. Pomerleau, Adkins, & Pertschuk, 1978). Moreover, the two-factor (physical dependence and self-medication) model (D. G. Gilbert, Meliska, Welser, et al., 1992) predicts that this high-psychopathology group is characterized by abstinence responses that do not return to preabstinence baseline levels. Thus, abstinence response curves may seriously misrepresent the responses of a large segment of the population attempting to quit. Hypothetical abstinence curves of self-medicators (neurotics, depression-prone, etc.) and those of the more traditional, successful non-self-medicators are plotted in Figure 5.1.

The size of this selective sample bias may be quite large given that a majority of individuals starting such studies do not successfully abstain for the full period of the study. For example, in a study by Hughes (1992) of 830 individuals initially indicating plans to quit, only 178 reported abstinence for 30 days. In an attempt to minimize selective sample attrition, D. G. Gilbert, Meliska, Welser,

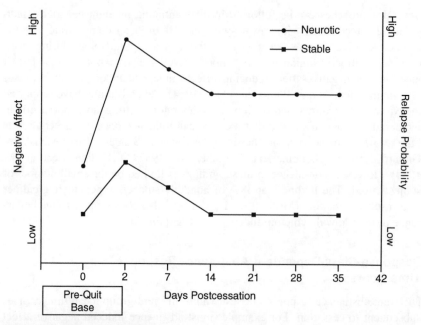

Figure 5.1 Relapse probabilities and negative affect across time subsequent to smoking abstinence in neurotic (self-medicating depression-, anxiety, or irritability prone) and in stable individuals.

et al. (1992) paid individuals $400.00 if and only if they completed a month of abstinence without relapse. Those high in negative affect, trait depression, and neuroticism at baseline did not return to baseline levels of negative affect, electrocortical arousal, or right and left frontal EEG symmetry even after a month of abstinence. Only 5 of the 33 individuals randomly assigned to quit for a month relapsed before 31 days. Thus, time courses of various abstinence responses have not been accurately characterized. Definitive statements concerning the prevalence and time course of abstinence responses are precluded by differential relapse rates in those with differing degrees and types of abstinence response, unstable baselines, and cessation-related environmental and lifestyle changes.

Hughes (1992) performed one of the few factor-analytic studies of withdrawal symptoms. He found that three factors accounted for most of the common variance: mood (anxiety, difficulty concentrating, irritability, and restlessness), appetite (hunger and weight gain), and insomnia (awakenings at night). Factor analysis can be a useful tool in assessing individual differences in smoker responses to abstinence and in identifying common variance and potential common mechanisms across variables. Nonetheless, there is also value in assessing the unique variance associated with each variable. For example, it appears that increased depression subsequent to abstinence is more important than other affective changes because depression appears to be more predictive of relapse

(Hughes, 1992). Specific affective changes frequently associated smoking abstinence are discussed below.

Negative Affect *Anger and Irritability* Cessation studies have consistently shown transient increases in mean self-reported and spouse-reported daily anger and irritability in smokers, peaking within the first day or two of deprivation and declining over the next 2 weeks to near baseline levels (D. G. Gilbert, Meliska, Welser, et al., 1992; Hatsukami, Dahlgren, Zimmerman, & Hughes, 1988; Hutsukami, Gust, & Keenan, 1987; Hatsukami, Hughes, & Pickens, 1984; Hughes, 1992; Hughes & Hatsukami, 1986; Hughes et al., 1984, 1986; Hughes et al., 1991; Stitzer & Gross, 1988; M. M. Ward, Swan, & Jack, 1994; West, Hajek, & Belcher, 1987; West et al., 1991; West et al., 1984). In one of the few studies assessing individual differences, Clavel, Benhamou, and Flamant (1987) observed that exsmokers felt more irritable compared with subjects still smoking even 1 year after quitting and that increases in irritability and weight gain were more frequent among high-dependent than low-dependent exsmokers.

Nicotine deprivation contributes to increases in anger and irritation associated with smoking cessation because such increases are attenuated by nicotine gum (Brantmark, Ohlin, & Westling, 1973; Hughes, Hatsukami, Pickens, Krahn, Malin, & Luknic, 1984; Hughes, Hatsukami, & Skorg, 1986; Schneider & Jarvik, 1985; Stitzer & Gross, 1988; West, Russell, Jarvis, & Feyeraband, 1984). Moreover, the findings of West, Russell, Jarvis, Pizzey, & Kadam (1984), showing that individuals who switched to low-nicotine cigarettes did not experience increased anger and irritation, suggested that relatively low doses of nicotine may substantially reduce anger and irritation associated with smoking cessation.

In contrast to studies of normal to frequently irritating living environments, those of less irritating settings have generally observed minimal or no increases in state anger and irritability subsequent to deprivation. Arci and Grunberg (1992) found an increase in irritability during abstinence only when an irritating stimulus (noise) was presented. Smokers in an inpatient ward did not exhibit increased argumentativeness subsequent to cessation (Hatsukami et al., 1984), and smoking abstinence in a sensory deprivation environment was experienced with minimal subjective distress by heavy smokers (Suedfeld & Ikard, 1974). The functionally important common denominator across these controlled environment studies may be that the situation was of relatively lower irritation potential.

In summary, increases in anger irritability occur in nicotine-deprived habitual tobacco users only when they are in an irritating environment. Whether such increases are more intense in those high in trait anger and irritability has not been determined.

Impatience and impulsivity Transient increases in self-reported and observed impatience have been repeatedly observed subsequent to cessation (Gross

& Stitzer, 1989; Hughes Hatsukami, Pickens, Krahn, Malin, & Luknic, 1984, 1986; Hughes, Hatsukami, & Skoog, 1986; Hughes et al., 1990; Hughes et al., 1991; Rodin, 1987). These increases appear to be in part a function of nicotine deprivation, as nicotine gum attenuates the magnitude of increase (Gross & Stitzer, 1989; Hughes et al., 1984a, 1986a, 1986b; Stitzer & Gross, 1988). Smoking deprivation has generally not altered errors of commission in rapid information-processing vigilance tasks (Jiang, 1987; Parrott & Craig, 1992; Wesnes, Warburton, & Matz, 1983). In contrast to these studies with human participants, Nelson and Goldstein (1972, 1973) observed an increased frequency of false positive errors in rats subsequent to cessation from chronic nicotine administration.

It is not clear whether individuals high in trait impatience and impulsivity typically experience more intense subjective impatience and impulsivity during tobacco cessation. Behavioral measures of impulsivity used in smoking abstinence studies to date have been limited to vigilance tasks that may not tap the types of impatience and impulsivity putatively associated with smoking abstinence.

Anxiety and Tension   In natural environment studies, anxiety and tension scores generally increase to maximum values within the first day or two of abstinence and then gradually return toward baseline levels over the next 2 weeks (D. G. Gilbert, Meliska, Welser, et al., 1992; Hatsukami et al., 1984, 1987, 1988; Hughes & Hatsukami, 1986; Hughes et al., 1990; Hughes, Hatsukami, & Skoog, 1986, 1991; Puddey, Vandongen, Berlen, & English, 1984; Puddey, Vandongen, Beilin, English, & Ukich, 1985; Rodin, 1987; Schneider & Jarvik, 1985; M. M. Ward et al., 1994). In general, these studies have tended to find reasonably high prevalences of increased anxiety. For example, a sizable study by Hughes et al. (1991) found abstinence-related incidences of self-reported increases in anxiety to be 59%, higher than for other negative affects (e.g., angry and irritable, 52%; impatient, 52%; restless, 55%; and drowsy, 40%. In contrast, in controlled-environment, minimally stressful studies anxiety does not increase after nicotine deprivation of up to 12 hours or more (D. G. Gilbert, Meliska, Williams, & Jensen, 1992; Meliska & Gilbert, 1991; Parrott & Craig, 1992; Parrott & Winder, 1989) and possibly not after any period of deprivation (Gilbert, 1994). Most investigations have looked only at group means. Although a majority of such studies have found nicotine gum to attenuate smoking-cessation-related anxiety (e.g., Gross & Stitzer, 1989; Hughes, Hatsukami, Pickens, Krahn, Malin, & Luknic, 1984a, 1986; Hughes, Hatsukami, & Skogg, 1986; Schneider & Jarvik, 1985; Stitzer & Gross, 1988), several have not (Brantmark et al., 1973; West & Russell, 1985; West, Russell, Jarvis, & Feyeraband, 1984). Hughes et al. (1990) noted that the studies not observing increases in mean anxiety used either short cessation periods (West, Russell, Jarvis, & Feyerabend, 1984a) or smokers not trying to quit smoking permanently (Weybrew & Stark, 1967).

Depression and Dysphoria   The incidence of depressive affect subsequent
to abstinence is much higher in those with a clinical history of depression and in
those scoring high in trait measures of depressed affect (Covey, Glassman, &
Stetner, 1990; S. M. Hall, Munoz, & Reus, 1991; Kinnunen, Doherty, Militello,
& Garvey, 1994; M. A. H. Russell, 1994). Smoking cessation has been associated with increases in group mean self-reported depression and dysphoria during the first week of cessation (Hatsukami et al., 1984; Schneider & Jarvik,
1985; M. M. Ward et al., 1994; West, Russell, Jarvis, & Feyerabend, 1984a;
West et al., 1987, 1991; Weybrew & Stark, 1967). Moreover, in a study by
Covey et al. (1990) depressive symptoms occurred in 75% of those with a history
of depression, but in only 31% of those without such a history. Those with a
history of depression reported more and more intense cessation-related effects.
S. M. Hall et al. (1991) found larger increases in negative affect in individuals
with a history of high trait or clinical depression. Smokers depressed immediately
before quitting reported larger increases in dysphoric response to abstinence, but
nicotine gum attenuated dysphoric response in these individuals (Kinnunen et
al., 1994).

Some studies have found no effect of cessation on depressed mood (Hatsukami et al., 1987, 1988; Hughes & Hatsukami, 1986; Lawrence, Amodci, &
Murray, 1982; Rodin, 1987). However, most of those individuals who become
depressed while attempting to quit relapse and are thus systematically excluded
from many studies. Moreover, Hughes et al. (1990) noted that most studies
failing to observe effects on dysphoria used the Profile of Mood States questionnaire, whereas studies finding effects have typically used a single-item (e.g.,
5-point) scale that may assess a broader construct than the Profile of Mood States
sadness and dejection measure.

Administration of nicotine versus placebo gum during smoking cessation
has attenuated depression and dysphoria in some studies (Hughes, Hatsukami,
& Skoog, 1986; Kinnunen et al., 1994; Schneider & Jarvik, 1985; West, Russell,
Jarvis, & Feyeraband, 1984), but not in others (Brantmark et al., 1973; Hatsukami, Huber, Callies, & Skoog, 1993). *D*-Fenfluramine, a serotoninergic agonist
with antidepressant properties, tended to prevent a rise in depression during the
first week of smoking cessation in a study by Spring, Wurtman, Gleason, Wurtman, and Kessler (1991).

Arousal, Activation, and Motivation and Energy   Nicotine and tobacco
abstinence influence a number of arousal and motivation-related constructs, including feelings of arousal, energy, drowsiness, fatigue, motivation, drive, and
ability to concentrate. Because these constructs are conceptually and empirically
associated (Strelau & Eysenck, 1987), there would be the advantage of parsi-
mony in aggregating them to the degree that they overlap.

Drowsiness and Alertness   Decrements in alertness have been observed in
a number of studies subsequent to cessation (Hatsukami et al., 1987, 1988;

Hughes et al., 1991), but not in others (e.g., Hatsukami et al., 1984; West, Russell, Jarvis, & Feyeraband, 1984; Weybrew & Stark, 1967). Effects of nicotine gum on self-reported drowsiness are also variable (Hughes et al., 1990). Nevertheless, studies of short-term deprivation in laboratory settings have relatively consistently found that nicotine deprivation increases drowsiness relative to smoking conditions (D. G. Gilbert, Meliska, et al., 1994; Meliska & Gilbert, 1991; O'Neill & Parrott, 1992).

The inconsistent effects of tobacco cessation on reported alertness in the natural environment may be a function of the measures of alertness and drowsiness used, as well as of the smoker's personality and the environmental conditions in the smoker's life. If cessation is associated with diminished functioning of homeostatic mechanisms, then individuals in environments providing an ideal level of stimulation would experience little or no alteration of alertness. In contrast, increases in drowsiness would be expected in individuals functioning primarily in an unstimulating environment in which they are required to maintain sustained vigilance. Finally, environments providing high levels of stimulation might result in excessively high arousal in recent abstainers. The net result of such environment-specific abstinence effects on group means of self-reports would depend on the proportion of individuals experiencing the different types of environments.

Concentration   Cessation is consistently associated with reported lessening of ability to concentrate over the first week or two of abstinence (Hughes et al., 1990; M. M. Ward et al., 1994; West et al., 1991). D. G. Gilbert, Meliska, Welser, et al. (1992) found the severity of vigilance decrements during the first few days of abstinence to be a function of habitual nicotine intake and neuroticism. Although the vigilance of most individuals had fully recovered within 31 days of cessation, individuals who scored high in neuroticism had not returned to baseline levels. Nicotine substitution by means of gum generally appears to attenuate the effects of cessation on concentration (for a review, see Hughes et al., 1990).

Vigor and Drive   Vigor is functionally distinct from alertness and drowsiness and from ability to concentrate. For example, Hughes and Hatsukami (1986) found self-reported decreases in vigor after cessation; the same individuals reported no changes in drowsiness. Alertness and ability to concentrate are cognitive information processing constructs, whereas vigor as assessed by the Profile of Mood States is associated with drive and a high motivation or impulse toward motor activity. There are few studies assessing the effects of cessation on vigor, and no studies assessing effects on drives other than hunger. In summary, the limited evidence supports the view that vigor may be transiently decreased subsequent to cessation.

Activity   Although P. Smith and Lombardo (1986) found that pedometer scores were 14% lower on a deprived day than on a smoking day, most studies have found no changes in monitored activity subsequent to cessation (S. M. Hall, McGee, Tunstall, Duffy, & Benowitz, 1989; Hatsukami et al., 1984; Hofstetter, Schultz, Jequier, & Wahren, 1986; Leischow & Stitzer, 1991; Puddey et al., 1984, 1985; Rodin, 1987). In contrast to humans, in rodents acute doses of nicotine in the range of 0.1–0.5 mg/kg generally produce a biphasic effect on locomotor activity, with an initial phase of suppression followed by a subsequent period of stimulation (Balfour, 1991a; E. H. Y. Lee, 1985). High doses result in decreases in rodent locomotor activity owing to the toxic effects of nicotine. Rodents do not appear to become tolerant to these stimulant effects of nicotine (Balfour, 1991b).

Fatigue   Fatigue does not appear to be influenced by cessation in most people (Hatsukami et al., 1984, 1987, 1988; Hughes & Hatsukami, 1986; Lawrence et al., 1982; Rodin, 1987; West & Russell, 1987; West, Russell, Jarvis, & Feyeraband, 1984; Weybrew & Stark, 1967). Thus, fatigue appears to be a different psychobiological construct than vigor and alertness and drowsiness. To the degree that fatigue is one end of a bipolar dimension of activity and fatigue, these results are consistent with those on activity.

Pleasure and Euphoria   Smoking cessation studies largely have not assessed changes in positive affect or the euphoriant effects of stimuli as a function of cessation. Appetite and food preference changes subsequent to cessation is the one related area that has received systematic study. Smokers say food tastes better and their appetite increases subsequent to quitting (Grunberg, 1985). Well-controlled experimental work has suggested that calorie and carbohydrate intake increase after quitting (Spring et al., 1991). It is possible that tobacco abstinence results in increases in drives and appetites for a variety of other pleasurable stimuli. The one study assessing the effects of acute smoking on sexual responsivity produced inconclusive results (D. G. Gilbert, Hagen, & D'Agostino, 1986).

Physical Symptoms   Unlike withdrawal from prototypic drugs such as heroin and alcohol, abstinence from tobacco does not induce specific physical withdrawal symptoms for most abstainers (for a review, see Hughes et al., 1990). The effects of nicotine abstinence are more psychological in nature. When physical symptoms do occur, the Situation × Trait Response hypothesis predicts they will be more likely to occur in those who typically respond to stress with physical symptoms.

Situational and Class Dependence of Responses to Abstinence   *Negative Affect and Arousal*   The finding that tobacco deprivation for as long as 12 hours increases drowsiness but not negative affect in a relaxing laboratory setting

(D. G. Gilbert, Estes, Meliska, Plath, & Welser, 1994; D. G. Gilbert, Meliska, et al., 1992; Meliska & Gilbert, 1991; Parrott & Craig, 1992; Parrott & Winder, 1989) indicates that the negative affect associated with nicotine abstinence depends on environmental factors. D. G. Gilbert and associates did not find increases in tension, worry, fear, anger, sadness, or unpleasantness in deprived smokers relative to nondeprived smokers. Environment-dependent effects are also implied by Suedfeld and Ikard's (1974) findings, in which smokers undergoing prolonged sensory deprivation experienced much milder withdrawal symptoms than anticipated. This evidence suggests that what are commonly referred to as withdrawal symptoms are not inherent effects of nicotine abstinence, but occur only in certain situations in predisposed individuals. Withdrawal symptoms may reflect a psychophysiological overreactivity or biases in bioinformation processing rather than a time-locked inherent biological syndrome. Future studies of abstinence response would benefit from contrasting affect during affect-promoting and performance-demanding tasks.

Urge to smoke   The urge to smoke continues with large degrees of fluctuation in intensity and occurrence for months or years after cessation in most quitters (Fletcher & Doll, 1969). Conditioning and expectancies related to hundreds of thousands of pairings of smoking cues with reinforcing psychobiological processes likely contribute to the activation of cigarette-seeking urges.

Individual Differences in Response to Abstinence

The STAR model of smoking (detailed in Chapters 7 and 9) suggests that the large individual differences observed in response to tobacco abstinence (A. L. Murray & Lawrence, 1984; see Chapter 7) can be conceptualized as a function of three partially independent factors: (a) Biological Dependence (preabstinence history of nicotine exposure and associated neurobiological adaptation to nicotine), (b) Individual Disposition (individual differences in psychobiologically influenced personality traits, dispositions to psychopathology, and biological differences), and (c) Environmental Risk and Support factors (social support, stress, and smoking cues unique to the individual). To the degree that tobacco abstinence effects are transient and that their offset results from neurobiological restoration of a new homeostasis, abstinence symptoms are a function of physical dependence, a nicotine-induced biological adaptation. To the degree that abstinence symptoms are offset effects, they are likely a function of individual differences in personality, psychopathology, and biological disposition toward negative affective states and impaired cognitive functioning. Although environmental influences would be expected to wax and wane variably in response to changes within and across situations, environmental risk and support factors are relatively stable and therefore traitlike. Also, it seems reasonable to hypothesize that individual differences in tendency toward neurobiological adaptation to nicotine may to some extent be related to individual differences in personality and psychopathology. For example, genetically based biological dispositions toward certain types of negative affect and neurotic processes may dispose one toward physical, as well as psychological, dependence on nicotine. Finally, biological dependence on nicotine is expected to correlate with individual differences in biological and psychological disposition to the degree that personality and psychopathology dispose one to smoke more or less heavily.

Individual Differences in Time Course and Intensity   The 1988 SGR (USDHHS, 1988) concluded that retrospectively collected data

> suggest that most cigarette smokers experience at least one symptom of the tobacco withdrawal syndrome, that between one-fourth and one-half show significant withdrawal, and that about one-fourth report no withdrawal at all. Of those persons who report no withdrawal symptoms, it is unclear whether they were not physically dependent, whether the assessment instruments were not sensitive, or whether some persons are less impaired or discomforted by withdrawal symptoms. (pp. 200–201)

Symptom-free persons may be so well psychobiologically balanced that their natural biological homeostatic systems efficiently adapt to their nicotine-free state. Another possibility is that such individuals are so psychologically or behaviorally adaptive that they avoid conditions that contribute to such negative states.

As mentioned previously, neuroticism, as well as habitual nicotine intake, correlated significantly with degree of vigilance impairment after 1 day of abstinence; however, only neuroticism was associated after 31 days of abstinence (D. G. Gilbert, Meliska, Welser, et al., 1992). Thus, degree of habitual nicotine intake correlated with degree of transient cognitive impairment, whereas neuroticism was associated with a failure to fully return to baseline (see Fig. 5.1).

Pre-Abstinence Nicotine Intake and Abstinence Response   Abstinence response intensity has been found to correlate with preabstinence nicotine intake and reported daily cigarette consumption in some studies, but not in others. The number of cigarettes smoked per day is at best a weak predictor of abstinence response severity (for a review, see Hughes et al., 1990; USDHHS, 1988), in part because this measure correlates poorly with daily nicotine intake. Objective measures of daily nicotine intake are somewhat more strongly associated with symptom severity. Plasma cotinine, nicotine's major metabolite, provides a better estimate of daily nicotine intake than does plasma nicotine itself, because cotinine has a much longer half-life than does nicotine. D. G. Gilbert, Meliska, Welser, et al. (1992) found that vigilance task performance decrements, brainwave slowing, and self-reported negative affect increases correlated with precessation plasma cotinine concentration. West and Russell (1985) found that preabstinence plasma nicotine, but not habitual daily cigarette number, correlated with overall withdrawal symptom severity, craving, and irritability. An earlier study by O. F. Pomerleau, Fertig, and Shanhan (1983) found that preabstinence baseline cotinine correlated with abstinence-associated craving, and Zeidenberg et al. (1977) found similar correlations in men but not in women. Preabstinence blood nicotine concentration is predictive of difficulty in maintaining abstinence (e.g., M. A. H. Russell, 1994).

LABORATORY STUDIES OF AFFECT MODULATION BY SMOKING AND NICOTINE

Studies of the acute effects of smoking have less reliably demonstrated negative-affect-attenuating effects than have the nonlaboratory studies of nicotine gum. Most experimental studies comparing the effects of nicotine gun with those of placebo gum have concluded that nicotine gum reduces negative affect in nicotine-deprived habitual smokers (Hughes, Hatsukami, Pickens, Krahn, Malin, & Luknic, 1984; Jarvis, Raw, Russell, & Feyeraband, et al., 1982; West, Jarvis, et al., 1984). A likely explanation for the reliable results of nicotine gum studies is that they assessed aggregate mood across the entire day in the natural environment. Averaging across time and situations generally increases not only the reliability and validity of measures (S. Epstein, 1979), but also the probability that situations in which nicotine can reduce negative affect will occur.

Table 5.1 differentiates studies according to the nature of the experimental stressor-situational complex and provides state and trait information when available. The categories used to differentiate situational characteristics are based on the conclusion (D. G. Gilbert & Welser, 1989) that nicotine modulates affect primarily when stressor stimuli are ambiguous, temporally distal, and of mild or moderate intensity. In addition, the present differentiation of studies includes the dimension of attentionally engaging situational distractor stimuli. This situational–distractor dimension is hypothesized to interact with nicotine-induced, cognitive–affective information-processing biases in the determination of many of nicotine's affect-modulating effects.

Unless otherwise stated, studies referred to were performed by comparing the smoking of normal nicotine-delivery cigarettes with very low nicotine-delivery cigarettes. Most other studies compared the smoking of normal nicotine-delivery cigarettes with not smoking over the corresponding period of time.

Effects of Nicotine on Specific Affects

Anxiety, Tension, and Fear   Experimental studies have shown smoking and nicotine to reduce anxiety and tension and other forms of negative affect when ambiguous and distal stressor stimuli are present (Table 5.1). Exceptions to this tendency are generally found in studies using rapid smoking procedures that produce nausea and other subjective distress because of nicotine overdose (D. G. Gilbert, Meliska, Williams, & Jenson, 1992). Affective responses in situations involving proximal stressors (Table 5.2) and minimally stressful stimuli (Table 5.3) are generally not influenced by nicotine. The clearest example of the importance of the nature of the anxiety-inducing situations in smoking and anxiolytic effects comes from the work of Jarvik, Caskey, Rose, Herskovic, and Sadeghpour (1989). Using a within-subjects design and minimal abstinence, they observed that smoking (a) reduced subjective anxiety while anticipating performing an unsolvable anagrams task, (b) resulted in a borderline significant reduction in anticipatory anxiety in a cold pain test, and (c) had no effect on anxiety resulting from white noise and auditory vigilance tasks. Pain endurance and threshold was not influenced by smoking. Posttask retrospective reports of anxiety experienced during the tasks were not attenuated for any of the four tasks. Thus, either nicotine's anxiolytic effects are very short lived, as suggested by Perkins, Grobe, Fonte (1992), or something about the anticipatory but not the direct-task coping-related processes is attenuated by nicotine. The anagrams and cold pain tasks may have generated more social performance anxiety, whereas the white noise task simply generated mild fear of a physical nature. Although both the auditory vigilance and the anagrams task demanded a great deal of active information processing, participants in the vigilance task achieved some success in practice sessions and thus may have experienced a more positive form of competitive anxiety. Anticipatory anxiety induced by the unsolvable anagrams task was also attenuated by smoking in a study by O. F. Pomerleau, Turk, and Fertig (1984). C. S. Pomerleau and Pomerleau (1987) found a similar outcome using a difficult mental arithmentic task.

Movie-induced anxiety was reduced by normal relative to low-nicotine cigarettes and relative to habitual nonsmokers in a study by D. G. Gilbert, Robinson, Chamberlin, and Spielberger (1989). The movie depicted three brief bodily injury scenes embedded in a discussion of industrial safety and accidents. Thus, the movie's anticipatory cues combined with an intellectual discussion and a related story line to generate the distal and distractor stimulus components hypothesized to contribute to nicotine's anxiolytic effects.

Anxiety induced by social interaction was attenuated in a study by D. G. Gilbert and Spielberger (1987) in which participants debated an issue on which they disagreed strongly. This complex social situation both generated moderate increases in anxiety and required active coping, including attention to the other participant, the situational components hypothesized to result in anxiolytic effects. In contrast, when these components were absent social anxiety was not reduced by smoking; for example, in a study by Hatch, Bierner, and Fisher (1983) in which smokers prepared for and performed an extemporaneous speaking task.

Pain endurance is in part a function of anxiety, and a number of studies have used pain thresholds as dependent variables in assessing the effects of smoking on anxiety. Two studies that tested the effects of smoking cigarettes of different nicotine delivery on electric shock endurance reported elevated endurance thresholds in subjects who smoked relative to nonsmokers and in the high-

Table 5.1 Experimental Stress Paradigms Using Distal, Ambiguous, and Anticipatory Stressors

Study and description	N and cigarettes per day	Deprivation (1), design (2), and coping (3)	Smoking and nicotine treatment	Conclusions
Cherek (1981): Effects of smoking different doses of nicotine on human aggressive behavior were assessed. Ss attended 10–12 60-min sessions and accumulated 3–4 sessions in each of 3 smoking conditions. Ss could deduct money or send white noice blasts to an imputed other S in response to the imputed other deducting money from S.	7 men & 1 woman; no information	1. No information 2. Within & between 3. Active	Nonsmoking vs. 0.42 mg vs. 2.19 mg nicotine cigarettes	The more nicotine, the less the aggressive behavior. This was not due to a nonspecific depressant effect.
Cherek (1984): Ss smoked either low or high nicotine cigarettes or did not smoke in paradigm described for Cherek (1981).	1 man 5 women; no information	1. No information 2. Within & between 3. Active	30 min to 60 min before session. Ss smoked 2 cigarettes (either 0.42 or 2.19 mg of nicotine) or did not smoke. Ss attended 10–12 sessions.	Nicotine administered by smoking reduced aggressive responses. Higher levels of nicotine produced bigger reductions in aggressive responding and the nicotine administered by smoking reduced reduction of money from imputed other more so than sending noise blasts.

Study	Subjects	Method	Dose	Results
D. G. Gilbert & Spielberger (1987): Social anxiety was assessed during 3 sessions of social interaction between same-gender partners alternating on discussion of topic of moderate to large disagreement. No smoking occurred in 1st session, 1st partner smoked in 2nd session, and 2nd partner in 3rd session. Sessions were on different days.	6 men, 6 women; 10+	1. 60 min 2. Within 3. Active & passive	1 cigarette at either 2nd or 3rd session	Smoking was associated with less anxiety and enhanced feelings of being successful in both changing the opinions of others and expressing oneself. The effects of smoking and social interaction appeared additive. Smoking increased heart rate only about half as much as typically reported for quiescent smokers in nonsocial situations.
D. G. Gilbert et al. (1989): Starting 10 min after smoking, smokers and a group of nonsmokers (who did not smoke) viewed a 15-min stressful movie.	40 men, 40 women; 10+	1. Overnight 2. Between 3. Passive	1 cigarette, 0.8 or 0.1 mg nicotine	Smoking the normal nicotine cigarette decreased anxiety while viewing a stressful movie relative to smoking low-nicotine cigarette and relative to habitual nonsmokers who did not smoke.
Hasenfratz & Bättig (1993): Anxiety was assessed before and after experimental sessions involving stressful tasks.	24 women; 15+	1. Overnight 2. Mixed 3. Active & passive	2 of own cigarettes	Smoking prevented the pre- to postsession increase in anxiety seen during non-smoking sessions.
Jarvik, Caskey, et al. (1989): Pre- and postsmoking changes in anxiety associated with the anticipation of four tasks (anagrams, cold pain, noise, and auditory vigilance) were assessed, as was recalled anxiety experienced during tasks.	11 men, 4 women; 15+	1. None 2. Within 3. Anticipatory & recalled active	Smoked or did not smoke 1 of own cigarettes	Smoking was associated with reduced anxiety in anticipation of the anagrams task and of the cold-pain task, but not of the noise or vigilance tasks. Retrospective reports of anxiety experienced during each of the tasks did not differ as a function of smoking. Note that anagrams and cold-pain tasks are passive-, hopeless-, and failure-related.

Table 5.1 Experimental Stress Paradigms Using Distal, Ambiguous, and Anticipatory Stressors

Study and description	N and cigarettes per day	Deprivation (1), design (2), and coping (3)	Smoking and nicotine treatment	Conclusions
Perkins, Grobe, Fonte, & Breus (1992): Ss smoked and then completed a mood questionnaire just before engaging in a high- or low-challenge task; mood was assessed a 2nd time halfway through the task.	16 male smokers, 16 female smokers, 6 male nonsmokers, 6 female nonsmokers; $M = 20$	1. 1–2 hr 2. Between 3. Active	Cued puffing (4/min) for 2 min on lit or unlit cigarette	Smokers reported less stress and annoyance and more relaxation than sham smokers shortly after smoking, but this effect disappeared in men shortly after smoking but was sustained in women.
C. S. Pomerleau & Pomerleau (1987): Performance anxiety was induced by a mental arithmetic task. Changes in anxiety from pre- to post-smoking were assessed.	7 men; $27.8 +/- 3$	1. 30 min 2. Within 3. Active	1 of own cigarettes smoked and 1 sham smoked unlit	While anticipating the stressor, less anxiety was reported subsequent to smoking than subsequent to sham smoking

Study	Sample	Design	Smoking Condition	Results
O. F. Pomerleau, et al. (1984; M = 25.8), Study 2: Ss attempted to solve unsolvable anagrams (threat of failure stress) during practice session and 2 subsequent experimental sessions. Ss smoked immediately before the anagrams task on the 2 experimental days. Anxiety was assessed immediately before and after smoking.	5 men; SD = 5.7	1. 30 min 2. Within 3. Anticipatory	1 of own brand (M = 1.4 mg nicotine) or nicotine-free.	Smoking usual cigarette decreased anxiety relative to nicotine-free cigarette in all Ss.
Schechter & Rand (1974): Ss either smoked or not during 3 4-min intervals while doing a teaching task. Ss administered shock to imputed learner on a Buss Aggression machine.	26 Ss (about half were male & half female); no information	1. None 2. Between 3. Active	Smoked ad lib own cigarette during 3 4-min intervals.	There was a significant increase in aggression for chronic smokers in the nonsmoking (deprivation) session compared with the smoking session.
Schultze (1982): Ss participated in 4 emotion-inducing tasks while either smoking or not smoking.	59 men & women; 20+/day	1. No information 2. Between 3. Active	Habitual smokers who either smoked or did not and nonsmokers.	Greater calm was experienced by smokers than by abstaining smokers and nonsmokers. This effect was limited largely to situational cuer smokers, whereas self-cuer smokers tended to show the opposite pattern.

Table 5.2 Experimental Stress Paradigms Using Proximal Stressors

Study and description	*N* and cigarettes per day	Deprivation (1), design (2), and coping (3)	Smoking and nicotine treatment	Conclusions
Fertig et al. (1986): Minimally deprived habitual smokers and as exsmokers were given nicotine through smoking and snuff, respectively, or a placebo, in counter-balanced order. Pain endurance threshold was assessed by the cold-pressor test.	10 smokers, 15 exsmokers; 30.7	1. 1 hr 2. Within 3. Active	Nicotine free cigs. vs. 2.9 mg nicotine. 10 mg snuff vs. Postum (nicotine-free) control.	Results suggest that nicotine can result in effects relevant to reinforcement that are independent of the state of nicotine withdrawal. That is, nicotine resulted in longer endurance in cold water. However, this effect may be due to an elevated perceptual threshold, rather than to reduced anxiety.
Fleming & Lombardo (1987): In a counterbalanced order, smokers and nonsmokers smoked and were smoking deprived while they approached a large, unrestrained rat. All were rat phobic.	17 female smokers & 17 female nonsmokers; no information	1. 8 hr 2. Within & between 3. Active	No-smoking vs. smoking No information on nicotine content.	Smoking had no effect on fear or anxiety as assessed by approach e or self-report. The study was probal more stressful than previous stuc ts assessing nicotine's effects. Many were visibly trembling as they approached the rat.
D. G. Gilbert & Hagen (1980): Just before, 10 min into, and 20 min into a series of 9 stressful movie scenes habitual smokers smoked high- or low-nicotine cigarettes. Only responses to the 3 most stressful scenes were assessed.	24 men, 24 women; 6–28	1. 60 min 2. Within 3. Pasive	3 cigarettes at 15-min intervals	No effect of nicotine content of cigarette on self-reported emotional responses. However, the rapid smoking of high-nicotine cigarettes may have cause stressful nicotine-overdose toxicosis in some smokers and counteracted any tranquilizing effects. The 30-s duration scenes included minimal anticipation (3–10 s) before stressor.

Study	Subjects	Design	Treatment	Results
Same as D. G. Gilbert and Hagen (1980) except only responses to the 3 moderately stressful scenes were assessed.	24 men, 24 women; 6–28	1. 60 min 2. Within 3. Passive	3 cigs. at 15-min intervals	No effect of nicotine content of cigarette on D. G. Gilbert & Hagen (1980) emotional responses. However, the rapid smoking of high-nicotine cigarettes may have caused stressful nicotine-overdose toxicosis in some smokers and counteracted any tranquilizing effects. The 30-s duration scenes included minimal anticipation (3–10 s) before stressor.
Hatch et al. (1983): Ss smoked either high-or low-nicotine cigarettes or did not smoke before giving an extemporaneous speech.	9 men, 21 women; 26.1	1. 4 hr 2. Between 3. Active	No smoking vs. 1.25-mg vs. 0.09-mg nicotine cigarette	Neither smoking ritual or nicotine content had a significant effect on emotional behavior measured by self-report, physiological, or observation methods.
Myrsten et al. (1972): Each S was tested under 4 experimental conditions: low arousal–no smoking, low arousal–smoking, high arousal–no smoking, & high arousal–smoking. Low and complex vigilance tasks were used.	Of 90 smokers, 8 low arousal and 8 high arousal smokers; 5–15	1. 15 hr 2. Within & between 3. Active	2 cigarettes of 1.8 mg nicotine smoked at 30 and 60 min, respectively, after session began.	In low arousal, smokers' general well-being was favorably affected by smoking in the low-arousal situation only. Conversely, well-being of high-arousal smokers was enhanced by smoking in the high-arousal situation only.
Nesbitt (1973): Electrical shock endurance threshold was used as an index of anxiety. An ascending series of shock intensities with puffs before every other shock was used.	60 men, (30 smokers and 30 nonsmokers); 20+	1. No information 2. Within 3. Coping	1.6 mg nicotine, 0.3 mg nicotine, sham smoke 1 + each	Shock endurance threshold increased in habitual smokers (but not in nonsmokers) as a function of nicotine intake. Nesbitt interpreted findings as indicating that nicotine reduced anxiety; however, self-reported anxiety was apparently not reduced as, although it was assessed, nicotine's-effects on it were not reported.

Table 5.2 Experimental Stress Paradigms Using Proximal Stressors

Study and description	N and cigarettes per day	Deprivation (1), design (2), and coping (3)	Smoking and nicotine treatment	Conclusions
Perlick (1977): Study assessed the effect of smoking high- and low-nicotine cigarettes in heavy and light (11.5 cigarettes/day) smokers.	Restrained & nonrestrained smokers; no information	1. No information 2. Between 3. No task	No vs. 0.3 vs. 1.3 mg nicotine cigarettes	1.3-mg nicotine cigs reduced annoyance to noise stimuli in heavy, but not light, smokers.
O. F. Pomerleau, Turk, & Fertig (1984; Study 1): 5 min before immersing hand and arm in cold water, smokers smoked either usual or nicotine-free cigarette	5 men; M = 25.8, SD = 5.7	1. 30 min 2. Within 3. Active	One of own brand (M = 1.4 mg nicotine)	Smoking usual cigarette increased pain threshold in all Ss and pain tolerance in 4 of 5.
Schori & Jones (1974): Ss were assigned to 1 of 3 smoking conditions: smoker, smoker-deprived, or nonsmoker. Half of each condition did the low-level-of-complexity task and the other half the high-level-of-complexity task.	76 men, 44 women; 10+	1. No information 2. Between 3. Active	Ss in the smoker condition smoked at least 1 cigarette at 3 specified times while completing the task.	For all practical purposes, smoking had no effect on performance. Smokers experienced fewer significant mood changes compared with deprived smokers or nonsmokers at the low level of task complexity. At high-complexity-task level, smokers experienced more mood changes.
Silverstein (1982): Ss were exposed to a series of escalating shocks while smoking either high- or low-nicotine cigarettes or not smoking.	38 male smokers, 13 male nonsmokers; 15+	1. None 2. Between 3. Coping	0.29- or 0.50- vs 1.09- or 1.2-mg nicotine cigarettes or not smoke.	Smokers who smoked high nicotine cigarettes experienced lower levels of anxiety compared with low-nicotine and nonsmokers. Non-smokers were calmer than deprived and low-nicotine smokers.

nicotine cigarette condition relative to the low-nicotine cigarette condition (Nesbitt, 1969; Silverstein, 1982). Other studies used the length of time that individuals are willing to endure pain associated with immersion of a hand or foot in ice water (the cold-pressor test) as an indicator of anxiety. These studies also showed that smoking and another means of nicotine administration (snuff) increase endurance in this test in smokers, as well as in exsmokers (Fertig, Pomerleau, & Sanders, 1986; O. F. Pomerleau et al., 1984). Similarly, pain detection threshold has been found to be elevated by nicotine (nasal spray) in nonsmokers, as well as in smokers (Perkins, Grobe, et al., 1994). The fact that nicotine increased pain detection threshold more in nonsmokers than in smokers (Perkins, Grobe, et al., 1994) suggests that this effect is not due to nicotine withdrawal.

However, many studies have failed to find increased shock endurance thresholds associated with smoking (Knott, 1990; Knott & De Lugt, 1991; Milgrom-Friedman, Penman, & Meares, 1983; Mueser, Waller, Levander, & Schalling, 1984; Shiffman & Jarvik, 1984; Sult & Moss, 1986; Waller, Schalling, Levander, & Erdman, 1983). It is possible that smoking and nicotine only increase pain thresholds when the doses of nicotine are sufficiently high to cause the release of beta-endorphin, a substance known to attenuate pain. Such a possibility might explain why nicotine produced larger increases in threshold in nonsmokers than in smokers in the Perkins, Grobe, et al. (1994) study. Studies finding that nicotine and smoking elevate pain thresholds may have used experimental procedures that were more stressful (nasal nicotine administration) or higher doses of nicotine than those failing to observe such effects. Finally, it may be that in pain threshold studies nicotine simply reduces sensitivity to pain directly, but Hazenfratz and Bättig (1993) found smoking to decrease anxiety associated with repeated electrical shocks but to have no effect on shock-induced pain.

Balfour (1991a) and Gray (1990) have concluded that nicotine does not exhibit the pharmacobehavioral profile of classical anxiolytic compounds such as benzodiazepine-related compounds. However, Stolerman (1990) has noted that the traditional animal models of anxiety are very selective for benzodiazepine-like effects, but are also insensitive to the newer nonbenzodiazepine anxiolytic drugs.

Recent work has supported the view that the sensory impact of cigarettes also contributes to reductions of anxiety and other forms of negative affect (Behm et al., 1993; Levin, Rose, Behm, & Caskey, 1991). The possible influence of sensory impact on affect modulation emphasizes the importance of controlling for these factors when designing controls in experimental investigations.

In conclusion, careful evaluation of studies of the effects of nicotine on anxiety supports the view that nicotine can contribute to the reduction of anticipatory anxiety in situations characterized by ambiguous, distal psychological stressors, especially in situations in which threat is not great and a distracting stimulus or activity can compete with anxiogenic cues.

Aggression and Irritability   Smoking-delivered nicotine lessens reported anger and irritation (Cetta, 1977; Heimstra, 1973; Neetz, 1979; Perkins, Grobe,

Table 5.3 Effects of Nicotine on Positive Affect and Subjective State During Relaxing or Minimally Stressful Conditions

Study and description	N and cigarettes per day	Deprivation (1), design (2), and coping (3)	Smoking and nicotine treatment	Conclusions
Ague (1973): Ss smoked 4 experimental cigarettes (lettuce leaf, low nicotine, medium nicotine, or high nicotine) in either the morning or the afternoon while physiological recordings were made.	24 men; 5+	1. 8 hr 2. Within & between 3. Relaxing	Each S smoked 4 cigarettes (lettuce leaf, 0.75-mg nicotine, 1.02-mg nicotine, & 2.11-mg nicotine cigarettes) in controlled manner.	Nicotine intake was closely related to puff length and rate but only when smoking in the afternoon. Greater mood lability was present in the afternoon.
Chait & Griffiths (1984): Effects of methadone and dextromethorphan on smoking and subjective state were assessed.	5 male methadone patients, 20–40/day	1. 30 min 2. Within 3. Relax	Ad lib. smoking of as many of own cigarettes as desired over 2 hr.	Methadone increased smoking and smoking satisfaction in a dose-dependent manner.
Cinciripini, Benedict, Van Vunakis, Macen & Nezami (1989): Mood was assessed before and after smoking each of 2 cigarettes, during relaxing conditions.	58 male smokers, 30 heavy (M = 30) 28 light (M = 23.5)	1. Overnight 2. Between 3. Relax	1 0.5-mg nicotine cigarette after overnight deprivation, a 2nd one when desired. No smoking control.	Smoking was associated with reductions of anger and tension and with increases in vigor. However, there were no sham-smoking or nicotine-free controls.

Study	Subjects	Conditions	Procedure	Results
Meliska & Gilbert (1991): The effect of smoking the first 5 normal nicotine cigarettes of the day on serum cortisol, plasma beta-endorphin, and mood.	8 male & female smokers, 8 male & female nonsmokers; 15+	1. Overnight 2. Between & within 3. Relaxed	On day 1 Ss smoked ad lib 5 cigarettes at 30-min intervals. On 3 subsequent sessions, Ss smoked via Quantified Smoke Delivery System a 1.0-mg (men) or 0.7-mg (women) nicotine cigarette or placebo.	Smoking 5 of smokers' usual cigarettes produced small but reliable increases in serum cortisol; beta-endorphin was elevated after 2 but not after 4 or 5 cigarettes. The increases in serum cortisol were associated with decreases in drowsiness. Nicotine deprived women were more drowsy at baseline compared with men and female nonsmokers.
Henningfield & Goldberg (1983): Smokers were given the opportunity to press a lever that resulted in intravenous injection of nicotine or saline over several occasions.	6 men (4 with drug abuse history); no information	1. 1 hr 2. Within & between 3. Relaxing	1.0 ml of nicotine or saline injection	Nicotine injections were taken in orderly patterns that were dose related. Nicotine produced subjective effects similar to those produced by abused drugs like morphine or cocaine.

& Fonte, 1992) in provoking situations. Movie-induced aggressive feelings were attenuated in smokers allowed to smoke relative to those not allowed to smoke during a negative-affect-inducing film (Heimstra, 1973). The movie was abstract, open to interpretation, and provided anticipatory anxiety cues, combined with intermittant potent proximal distressing scenes; thus, combining the distal, ambiguous, and distractor stimulus components hypothesized required for at least some forms of negative affect attenuation by nicotine.

Overt aggression and irritability have also been reduced by smoking normal nicotine-delivery relative to low nicotine-delivery cigarettes. For example, reduced aggressive responding has been observed subsequent to smoking and to nicotine gum use (Cherek, 1981; Cherek, Bennett, & Grabowski, 1991). In one of the best designed studies, Hughes, Hatsukami, Pickens, & Krahn, et al. (1984) randomly assigned abstainers to chew placebo or nicotine gum. Individuals who chewed the placebo gum were rated by their spouses as exhibiting significantly more anger and tension after quitting, whereas those who chewed nicotine gum showed little change in these emotional states.

Although Bell, Warburton, and Brown (1985) concluded that nicotine inhibits a variety of different forms of aggression in several rat species, they failed to note that all but one of their reviewed studies used doses of nicotine exceeding the threshold that produces conditioned taste aversion (Jensen et al., 1990; Kumar et al., 1983). High acute doses of nicotine frequently decrease all motor behavior, something that has been referred to as the rat equivalent of a vomit response (A. P. Silverman, 1971). Nonetheless, A. P. Silverman (1971) found that a "smoking-sized" dose reduced aggression in albino and hooded rats. In a similar vein, Hutchinson and Emley (1973) reviewed a number of studies in their laboratory that assessed effects of nicotine on biting responses subsequent to tail shock in squirrel monkeys. Acute oral administration of small doses of nicotine (0.04–0.80 mg/kg) and the chronic oral administration of even smaller doses (as small as 0.002 mg/kg) reduced postshock biting in monkeys while simultaneously increasing preshock anticipatory motor behaviors. These two simultaneous effects were also produced by major and minor tranquilizers (chlorpromazine and chlordiazepoxide) and may be characteristic of tranquilizing compounds (Emley & Hutchinson, 1972).

Sadness and Dysphoria   Little is known about the effects of smoking or nicotine on experimentally induced sadness and dysphoria. Unpleasantness and sadness are not changed by smoking nicotine, relative to control cigarettes, in nonstressful, no-demand laboratory settings (D. G. Gilbert, Meliska, Williams, & Jensen, 1992; Meliska & Gilbert, 1991). This failure of nicotine to attenuate sadness and dysphoria may have resulted from a floor effect, given the extremely low levels of sadness exhibited in these relatively sad-stimulus-free settings.

Drowsiness, Alertness, and Arousal   During low-arousal conditions, nicotine clearly has a stimulating effect on subjective and vigilance performance measures. Subjective alertness is enhanced and drowsiness is decreased by smoking in smoking-deprived smokers (D. G. Gilbert, Meliska, Williams, & Jensen, 1992; Meliska & Gilbert, 1991; Parrott & Craig, 1992; Perkins, Grobe, Epstein, Caggiula, & Stiller, 1992). Nicotine administered by gum or intravenously also has stimulant effects on subjective and vigilance measures in habitual tobacco users (Parrott & Winder, 1989; Warburton, 1992) and in some cases in nonusers (Kerr, Sherwood, & Hindmarch, 1991; Sahakian, Jones, Levy, Gray, & Warburton, 1989; Wesnes & Warburton, 1978). However, several studies that used larger nicotine doses (Perkins et al., 1993, in press; Newhouse et al., 1990) found decreases in arousal, vigor, and relaxation or increased confusion in nonsmokers. These effects likely resulted from the overdose-response syndrome. More generally, nicotine may decrease arousal either in conditions of high dose or when the individual is in a state of heightened arousal (H. J. Eysenck, 1973).

Consistent with this pre-nicotine-arousal state-dependency hypothesis, Rose (1986; Rose & Behm, 1991) observed smoking-produced reductions in arousal in habitual smokers who had previously been administered caffeinated coffee, but not in those given decaffeinated coffee. However, recent studies have found additive effects of caffeine and nicotine on arousal (Lane & Rose, 1994; Perkins, Sexton, et al., 1994), but Perkins, Sexton, et al. (1994) did find that nicotine increased arousal during rest but not during activity. Perkins et al. (in press) also found an inverted-U relationship between subjective arousal and nicotine dose in tobacco users and nonusers.

The convergence of findings show smoking and nicotine to have state-dependent effects on arousal. During low-arousal conditions, smoking and nicotine stimulate. During some conditions of intermediate arousal, little or no effects on arousal occur. During certain high-arousal situations, certain dimensions of arousal may be decreased by smoking. However, the effects of nicotine under high-arousal conditions have not been adequately characterized.

Fatigue The small number of experimental studies assessing fatigue have found that nicotine has small antifatigue effects (Perkins et al., 1993) except when doses significantly exceed individual tolerance levels (Newhouse et al., 1990) and result in a generalized distress syndrome (D. G. Gilbert, Meliska, Williams, & Jensen, 1992).

Vigor and Activity Nicotine has stimulant effects in rodents with doses at or slightly above those relevant to smoking (Stolerman, 1990). Although the effects of acute smoking on motor activity in humans have not been assessed, smoking abstinence over several days or more appears to have little or no effect on motor activity (Leischow & Stitzer, 1991; Oliveto et al., 1992). In contrast with normal smoking-sized doses, high doses of nicotine reduce locomotor activity in animals (A. P. Silverman, 1971; Stolerman, 1990) and reduce subjective vigor in humans (Newhouse et al., 1990; Perkins et al., 1993), likely due to the toxically high doses of nicotine. However, it is not clear why humans do not exhibit the motor stimulant effects observed in subhuman species. Possibly the vigilance enhancement observed in humans is a behavioral analog to the increased motor behavior observed in rodents. During rest but not activity, subjective vigor has been increased by nicotine (Perkins, Sexton, et al., 1994).

Pleasure, Pleasantness, and Euphoria With few exceptions, nicotine has consistently failed to increase pleasantness and euphoria in experimental studies. For example, smoking in a quasi-ad-libitum manner as many as five normal nicotine-delivery cigarettes throughout the morning failed to alter Likert-type scale pleasantness ratings in any of three studies (D. G. Gilbert, Meliska, Williams, & Jensen, et al., 1992; D. G. Gilbert, Meliska, Welser, et al. 1994; Meliska & Gilbert, 1991). In tobacco nonusers, intravenous nicotine can decrease happiness and increases displeasure, anxiety, tension, discomfort, fatigue, depression, and confusion (Newhouse et al., 1990; Perkins et al., 1993) in a manner similar to excessively rapid smoking in habitual smokers (D. G. Gilbert, Meliska, Welser, et al. 1992).

The possible exceptions to this general rule include investigations by Henningfield and associates (Henningfield et al., 1985; Henningfield & Keenan, 1993), using iv nicotine administered to heavy drug users. These studies found higher levels of drug "liking" for nicotine than for saline placebo iv. Henningfield's findings contrast with the increased poor mood and negative affect noted in the larger study by Newhouse et al. (1990), using tobacco or drug nonusers. Finally, C. S. Pomerleau and Pomerleau (1992) asked smokers to indicate while smoking when they felt a rush, a buzz, or a high, but they did not differentiate simple sensations from pleasure and euphoria.

There is a clear need for studies assessing the likable, pleasurable, and related hedonic effects of smoking and nicotine with that for other substances (food, coffee, drugs, etc.). Experimental studies have not adequately characterized times of special enjoyment (e.g., postprandial, postsex, and postdeprivation; with alcohol; and morning vs. afternoon). Smoking may enhance the satisfaction and pleasure associated with having consumed a good meal or may facilitate pleasure indirectly, such as by enhancing concentration on the reading of an enjoyable book.

Duration of Affect-Modulating Effects

The duration of nicotine's affect-modulating effects has been given little attention. In one of the few studies assessing the duration of effects resulting from the smoking of a single cigarette, Perkins, Grobe, Fonte, and Breus (1992) found subjective stress and annoyance to be attenuated immediately subsequent to smoking but observed minimal effects 10 minutes later. The transient nature of these "distressolytic" effects may reflect the fact that subjects were only deprived for 1.5 hours. However, during natural conditions smokers are rarely deprived for periods longer than this. The anxiolytic effects observed by D. G.

Gilbert, Robinson, et al. (1989) 13 to 23 minutes subsequent to smoking may have been a function of their overnight smoking deprivation. The effects of a single cigarette on plasma nicotine concentration and physiological processes after overnight deprivation are percentagewise much greater than after briefer deprivation. Furthermore, C. S. Pomerleau and Pomerleau (1992) found the duration of smoking-associated sensations to constitute only 10% of the time during which the cigarette was being smoked.

Individual Differences in Affect-Modulating Effects of Nicotine

Nicotine Tolerance and Physical Dependence and Nonsmokers   Very little is known about the effects of smoking and nicotine on affect as a function of nicotine exposure history and nicotine tolerance and dependence. Although occasional smokers (chippers) report experiencing calming effects from smoking (McNeill et al., 1987; Shiffman, Paty, Kassel, & Gnys, 1993; Spielberger, 1986), experimental studies have not assessed these claims. To the degree that nicotine reduction of negative affect is a result of nicotine dependence, measures of habitual nicotine intake should correlate with degree of negative affect modulation. In an early study, very heavy smokers responded to smoking a regular cigarette with reductions in experimentally induced irritability, whereas more moderate smokers did not exhibit such effects (Perlick, 1977). More recent studies have generally assessed smokers in the 10–20 cigarette per day range in which Perlick found no effects. Nonetheless, many studies using lighter smokers have found that smoking attenuates negative affect when the experimental situation includes distal, ambiguous, and nonextreme stressors.

As noted earlier, preabstinence nicotine intake correlates only slightly with abstinence discomfort. This small correlation may be mediated by the association between nicotine intake and neuroticism (D. G. Gilbert, Meliska, et al., 1994) rather than by nicotine dependence. The finding that nicotine reduced anxiety in exsmokers (Fertig et al., 1986) is consistent with the view that nicotine can produce withdrawal-independent negative affect reduction. In addition, recent findings by E. D. Levin and associates (personal communication, September 25, 1994) indicate that patch-delivered nicotine can increase relaxation and improve concentration in youth with attention deficit disorder who do not use tobacco. Reports that nicotine increased or had no effects on negative affect in tobacco nonusers (Newhouse et al., 1990) should not be taken as evidence against potential negative-affect-reducing effects as these studies used excessively high doses that produced toxic effects and did not elevate prenicotine levels of negative affect. Nonetheless, the possibility exists that exsmokers and smokers may experience negative-affect-attenuating effects from nicotine that most nonsmokers do not, because of either a sensitivity to nicotine's aversive effects or an insensitivity to its affect-modulating effects.

Personality, psychopathology, and other genetically mediated traits appear to influence the degree and nature of any affect-modulating effects of nicotine. Evidence has suggested that depression-prone individuals obtain antidepressant effects from nicotine, whereas anxiety-prone individuals may experience relatively stronger anxiolytic effects (see Chapter 7). Such trait-dependent affect responses to nicotine and nicotine deprivation may be limited to individuals sensitive to nicotine's rewarding or affect-modulating properties. Individuals who are insensitive to these effects would be expected to find smoking unrewarding and, in the present antismoking social context in the United States, would be unlikely to become smokers. Chippers may be motivated to a lesser degree or by a relatively different balance of smoking motivations than are heavier smokers (Shiffman et al., 1993).

Gender differences in affective responses to smoking have not been adequately characterized. Nonexperimental designs have found women to report smoking more for negative affect reduction, whereas men smoke for stimulation (see Chapter 8). Also, processes associated with aging may mediate affect modulation and the motives for smoking. Tentative evidence has suggested that nicotine may enhance cognitive processes in individuals with Alzheimer's disease (R. W. Parks et al., 1994). The general alertness and concentration-enhancing effects observed in younger populations may be especially rewarding to elderly individuals with attentional deficits, as well as to others with attention disorders. Similarly, elderly individuals suffering from relationship loss or depression may find that smoking reduces their depression (see Chapters 7 and 9).

Summary of Affect-Modulating Effects of Smoking and Nicotine

Evidence from experimental studies has suggested that tobacco use decreases negative affect in habitual tobacco users in certain situations. Nicotine appears to produce some of these effects by mechanism(s) independent of withdrawal symptom alleviation. Although the precise conditions requisite for nicotine to attenuate negative affect have yet to be clearly established, the experimental literature suggests that nicotine reduces negative affect most effectively in situations involving mild or moderate distal (anticipatory) anxiety, or ambiguous stressors, or both. The roles that individual differences in personality, temperament, and psychopathology appear to play in determining the nature and degree of the stress-reducing effects of nicotine have yet, however, to be adequately characterized.

Taken as a whole, evidence supports a Situation × Trait formulation of nicotine's affect-modulating effects. That is, withdrawal effects and nicotine's effects on affective and other information-processing states are a function of situational and trait factors. Animal studies have suggested that nicotine's effects are not parallel to those of classical anxiolytics but may be more akin to antidepressants or new-generation anxiolytics. The possibility that nicotine's affect-modulating effects parallel those of low-dose stimulants also needs further evaluation.

COGNITION AND PERFORMANCE MODULATION AND ENHANCEMENT

Visual Thresholds

Smoking and nicotine have increased perceptual sensitivity of abstinent smokers as assessed in some critical-flicker-fusion-threshold and two-flash-fusion studies (Larson, Finnegan, & Hoag, 1950; Sherwood, Kerr, & Hindmarch, 1992; Tong, Knott, McGraw, & Leigh, 1974; Waller & Levander, 1980; Warwick & Eysenck, 1963; Wesnes & Warburton, 1983). Some investigators have also found increases in critical-flicker-fusion thresholds in nonabstinent smokers (Fabricant & Rose, 1951). Although a study of subcutaneous nicotine resulted in increased critical-flicker-fusion-threshold frequency in patients with Alzheimer's disease (Sahakian et al., 1989), most studies administering nicotine by gum to nonsmokers have not found elevated critical-flicker-fusion thresholds (Hindmarch, Kerr, & Sherwood, 1990; Kerr et al., 1991; Sherwood, Kerr, & Hindmarch, 1990). However, nicotine gum generally results in nausea and other forms of malaise in nonsmokers, and these effects may have overshadowed any enhancing effects of nicotine.

Reaction Time and Performance Speed and Accuracy

Reaction times were decreased by smoking relative to abstinence in vigilance tasks (Heimstra, Bancroft, & DeKock, 1967 [smoking]; Wesnes & Warburton, 1983, 1984); visual choice reaction times (Frankenhaeuser, Myrsten, Post, & Johansson, 1971 [smoking]); auditory choice reaction times (Myrsten, Andersson, Frankenhaeuser, & Elgerot, 1975 [smoking]); decision reaction time (Lyon, Tong, Leigh, & Clare, 1975 [smoking]; Smith, Tong, & Leigh, 1977 [smoking]; Parrott & Winder, 1989 [gum]); and logical-reasoning, letter-search, and mental arithmetic reaction times (F. R. Snyder & Henningfield, 1989 [gum]). Timed letter-cancellation task performance is generally speeded by smoking in abstinent smokers (Parrott & Craig, 1992 [smoking]; D. G. Williams, Tata, & Miskella, 1984 [smoking]), as are short-term memory-scan reaction times (West & Hack, 1991 [smoking]). Hatsukami, Skoog, Huber, and Hughes (1991) found increased errors of commission in association with cessation from 4-mg nicotine gum, relative to placebo gum. However, they failed to find nicotine gum cessation effects for errors of omission or reaction time.

Reaction times and performance have been improved by smoking or nicotine gum in nonabstaining smokers on a number of tasks: simple and visual choice reaction time tasks (Myrsten, Post, Frankenhausa, & Johansson, 1972 [smoking]; Pritchard, Robinson, & Guy, 1992 [smoking]), odd-man-out reaction time (Frearson, Barrett, & Eysenck, 1988 [smoking]), and movement reaction time (Hindmarch et al., 1990 [gum]; Sherwood et al., 1992 [gum]). The number of studies failing to find significant effects of nicotine on reaction times in nonabstinent smokers roughly equals the number finding such effects (for a review, see Sherwood et al., 1992).

Finger-tapping rate was boosted by nasally administered nicotine in nonsmokers in a study by West and Jarvis (1986). Frith (1967) observed similar effects of nicotine tablets. Perkins et al. (1990), however, failed to observe any effects of nicotine spray in finger-tapping rate. Visual four-choice reaction time in tobacco nonusers was speeded by 0.8-mg subcutaneous nicotine, but not by placebo (Le Houezec et al., 1994). Nicotine gum speeded movement reaction time and enhanced tracking accuracy in nonsmokers in a study by Sherwood et al. (1990) and short-term memory-scanning speed in reports by Kerr et al. (1991) and Sherwood, Kerr, and Hindmarch (1991). Short-term memory-scanning speed was also increased in occasional smokers by smoking a nicotine cigarette, regardless of degree of abstinence (West & Hack, 1991).

Vigilance and Selective Attention

Various forms of nicotine administration have relatively consistently been found to increase vigilance performance in abstaining smokers (J. A. Edwards, Wesnes, Warburton, & Gale, 1985; Hasenfratz, Michel, Nil, & Bättig, et al., 1989; Parrott & Winder, 1989; Petrie & Dreary, 1989; Revell, 1988; Wesnes & Warburton, 1983, 1984b). Nicotine gum and tablets also appear to facilitate vigilance performance in nonsmokers (Provost & Woodward, 1991; Wesnes & Warburton, 1978; Wesnes et al., 1983). The effect of nicotine on these tasks is to help sustain vigilance and to prevent the normal vigilance decrement over time. Errors of commission have generally not been influenced by nicotine.

Attentional Allocation

Andersson and Hockey (1977) observed that task-irrelevant spatial location memory was poorer in smokers in smoking sessions than in nonsmoking sessions after overnight deprivation. These findings could be interpreted as indicating that smoking acts as a chemical filter to screen irrelevant information. They are also consistent with the view that in these conditions the right, visio-spatial-dominant hemisphere was inhibited by nicotine during the primary, left-dominant serial recall task. However, in a different condition, Andersson and Hockey (1977) found that smoking tended to facilitate recall of relevant spatial location (location of words on monitor screen). Task-irrelevant (incidental) memory was not influenced by smoking in studies in which the incidental memory was of word color (Jubis, 1986) or word recall and recognition (Peeke & Peeke, 1984). Thus, the

Andersson and Hockey findings of a decrement in incidental memory may have resulted from the use of a spatial-location task where decreased right-hemisphere spatial processing was inhibited by smoking combined with focusing on the primary task.

Short-Term Memory

Although nicotine appears to generally speed short-term memory scanning in smokers, it has inconsistent effects on short-term memory capacity. D. G. Williams (1980) found that after overnight abstinence, smoking increased errors during an auditory digit-span task assessing short-term memory capacity. In a digit-recall short-term memory task, F. R. Snyder and Henningfield (1989) found no effects of smoking deprivation or nicotine gum on response accuracy, but observed slowing of reaction time in the placebo condition relative to the pre-smoking abstinence baseline. Nicotine gum returned reaction time to baseline levels. Mangan and Golding (1978) also reported no short-term-memory-mediated recency effect in their serial learning study. In contrast, nicotine-mediated increases in recency recall have been observed by others (Warburton, Rusted, & Fowler, 1992; Warburton, Rusted, & Muller, 1992). Warburton, Rusted, and Muller (1992) interpreted their findings and the literature as suggesting that nicotine enhances storage of information, but only information on which the individual intentionally focuses.

Nicotine gum administered to nontobacco users resulted in more rapid responding, but decreased accuracy in a digit-recall task (Heishman et al., 1990). However, the nicotine gum increased Profile of Mood States total mood disturbance that may have interfered with their ability to concentrate and recall effectively.

Long-Term Memory

Effects of smoking on immediate recall from long-term memory in overnight-abstinent smokers have been variable. Smoking, relative to abstaining, impaired rote learning but improved recall of nonsense syllables previously learned and presented in a fixed order (Andersson, 1975). Mangan and Golding (1978) observed similar tendencies for smoking-impaired learning but facilitated recall. In a paired-associate task, trials-to-criterion were nonsignificantly increased by smoking in 1-hour abstinent smokers. However, 30 minutes subsequent to smoking recall was better in the smoking than in the abstaining condition. In a different experiment, Mangan and Golding found that smoking improved recall of words from the beginning portions of the word list but not from the later portions. Improved memory has also been observed in a number of other delayed-recall tests (Colrain, Mangan, Pellett, & Bates, 1992; Mangan, 1983; Peeke & Peeke, 1984; Warburton, Wesnes, Shergold, & James, 1986; Warburton, Rusted, & Fowler, 1992; Warburton, Rusted, & Miller, 1992).

Effects of smoking and nicotine on immediate recall have varied across studies. Positive effects on recall were reported by Peeke and Peeke (1984), Jubis (1986), Warburton et al. (1986), and Rusted and Eaton-Williams (1991). No effects of nicotine or smoking on immediate recall have been found by Andersson and Hockey (1977), Peters and McGee (1982), Kunzendorf and Wigner (1985), or Williams (1980). Impaired immediate free recall resulted from smoking in studies by Dunne et al. (1986) and Houston et al. (1978). While immediate recall was not improved by nicotine in patients with Alzheimer' disease (Sahakian et al., 1989; Jones et al., 1992), semantic memory was increased in this group, but not in controls (Parks et al., 1994). Perkins et al. (in press) observed enhanced memory performance due to nicotine in nonsmokers.

State-Dependent Memory, Incidental Learning, Free-Recall Organization, and Levels of Information Processing

Nicotine appears to have state dependent effects (Kunzendorf & Wigner, 1985; Peters & McGee, 1982; Warburton et al., 1986) but no effects on incidental learning (Jubis, 1986; Peeke & Peeke, 1984), free-recall memory organization (Houston et al., 1978; Warburton, Wesnes, Shergold, & James, 1986), or levels of information processing (Peeke & Peeke, 1984).

Lateralized and Arousal-Dependent Effects of Nicotine on Information Processing and Performance

I previously concluded that evidence suggests that the effects of nicotine on cognition and performance may be a function of the relative lateralization of the cognitive processing systems involved in the task and upon the stressfulness of the task (D. G. Gilbert, Robinson, et al. 1989; D. G. Gilbert & Welser, 1989). This conclusion is consistent with the observation that cognitive and affective subprocessing systems to some extent rely on differentially localized and lateralized neurotransmitter systems and neurocircuitry (Tucker & Williamson, 1984) and on evidence indicating that nicotine and smoking have resulted in localized and lateralized effects on electrocortical activity (D. G. Gilbert et al., 1989; D. G. Gilbert, Gehlbach, Estes, Rabinovich, & Detwiler, 1994; D. G. Gilbert, Meliska, et al., 1994; Pritchard, 1991a). During mildly or moderately stressful tasks, predominantly left-hemisphere-based performances appear to be enhanced by nicotine, whereas right-hemisphere-based processes, including those hypothesized to be associated with negative affect, are relatively impaired.

Schultze (1982) found that smoking improved anagram performance, a left-hemisphere verbal task, but decreased performance on digit symbol substitution and recall of Bender-gestalt form (both primarily right hemisphere based). Similarly, Stroop task performance enhancements subsequent to nicotine (Wesnes

& Warburton, 1978) can be seen as mediated by the left hemisphere (Tucker & Williamson, 1984). Decrements in right-hemisphere processing efficiency subsequent to smoking is also suggested by the finding that smoking decreased performance on jigsaw puzzles (Schneider, 1978), accuracy in identifying facial emotional cues (Hertz, 1978), and recall of incidental spatial location cues (Andersson & Hockey, 1977),

Evidence concerning nicotine's effects on right-hemisphere-based performance during minimally stressful conditions is minimal. Nicotine's apparent ability to facilitate habituation to simple stimuli during relaxing conditions (Friedman, Horvath, & Meares, 1974; Golding & Mangan, 1982) may reflect enhanced right-hemisphere activation during such situations (Tucker & Williamson, 1984).

Summary of Smoking and Nicotine Effects on Cognition and Memory

The overall evidence has suggested that nicotine enhances voluntary, conscious, attention, vigilance-focusing processes. Effects of nicotine on memory have been interpreted as consistent with this conclusion (Peeke & Peeke, 1984; Warburton, Rusted, & Miller, 1992). These attention-enhancing effects result in enhanced performance on a number of tasks in abstaining tobacco users and frequently in nonabstainers and nontobacco users.

CONCLUSIONS AND RECOMMENDATIONS

1 Nicotine attenuates negative affect in certain situations, but not in others.
2 It appears that in certain conditions nicotine reduces negative affect by means independent of withdrawal symptom relief. In addition to directly reducing negative affect, nicotine may improve subjective well-being by enhancing concentration and task performance.
3 Nicotine's effects appear to be different from traditional anxiolytic and antidepressant medications, but may have some commonalities with newer anxiolytics and antidepressants. Nicotine also has a number of stimulantlike effects.
4 There is a need for more sophisticated and tightly controlled research that systematically manipulates and controls nicotine dose, personality, smoker type, and different types and intensities of stressors and emotions.
5 Abstinence-related increases in negative affect have not been adequately characterized. Individual differences in abstinence response patterns across time need to be determined. Furthermore, there is a need for characterization of the nature of the specific stimuli that elicit various moods and emotions in abstinent smokers. It is still not clear whether it is better to conceive of abstinence as leading to a disposition to certain moods or simply to enhanced emotionality or as leading more indirectly to cognitive and appetitive changes that interact with specified environmental factors that contribute to negative affect.

Mechanisms hypothesized to mediate the affect-modulating, performance-enhancing, and reinforcing effects of nicotine and smoking discussed in this chapter are explored in Chapter 6. Testing hypothesized mechanisms will generate new findings that will further articulate when and in whom various effects occur.

Chapter 6

Mechanisms Underlying Nicotine's Reinforcing and Affect-Modulating Effects

This chapter assesses mechanisms hypothesized to mediate nicotine's reinforcing and mood-modulating effects. Single-mechanism models of tobacco use and of nicotine's reinforcing and affect-modulating properties have been criticized (e.g., Ashton & Golding, 1989; O'Connor, 1989; O. F. Pomerleau & Pomerleau, 1984, 1989; J. H. Robinson & Pritchard, 1992; Warburton, 1990). Tomkins (1966) and H. J. Eysenck (1973, 1980) argued that individuals smoke for a number of reasons and that some smokers are more likely to smoke for some of these reasons than for others. In spite of their conceptual advancement over unifactorial models, most multireinforcer–multimechanism approaches to date have been limited by their failure to specify when nicotine results in what effects in what individuals and by failures to note interactions among multiple mechanisms. The questions of in whom, after what dose history, and in what circumstances does what dose of nicotine result in what type of affect-modulating and reinforcing effects is much more likely to produce useful answers than more simplistic questions as, "Why do people smoke?" and associated answers such as "They are addicted or dependent." Chapter 6 assesses support for many of the numerous psychological and biological mechanisms hypothesized to underlie nicotine's reinforcing and affect-modulating properties. However, discussion of a number of indirect mechanisms that may underlie these effects is deferred until Chapter 9, where an overall integrated biopsychosocial STAR model of the affect-modulating and reinforcing effects of smoking is presented.

The wide range of mechanisms hypothesized to mediate nicotine's affect-modulating and reinforcing effects reflects the large number of effects produced by the drug. Nicotinic cholinergic receptors, in addition to constituting a primary component of cholinergic neurons, are also located on a variety of noncholinergic neurons (Rosecrans & Karan, 1993). The pervasiveness of these cholinergic receptors allows nicotine to influence almost all of the body's biological systems and subsystems. Moreover, different systems have different sensitivities to nicotine's effects, and thus the effects of nicotine are dose dependent and biological and psychological state dependent.

CNS HEDONIC AND REINFORCEMENT SYSTEMS MODELS

It may seem circular logic to suggest that nicotine is reinforcing because it stimulates CNS reinforcement systems or that nicotine increases pleasure or decreases negative affect because it modulates brain pleasure and pain systems. However, understanding and theoretical utility are gained to the degree that reinforcement and punishment systems are defined in specific anatomical and biological terms that can be influenced independently of their operational definitions. Early investigators (e.g., H. J. Eysenck, 1973; Jarvik, 1973; Seevers, 1968) noted that nicotine-induced modulation of one or more systems in the brain putatively associated with pain, pleasure, and reinforcement may account for nicotine's capacity to reduce negative affect and increase feelings of well-being. On the basis of work on the brain's reward and pain systems (Olds & Milner, 1954; Olds & Olds, 1965), H. J. Eysenck (1973) suggested that feelings of well-being produced by nicotine and other means could be due to influences on three hedonic systems: the primary reward system, the primary aversion system, and the secondary reward system. These early models were based on evidence interpreted as suggesting that activating the primary reward system produces pleasure and reinforcement directly, whereas secondary reward system activation results from inhibition of the aversion system, which in turn releases the primary rewarding system from inhibition. Berlyne (1971) argued that reduction of uncomfortably high levels of physiological arousal results in reinforcement through activation of the secondary reward system. On the basis of Berlyne's proposals, H. J. Eysenck (1973) hypothesized that nicotine's apparent ability to reduce CNS arousal when prenicotine arousal is excessively high results in reinforcement of tobacco use by means of the secondary reward system, whereas nicotine results in activation of primary reward systems when CNS arousal is lower than optimal.

According to Eysenck's (H. J. Eysenck, 1967; H. J. Eysenck & Eysenck, 1985) model, extraverts have a temperamental disposition toward low cortical arousal that promotes a desire to seek sources of stimulation to achieve a hedonically ideal state of arousal. Thus, he hypothesized that extraverts smoke more often to achieve pleasurable stimulation of the primary reward centers. Introverts and neurotics (who are seen as genetically predisposed toward high arousal) were seen as smoking more often to achieve lower CNS arousal, that is, to obtain reinforcement through the negative reinforcement system. Supporting these hypotheses, smoking doses of nicotine induce cortical activation of the EEG in cats; bilateral lesions in the tegmental region of the midbrain prevent such effects even at high doses (Domino, 1967; Kawamura & Domino, 1969). Because the ventral tegmental region is associated with reinforcement and reward, one might ask whether nicotine's electrocortical activating properties are intimately related to its rewarding effects. Evidence related to Eysenck's hypotheses is assessed in the *Cortical Arousal Modulation Model* section and in Chapter 7.

H. J. Eysenck's (1973) CNS reward system model of smoking reinforcement was somewhat unique in that, until the 1980s, most models of drug use stressed only the roles of individual differences or physical dependence as predisposing factors. Unlike H. J. Eysenck's model, such models do not integrate personality traits or stress with biological mechanisms of reinforcement. Individual differences models range from addictive personality (Khantzian & Treece, 1977) and psychological stress (Shiffman & Wills, 1985) to genetically based biological disposition explanations (Tarter & Edwards, 1988). Some models focus exclusively on physical dependence on drugs such as heroin and the reinforcement of drug use by the relief of withdrawal symptoms (Himmelsback, 1943; Solomon & Corbit, 1974). Since the 1980s, a growing number of researchers have argued that the direct, positively reinforcing effects of drugs are the primary determinant of drug use.

Mesolimbic Dopaminergic Activation System: Influences on Reinforcement and Affect

Currently, many investigators have argued that nicotine and many other drugs are self-administered because they activate a dopaminergic mesolimbic positive reinforcement system (Bozarth, 1987, 1991; Wilner & Scheel-Kruger, 1991; Wise, 1989). A mesolimbic dopaminergic psychomotor activation-reinforcement system has been partially characterized. Under certain conditions this system (a) can contribute to the activation and reinforcement of behavior; (b) can promote conditioned place preference when stimulated by drugs of abuse; (c) is dopamine dependent; (d) anatomically includes ventral tegmental dopaminergic neurons that project to the nucleus accumbens, limbic structures, and the neocortex; (e) involves response activation; and (f) is activated by stimulant drugs, opiates, alcohol, nicotine, and electrical self-stimulation of various brain structures (Bozarth, 1987, 1991; Salamone, 1992; Wise, 1988).

Psychomotor Stimulant Theory of Drug Self-Administration   Wise and Bozarth (1987) initially promoted the hypothesis that the common denominator across a wide variety of addictions is their ability to produce psychomotor stimulation through mesolimbic system activation. This theory has been modified and now proposes that although all rewards are not mediated by the mesolimbic dopaminergic system or even dopaminergic activation, if the mesolimbic system is activated then reward occurs (Bozarth, 1991). Psychomotor stimulants, alcohol, opiates, nicotine, a variety of other abused substances, reinforcing brain electrical stimulation, and some naturally rewarding stimuli activate this system. Wise (1988) stated that activation of a common underlying mechanism should result in similar subjective euphoriant effects across different reinforcing drugs. Finally, the psychomotor stimulant model assumes that negative reinforcement and punishment are mediated by a different mechanism than is positive reinforcement. In addition, there are reasons to believe that a number of brain reward–reinforcement systems exist and that a given behavior may involve several reinforcement systems (Bozarth, 1987, 1991).

Mesolimbic Dopaminergic Systems: The New Synthesis   A number of recent reviews (Morgenson, 1987; Salamon, 1991; Scheel-Kruger & Williner, 1991) have concluded that evidence does not support the view that the mesolimbic dopaminergic system is uniquely associated with positive reinforcement or is the primary biological mediator of reward and euphoria. Aversive stimuli can increase dopamine activity in the accumbens and frontal cortex (Abercrombie, Keefe, DiFrischia, & Zigmond, 1989; Fada et al., 1978; Thierry, Tassin, Blanc, & Glowinski, 1976). Dopaminergic neurons are stimulated by the same stimuli that arouse the whole organism: stressors, cues associated with aversive states, incentive stimuli, and cues associated with positive affect (Salamone, 1991; Scheel-Kruger & Willner, 1991). In Salamone's new synthesis of the mesolimbic dopaminergic literature, he concluded that mesolimbic dopamine is involved in the coping and engagement processes common to both positive and negative emotional states. That is, the mesolimbic dopaminergic system is seen as a mechanism to "promote interaction with, and adaptation to, the environment" (Salamone, 1991, p. 609). Salamone, like Wilner (1985), noted that a slight increment in dopaminergic activity in the accumbens and striatum, such as that produced by low doses of stimulant drugs, would be expected to increase the ability of the organism to avoid aversive stimuli and to obtain positive ones. Reductions in mesolimbic dopamine would be expected to have the opposite effects. Thus, the mood-modulating effects promoted or precluded by alterations in dopamine in this system would be indirect, resulting from interactions with the environment (Salamone, 1991, pp. 607–609).

There are a number of important nicotine-related implications of this new intepretation of the function of the mesolimbic dopaminergic system. First, activation of this system should no longer be viewed as activation of a biological substrate unique to reward. Second, activation may be a function of its promoting successful avoidance of aversive (negative reinforcment) or gaining of desired stimuli (positive reinforcement). In situations in which nicotine does not allow the achievement of more successful active coping, the currently proposed extension of Salamone's (1991) model predicts that nicotine would have no affect-modulating effects. Although there has been no direct test of this hypothesis for nicotine and smoking, recent evidence has supported the situation-specific view of caffeine. Whether caffeine is reinforcing in humans is a function of the user's situation-related goals (K. Silverman, Mumford, & Griffiths, 1994).

Stressors and incentive stimuli organize behavior, as well as activate and amplify it. Although it has been suggested that the dopaminergic systems are primarily involved in the amplification or activation process (Salamone, 1991; Scheel-Kruger & Willner, 1991), they are also involved in affect-, cognition-, and motivation-related hierarchically organized loops throughout the brain. This pervasive influence modulates central motivational states that bias perceptual processing, response output classes, and autonomic and neuroendocrine activity (Scheel-Kruger & Willner, 1991).

The nucleus accumbens appears to promote adaptation to the external environment by influencing attention, response selection, and response activation. Toan and Schultz (1985) concluded that dopamine contributes to a focusing process in which "information from the strongest cortical and limbic inputs pass to the pallidum and less prominent activity is lost" (p. 683). Candor et al. (1991) interpreted the literature as indicating "that amygdala- and [dopamine]-dependent processes in the ventral striatum appear jointly to determine, respectively, response choice and the 'gain-amplifying' effect of enhanced activation on this choice" (p. 243). Finally, Pulvirenti, Swerdlow, Hubner, and Koob (1991) noted that sensory (amygdalar) and mnemonic (hippocampal) information may gain access to the motor effectors of the mesocorticolimbic system by means of a dopaminergic gating mechanism in the nucleus accumbens. Nicotine-induced alterations of the relative gating of hippocampal and amygdalar information may account for a number of nicotine's effects on attentional, cognitive, coping, motivational, and affective processes.

Efforts to integrate the mesolimbic dopaminergic system's involvement with negative, as well as positive, reinforcement and affective processes have led to models that view the nucleus accumbens as a center for limbic-motor integration. (See Morgenson, 1987; Salamone, 1991; and Scheel-Kruger & Willner, 1991, for excellent reviews of interactions of limbic-motor integration, including influences of the mesolimbic system on hormones and sensory process.) These models suggest that mesolimbic systems are involved in a range of adaptive processes, including selective attention, active coping, and behavioral activation. If these more general formulations are accurate, the search for specific mechanisms of reinforcment of smoking and tobacco use will require characterization of complex, environment-dependent, psychobiological mechanisms. Thus, the mesolimbic dopaminergic system may be an important system within a larger reinforcement system or set of systems that contribute to nicotine reinforcement.

Phillips, Pfaus, and Blaha (1991, pp. 218–219) have noted that although extracellular dopaminergic activity increases before feeding and sexual behavior in male rats, there may be a decrease in dopaminergic activity following consumption of a signaled meal and ejaculation. Thus, Phillips et al. tentatively suggested that rather than increased dopaminergic activity being a correlate of reward, "the opposite relationship may hold. Anticipation of reward may enhance dopaminergic activity, producing a concomitant increase in arousal, which is rapidly reduced" (p. 219) by the culmination of the rewarding event. Similarly, smoking-delivered pulses (boli) of nicotine may produce phasic changes in dopamine that result in rapid dopamine reduction produced reinforcement.

Nicotine-Induced Activation of Mesolimbic Dopaminergic Psychomotor Activation Systems

It has been suggested that some, if not all, of nicotine's positively reinforcing effects are related to its capacity to promote dopaminergic activity in the nucleus accumbens (Balfour, 1991b; Clarke, 1990; Corrigall, Franklin, Coen, & Clarke, 1992; Imperato, Mulas, & DiChiara, 1986). A number of lines of evidence have been interpreted as converging to support this view. First, physiological, subjective, and behavioral effects of nicotine are significantly reduced or blocked by CNS nicotinic blockers (e.g., mecamylamine), but not by the peripheral administration of nicotinic blockers that do not cross the blood–brain barrier (USDHHS, 1988). Thus, nicotine's primary behavioral effects appear to be directly centrally mediated. Second, among rats there is a relatively high density of nicotine binding sites in the tegmental area (for a review, see Corrigall et al., 1992). Third, smaller doses of nicotine are required to increase dopaminergic turnover and release in the mesolimbic system than in most other brain areas (Balfour, 1991b). Fourth, systemic as well as direct local administration of nicotine into the ventral tegmental area increases locomotor activity (Reavill & Stolerman, 1990). Fifth, lesions of the nucleus accumbens by injection of 6-hydroxydopamine block nicotine-induced increases in locomotor activity (Clarke, Fu, Jakubovic, & Fibiger, 1988; Corrigall et al., 1992) and nicotine self-administration (Corrigall et al., 1992). Sixth, nicotine excites dopaminergic cells in the ventral tegmental area (Calibresi, Lacey, & North, 1989) and increases extracellular dopamine in this region (Imperato et al., 1986) and in the nucleus accumbens (Benwell & Balfour, 1992). Seventh, positron emission tomography scans indicate that in rats nicotine significantly increases glucose metabolism in the ventral tegmental area (London, Connolly, Szikszay, & Wamsley, 1985; London et al., 1986). Finally, although significantly weaker in nature, a number of nicotine's effects are similar to those of cocaine and d-amphetamine, prototypic stimulants known to act primarily by activation of dopaminergic activity (Balfour, 1991b). (The first six of these points must be qualified by noting that these effects have been found almost exclusively in studies on rats and mice.)

Critique of the Dopaminergic Reward Model of Nicotine Reinforcement

Although the convergence of evidence suggests involvement of mesolimbic dopamine in nicotine self-administration and affect modulation, the evidence is weak and equivocal for a variety of reasons. It is not clear whether increases in mesolimbic dopamine reflect any or a combination of (a) stress resulting from overdose toxicosis, (b) generalized increase in affect-nonspecific arousal or activation and engagement with the environment, or (c) a rewarding state associated with activation of positive reinforcement or reward-specific mechanisms. As noted earlier, the role of dopamine in reinforcement and affect modulation is far from clear (Salamone, 1991; Scheel-Kruger & Willner, 1991).

It is yet to be reliably demonstrated that positive-reinforcement-related doses of nicotine increase mesolimbic dopaminergic activity. Although both acute and chronic in vivo administration of nicotine has frequently resulted in dopamine release in the nucleus accumbens (e.g., Balfour, Benwell, & Vale, 1991; Benwell & Balfour, 1992; Mitchell, Smith, Joseph, & Gray, 1992), these studies have consistently used high doses that may have been aversively stressful rather than rewarding. In acute administration studies, doses found to cause elevated dopamine have exceeded the 0.046 mg/kg intraperitoneal dose found by Jensen et al. (1990) to result in conditioned taste aversion and stress hormone release. Studies demonstrating nicotine-induced increases in mesolimbic dopamine have used a single acute administration of nicotine in doses generally in the stressful range: 0.5mg/kg (Grenhoff, Aston-Jones, & Svensson, 1986), 0.4 to 0.8mg/kg (Mitchell et al., 1992), 0.6 mg/kg (Imperato et al., 1986), and 0.025 to 0.50 mg/kg (Mereu et al., 1987).

Conclusions   Although the mesolimbic dopaminergic system is clearly an important link in a set of reinforcement-related mechanisms, the possible role of the mesolimbic dopaminergic system in nicotine reinforcement in humans is not clear, but appears more likely than not.

Sensory Gratification and Sensation Seeking

Studies by Rose and colleagues have shown sensory aspects of smoking to be both rewarding and sought after (Behm et al., 1990; Rose & Behm, 1987; Rose, Tashkin, Ertle, Zinser, & Lafer, 1985). They may also be capable of reducing negative affect (Levin et al., 1991). Smokers enjoy inhaling cigarette smoke (Reasor, Reynolds, & Ferris, 1988), and nicotine appears important to this sensory enjoyment as it is the irritant primarily responsible for the throat scratch and lung feeling found to be pleasing by many smokers (Levin et al., 1991). Like the carbonation in soft drinks, the mild irritation associated with smoking is generally desired by smokers, and when combined with tobacco and additive flavors, this sensory complex is clearly wanted by smokers (Behm et al., 1990; Rose & Behm, 1987).

However, the degree to which such sensations are inherent, unconditioned stimuli, as opposed to conditioned reinforcers, is not clear. Smoking may in part be used like chewing gum, soft drinks, and decaffeinated coffee—for pure and rewarding sensory stimulation. Moreover, the rewarding sensory stimulation associated with smoking may in certain circumstances reduce negative affect by distracting attention from threatening internal or external stimuli.

Urge Attribution Model of Positive Affect

The urge to self-administer nicotine may largely be mediated by neurophysiological drives, independent of significant positive subjective consequences other than the relief of the urge. Thus, reports by individuals that they smoke because it is pleasurable may result from people's tendency to say that anything they have the urge to do is pleasurable. Attributions such as "I have the urge to do it, so it must feel good" may play a role in a number of behaviors including fingernail biting, pencil biting, hair pulling, and other nervous habits. Attributions and misattributions related to nicotine and smoking may be especially likely to occur because the effects of nicotine appear largely to make individuals feel more "normal."

MECHANISMS UNDERLYING NEGATIVE-AFFECT-REDUCING EFFECTS

In contrast to most drug users, smokers report that negative affect reduction is one of the major reasons they smoke (see Chapter 5). B. S. Segal, Huba, and Singer (1980) found negative affect reduction to be the reported reason given by only 6–12% of drug users for all drugs except depressants (alcohol, barbiturates, and tranquilizers), for which 21% gave this reason. Thus, a major difference in perceived reasons for tobacco versus other drug use is negative affect reduction. Differences in attributed motivation for use may result from a variety of sources: (a) purely psychological processes involved in making attributions of effects of legal, as opposed to illegal, drugs; (b) basic biological differences between nicotine and illegal drugs; or (c) frequency and setting differences associated with nicotine, as opposed to other drugs.

The past decade has generated more theory and research looking at the possibility that nicotine stimulates the brain's positive reinforcement systems than at the possibility that it influences negative reinforcement and negative affect systems. This fact is interesting because (a) smokers more often say they smoke to alleviate negative affect than to increase positive affect, (b) negative affect is more predictive of relapse than is positive affect, and (c) withdrawal is characterized by increases in negative affect but not by clear deficits in positive affect (although this interesting question has not been thoroughly assessed).

Negative Reinforcement by Means of Withdrawal or Neuroadaptation Mechanisms

It appears that a number of brain systems mediate negative reinforcement and that different drugs and environmental stimuli activate different withdrawal or aversion systems (Wise, 1988). Different drug classes result in different results in different withdrawal syndromes (G. Edwards, Arif, & Hodgson, 1981). For example, barbiturates, benzodiazepines, and alcohol result in withdrawal responses that are similar to but different from those associated with opiates (Kalant, 1977; Wise, 1988), whereas nicotine (Hughes & Hatsukami, 1986; Shiffman, 1979), cocaine (R. T. Jones, 1984), and cannabis (R. T. Jones, 1980) cause markedly different and weaker withdrawal symptoms (Wise, 1988). Overarousal is characteristic of withdrawal from barbiturates, opiates, and alcohol, but underarousal is associated with withdrawal from nicotine, caffeine, amphetamines, and cocaine.

The Expert Committee of the World Health Organization (G. Edwards et al., 1981) suggested that the term *neuroadaptation* is a better term than physical dependence and that withdrawal syndromes are "characteristic for the particular drug (or category of drugs) and for the specific biological systems or species" (p. 239). Wise (1988) has noted that there is clear evidence for multiple mechanisms of negative reinforcement even with a single drug class. Opiates are likely to reduce withdrawal cramps at opiate receptors in the gut itself. They can also alleviate pain by means of mechanisms at the spinal, mesencephalic, and diencephalic levels (for a review, see Wise, 1988) and can reduce social isolation distress (B. H. Herman & Panksepp, 1978, 1981).

Increased irritability, anxiety, difficulty concentrating, and appetite are the most common responses to the cessation of habitual nicotine or smoking administration (Hughes et al., 1990; A. L. Murray & Lawrence, 1984). These are the psychological states most consistently reduced by acute doses of nicotine in nicotine-deprived smokers. Thus, it is reasonable to question whether nicotine-abstinence-related increases in such aversive states are simply a function of physical dependence on nicotine.

Some have argued that nicotine's negative-affect-reducing effects are solely a result of its reducing internally driven, physiologically based withdrawal symptoms (Perlick, 1977; Schachter, 1979). Consistent with withdrawal-symptom-alleviation formulations, Perlick (1977) found that normal nicotine-delivery cigarettes alleviated experimentally manipulated annoyance in heavy but not in light smokers. He interpreted these findings as indicating that individuals who are not addicted to nicotine experience no withdrawal symptoms or negative-affect-reducing effects from nicotine. However, other interpretations of Perlick's findings are possible as they are confounded to the degree that heavy smokers are different from light smokers in terms of personality and temperamental traits, including irritability.

Hypotheses that can be derived from the most extreme version of the withdrawal-symptom-alleviation model include the following:

1a All physically dependent tobacco users experience increased irritability, anxiety, difficulty concentrating, depression, and other withdrawal symptoms subsequent to abstinence.

b Withdrawal responses are relatively time locked and inevitable without pharmacological intervention.

2a Withdrawal responses vary between people exclusively as a function of the individual's degree of physical dependence.

b Individual differences in personality, temperament, and environment are only important in predicting response to nicotine abstinence and effects to the degree that they correlate with physical dependence and nicotine exposure.

3 Individuals not currently physically dependent on nicotine will experience no negative-affect-reducing effects from nicotine.

4 Individuals in a state of minimal nicotine deprivation and who are not currently experiencing nicotine withdrawal symptoms will experience no negative-affect-reducing effects from nicotine administered at that time.

5 All of nicotine's negative-affect-reducing effects result from alleviation of withdrawal symptoms.

6 Environmental factors play a minimal or no role in determining affective response to nicotine and abstinence.

7 Expectations, habit interference, response to loss of positive reinforcement, and other higher order psychological processes play little or no role in the experience of negative affect subsequent to nicotine abstinence.

Most of these hypotheses can be rejected, and none has strong support. Hypothesis 1a is generally argued in a circular fashion, that is, only those who experience negative affect and related physical symptoms on abstinence are physically dependent. To the degree that inevitable symptoms (Hypothesis 1b can be shown to be invalid, Hypothesis 1a is also disproven. Evidence that many heavy smokers can abstain while on vacations, during religious holidays, and in situations in which smoking is prohibited with little or no distress demonstrates that some heavy smokers avoid becoming physically dependent or are dependent but experience no reliable negative affect during abstinence.

Contrary to Hypothesis 2a, negative affect response severity associated with nicotine cessation has only an inconsistent slight to moderate correlation with habitual nicotine intake. In addition, individual differences in affective response to abstinence varies as a function of a number of variables beyond those reflective of physical dependence. Personality and environmental factors predict response to nicotine and nicotine abstinence even after habitual nicotine intake and self-reported nicotine tolerance or dependence have been controlled for (D. G. Gilbert, Meliska, Williams, & Jenson, 1992; Gilbert, Meliska, et al., 1994; Masson & Gilbert, 1990). In addition, the finding that affective response to cessation is a function of history of psychopathology (Covey et al., 1990) is not predicted by the strong version of the withdrawal symptom model.

Contrary to Hypothesis 3, nondependent smokers report experiencing negative affect reduction from nicotine. Very light smokers experience negative-affect-reducing effects from smoking during stressful conditions (McNeill et al., 1987; Shiffman, 1989). Furthermore, although almost all smokers report that smoking tranquilizes them and attenuates negative mood states, more than a third of the individuals who quit smoking report no postcessation symptoms other than the desire to smoke.

Contrary to Hypothesis 4, individuals in a state of minimal nicotine deprivation and who are not currently experiencing withdrawal symptoms do experience negative-affect-reducing effects from nicotine. In a similar vein, contrary to Hypothesis 5, nicotine's negative-affect-reducing effects can occur when the individual is minimally deprived. Thus, when there are no withdrawal symptoms to alleviate, it is difficult to suggest that smoking's negative-affect-attenuating effects result simply from alleviation of withdrawal syptoms. However, to the degree that abstinence responses are elicited by stress one can interpret such studies as potentially reflecting nicotine-induced attenuation of abstinence-related emotional lability.

Contrary to Hypothesis 6, there is a great deal of evidence indicating that environmental factors play important roles in determining responses to nicotine deprivation (see Chapter 5). Nicotine abstinence in relaxing environments does not increase negative affect (D. G. Gilbert, Meliska, Williams, 1992; Perkins, Grobe, Fonte, & Breus, 1992; Suedfeld & Ikard, 1974), although abstinence during stressful conditions amplifies distress.

Hypothesis 7, that expectations, habit interference, subjective loss of positive reinforcement, and other higher order psychological processes play little or no role in abstinence-related negative affect is contrary to experimental evidence. For example, Hughes, Gulliver, et al. (1989) found that nicotine chewing gum was reinforcing only when individuals believed they were receiving nicotine. Furthermore, the loss of access to many positive reinforcers (e.g., relationship loss or frustrated goal obtainment) results in a negative affect syndrome largely similar to, and frequently more intense than, that observed during nicotine abstinence (Gilbert, Gilbert, & Schultz, 1994).

Clearly the strong form of the withdrawal-symptom-alleviation hypothesis of nicotine's reinforcing and negative-affect-reducing properties is invalid. Nonetheless, significant neurobiological and other physiological adaptations resulting from prolonged nicotine administration clearly contribute to some of nicotine's affect-modulating properties. The transient nature of the increase in negative affect subsequent to smoking cessation combined with the attenuation of cessation-associated negative affect by nicotine replacement therapy provide the strongest evidence that some of nicotine's negative-affect-reducing effects are a function of abstinence-related processes. However, the large within-smoker and between-smokers variability in severity and type of affective response requires a more sophisticated explanatory model.

Critique of Withdrawal Alleviation Models   The negative-affect-alleviating and performance-enhancing effects of nicotine have frequently been interpreted as resulting from withdrawal alleviation rather than from psychomotor stimulant or other inherent effects (Schachter, 1979; USDHHS, 1988). However, Wise and Bozarth (1987) have criticized models of drug use based on withdrawal alleviation and other forms of negative reinforcement on a number of empirically based grounds. Wise and Bozarth argued that "physical dependence has not proved to have actual heuristic value as the foundation of a general theory of addiction'' (p. 470). Nonetheless, the negative-affect-reducing and reinforcing effects of smoking almost certainly result from a combination of mechanisms, one of which is biologically based on altered neurobiological functioning. Drug withdrawal theory suggests that drug exposure elicits negative feedback mechanisms that counter the drug's primary effect (Solomon & Corbit, 1974). Repeated drug exposure results in increased negative feedback responses that result in drug tolerance. Thus, when one ceases drug use such opponent processes are not countered by the drug, and drug abstinence responses occur (Solomon & Corbit, 1973).

Consistent with this opponent process model, most drugs' withdrawal symptoms are the opposite of those associated with acute drug effects. Many of the effects of tobacco cessation are the opposite of those of tobacco or nicotine. For example, nicotine increases alertness, concentration, electrocortical activation, and heart rate and decreases anger, anxiety, drowsiness, irritability, appetite, and weight, whereas the effects of cessation are in the opposite direction. However, some of the effects of tobacco abstinence are not the opposite of the direct effects of nicotine (Hughes et al., 1990), for example, depression, restlessness, and insomnia. Furthermore, whereas nicotine has been found to elevate pain thresholds and to increase motor activity, decreases in these measures have not been reported subsequent to abstinence (Hughes et al., 1990). Thus, the opponent process model appears to account for some, but not all, of the effects resulting from nicotine abstinence. In addition, the withdrawal model does not account for the individual and situational specificity of occurrence of abstinence-related negative affect.

Hughes (1991) proposed a number of means of distinguishing withdrawal relief from direct effects of smoking. The first solution is that of comparing nonsmokers with deprived and nondeprived smokers. However, as he noted, the nonsmoker control group is not an adequate comparison group as prospective studies show that individuals who later become smokers are more anxious, depressed, neurotic (Cherry & Kiernan, 1976), attention-disordered (Hartsough & Lambert, 1987), and predisposed toward distress and psychopathology than are those who do not take up the habit. Exsmokers also fail as an adequate control group as they differ from continuing smokers on the same psychological dimensions as smokers and nonsmokers. The third possible solution is that of using minimally deprived smokers. Several studies (e.g., Pomerleua, Turk, & Fertig, 1984) have suggested that abstinence effects can occur after only 6–12 hours of deprivation, thus making the distinction between inherent and withdrawal relief effects difficult. Smokers deprived for 1 or 2 hours before testing would avoid this problem; however, such a short period of deprivation may be inadequate to demonstrate additional effects of smoking. The final solution suggested by Hughes is that of comparing the morning mood, performance, and other functioning of smokers, exsmokers, and those who have never smoked. If no differences are observed when using well-matched groups, then withdrawal would not occur after overnight deprivation, according to Hughes. He concluded that until such studies are performed, the best hope of demonstrating any inherent effects of nicotine would be to use minimally deprived smokers and to demonstrate that they exhibit less negative affect subsequent to smoking and that their postsmoking negative affect is less than that of those who have never smoked and exsmokers. Unfortunately, the latter requirement does not address the fact that smokers are more disposed toward negative affect, so that any decrement in negative affect produced by nicotine would have to overcome this constitutional difference in baseline levels.

Although experimental paradigms used to detect behavioral effects of classical anxiolytics in rodents have typically failed to observe anxiolyticlike effects of nicotine, a small number of studies using paradigms sensitive to newer forms of anxiolytics have observed such effects. New paradigms may need to be sensitive to the detection of anxiety involving the distal and ambiguous stimuli combined with distractors found to be required for nicotine's anxiolytic effects. Finally, nicotine may reduce negative affect in humans by means not found in lower species.

The strongest evidence supportive of withdrawal symptom alleviation is that negative affect increases and then decreases in a relatively predictable manner during the month subsequent to cessation in habitual smokers who quit. However, this return may occur through a number of mechanisms other than neuroadaptation. Such changes may result from new psychological and behavioral coping techniques, including general lifestyle changes. In addition, effects of simply self-reporting negative affect may result in decreases in reported affect over time independent of any intervention owing to less attention being paid to actual state over time. Finally, and most important, return to baseline levels of negative affect occur only in those quitters, frequently a minority, who successfully abstain for the length of the study. Those failing to abstain might not have returned to baseline values. Thus, without carefully designed control groups, the return to precessation baseline levels of negative affect cannot be attributed solely to changes in neuroadaptation to the lack of nicotine.

Finally, evidence reviewed in Chapter 5 clearly indicates that the affect-modulating effects of nicotine and smoking are a function of environmental, personality, and state factors not predicted by the extreme version of the withdrawal-symptom-alleviation model. The withdrawal model cannot fully account for these observed findings. The mechanisms reviewed in the following pages generally do not make any assumptions as to whether nicotine is alleviating negative affect associated with withdrawal or whether nicotine has inherent negative-affect-attenuating effects.

Cortical Arousal Modulation Model

H. J. Eysenck (1973, 1980) proposed that nicotine is rewarding because it can increase cortical arousal when one is underaroused and can, in other situations, reduce cortical and subjective arousal when one is excessively aroused, as when in a state of emotional distress. Consistent with this bidirectional (inverted-U) hypothesis, a large number of studies (Church, 1989; J. A. Edwards et al., 1985; Knott, 1990) have shown that in low-arousal situations modest doses of nicotine increase cortical activation and alertness. Armitage and his coworkers (Armitage, Hall, & Morrison, 1968; Armitage et al., 1969) found that nicotine administered to cats and rats resulted in decreased electrocortical and behavioral measures of activation in animals who were initially highly aroused, but increased arousal in initially less aroused animals. Consistent with the arousal-modulation hypothesis, Rosecrans (personal communication, May, 1994) found nicotine to reduce dopamine concentrations in rats high in baseline dopamine and to increase brain dopamine in rats with low baseline levels.

Few studies have assessed the effects of smoking and nicotine simultaneously on negative affect and arousal during stressful conditions. Golding and Mangan (1982) found that smoking during stressful noise blasts increased alpha power, whereas smoking during relaxing conditions decreased alpha power. They interpreted these findings as consistent with the hypothesis that nicotine stimulates cortical arousal when arousal is low, but decreases arousal when cortical arousal is high. D. G. Gilbert, Robinson, et al. (1989) found smoking-delivered nicotine to enhance alpha power, especially in the right hemisphere, during stressful accident scenes in a woodshop safety film. During low-stress conditions, nicotine reduced alpha power in both hemispheres. These findings were interpreted as supportive of a right hemisphere sedative effects during stress and stimulant effects during low stress. However, alpha is a questionable measure of cortical activation level. Thus, neither the Golding and Mangan or D. G. Gilbert et al. studies provides strong support for this view.

Finally, effects of nicotine on EEG power and dimensional complexity (a dynamical modeling) vary as a function of baseline power and complexity (Pritchard & Duke, 1992; Pritchard, Gilbert, & Duke, 1993). Individuals with high baseline activation or complexity exhibited reductions in complexity or activation, whereas those low on these dimensions exhibited corresponding increases. However, contrary to the view that smoking decreases cortical activation when activation is high, Knott (1990) found that smoking increased cortical event-related potentials to electrical shock stimuli and to auditory stimuli during a stressful, shock-stress paradigm (Knott & De Lugt, 1991) . Also contrary to the arousal-reduction hypothesis, Hasenfratz and Bättig (1993) found that smoking decreased anxiety but simultaneously increased EEG activation during stressful tasks. Consistent with both cortical and peripheral arousal-reduction models, smoking-delivered nicotine decreases skin conductance response magnitude, especially to highly arousing or emotional stimuli (D. G. Gilbert & Hagen, 1980, 1985; Knott, 1984). P. H. Morris and Gale (1993) found that smoking increased electrodermal arousal during a monotonous vigilance task, but decreased electrodermal arousal during a demanding cognitive task.

In summary, although some studies have observed nicotine-induced decreases in electrocortical and electrodermal arousal when presmoking arousal is high, other findings have observed smoking-induced increases in both electrocortical and subjective arousal during stressful and high-arousal conditions even though subjective anxiety is decreased. Finally, an inverted-U model is also supported by a number of studies showing that nicotine's effects depend on baseline behavior rates. Nicotine tends to transpose behavior. That is, it increases behavior when baseline levels are low and decreases the same behavior when baseline levels are high (for a review, see Hendry & Rosecrans, 1982).

An alternative form of the arousal-modulation hypothesis is that cortical sedation may be obtained from smoking and other forms of nicotine intake because users increase their dose of nicotine during stress. Dose determines cortical response to nicotine. Norton, Howard, and Brown (1991) and Norton and Howard (1988) observed smoking-associated attenuations of cortical event-related potential amplitude in individuals with large nicotine intakes but observed amplitude enhancements in low-dose smokers. The low-nicotine group reported increases in subjective arousal subsequent to smoking, whereas high-dose smokers reported decreases. Ashton, Millman, Telford, and Thompson (1974) also found high-dose-dependent attenuations of electrocortical activity. Although low and moderate doses of nicotine increase cortical arousal, very high doses decrease CNS arousal in animals (Armitage et al., 1969; Guha & Pradhan, 1976). Similarly, low doses of nicotine stimulate peripheral receptors, and very high doses block them (Lippiello, Sears, & Fernades, et al. 1987).

Evidence contrary to both forms of the cortical sedation model is provided by findings that nicotine can decrease negative affect while concomitantly increasing subjective arousal (O'Neill & Parrot, 1992; Perkins, Grobe, Fonte, & Breus, 1992). O'Neill and Parrot had 18 sedative and 9 stimulant smokers report their level of stress and arousal just before and subsequent to smoking each cigarette. Self-reported stress was reduced subsequent to smoking in both groups of smokers throughout the day. Arousal was simultaneously increased throughout the day for stimulant smokers, but only subsequent to the first cigarette of the day for sedative smokers. Perkins, Grobe, Fonte, & Breus, et al. (1992) found smoking-induced decreases in experimentally induced stress to occur concurrently with smoking-induced increases in subjective arousal.

Thus, in contrast to the arousal-modulation model, smoking can lead to simultaneous increases in subjective alertness and increased EEG arousal combined with decreased stress. O'Neill and Parrot (1992) noted that another problem with this model is the finding that during smoking abstinence, subjective and electrocortical indexes of arousal decrease, but irritability and anxiety frequently increase. Therefore, these findings do not support the assumption that subjective stress covaries with high arousal. Instead, consistent with most factor-analytic results, these findings suggest that stress and arousal are orthogonal dimensions (Ashton & Golding, 1989; Surawy & Cox, 1987).

Cortisol and Glucocorticoid Models

Nicotine can increase the release of corticosteroids (primarily cortisol in humans and corticosterone in rodents) from the adrenal cortex. Their observation that rats can become dependent on nicotine for successful shock avoidance performance led G. H. Hall and Morrison (1973) to suggest that corticosteroid activity modulates nicotine-stress interactions. On the basis of their finding that nicotine directly activated isolated adrenocortical cells, Rubin and Warner (1975) proposed that in individuals with an inadequate response to stress, smoking may enhance ability to cope with stress by increasing steroid output. Noting the similar effects of glucocorticoids and smoking on behavioral, electrocortical, and perceptual processes, D. G. Gilbert (1979) proposed that nicotine's reinforcing and stress-alleviating effects are in part mediated by changes in arousal-, sensory-threshold-, and information-processing-related brain activity resulting from nicotine-induced increases in glucocorticoid release.

Smoking and Nicotine-Induced Glucocorticoid Release   The effects of smoking typical commercial cigarettes in a normal fashion are relatively small, somewhat unreliable, and probably state- and trait-dependent. Smoking nicotine cigarettes frequently results in slight elevations in serum cortisol relative to nicotine-free cigarette smoking (D. G. Gilbert, Meliska, Williams, & Jensen, 1992; Kirschbaum, Wust, & Strasburger, 1992; Meliska & Gilbert, 1991). However, some studies assessing individuals in more normal and somewhat active environments observed no increases when comparing own-cigarette smoking with control conditions (Benowitz, Kuyt, & Jacob, 1984; Cherek, Smith, Lane, & Brauchi, 1982). Two studies have assessed the effects of smoking and stress, separately and in combination, on blood cortisol concentrations. O. F. Pomerleau et al. (1987) found that smoking a single cigarette had no effect on cortisol either after a period of inactivity or immediately after a period of extreme exercise stress. O. F. Pomerleau and Pomerleau (1990) found modest additive effects on serum cortisol for smoking and psychological stress. Yeh and Barbieri (1989) also failed to find differences between habitual smokers and nonsmokers in their 24-hour urine samples. A majority of studies have observed decreased blood cortisol concentrations subsequent to abstinence (Puddey et al., 1984; West, Russell, Jarvis, Pizzey, & Kadam, 1984); however, others have found no changes or an increase in cortisol (for a review, see Hughes et al., 1990).

Affect Modulation by Glucocorticoids   Effects of glucocorticoids on measures of emotion and affect in humans have produced inconsistent results, suggesting that these effects are complex and a function of a number of variables. Effects of nicotine have been mimicked by acute cortisol and cortisollike substances administered to healthy humans, including elevated mood, increased concentration, and reduced tiredness during task performance (Born, Hitzler, Pietrowsky, Paushinger, & Fehm, 1988; Carpenter & Gruen, 1982). In contrast,

Wolkowitz et al. (1988) found exogenous administration of glucocorticoids in healthy humans to have rather minimal subjective effects, but to reliably decrease cerebrospinal fluid beta-endorphin and ACTH and to decrease EEG activation— effects opposite these of nicotine.

Depression is characteristic of Addison's disease, a condition characterized by a low cortisol: ACTH ratio due to a failure of the adrenal cortex to produce normal amounts of cortisol, which then results in heightened output of ACTH owing to a lack of negative feedback (Cleghorn, 1951). Patients with Addison's disease report experiencing concentration difficulties, drowsiness, restlessness, insomnia, and irritability (Carpenter & Gruen, 1982), the same set of symptoms frequently observed subsequent to smoking cessation. However, contrary to simple linear views of cortisol concentration, patients with Cushing's syndrome (hypersecretion of cortisol) also frequently exhibit depressed mood and concentration and cognitive dysfunctions (Carpenter & Gruen, 1982; Starkman, Schteingart, & Schork, 1981, 1986). Many clinically depressed individuals have elevated CNS and peripheral cortisol concentrations (Gerner & Wilkins, 1983).

The contrast between the subjective effects observed with acute administration of cortisol to healthy individuals compared with chronic excessive levels in cases of disease suggests that acute, moderate elevations of cortisol may promote a euphoric state, whereas chronic high levels may promote dysphoria (D. M. Barnes, 1986). It may be that cortisol and related glucocorticoids in doses appropriate to the conditions exert a stress-attenuating effect, but at excessive levels they dampen a number of biological processes leading to physiological and psychological depression (outlined below).

A number of studies have suggested that acute glucocorticoid administration attenuates emotion-related behavior in animals. It has been concluded that glucocorticoids reduce anxiety and fear-motivated behavior, whereas ACTH enhances them (Bohus, De Kloet, & Veldhuis, 1982; DeWied, 1980; File, Vellucci, & Wendlandt, 1979). Glucocorticoids can also facilitate extinction of conditioned avoidance responses (for a review, see H. J. Eysenck & Kelley, 1987). However, the leap from discussion of rodents to humans is risky as the primary glucocorticoid in rodents is corticosterone, whereas that for humans is cortisol and because functional relations between food, stress, and neuromodulators in rodents do not always parallel those observed in humans (Munck et al., 1984).

Homeostatic, Negative Feedback Model of Effects of Nicotine, Stress, and Cortisol Glucocorticoids have long been known to attenuate the effects of a variety of stress-related physiological processes (for a review, see Munck et al., 1984). Consistent with the notion that nicotine's stress-reducing effects may be mediated by cortisol, Munck et al. provided evidence supporting the view that (a) the physiological function of stress-induced increases in glucocorticoid levels is to protect against the normal defensive reactions activated by stress and not against the source of stress and (b) the glucocorticoids accomplish this function by turning off those defensive reactions, thus preventing overshooting and threats to homeostasis. Cortisol counteracts the effects of numerous stress-related physiological processes and appears to promote normalization of physiological functioning after stress (Munck et al., 1984). Thus, it is reasonable to hypothesize that cortisol and other glucocorticoids attenuate negative affect by facilitating recovery from stress-induced neuromodulator elevations.

It is generally assumed that the effects of glucocorticoids are direct central effects, as these substances readily pass through the blood–brain barrier and the brain has numerous glucocorticoid receptors in a wide range of areas (Fuxe et al., 1990). Mesolimbic dopaminergic pathways are apparently modulated by glucocorticoids (Fuxe et al., 1990). Effects of glucocorticoid administration have been found to include EEG slowing (Glaser, Kornfield, & Knight, 1955; Wolkowitz et al., 1988), reduced hippocampal electrical activity in rats (Pfaff, Silva, & Weiss, 1971), lowered cortical sensitivity to stimuli and stimulus change (Born, Kern, Fehm-Wolfsdorf, & Fehm, 1987), elevation of sensory thresholds (Beckwith, Lerud, Antes, & Reynolds, 1983; Henkin, 1970; Korbacher, Arndt, Maier, & Fehm-Wolfsdorf, 1993), and elevation of thresholds for stress-induced cortisol secretion (Fehm-Wolfsdorf & Nagel, 1993). Evidence has suggested that metabolites of cortisol include barbituratelike modulators of the GABA–benzodiazepine receptor complex that may decrease CNS excitability and produce tranquilizing effects (Majewska, Harrison, Schwartz, Barker, & Paul, 1986).

Consistent with the view that cortisol and other glucocorticoids attenuate many physiological functions, evidence has suggested that elevated glucocorticoid concentrations decrease binding of nicotine at receptor sites in mice (Pauly, Ullman, & Collins, 1988). Thus, stress-induced elevations of cortisol may attenuate bioavailable nicotine and produce a state equivalent to nicotine withdrawal, the subjective effects of which add to those of the stressor itself. In a state of heightened negative affect, this model suggests that part of the negative affect would be withdrawal related. It has been suggested that increased smoking in response to stress might result from cortisol-induced decreases in CNS sensitivity to nicotine (Pauly et al., 1988).

In contrast to the hypothesis that glucocorticoids decrease CNS sensitivity to nicotine, glucocorticoids may enhance sensitivity of mesolimbic dopamine release to nicotine and thereby enhance its reinforcing effects. Glucocorticoids increase amphetamine-induced dopamine release in the nucleus accumbens in rodents (Imperato, Puglisi-Allegra, Casolini, Zocchi, & Angelucci, 1989), and there are a number of behavioral and pharmacologic similarities between nicotine and amphetamines. Thus, individuals high in stress and personality traits such as depression and neuroticism may have high prevalences of smoking because these traits are characterized by elevated cortisol concentrations that enhance nicotine's reinforcing effects. This cortisol-enhanced dopamine release model could also explain the special pleasure associated with smoking immediately after a meal, as cortisol is elevated after eating (Munck et al., 1984).

Summary and Critique of Glucocorticoid Models   The above-reviewed findings suggest a number of means by which cortisol and other corticosteroids may mediate and moderate the effects of nicotine on affect and cognition. The limited number of studies assessing this model are suggestive, but allow no definitive conclusions to be drawn.

The fact that smokers report tranquilizing effects within the first few puffs (Warburton, Revell, & Walters, 1988) although cortisol release is delayed for 5 or 10 minutes subsequent to the onset of smoking confirms that cortisol does not account for all tranquilizing effects associated with smoking. Nonetheless, it is tempting to suggest that cortisol contributes to some of nicotine's distressolytic effects given the similarity of a number of the effects and associations of cortisol and nicotine. The possibility that smoking results in cortisol-induced (emotional) prophylaxis (CIP) or cortisol-induced homeostasis (CIH) is an intriguing one. Smoking-induced elevations in cortisol may decrease subsequent emotional and physiological responses to stress. Deductions from the CIP–CIS model include (a) smoking subsequent to stress will have minimal effects on immediate subjective and behavioral measures because the cortisol response lag to smoking is a number of minutes, (b) smoking 10–15 minutes before stressor presentation will reduce physiological and subjective responses to stress; (3) CIP occurs only with emotional or physiological overactivation to a stimulating stressor (as opposed to dysphoria associated with underarousal), (d) other substances and situations resulting in the release of cortisol (e.g., eating, stress, and exercise) should also result in CIP–CIH, and (e) positive as well as negative emotional states may be influenced by CIP.

Endogenous Opioid Mechanisms and Models

The hypothesis that nicotine's affect-modulating properties are mediated in part by beta-endorphin (D. G. Gilbert, 1979) was initially promoted by studies showing rapid and high-dose smoking-induced elevations of peripheral blood concentrations of beta-endorphin (D. G. Gilbert, Meliska, Williams, & Jensen, 1992; Karras & Kane, 1980; O. F. Pomerleau et al., 1983; Seyler, Pomerleau, Fertig, Hunt, & Parber, 1986). High doses of nicotine can also increase central release of β-endorphin (O. F. Pomerleau & Rosecrans, 1989). However, normal smoking during relaxing laboratory conditions does not reliably increase peripheral concentrations of β-endorphin (D. G. Gilbert, Meliska, Williams, & Jensen, 1992; Meliska & Gilbert, 1991). Nonetheless, smoking may result in the release of β-endorphin in certain moderately stressful conditions that do not by themselves cause elevated β-endorphin concentrations.

The increased concentrations of β-endorphin subsequent to smoking high nicotine-delivery-cigarettes have been associated with nausea and other signs of subjective distress, but not to pleasure or pleasantness (D. G. Gilbert, Meliska, Williams, & Jensen, 1992; Seyler et al., 1986). However, it should be noted that peripheral concentrations of β-endorphin do not always correlate highly with central levels (Finck, 1989; Post et al., 1982). Thus, the failure of ecologically valid smoking to elevate peripheral β-endorphin does not preclude the possiblity that normal smoking elevates central β-endorphin concentrations.

The importance of central as well as peripheral β-endorphin in mediation of nicotine's subjective and reinforcing effects has been assessed in several studies using naloxone, a substance that blocks central and peripheral opioids. Although a pilot study by Palmer and Berens (1983) demonstrated naloxone-induced blockade of subjective pleasure from smoking, subsequent studies (Gorelick, Rose, & Jarvik, 1989; Nemeth-Coslett & Griffiths, 1986) failed to detect any effects of naloxone on craving or subjective response to smoking or any evidence that it resulted in withdrawal symptoms.

A pilot study by Karras and Kane (1980) found naloxone to reduce the number of cigarette puffs taken over a 3-hour period. Similarly, Gorelick et al. (1989) observed that naloxone decreased smoking. However, a well-designed study by Nemeth-Coslett and Griffiths (1986) that used a wide range of naloxone doses failed to find any effects of CNS opioid receptor blockade on smoking or withdrawal symptoms. The findings of this better controlled study are inconsistent with the view that β-endorphin is involved in smoking rate. Similarly, rats trained to self-administer nicotine were unaffected by the same naltrexone treatment that decreased cocaine administration in a parallel group of rats (Corrigall & Coen, 1991). However, naltrexone antagonized nicotine-influenced behavior in a study of mice by Corrigall, Herling, and Coen (1988).

Overall, evidence fails to support the importance of peripheral β-endorphin in modulating smoking's effects, and the evidence concerning the importance of central β-endorphin in mediating smoking's reinforcing and affect-modulating effects is not clear.

Mechanisms Based on Altered Perceptions of Bodily Activity

Three distinct mechanisms based on altered perceptions of bodily activity have been proposed to account for nicotine's stress-reducing effects. They are the elevated perceptual threshold model, the muscular relaxation model, and the reduced phasic response or facilitated homeostatic control model.

Elevated Perceptual Threshold   Nicotine may reduce the intensity of emotional experiences by increasing perceptual thresholds for emotion-related bodily tension and arousal (D. G. Gilbert, 1979). This suggestion was based on evidence indicating that in some situations nicotine increases the threshold for electric shock (Mendenhall, 1925; Wenusch & Schöller, 1936) and that nicotine-induced increases in cardiovascular activity typically do not produce corresponding increases in perceived heart activity (D. G. Gilbert & Hagen, 1980).

Evidence assessing this hypothesis is mixed. Levine and Lombardo (1985) found that smoking interfered with the perception of electromyographic activity of the corrugator muscle, a muscle tensed during a number of negative affective states (Fridlund & Izard, 1983). Epstein, Dickson, McKenzie, and Russell (1984) observed reduced sensitivity to muscle activity subsequent to smoking in women and enhanced sensitivity in men. The perception of auditory stimuli was not altered. Dengerink, Lindgren, and Axelsson (1992) found that smoking reduced temporary auditory threshold shifts following noise exposure in habitual smokers, but that nicotine gum increased shifts (elevated thresholds) in non-smokers. Although a study by Lombardo and Epstein (1986) failed to find any effects of nicotine on the perception of heartbeat, the study did not control for increased cardiac contractility or increases in other cardiac measures that would normally result in increased perception of heart activity.

Evidence of elevated detection and pain thresholds for electrical shock include several additional studies showing smoking-delivered nicotine to elevate such thresholds (Mendenhall, 1925; Nesbitt, 1969; O. F. Pomerleau et al., 1984; Silverstein, 1982). However, a number of studies have observed no effect of smoking on pain (Milgrom-Friedman et al., 1983; Mueser et al., 1984; Shiffman & Jarvik, 1984; Waller et al., 1983; Sult & Moss, 1986). Knott and De Lugt (1991) found that smoking did not alter either self-reported pain intensity or cortical event-related potentials to electrical shock stimuli.

The convergence of evidence suggests the probability that under certain conditions nicotine can attenuate sensory perceptual processes. Mendenhall (1925) found that smoking elevated thresholds in more individuals than it lowered them and that smoking elevated thresholds when they were low, but lowered thresholds when they were high. Similar effects were observed in both habitual smokers and nonsmokers. High doses of nicotine exert a potent antinociceptive effect in rats (Sahley & Berntson, 1979).

Mechanisms possibly mediating any such alterations of perceptual thresholds may vary as a function of type of threshold. Beta-endorphin may mediate elevated pain thresholds in the subgroup of studies showing such elevations. Although smoking does not appear to generally increase β-endorphin in nonstressful conditions, the stressful nature of pain tests may combine with nicotine to elevate β-endorphin and perceptual thresholds in situations in which the pain stress or associated anxiety has not already so elevated β-endorphin as to make any contribution of nicotine insignificant. In contrast, cortisol has been found to be a more reliable correlate of tobacco use than β-endorphin and thus may elevate thresholds in low-dose and low-stress situations and potentially alter perceptual processes in more normal conditions.

Muscle Relaxation   The second hypothesized mechanism to account for the stress-reducing effects of nicotine is that nicotine produces a state of tranquility by reducing the level of tonic or phasic muscular activity (D. G. Gilbert, 1979). Hence, individuals may report that smoking relaxes them because smokers are more sensitive to nicotine's muscle-relaxing effects than to its autonomic-, neuroendocrine-, and CNS-arousing effects. Nicotine has been found to reduce resting muscle tone in spastic patients (Webster, 1964). Experimental evidence has strongly supported the view that nicotine in smoking-sized doses depresses patellar reflexes and startle responses (Clark & Rand, 1968; Domino, 1973; Hutchinson & Emley, 1973). Fuller and Forrest (1977) observed reduced electromyographic activity in both low- and high-stress conditions. The failure of several studies (e.g., Fagerstrom & Gotestam, 1977; D. G. Gilbert & Hagen, 1980) to observe decreased muscular tension subsequent to smoking may be a result of the subjects in these studies smoking high-nicotine cigarettes at excessively rapid rates which was highly stressful for them.

It has generally been assumed that these muscle-relaxing effects result from nicotine's stimulation of the Renshaw inhibitory neurons in the spinal cord (Domino, 1973). Recent findings (Ginzel, 1988) have suggested the intriguing possibility that nicotine may also contribute to muscular relaxation and simultaneous cortical arousal by reflex actions initiated by nicotine's stimulation of vagal afferents in the lower respiratory tract.

Reduced Phasic Response and Enhanced Homeostatic Control   Nicotine may reduce emotional experience by attenuating emotion-induced phasic increases in ANS end-organ activity (Schachter, 1973) or CNS emotion-induced arousal. Because nicotine typically increases activation of the ANS, this increase in tonic ANS activation may produce a ceiling effect such that the additional arousal increase associated with the onset of emotional stimulation is less than the emotion-induced arousal that occurs without nicotine. This hypothesis assumes that phasic, rather than tonic, activation of the ANS is an important contributor to the subjective experience of emotion. Consistent with this model, nicotine reliably increases tonic heart rate, but reduces phasic heart rate responses to stressors (D. G. Gilbert, Robinson, et al., 1989; Schachter, 1973; Woodson, Buzzi, Nil, & Battig, 1986). Thus, nicotine may reduce the perception of cardiovascular and other ANS end-organ activity because phasic increases in such changes are in fact reduced. However, at most this model accounts for some of the tranquilization observed in response to acute emotional stressors as smokers report obtaining relaxation from smoking in a number of situations not involving phasic cardiovascular or other autonomic arousal. Moreover, effects of nicotine on mood and feeling states would have to be accounted for by some other mechanism.

Nutritional and Consummatory Drive-Related Models

Relationships between stress, mood, food consumption, appetite, body weight, and nicotine and smoking are functionally important. Nicotine reduces body weight in humans and rodents, and withdrawal from nicotine leads to increases in weight (Levin, Briggs, Christopher, & Rose, 1993). The tendency of smoking to lower body weight is perceived by many smokers as a beneficial effect of smoking that contributes to the decision of some individuals, especially women, to start smoking (Klesges & Klesges, 1988), to continue smoking (Klesges & Shumaker, 1992; Pirie, Murray, & Luepker, 1991), and to relapse subsequent to quitting (Pirie et al., 1991). Food consumption, like smoking, reduces anxiety and other forms of negative affect (Schachter, 1971; Spring, Chiodo, & Bowen, 1987; Spring et al., 1989). In addition, negative affect promotes both smoking (O. F. Pomerleau & Pomerleau, 1989; Rose et al., 1983) and eating (Cooper & Bowskill, 1986; C. P. Herman & Polivy, 1975; McKenna, 1972; Morley, Levine, & Rowland, 1983). Cigarette craving is also enhanced immediately after a meal, and cigarettes immediately after a meal are rated as tasting better and being more satisfying (Jarvik, Saniga, Herskovic, Weiner, & Oisboid, 1989). Smoke intake also increases subsequent to food deprivation (Zacny & De Wit, 1990). Finally, a common serotonin-modulated mechanism may mediate the commonly observed increases in negative affect and weight or appetite subsequent to smoking cessation (Spring et al., 1991). The following paragraphs review evidence and models of relationships of smoking, nicotine, and mood modulation to nutrient intake, body weight, and metabolism.

Hypoglycemic Model   Hickey and Harner (1973) proposed that alleviation of feelings of hunger may contribute to smoking reinforcement and that nicotine alleviates negative affect in certain individuals by attenuating hypoglycemia. Hypoglycemia is associated with subjective symptoms of nervousness, tremulousness, palpitation, faintness, weakness, and hunger (Messer, Morris, & Gross, 1990). Elevated blood concentrations of counterregulatory hormones (adrenaline, glucagon, cortisol, and growth hormone) resulting from decreased blood sugar levels may promote the onset of these adrenergic symptoms (Messer et al., 1990). The CNS symptoms sometimes associated with more acute hypoglycemia include impaired problem-solving and concentration as well as headache, confusion, and perceptual disturbances (Hale, Margen, & Rabak, 1982). These CNS and adrenergic symptoms overlap to a significant degree with those most commonly exhibited during nicotine withdrawal. Hickey and Harner viewed smoking as counteracting hypoglycemia through nicotine-induced epinephrine release that in turn releases glucose from liver glycogen stores.

Hickey and Harner (1973) based their hypothesis on animal and human studies showing that nicotine elevated blood glucose concentrations. However, although some evidence has suggested that smoking can elevate blood glucose levels (Glauser, Glauser, Reidenberg, Rusy, & Tallarida, 1970; McCormick, 1935), better controlled, ecologically valid studies have failed to observe such effects (D. G. Gilbert, Estes, et al., 1994). However, effects of smoking in a variety of situations (e.g., stressful and high activity) have not been assessed. Thus, no definitive conclusion pertaining to the role of glucose in mediating effects of smoking can be drawn at this time.

Consummatory Drive and Body-Weight Control Model   Mechanisms contributing to the weight-reducing effects of nicotine and smoking have not been fully elucidated. In attempting to explain the facts that many individuals gain weight when they quit smoking and that smokers weigh less than non-smokers of the same age (S. M. Hall, Ginsberg, & Jones, 1986; Williamson et al., 1991), Grunberg (1985) suggested that nicotine may relieve the hunger drive. Although some evidence has suggested that nicotine may reduce appetite by the reduction of carbohydrate preference (Grunberg, 1982, 1985; Spring et al., 1991), these effects have frequently not been replicated (B. L. Lee, Jacob, Jarvik, & Benowitz, 1989; Perkins, 1992; Perkins, Epstein, et al., 1992; C. S. Pomerleau, Garcia, Drewnowski, & Pomerleau, 1991). Thus, nicotine's effects on hunger appear to be at most modest and situationally specific.

Cortisol is intimately involved in carbohydrate metabolism, smoking, and eating. Both eating and smoking elevate blood cortisol concentrations. The influence of nicotine and smoking on appetite and weight gain and the similarity of nicotine's and food's effects suggest that some of nicotine's reinforcing effects may be mediated by mechanisms mediating food reinforcement. Consistent with the view that eating and smoking are to some extent exchangable behaviors, individuals tend to gain weight, and possibly eat more, after they quit smoking (Perkins, 1992).

Serotonergic Model   Serotonin is intimately related to eating, mood, and negative affect (Spring et al., 1991). Serotonergic activity inhibits feeding behavior in a variety of species, including humans (Levin et al., 1993; Spring et al., 1991). Smoking-cessation-related weight gain, overeating, and dysphoric mood were suppressed by the serotonin-releasing drug D-fenfluramine in a study by Spring et al. (1991). Fat and protein intakes did not change in the placebo group, but carbohydrate intake increased (from 30% to 40%). Carbohydrate intake increased most in quitters, who became most anxious after cessation. D-fenfluramine prevented an increase in hostility and tended to attenuate depression during the first week of abstinence. These findings are consistent with the view that a common serotonin-modulated mechanism may mediate the commonly observed increases in negative affect and weight or appetite subsequent to smoking cessation (Spring et al., 1991). Evidence has suggested that carbohydrates, including sweets and chocolate, can increase brain concentrations of serotonin (Fernstrom & Wurtman, 1971; Wurtman & Wurtman, 1983), that some individuals self-medicate negative affect (especially anger) by eating sweets (Schuman, Gitlin, & Fairbanks, 1987), and that such self-medication takes place more often in individuals scoring high in two neurotic traits, depression and hysteria (Schuman et al., 1987). Smoking is associated with the same personality traits, as well as with self-medication of negative affect and the alterations in brain concentrations of serotonin (Benwell, Balfour, & Anderson, 1990).

Similarly, a serotonin reuptake inhibitor, fluoxetine, reduced smoking-cessation-induced weight gain in a study by O. F. Pomerleau, Pomerleau, Morrell, and Lowenbergh (1991). The serotonin reuptake inhibitor, sertraline, has also been found to attenuate nicotine-withdrawal-induced hyperphagia and rapid weight gain in rats (Levin et al., 1993).

Insulin Grunberg and Raygada (1991) have explored the possibility that insulin mediates some of nicotine's effects on food preferences and body weight. Grunberg's work has shown that high daily nicotine administration (6 mg/kg/day or 12 mg/kg/day) in rats decreases circulating and pancreatic insulin while slightly elevating concentrations in the hypothalamus. Decreased insulin should decrease lipolysis and lipogenesis, which in turn should account for the observed decrease in consumption of sweets associated with nicotine.

Energy Expenditure Nicotine administration (6 mg/kg/day or 12 mg/kg/day) increases the energy expenditure of rats, and cessation of nicotine administration reverses this increase (Grunberg & Raygada, 1991). However, these are relatively high doses. Studies in humans have found that the relatively small increases in metabolic rate caused by nicotine in individuals at rest are enhanced during light exercise (Perkins, Epstein, Marks, Stiller, & Jacob, 1989).

Summary of Nutritional and Consummatory Drive-Related Models Although the above-reviewed commonalities and interactions of smoking and nicotine to eating and appetitive mechanisms to each other and to negative affect is striking, there are a number of important divergences between negative affect and food and weight-gain mechanisms. The divergence is seen most clearly in smoking cessation studies in which the cessation response-time curves for negative affect and food craving differ dramatically. Although mean self-reported increases in negative affect subsequent to smoking abstinence return to baseline levels within 2 or 3 weeks, cessation-related increase in hunger is sustained for over a month, and possibly indefinitely. However, it is interesting that the urge to smoke also continues for years subsequent to cessation. Thus, the urge to smoke and increases in appetite may have more in common than do negative affect and increases in appetite.

SUMMARY AND CONCLUSIONS

Evidence has supported the view that a number of the mechanisms reviewed here contribute to nicotine's reinforcing and mood-modulating effects and that different mechanism's are relatively more important in some individuals than in others. There is also good reason to believe that a number of indirect and relatively more psychological mechanisms are required to provide a full account of nicotine's reinforcing effects. The fingertip control that smokers have over timing and dose allows a degree of psychobiological control and conditioning not found in other forms of substance use. Nicotine's multiple reinforcing effects appear to be in large part a function of the smoker's ability to modulate a number of different biological systems that have cholinergic receptors. In addition, nicotine's ability to act as a cholinergic agonist initially and in lower doses while acting as cholinergic antagonist in other conditions may mediate a number of its reinforcing effects (Rosecrans & Karan, 1993).

Chapter 9 reviews interactive and adaptive models of smoking reinforcement and affect modulation and concludes with the articulation of an integrative biopsychosocial STAR model. The STAR model builds on evidence that although a number of the mechanisms proposed in this chapter are operative in some individuals in some circumstances, a complete, accurate, and maximally useful model must articulate when and in whom what processes occur. Thus, Chapters 7 and 8 articulate individual differences in smoking and the effects of nicotine as a function of personality, psychopathology, and gender as a foundation for articulation and discussion of the STAR model in the final two chapters.

Personality, Psychopathology, Tobacco Use, and Individual Differences in Effects of Nicotine

Personality and psychopathology are predictors, in some cases very good ones, of smoking prevalence. In the United States, people with schizophrenia or alcoholism are approximately three times as likely to smoke as other U.S. citizens. Similarly, those experiencing frequent depression, anxiety, and other neurotic traits and disorders are roughly twice as likely to smoke as those without these traits. Moreover, there is reason to believe that the association of smoking with psychopathology is becoming stronger as smoking becomes less socially acceptable. This chapter first reviews evidence on how smoking is associated with psychopathology and personality and then evaluates genetic, biological, and psychological mechanisms that may mediate those relationships.

INDIVIDUAL DIFFERENCES AND TOBACCO USE

The major higher order personality dimensions are predictive of smoking prevalence. Each of the three super factors P-IUSS, N, and E, as well as a number of their component factors, correlate positively with probability of smoking (see Tables 7.1–7.6). Intelligence–education (IE) and general socioeconomic status are also linked (inversely) to smoking. Culture–openness (CO), conscientiousness, and agreeableness have received less attention than the other personality superfactors (see Chapter 4).

Table 7.1 Smoking's Relationship with Extraversion

Study	Association	Type
Cherry & Kiernan (1976)	+	pro
Seltzer & Oechsli (1985)	+	pro
Kellam, Ensminger, & Simon (1980)	+	pro
Sieber & Angst (1990)	+	pro
G. M. Smith (1970; 22 of 25 studies to 1969)	+	cro
Angst (1979)	+	cro
Brackenridge & Block (1972)	+	cro
Coan (1973)	+	cro
A. K. Gupta, Sethi, & Gupta	+	cro
Heath & Madden (1993)	+	cro
Jamison (1979)	+	cro
Kanekar & Dolke (1970)	+	cro
Koopmans, Boomsma, van Doornen, & Orlebeke (1993)	+	cro
K. R. Parks (1984)	+	cro
Patton, Barnes, & Murray (1993)	+	cro
Rae (1975)	+	cro
Rustin, Kittel, Dramaix, Kornitzer, & de Backer (1978)	+	cro
Spielberger & Jacobs (1982)	+	cro
Surawy & Cox (1987)	+	cro
Wijatkowski Forgays, Wrzesniewski, & Gorski (1990)	+	cro
Bass (1988)	0	cro
Breslau, Kilbey, & Andresk (in press)	0	cro
Floderus (1974)	0	cro
D. G. Gilbert (1988)	0	cro
Golding et al. (1983)	0	cro
Kassel, Shiffman, Gnys, Paty, & Zettler-Segal (in press)	0	cro
Lyvers, Boyd, & Maltzman (1987)	0	cro
McCrae et al. (1978)	0	cro
McManus & Weeks (1982)	0	cro
Powell, Stewart, & Grylls	0	cro
Stanaway & Watson (1981)	0	cro

Note. Plus signs = positive correlation; zeros = no significant association; pro = prospective study; cro = cross-sectional study.

Tables 7.1–7.8 summarize studies published subsequent to those reviewed in G. M. Smith's 1970 summary of the personality correlates of smoking. G. M. Smith found smokers to be more extraverted, neurotic (of poorer mental health), impulsive, and antisocial than nonsmokers. Studies subsequent to 1970 have generally supported and expanded on G. M. Smith's observations.

Extraversion

Extraversion was predictive of smoking in 22 of 25 studies through 1969 (G. M. Smith, 1970) and in a slight majority of studies subsequent to that time (see Table 7.1). Several more recent studies have failed to find smoker–nonsmoker differences in extraversion. It seems likely that as a group smokers have become less extraverted during the past 2 decades. In addition, the typical means of measuring extraversion has changed during this period of time. It appears that in contrast to earlier times, the current U.S. population of smokers is only slightly but not consistently more extraverted than nonsmokers.

Neuroticism

There is reason to believe that smoking's association with neuroticism and the neurotic–depressive disorders has grown stronger during recent decades in countries in which the overall prevalence of smoking has substantially decreased. Although Smith (1970) found only 24 of 49 comparisons showed neuroticism and poor mental health to be positively correlated with smoking, subsequent investigations have shown stronger and in some cases very high smoking prevalences among those with poor mental health (see Table 7.2). Recent investigations have consistently shown neuroticism to be predictive of smoking.

Most prospective studies found that high N assessed in childhood or early adolescence before smoking predicts smoking. For example, Cherry and Kiernan (1976) found high-N youth to have a 1.3 times larger odds ratio (65% vs. 50%) of smoking in their mid-20s. Moreover, Lerner and Vicary (1984) found that "difficult temperament" at age 5 was predictive of smoking in young adults. Other studies have found similar results (Kandel & Davies, 1986; Sieber & Angst, 1990). (Note: Although Kandel and Davies characterized their self-report scale as a measure of depression, results of their factor analysis indicate that it was also a measure of the broader construct of N.) In contrast to these studies, Seltzer and Oechsli (1985) found that a mother's rating of her child's neurotic behaviors at age 10 did not predict smoking approximately 8 years later. In conclusion, the aggregate of findings indicate that N is a risk factor for smoking that precedes the onset of smoking and the association in the United States between N and smoking appears to have grown stronger over the past 2 decades.

Depression and Major Depressive Disorder (MDD)

Depression's substantial association with smoking and failure to maintain smoking abstinence have generated a great deal of interest. In a prospective study, Kandel and Davies (1986) found the odds ratio of smoking to be 1.90 times greater in men and 1.47 times greater in women with a history of adolescent depression or neuroticism. Similarly, Breslau, Kilbey, and Andreski (1991) observed that after controlling for effects of other substances, individuals with nicotine dependence had higher rates of major depression (4.66 times) and anxiety disorders (4.18 times) than did controls. A number of cross-sectional studies have discovered higher odds ratios of smoking in individuals with major depressive disorder than in nonpsychiatric controls (see Table 7.3). For example, of persons with a history of major depressive disorder at some time in their lives,

Table 7.2 Smoking's Relationship with Neuroticism

Study	Association	Type
Cherry & Kiernan (1976)	+	pro
Kandel & Davies (1986; 57% neurotic men, 30% nonneurotic men, 50% neurotic women, and 34% nonneurotic women)[a]	+	pro
Lerner & Vicary (1984)	+	pro
Seltzer & Oechsli (1985)	0	pro
Seiber & Angst (1990)	+	pro
Smith (1970); 24 of 50 studies to 1969)	+	cro
Angst (1979)	+	cro
Breslau et al. (1994)	+	cro
Floderus (1974)	+	cro
A. K. Gupta et al. (1976)	+	cro
Heath & Madden (1993)	+	cro
Kanekar & Dolke (1970)	+	cro
Koopmans et al. (1993)	+	cro
McCrae et al. (1978)	+	cro
McManus & Weeks (1982)	+	cro
Patton et al. (1993; men and women)	+	cro
Powell et al. (1979)	+	cro
Rustin et al. (1978)	+	cro
Spielberger & Jacobs (1982)	+	cro
Stanaway & Watson (1981)	+	cro
Von Knorring & Oreland 91985)	+	cro
Waters (1971)	+	cro
Wijatkowski et al. (1990)	+	cro
Bass (1988)	0	cro
D. G. Gilbert (1988)	0	cro
Golding et al. (1983)	0	cro
Jamison (1979)	0	cro
Lyvers et al. (1987)	0	cro
K. R. Parks (1984; NxP and NxE)	0	cro
Rae (1975)	0	cro
Surawy & Cox (1987)	0	cro

Note. Plus signs = positive correlation; zeros = no significant association, pro = prospective study, cro = cross-sectional study; NxP = interaction of N and P NxE = interaction of N and E.
[a]This study is also reported in the Depression Section. See text for a full description.

Glassman et al. (1990) found 74% had a history of regular smoking as compared with only 53% of those without a psychiatric history. Moreover, Breslau, Kilbey, and Andreski (1993a) found that individuals with a history of nicotine dependence were more likely to experience the first incidence of major depressive disorder during a 14-month prospective study. Also noteworthy, Covey et al. (1990) found that the frequency and intensity of smoking withdrawal symptoms, especially depressive mood, were higher in smokers with a history of major depressive disorder.

Psychometrically assessed depression is also consistently higher in smokers than in nonsmokers (Table 7.3). Covey and Tam (1990) found questionnaire-

Table 7.3   Smoking's Relationship with Depression

Study	Association	Type
Continuous-dimension-assessed depressive traits		
Anda et al. (1990; 56% depressed men, 41% nondepressed men, 44% depressed women, and 32% nondepressed women)	+	cro
Covey & Tam (1990; odds ratio of depression = 3.86, odds ratio of controls = 1.0)	+	cro
Kandel & Davies (1986; 57% depressed men, 30% nondepressed men, 50% depressed women, and 34% nondepressed females)	+	pro
Brook et al. (1983; adolescent boys)	+	cro
Brook et al. (1987; adolescent girls)	0	cro
Leon et al. (1979)	+	cro
Perez-Stable et al. (1990; nonsmoker controls = 1.0, odds ratio former smokers = 1.1, and odds ratio with current smokers = 1.7)	+	cro
Schubert (1965)	0	cro
Stefanis & Kokkevi (1986)		cro
Women	+	
Men	0	
Waal-Maning, de Hammel (1978)	+	cro
Wang (1994), Fitzhugh, Westerfield, & Eddy	+	cro
Categorical major depressive disorder		
Breslau et al. (1991; odds ratio with mild nicotine dependence = 1.86, odds ratio with moderate nicotine dependence = 4.66)	+	cro
Breslau et al. (1993a; odds ratio with nicotine dependence = 2.89)	+	pro
Cohen, Schwartz, Bromet, & Parkinson (1991)	+	cro
Covey et al. (1990; history present: psychological abstinence symptoms, especially depressed mood, more intense; history absent: psychological symptoms less intense and little depressed affect)	+	cro
Covey & Tam (1990; depressive disorder, 53% prevalence controls, 32% prevalence)	+	cro
Glassman et al. (1990; depressive disorder, 74% ever smoked; no psychiatric problem, 53% ever smoked)	+	cro
Hughes, Hatsukemi, Mitchell, & Dahlgren et al. (1986; 49% smokers depressed, 30% controls depressed)	+	cro
Kendler et al. (1993; odds ratio ever smoking given lifetime major depressive disorder = 1.48, odds ratio of major depressive disorder given ever smoker = 1.60)	+	cro

Note. Plus signs = positive correlation; zeros = no significant association; pro = prospective study; cro = cross-sectional study.

assessed depression and worry to be higher and life satisfaction lower in smoking than in nonsmoking 11th graders. Smokers were 3.9 times more likely to be above the group mean than nonsmokers. A number of other studies have reported similar outcomes (Anda et al., 1990; Covey & Tam, 1990; Kandel & Davies, 1986; Kendler et al., 1993; Leon, Kolotkin, & Korgeski, 1979; Perez-Stable, Marin, Marin, & Katz, 1990; Stefanis & Kokkevi, 1986; Waal-Manning & de Hammel, 1978). Consistent with the strong association of depression with smoking, individuals who commit suicide are much more likely to be smokers (Cederlof, Friberg, & Lundman, 1977).

Anxiety and Anxiety Disorders

High trait anxiety and anxiety disorders are higher in smokers than in nonsmokers (see Table 7.4). A Detroit study of young adults found that those who smoked were 4.18 times more likely to have an anxiety disorder than were nonsmokers (Breslau et al., 1991). A 47% prevalence of smoking was found in an inpatient sample diagnosed with anxiety disorders, relative to 30% in controls (Hughes, Hatsukami, Mitchell, et al., 1986). Also, women with panic disorder had a significantly higher smoking prevalence than controls, but no differences were observed between men with panic disorder and their controls (Pohl, Yeragani, Balon, Lycaki, & McBride, 1992).

Measures of trait anxiety level have been significantly higher in smokers than in nonsmokers in a number of studies (Angst, 1979; Matarazzo & Saslow, 1960; McCrae, Costa, & Bosse, 1978; Spielberger & Jacobs, 1982 [women only]; Waal-Manning & de Hammel, 1978), but not in others (D. G. Gilbert, 1988; Schubert, 1965; Seltzer & Oechsli, 1985). Surprisingly, one investigation found trait anxiety to be higher in nonsmoking than in smoking men (Spielberger & Jacobs, 1982).

In summary, the aggregate of studies suggest a small to moderate association between smoking and increased trait anxiety. At very high levels of anxiety, such as those associated with clinical anxiety disorders, the probability of smoking is approximately 50% higher than that of the general U.S. population. Furthermore, among heavy smokers the prevalence of anxiety disorders is approximately four times that of nonsmokers.

Anger and Hostility

Anger and hostility are components of higher order N and another higher order factor, P-IUSS. The differences between N anger and hostility and P-IUSS anger and hostility is that the latter is more likely to be expressed and the former merely felt (Spielberger, 1986). A number of investigations have observed higher trait anger and hostility scores in smokers than in nonsmokers (Angst, 1979; D. G. Gilbert, 1988; Pritchard & Kay, 1993; Scherwitz & Rugulies, 1992; Seltzer & Oechsli, 1985; Thomas, 1960, 1973), but some have failed to find such differ-

Table 7.4   Smoking's Relationship with Anxiety

Study	Association	Type
Continuous—dimension-assessed anxiety traits		
Seltzer & Oechsli (1985)	0	pro
Angst (1979)	+	cro
Brackenridge & Bloch (1972)	0	cro
Brook et al. (1983; adolescent boy)	0	cro
Brook et al. (1987; adolescent girl)	+	cro
Koopmans et al. (1993)	+	cro
McCrae et al. (1978)	+	cro
Matarazzo & Saslow (1960)	+	cro
Pritchard & Kay (1993)	+	cro
Schneider & Houston (1970)	+	cro
Schubert (1965)	0	cro
Spielberger & Jacobs (1982; men and women)	0	cro
Tilley (1987)	+	cro
Waal-Manning & de Hamel (1978)	+	cro
S. G. Williams, Houston, & Redd (1982)	+	cro
D. G. Gilbert (1988)	0	cro
Categorical anxiety disorder		
Breslau et al. (1991; any DSM–III anxiety disorder: odds ratio with mild nicotine dependence = 1.46, odds ratio with moderate nicotine dependence = 4.18)	+	cro
Cohen et al. (1991)	0	cro
Hughes, Hatsukami, Mitchell, & Dahlgren et al. (1986; 47% anxiety disturbance, 30% controls)	+	cro
Pohl et al. (1992; panic disorder, 54% prev; controls, 35% prev)		cro
men	0	
women	+	
Sleep disturbance		
Seltzer & Oechsli (1985)	+	pro

Note. Plus signs = positive correlation; zeros = no significant association; pro = prospective study; cro = cross-sectional study.

ences (Muller, 1992; Witt, Kaelin, & Stoner, 1988). Thus, it appears that trait anger and hostility is somewhat higher in smokers, but the size and robustness of these differences have not been adequately characterized (see Table 7.5).

P-IUSS

P is a higher order personality dimension whose facets include impulsivity, sensation seeking, cynicism, tough-mindedness, disagreeableness, aggressiveness, coldness, antisocial attitudes, low conscientiousness, and unempathic responses (H. J. Eysenck, 1992c). P is consistently higher in smokers than in nonsmokers, and the prevalence of smoking among individuals high in P-IUSS

Table 7.5   Smoking's Relationship with Hostility and Anger

Study	Association	Type
Seltzer & Oechsli (1985)	+	pro
Angst (1979)	+	cro
D. G. Gilbert (1988)		cro
women	+	
men	0	
Koopmans et al. (1993)	+	cro
Pritchard & Kay (1993)	+	cro
Scherwitz & Rugulies (1992)	+	cro
Thomas (1960)	+	cro
Thomas (1973)	+	cro
Muller (1992, Study 1)	0	cro
Witt et al. (1988)	0	cro

Note. Plus signs = positive correlation; zeros = no significant association; pro = prospective study; cro = cross-sectional study.

is much higher than in the general population. Pritchard (1991b) has interpreted P as primarily reflecting impulsiveness and cynicism, whereas H. J. Eysenck and Eysenck (1976) used the term *tough-mindedness* to characterize this dimension but saw extremes as being associated with psychotic processes (see Chapter 4). As reviewed in Table 7.6, P was significantly higher in smokers than in nonsmokers in all but one of the studies. Facets of P—specifically measures of sensation seeking, impulsivity, and antisocial behavior—have also consistently differentiated smokers from nonsmokers.

Schizophrenic Disorders

In the United States, those with schizophrenia have consistently been found to have a nearly three times higher prevalence of smoking than the general population (see Table 7.7). Schizophrenics, like other individuals with higher prevalence of smoking, are also more prone to illicit drug use and alcohol abuse.

Drug and Alcohol Use and Abuse

In the United States and Great Britain, 90% or more of alcoholic individuals smoked during the 1970s and early 1980s (Golding, Harpur, & Brent-Smith, 1983; Istvan & Matarazzo, 1984), compared with about 30-35% of the general adult U.S. nonalcoholic population. The consistent association of smoking with other legal and illicit drugs (Breslau et al., 1991; Golding et al., 1983) suggests that in many cases substance use results in large part from common causes (T. N. Robinson et al., 1987). In a large sample of young adults in the Detroit area, Breslau et al. (1991) found the prevalence of cocaine dependence to be 9.7 times greater, cannabis 3.8 times greater, other drugs 6.7 times greater, and alcohol dependence 3.2 times greater in individuals with moderate nicotine dependence than in controls. The

Table 7.6 Smoking's Relationship with Psychoticism and its Component Facets

Study	Association	Type
Psychioticism		
Seltzer & Oechsli (1985)	+	cro
Bass (1988)	+	cro
Eaven (1989)	+	cro
D. G. Gilbert (1988)	+	cro
Golding et al. (1983)	+	cro
Jamison (1979)	+	cro
Lyvers et al. (1987)	+	cro
K. R. Parks (1984)	+	cro
Patton et al. (1993)	+	cro
Powell et al. (1979)	+	cro
Spielberger & Jacobs (1982)	+	cro
Stanaway & Watson (1981)	+	cro
Surawy & Cox (1987)	+	cro
Breslau et al. (in press)	0	cro
Impulsivity–self-control		
G. H. Smith (1970; 7 of 10 studies to 1969)	+	cro
Brook et al. (1981; adolescent boys)	+	cro
Brook et al. (1983; adolescent boys)	+	cro
Brook et al. (1987; adolescent girls)	+	cro
Chassin, Presson, & Sherman (1989)	+	cro
Geist & Herrmann (1990)	+	cro
Kassel et al. (in press)	+	cro
Sensation seeking		
Brook et al. (1983; adolescent boys)	0	cro
Brook et al. (1987; adolescent girls)	+	cro
Chassin et al. (1989)	+	cro
Golding et al. (1983)	+	cro
Heath & Madden (1993)	+	cro
Kassel et al. (in press)	+	cro
Kohn & Annis (1977)	+	cro
Koopmans et al. (193)	+	cro
Schubert (1965)	+	cro
von Knorring & Oreland (1985)	+	cro
Zuckerman, Ball, & Black (1990)	+	cro
Stanaway & Watson (1981)	0	cro
Antisocial		
G. M. Smith (1970; 27 of 32 studies to 1969)	0	cro
Kellam et al. (1980)	+	pro
Seltzer & Oechsli (1985)	+	pro

(Table continued on next page)

Table 7.6   Smoking's Relationship with Psychoticism and its Component Facets *(Continued)*

Study	Association	Type
Aggressiveness		
Brook et al. (1981; adolescent boys)	+	cro
Brook et al. (1987; adolescent girls)	+	cro
Kellam et al. (1980)	+	pro
Muller (1992)	0	cro
Disagreeableness–rebelliousness		
Brook et al. (1981; adolescent boys)	–	cro
Brook et al. (1983; adolescent boys)	+	cro
Brook et al. (1987; adolescent girls)	+	cro
Conscientiousness–deviance		
Brook et al. (1981; adolescent boys)	–	cro
Brook et al. (1983; adolescent boys)	–	cro
Brook et al. (1987; adolescent girls)	–	cro
Chassin et al. (1989)	+	cro

Note. Plus signs = positive correlation; minus signs = negative correlation; zeros = no significant association; pro = prospective study; cro = cross-sectional study.

tendency for users of one drug to use other drugs may have its origin in the association of high psychoticism and sensation seeking with drug use (Golding et al., 1983). The numerous studies demonstrating smoking's association with a substantially increased prevalence of other drug use are reviewed by a number of authors (Golding et al., 1983; Henningfield, Clayton, & Pollin, 1990).

Socioeconomic Status

Education and economic status are consistently lower in smokers than in nonsmokers (Adler et al., 1994; Marmot et al., 1991; McGee & Newcomb, 1992; Pierce, Fiore, Novotny, Hatziandreau, & Davis, 1989). In the United States, a negative association between smoking and education is growing stronger as individuals higher in education continue to quit smoking at a more rapid rate

Table 7.7   Smoking's Relationship with Schizophrenic Disorder

Study	Association	Type
Goff et al. (1992, 74% schizophrenics)	+	cro
Hughes, Hatsukami, Mitchell, & Dahlgren et al. (1986; 88% schizophrenics, 30% controls)	+	cro
Masterson & O'Shea (1984)	+	cro
O'Farrell, Connors, & Upper (1983; 88% schizophrenics)	+	cro

Note. Plus signs = positive correlation; cro = cross-sectional study.

than others (Pierce et al., 1989; USDHHS, 1988). More generally, socioeconomic status is a strong predictor of smoking and drug use (Marmot et al., 1991).

Individual Differences in Social Environment

A wide range of dysfunctional interpersonal problems in family and social environments correlate with prevalence of smoking (see Table 7.8). Parental smoking and alcohol and drug use; uninvolved, unsupportive, and conflicted parent–child relationships; and poor parental psychological adjustment are all predictive of child smoking behavior (Brook, Gordon, & Brook, 1987; Brook, Whiteman, & Gordon, 1981; Brook, Whiteman, Gordon, & Brook, 1983). Peer smoking predicts smoking; for example, the more one's peers smoke, the more likely one is to smoke (Chassin, Presson, Sherman, Corty, & Olshavsky, 1984).

Summary of Smoking and Individual Difference Associations

Findings reviewed above indicate that psychiatric disorders, as well as the higher order personality dimensions and their constituent facets, differentiate smokers from nonsmokers. Smokers differed most reliably on the P and related trait categories (impulsivity, antisocial behavior, sensation seeking, and aggression). N and its component factors, especially depression and anxiety, reliably predict smoking prevalence. The relationship between E and smoking is relatively weak and has not been consistently demonstrated in studies during the past decade. Extraversion may distinguish smokers from nonsmokers only in certain cohorts (e.g., among older smokers). Education, intelligence, and socioeconomic status are reliably inversely associated with smoking in the United States. The relationship of openness and culture to smoking has not been adequately assessed. The same individual differences in personality and psychopathology that are predictive of smoking are also predictive of use of other drugs (Bukstein, Brent, & Kaminer, 1989; Golding et al., 1983; T. N. Robinson et al., 1987). In addition, use of licit and illicit drugs is predictive of smoking (Biglan, Weissman, & Severson, 1985; Breslau et al., 1991). Thus, it appears that use of a variety of different psychoactive substances results from a common set of processes related to individual differences in personality, psychopathology, socioeconomic status, and past and current environments.

The fact that prospective studies have found associations between anxious, depressive, aggressive, and generally neurotic personality traits in childhood and smoking later in life supports the view that major personality and temperamental traits precede and contribute to the initiation and maintenance of smoking. There is, however, no strong evidence that smoking attenuates or promotes changes in personality, temperament, or psychopathology. Prospective and genetic studies assessing illegal drug use and smoking have indicated that early personality traits influence subsequent drug use, rather than the reverse (Kendler et al., 1993;

Table 7.8 Smoking's Relationship with Family and Social Environment

Study	Association	Type
Brook et al. (1981; adolescent boys)		cro
Maternal smoking	0	
Maternal expectations	−	
Maternal deviance rejection	−	
Maternal educational expectations for her son	−	
Maternal warmth	−	
Maternal identification	−	
Brook et al. (1983; adolescent boys)		cro
Paternal smoking	0	
Paternal impulsivity	+	
Paternal interpersonal difficulty	+	
Paternal masculinity	+	
Paternal attitudes to smoking	+	
Paternal affection	−	
Paternal child-centeredness	−	
Paternal communication	−	
Paternal identification	−	
Paternal time with son	−	
Paternal support	−	
Brook et al. (1987; adolescent girls)		cro
Paternal smoking	+	
Paternal attitudes toward smoking	+	
Paternal alcohol use	+	
Paternal cocaine use	+	
Paternal tolerance of daughter's smoking and marijuana use	+	
Paternal communication	−	
Paternal time with daughter	−	
Spielberger et al. (1983)		cro
Maternal or paternal smoking (female odds ratio = 1.53, male odds ratio = 1.52)	+	
Both parents smoked (female odds ratio = 1.39, male odds ratio = 1.21)	+	
Brother or sister smoked (female odds ratio = 2.03, male odds ratio = 1.68)	+	
Brother and sister smoked (female odds ratio = 2.45, male odds ratio = 1.96)	+	

Note. Plus signs = positive correlation;. zeros = No significant association; cro = cross-sectional study.

Stein, Newcomb, & Bentler, 1987). As in the case of smoking, the association between depression and the full range of licit and illicit drug use has long been noted (Stefanis & Kokkevi, 1986).

Individual differences in family and social environment correlated with and appear to have a causal influence on prevalence of smoking. Parental smoking and alcohol and drug use; uninvolved, unsupportive, and conflicted parent–child relationships; and poor parental psychological adjustment all predict child smoking. Similarly, peer smoking, peer and own drug and alcohol use, and nontraditional attitudes and behavior—including low religiosity, low academic orientation, rebelliousness, and disregard for the law—are predictive of smoking (McGee & Newcomb, 1992). Generally, deviant behavior is most typical of individuals scoring high in psychoticism and low in intellectual and economic attainment, but it has little correlation with neuroticism and extraversion.

MECHANISMS AND CAUSAL PATHWAYS UNDERLYING TOBACCO'S ASSOCIATION WITH PERSONALITY, PSYCHOPATHOLOGY, AND NICOTINE REINFORCEMENT

A variety of mechanisms may account for the associations of personality dimensions and psychological disorders with smoking prevalence, motivation, withdrawal responses, and relapse. Hypothesized general mechanisms include (a) genetic linkage of predisposing genes, (b) a common predisposition (e.g., emotional lability, low self-esteem, or stressful environment), (c) self-medication, (d) selective quitting, and (e) linkage of smoking to changes in personality and to psychopathology (H. J. Eysenck, 1980; Meyer, 1986; Hughes, 1986). The following discussion first evaluates the literature showing a genetic basis for smoking. It then discusses general, cross-dimensional, mechanisms and finally examines the mechanisms mediating smoking associations with specific dimensions of personality and psychopathology.

Genetics of Smoking and Its Correlates

Genetic Evidence   Twin studies have consistently indicated a substantial genetic, as well as environmental, contribution to smoking (Carmelli, Swan, Robinette, & Fabsitz, 1990, 1992; Eaves & Eysenck, 1980; H. J. Eysenck, 1980; Gynther, Hewitt, Heath, & Eaves, 1993; Hannah, Hopper, & Mathews, 1985; Hughes, 1986; Kaprio et al., 1982; Kendler et al., 1993; Madden et al., 1993; Pederson, 1981). For example, the pharmacological factor of Russell's Motives for Smoking Questionnaire has high heritability (h^2 = .48; Gynther et al., 1993), suggesting that this smoking motivation is largely genetically influenced. However, the fact that self-report indexes of nicotine dependence correlate with N (D. G. Gilbert, Meliska, et al., 1994; Masson & Gilbert, 1990) indicates that such genetic influences may be mediated by N or one of its facets.

One of the facets of N that has been found to be related to smoking generally, including the genetics of smoking, is depression. Using the cotwin control method, Kendler et al. (1993) assessed 1,566 female twins for lifetime daily cigarette consumption and for prospective 1-year prevalence of major depressive disorder. The best fitting model was one in which lifetime smoking and lifetime major depressive disorder resulted solely from common genes that predispose one to both depression and smoking. The Kendler et al. analyses revealed no evidence that depression caused smoking or smoking caused depression. There is reason to believe that N and its associated mechanisms mediate some of these common genetic influences. N exists before the onset of both smoking and depressive disorders (M. Martin, 1985). Thus, although depression did not appear to lead to smoking in the Kendler et al. sample, N may lead to smoking and high-N smokers may smoke more often for various N-related forms of negative affect, including depression, anxiety, and anger. Findings showing N, E, and P-IUSS to account for some (Eaves & Eysenck, 1980; H. J. Eysenck, 1980) and possibly half (Heath & Madden, in press) of the genetic determination of smoking support the view that N mediates some of the common genetic influence leading to both smoking and depression. Nonetheless, these three higher order personality traits leave a substantial portion of the genetics of smoking unaccounted for. Other genetically influenced psychological factors contributing to this association may include other personality factors and socioeconomic, educational, and intellectual factors. It seems very likely that the Socioeconomic Status–Education–Intelligence factor is responsible for a substantial portion of the genetics of smoking, given the strong genetic contribution to this factor and its strong inverse association with smoking. Unfortunately, the inclusion of measures of personality, psychopathology, and socioeconomic status–education–intelligence in studies of the genetics of smoking have been the exception rather than the rule. Individual differences in basic nicotine responsivity and sensitivity may also contribute to the genetics of smoking. These and other possible biological expressions of the genetics of smoking are discussed below.

Biological Expression of Genetic Differences Kendler et al.'s (1993) modeling of the causal and genetic relationship between depression and smoking is general enough to be consistent with a variety of common psychobiological pathways to smoking and depression. Genetically based individual differences in neurobiological structures result in individual differences in psychological and biological responses to nicotine. There are probably important genetically based individual differences in (a) rewarding or positively reinforcing effects of nicotine (possibly mediated by individual differences in mesolimbic dopaminergic-related biological structures); (b) aversive effects of nicotine; (c) nicotine distribution kinetics; (d) social-emotional and intellectual competence and temperament that predispose one toward or away from risk taking, sensation seeking, social alienation versus conventionality; and (e) individual differences in biological structures that mediate both personality dimensions and psychopathology and physiological and subjective responses to nicotine. Although there has been little research in this area, arguments in favor of the first three of the above differences have been made in recent reviews (O. F. Pomerleau, Collins, Shiffman, & Pomerleau, 1993; Rosecrans & Karan,

1993; Shiffman, 1989). Mechanisms that may mediate individual differences in these sensitivities are discussed later in this chapter.

Mechanisms Common to Multiple Dimensions and Pathologies

Psychological Resource and Self-Medication Model   The psychological resource model proposes that smokers as a group have a variety of motives for smoking and that smoking can provide a number of different situation and person-specific psychological benefits (Stepney, 1982; Warburton et al., 1988; Warburton, Wesnes, & Revell, 1983; Wills, 1985). On one occasion, an individual experiencing acute negative affect may smoke to reduce subjective distress. On another occasion, the same individual may feel drowsy and smoke to become more stimulated or to focus his or her attention to complete an important task. In other situations, impulsive individuals may smoke to reduce impulsivity and thereby increase rewards associated with restraint and minimize punishment associated with impulsivity (Pritchard, 1991b). If smoking is used as a psychological resource or coping mechanism, individuals with poor coping skills or with high degrees of chronic stress would be expected to have a higher prevalence of smoking. Consistent with the self-medication component of the psychological resource model, individuals predisposed toward various forms of affective, cognitive, and behavioral dysfunction are more likely to smoke. According to this model, they have stronger motives for smoking because they need to supplement their minimal psychological resources with those provided by smoking. Also supporting this model, smokers tend to smoke more during stressful situations (L. Epstein & Collins, 1977; Rose et al., 1983; Schachter, Silverstein, & Perlick, 1977), and those attempting to quit smoking tend to relapse during stressful situations, even months after withdrawal symptoms have subsided (Shiffman, 1986).

Selective Quitting: Attempts and Relapse   To the degree that a given personality dimension or psychological disorder is associated with a lower than normal success rate in quitting smoking permanently, the residual group of smokers will contain a higher proportion of individuals with that personality or psychopathology. Thus, groups with high relapse and low cessation attempt rates would be expected to have higher prevalences of smoking. This generally is the case. Both prevalence of smoking and probability of smoking relapse are greater in individuals scoring high on depression (Anda et al., 1990; Covey et al., 1990; Glassman et al., 1990; Kandel & Davies, 1986), N (Cherry & Kiernan, 1978; Guilford, 1966; Table 7.2), and perceived stress (M. P. Carey, Kalra, Carey, Halperin, & Richards, 1993). Although smoking cessation attempts and relapse rates have not been adequately characterized for schizophrenia, for most neurotic and personality disorders prevalences are high, and the characteristics of these groups lead one to predict that they have both lower rates of cessation initiation and higher relapse rates. In the single study assessing the relationship of psychoticism to success in giving up smoking, high P was associated with less success in quitting permanently (McManus & Weeks, 1982).

Negative affect appears to be an important common denominator underlying the high prevalence of smoking among those high in psychopathology. Negative affect was the only variable predictive of smoking status at 1 year after cessation in a study by O. F. Pomerleau et al. (1978). Only 26% of negative affect smokers were abstinent at 1 year, compared with 50% of those who were other types of smokers. In another study, high levels of negative affect during each of two assessments predicted relapse (S. M. Hall et al., 1983). Seventy-one percent of callers to a hot line for smokers who had relapsed or feared they might reported that their relapse crisis was preceded by negative affect (Shiffman, 1982). Furthermore, a number of studies have found negative affect to be predictive of acute relapse episodes (Lichtenstein, Antonuccio, & Rainwater, 1977; Marlatt & Gordon, 1980). The failure of some studies to observe a relationship between prospectively assessed negative affect and relapse to smoking may be due to their failure to assess negative affect frequently enough and immediately before relapse (S. M. Hall et al., 1990).

Overall, these findings are consistent with the hypothesis that selective relapse accounts for some of the smoking—negative affect/psychopathology association. However, it cannot account for all of this association as personality in children and adolescents is predictive of lifetime history of taking up the smoking habit.

Smoking Contributes to Personality and to Psychopathology   The fact that prospective longitudinal and genetic studies demonstrate a causal influence of genetics and personality on the disposition to smoke does not rule out the possibility that some of the smoking–personality/psychopathology relationship is caused directly or indirectly by smoking. Smoking and nicotine use might promote psychopathology by (a) fixation at a pharmacological coping level without development of alternative coping mechanisms, (b) alteration of biological mechanisms mediating personality and psychopathology, and (c) indirect, physical-disease-related distress. Evidence related to the smoking-causes-psychopathology hypothesis is very limited. Kendler et al.'s (1993) twin study failed to support the view that smoking causes depression. However, one can assume that individuals with major health problems related to smoking are not represented in most samples assessing potential causal relationships between smoking and psychopathology.

Nicotine Reinforcement Sensitivity   Biologically based individual differences in sensitivity or response to nicotine may help explain why some individuals do not continue to smoke after initial experimentation, others become heavily dependent, and some smoke lightly for years without becoming dependent (O. F. Pomerleau, Collins, et al., 1993; Rosecrans & Karan, 1993; Shiffman,

1989). On the basis of limited but relevant findings, O. F. Pomerleau, Collins, et al. (1993) hypothesized that vulnerability to nicotine dependence is related to high initial sensitivity to nicotine. The Pomerleau et al. model might best be characterized as a generalized nicotine sensitivity dimension or factor. Although it is likely that such a general dimension exists, there are almost certainly a number of somewhat independent factors that describe individual differences in nicotine sensitivity and responsivity. It is reasonable to postulate that there are a relatively small number of genetically influenced basic biological sensitivities and responsivities that relate to nicotinic cholinergic receptor number and type. Moreover, some of these individual differences are likely to contribute to basic dimensions of personality and psychopathology. Other individual differences in response to nicotine may be much less direct, yet nonetheless genetically influenced, and important determinants of nicotine's potential to act as a reinforcer. Some of these differences are related to variations in genetically influenced personality traits.

Nicotine response magnitude has been found to relate to personality and psychopathology in several studies. As noted earlier, neuroticism and depression have previously found to be associated with relatively attenuated EEG, hormonal, and subjective responses to nicotine even when nicotine dose and habitual nicotine intake are controlled (D. G. Gilbert & Meliska, 1992; Gilbert, Gehlbach, et al., 1994; D. G. Gilbert, Meliska, et al., 1994; Golding, 1988; Masson & Gilbert, 1990). Because depressed and neurotic individuals have very high prevalences of smoking and of nicotine dependence, this attenuated response of neurotic and depressive individuals appears contrary to the hypothesis that those prone to becoming dependent smokers are especially sensitive to nicotine's effects. Nonetheless, dimensions of personality and psychopathology would be expected to relate to nicotine response and sensitivity for a number of reasons, many of which are discussed in the following discussions of mechanisms mediating the associations of smoking with specific individual differences.

Mechanisms Mediating Smoking Associations with Specific Individual Differences

E *Reported Reasons for Smoking*   Unlike the other major personality dimensions, E has not been consistently related to specific reasons for smoking. Spielberger (1986) observed very small but statistically significant correlations between E and social–sensory motivations in men and negative correlations of E with anxiety, restful–relaxing, and automatic or habitual smoking in women. O'Connor (1980) found that high E scorers on his attentional factor smoked less, suggesting that introverts are more likely than extraverts to smoke during selective attention tasks. D. G. Gilbert (1980) found that extraverts reported smoking relatively more for stimulation than for tranquilization, but only on some measures. Knott (1979) found that high-arousal smokers were significantly more extraverted and neurotic than low-arousal smokers. In contrast, Bartol (1975) found extraverted female smokers to prefer smoking in stressful situations, whereas introverts preferred smoking in nonstressful conditions. These mixed findings led D. G. Williams et al. (1984) to conclude that questionnaires viewing stress and arousal as a single construct fail to discriminate between sedative and stimulant smokers. That is, sedative smokers smoke to reduce negative affect that may be either high or low in arousal, and stimulant smokers smoke to enhance arousal but are not influenced highly by negative affect. Adequate characterization of E's relationship to smoking motivation will require careful articulation of types of negative-affect- and arousal-related situations, as well as detailed characterization of positive and depressed affect.

Arousal Modulation   The relation of E to smoking was seen by H. J. Eysenck (1973) as a result of differential effects of nicotine on cortical arousal in extraverted people relative to introverted people. He hypothesized that extraverts have a biologically based tendency toward low cortical arousal, whereas introverts have a tendency toward high CNS arousal. Thus, extraverts are more often below their hedonically ideal level of cortical arousal, and introverts are relatively more often higher than their ideal level. The CNS stimulant effects of nicotine obtained during most nonstressful conditions were seen by H. J. Eysenck to result in a more hedonically pleasing level of arousal that is sought by extraverts as a major source of reinforcement. Under similar environmental conditions, introverts would more often be at or near their ideal level of arousal and thus would be less likely to benefit from nicotine's stimulant effects.

Given their putative tendency toward heightened arousal and arousability, introverted people are hypothesized by H. J. Eysenck (1973) to benefit more from nicotine's putative ability to reduce cortical arousal when arousal is high (D. G. Gilbert, Robinson, et al., 1989; Golding & Mangan, 1982). To the extent that extraverts are more often underaroused than introverts are overaroused, smoking would be expected to be more rewarding in extraverts and thus more prevalent.

H. J. Eysenck's (1973) model of smoking and extraversion appreciates the importance of both individual difference factors (extraversion) and environmental factors (outside stimulation, drug effects, etc.) in determining the effects of smoking and nicotine. H. J. Eysenck's hypothesis that individuals use smoking for stimulation when underaroused but for reduction of arousal when overaroused is a psychological tool–resource model of smoking motivation (Stepney, 1982; Warburton et al., 1988). As noted in Chapter 6, evidence provides mixed support for the hypothesis that nicotine's effects on cortical arousal vary in an inverted-U-shaped manner as a function of predose cortical arousal.

Nicotine's promotion of psychomotor engagement and approach behavior may be relatively more rewarding to extraverted than to introverted people because of their social competence and enjoyment of social and environmental interactions. Surawy and Cox (1987) found that smokers who reporting smoking primarily for stimulation were more extraverted than others and smoked more in social situations.

Dose-Dependent Effects of Nicotine Biphasic, dose-dependent effects of nicotine have been established for cell membranes when very large dose ranges are used. Small doses of nicotine stimulate, and large doses (generally in excess of normal smoking doses) have depressant effects on nervous system functioning (Ochoa, Li, & McNeamee, 1992). High doses of nicotine associated with rapid smoking cause a different set of physiological and subjective effects than do doses associated with normal smoking (Gilbert, Meliska, Williams, & Jensen, 1992), yet these effects appear to be correlated with nicotine-induced distress rather than simply with desired tranquilizing effects. The limited number of studies assessing dose-response functions makes any inferences of a biphasic nicotine dose-response curve within the normal smoking-dose range premature (O'Connor, 1989). Ashton, Millman, Rawlins, Telford, and Thompson (1978) reported finding a biphasic dose-response curve for electrocortical activity in humans administered nicotine, but replication of this study is needed.

Differential Effects of Smoking or Nicotine in Extraverts. There is some support for nicotine's having more electrocortical stimulant effects in extraverts but sedative effects in introverts in moderately stimulating environments (Ashton et al., 1974; H. J. Eysenck & O'Connor, 1979; D. G. Gilbert, Meliska, et al., 1994). However, the fact that several studies have failed to find such effects (e.g., Binnie & Comer, 1978; D. G. Gilbert, Robinson, et al., 1989) suggests that there is no cross-situationally robust effect mediating extravert-introvert differences in smoking prevalence. Extraverts, relative to introverts, exhibit larger increases in electrodermal levels and responses following caffeine (B. D. Smith et al., 1983) and smoking (D. G. Gilbert & Hagen, 1985). Extraverts, relative to introverts, have also been found to respond with larger cortisol, EEG, and subjective responses to quantified doses of nicotine (D. G. Gilbert, Meliska, et al., 1994). Thus, extraverts may be more likely to take up and maintain smoking because they are more sensitive to nicotine and its reinforcing effects than are introverts (O. F. Pomerleau, Collins, et al., 1993). Because extraverts are relatively more sensitive to reinforcement than introverts, they would be expected to be especially sensitive to the positive reinforcing effects of nicotine.

In extraverts, smoking a single cigarette increased the right-hemisphere EEG activation more than it did left-hemisphere EEG activation, whereas the left hemisphere was relatively more activated by smoking in introverts (D. G. Gilbert, 1987). To the extent that the introverts' left hemisphere is relatively activated by nicotine, smoking might promote left-hemisphere-based approach behaviors and positive affect (Davidson, 1984; Tucker & Williamson, 1984). O'Connor's (1982) finding that smoking differentially modulated motor readiness and motor processing in extraverts and introverts and of parallel electrocortical differences supports the hypothesis of lateralized and localized differences in response to smoking as a function of E.

N and Neurotic Disorders   To the degree that nicotine reduces emotionality or negative affect, smoking would be expected to be more reinforcing in neurotic than in stable individuals (H. J. Eysenck, 1973, 1980). N is characterized by high frequencies and intensities of negative affect, thereby offering numerous opportunities for negative affect reduction by smoking. Moreover, H. J. Eysenck saw smoking as a form of self-medication resulting from nicotine's ability to reduce cortical arousal and thereby reduce negative affect during periods of high stress. As noted earlier, the evidence testing this hypothesis is limited and mixed.

N and Reported Reasons for Smoking   Studies assessing the association of N to smoking motivation show that N correlates with smoking for stress or negative affect relief (Knott, 1979; McManus & Weeks, 1982; O'Connor, 1980; Spielberger, 1986; Surawy & Cox, 1987). Interestingly, studies have also suggested a weaker but also positive correlation between N and self-reported smoking for stimulation (McManus & Weeks, 1982; O'Connor, 1980). Neurotic individuals may have inefficient homeostatic self-regulatory mechanisms for affect and arousal modulation and thus use smoking to facilitate homeostasis.

Differential Effects of Smoking or Nicotine in Neurotics   Individuals high in N have been found to exhibit smaller or less stimulating responses to nicotine than those low in N. D. G. Gilbert, Meliska, et al. (1994) found N to correlate negatively with cortisol, EEG, and subjective responses to a quantified dose of nicotine even after controlling for habitual nicotine intake. Neurotic individuals tended to exhibit relatively smaller stimulant, and in some cases sedativelike, EEG deactivating effects in response to smoking. Similarly, Golding (1988) observed a negative correlation between N and smoking-induced changes in EEG photic driving balance. Finally, in a study of male smokers who were abstinent for 31 days, N predicted sustained vigilance decrements over 31 days. N was also correlated with cessation-induced EEG changes suggestive of a disposition toward depression (decreased left relative to right frontal activation; D. G. Gilbert, Meliska, Welser, et al., 1992).

The tendency of high-N individuals to have higher baseline serum cortisol concentrations may account for their attenuated responses to nicotine. Cortisol and related glucocorticoids reduce the behavioral effects of nicotine and the binding of nicotine to CNS receptor sites (Pauly, Grun, & Collins, 1992), and cortisol reduces binding of neurotransmitters to their receptors (Munck et al., 1984). Reduced sensitivity to nicotine may promote heavier and more habitual smoking among high-N individuals.

The importance of controlling for acute and habitual nicotine intake when assessing responsivity to nicotine as a function of N is underlined by studies showing that N correlates with biochemically assessed nicotine intake and self-reported nicotine dependence (D. G. Gilbert, Meliska, et al., 1994; Golding, 1988). Fagerstrom Tolerance Questionnaire scores correlate positively with N (D. G. Gilbert, Meliska, et al., 1994; Masson & Gilbert, 1990). Thus, studies observing that nicotine dependence assessed by the Fagerstrom Tolerance Questionnaire relates to various outcomes may erroneously attribute causal influences to dependence rather than to equally plausible mechanisms related to N.

Depression and Depressive Disorders   *Reported reasons for smoking*   I am not aware of any published studies characterizing relationships between reasons for smoking and depression. Because negative affect reduction is generally a reinforcing process, tobacco-associated reductions in depressive affect are expected to be reinforcing. Because depressed mood and other forms of negative affect occur more frequently and intensely in individuals predisposed toward depression (Covey et al., 1990), such individuals are likely to learn more readily that smoking attenuates depression from sources other than nicotine withdrawal (Anda et al., 1990). Moreover, depressive symptoms may trigger cravings for tobacco because they were previously alleviated by tobacco-administered nicotine.

Differential Effects of Smoking or Nicotine and Depression   Smokers scoring high in pre-abstinence depression or other dysphoric mood before quitting are less than half as likely to maintain abstinence for a month after quitting as are others (Anda et al., 1990; Covey et al., 1990; Rausch, Nichinson, Lamke, & Matloff, 1990; M. A. H. Russell, 1994; Zelman, Brandon, Jorenby, & Baker, 1992). However, nicotine replacement therapy (nicotine gum and patch) greatly reduces the probability of relapse in such dysphoric individuals (Kinnunen et al., 1994; M. A. H. Russell, 1994). Kinnunen et al. found that only 11% of their depressed smokers were able to quit without nicotine gum, whereas 32% quit with gum. Nicotine gum not only helped these individuals quit smoking, but it decreased their depressed mood during the first week of abstinence, possibly thereby lessening their urge to smoke.

Consistent with the antidepressant effects of nicotine replacement therapy, D. G. Gilbert, Gehlbach, et al. (1994) and D. G. Gilbert, Meliska, et al. (1994) found smoking to normalize depression-related frontal EEG asymmetries. Individuals scoring high in depression were also less sensitive to nicotine's stimulant effects (D. G. Gilbert, Meliska, et al., 1994). Depression correlated negatively with hormonal, EEG, and subjective responses to standardized doses of nicotine even after controlling for biochemically determined habitual nicotine intake. Depressive individuals exhibited relatively smaller stimulant, and in some cases sedativelike, EEG deactivating effects in response to nicotine. The tendency of depressed individuals to have higher baseline serum cortisol concentrations may account for their tendency to have attenuated responses to nicotine. As noted earlier, cortisol and other glucocorticoids reduce the behavioral effects of nicotine and the binding of nicotine and neurotransmitters to CNS receptors (Munck et al., 1984; Pauly et al., 1992). However, contrary to the hypothesis that cortisol blockade or some other mechanism attenuates all responses to nicotine, Masson and Gilbert (1990) found that the depressive trait correlated positively with heart rate boosts resulting from a quantified dose of smoke and nicotine. Gilbert, Gehlbach, et al. (1994) found that depressive trait correlated with degree of abstinence-related EEG slowing, especially in the left hemisphere.

As noted in Chapter 6, the finding that glucocorticoids increase mesolimbic dopamine release in response to amphetamines suggests that although cortisol attenuates some drugs' effects, it may enhance the effects of others, including those of nicotine.

Effects of Antidepressants on Cessation and Abstinence   To the degree that smokers smoke to self-medicate depression or to avoid smoking-cessation-related depressive affect, one would expect antidepressants to facilitate smoking cessation and to attenuate depressive affect subsequent to quitting. Given the association between history of major depressive disorder and depressive cessation-related symptomatology (Breslau, Kilbey, & Andreski, et al., 1992), one would predict antidepressants to be most effective in individuals with a history of major depression. Only a small number of studies have assessed the potential efficacy of antidepressant medications in these regards. N. B. Edwards, Simmons, Rosenthal, Hoon, and Downs (1988) found the antidepressant doxepin (150mg/day) reduced withdrawal symptom severity in nondepressed smokers. However, the control group did not receive placebo medication and cessation rates were not assessed. The selective serotonin reuptake inhibitor fluoxetine hydrochloride attenuated cessation-related dysphoria and prevented increased food intake in the first week after smoking cessation in a study by Spring et al. (1993). Finally, a large multicenter trial of fluoxetine failed to demonstrate any overall effects of this antidepressant on cessation in a group of individuals without depression or a history of psychiatric disorders (Eli Lilly Pharmaceutical Company, personal communication, April, 1993).

Anxiety and Anxiety Disorders   *Reported reasons for smoking*   Trait anxiety correlates positively with self-reported motivation to smoke during states of heightened anxiety. Spielberger (1986) observed that trait anxiety correlated significantly but modestly with reported smoking urge when anxious (r's $= .21$ and .26, for women and men, respectively), as well as when angry (r's $= .25$, for both women and men). Similarly, Pritchard and Kay (1993) found urge to smoke when anxious and when depressed to correlate (r's $= .34$ and .32, respectively) with trait anxiety.

Differential Effects of Smoking or Nicotine and Anxiety   Few investigations have assessed individual differences in response to smoking or nicotine as a function of trait anxiety or of history of anxiety disorder. One might expect trait anxiety to correlate with physiological and subjective responses to smoking and smoking cessation in a manner similar to that of N as N and anxiety are highly correlated. Trait anxiety was found to correlate positively with heart rate (but not blood pressure) boosts resulting from a quantified dose of smoke and nicotine in a study by Masson and Gilbert (1990).

Effects of Anxiolytics on Cessation and Abstinence If smokers smoke to self-medicate anxiety or to avoid smoking-cessation-related anxiety, anxiolytics should facilitate smoking cessation and attenuate anxiety subsequent to quitting. Newer generation anxiolytics such as buspirone and clonidine may attenuate smoking-cessation-related negative affect and facilitate abstinence. West, Hajek, and McNeill (1991) randomly administered buspirone or a placebo to 61 smokers 2 weeks before cessation and 4 weeks after quitting. Although there was no difference in withdrawal symptoms, smokers administered buspirone maintained abstinence at a rate of 47% compared with 16% of the placebo group. The lack of association between withdrawal symptoms and successful abstinence suggests a complex set of connections between nicotine use and relapse and serotonin pathways (West et al., 1991). Cinciripini et al. (1994) found an interaction between preabstinence anxiety level and the effects of the anxiolytic buspirone. Individuals high in anxiety before quitting were more likely to be abstinent on buspirone than on placebo, whereas those low in anxiety were less likely to maintain abstinence when on buspirone. Anxiety was also attenuated in the high-anxiety buspirone group relative to the corresponding placebo group.

Most studies have failed to observe a reduction of craving by clonidine (for a review, see Prochazka, DiClemente, & Norcross, 1992). Still, clonidine has been shown in several studies to reduce cigarette-cessation-related negative affect and to improve short-term success rates (Franks, Harp, & Bell, 1989; Glassman, Jackson, Walsh, Roose, & Rosenfeld, 1984; for a review, see Prochazka, Petty, et al., 1992). However, the aggregate of studies do not show a large effect of clonidine on smoking cessation (Prochazka et al., 1992). Moreover, approximately a quarter of individuals placed on the clonidine patch stopped taking the drug because of adverse effects. Differential attrition owing to clonidine-related side effects may bias the findings in favor of clonidine and thus give an undue favorable impression of this intervention's effectiveness. Overall, evidence provides some tentative support for the view that anxiolytics may facilitate continued smoking abstinence.

Anger *Reported Reasons for Smoking* Trait anger has been found to correlate positively with self-reported motivation to smoke during states of heightened anger (Pritchard & Kay, 1993; Spielberger, 1986). Spielberger's (1986) study of more than 900 smokers found correlations of .32 and .31 between trait anger and smoking when angry and of .27 and .25 between trait anger and smoking when anxious, for women and men, respectively. Similarly, using another large sample, Pritchard and Kay (1993) found correlations between trait anger and reports of smoking to reduce anger ($r = .32$) and to reduce anxiety ($r = .27$).

Differential Effects of Smoking or Nicotine and Anger   Trait anger directed inward has been found to correlate positively with heart rate (but not blood pressure) boosts resulting from a quantified dose of smoke or nicotine, whereas trait anger directed outward (expression) correlated negatively with nicotine-induced heart rate increase (Masson & Gilbert, 1990). Further information concerning differential effects of nicotine in those high in anger-inward versus anger-outward may be beneficial in understanding individual differences in smoking motivation.

Schizophrenia   *Reported Reasons for Smoking*   Glynn and Sussman's (1990) survey of schizophrenic patients indicated that a majority believed that smoking produced relaxation and relieved anxiety. Of these smokers, 20% also indicated that smoking reduced psychiatric symptoms, and the same percentage reported that smoking reduced medication side effects.

Hypothesized Reasons for the High Prevalence Smoking in Schizophrenic Individuals   A number of reasons have been proposed to account for the high rate of smoking in schizophrenic individuals. Smoking may attenuate schizophrenic psychopathology by enhancing concentration, reducing unpleasant hyperarousal, and providing one of the few pleasures available to many schizophrenics (Gopalaswamy & Morgan, 1986). If nicotine's effects in nonclinical populations are generalizable to schizophrenic populations, nicotine should reduce negative schizophrenic symptoms such as anhedonia, apathy, boredom, blunted affect, and emotional withdrawal while improving attentional processes. Nicotine-increased mesolimbic activity may help activate psychomotor processes typically lacking in negative-symptom schizophrenia, for example, active coping, environmental attention and engagement, and emotional responsivity. Negative-symptom schizophrenics appear to exhibit a reduction of frontal and prefrontal cortical activation (Lohr & Flynn, 1992), and smoking and nicotine attenuates such hypofrontality.

Positive schizophrenic symptoms may be reduced by chronic nicotine as a result of nicotine-induced reductions in active-symptom-related functional dopaminergic activity. Chronic nicotine use has complex direct and indirect effects on a variety of neuromodulators, including dopamine activity, as well as dopamine-influencing nicotinic cholinergic functioning (Balfour, 1991a, 1991b).

If schizophrenia is characterized by lability (as opposed to simple overactivity) in the responsivity and functioning of dopaminergic release and modulation, the fingertip control one has over nicotine administration during smoking may provide a parallel fine-grain modulatory control over dopaminergic activity. The ability of state-dependent smoking to modulate dopaminergic and other neuromodulators associated with schizophrenia may provide beneficial effects not possible with drugs administered infrequently in an all-or-none fashion.

As neuroleptic drugs taken by most schizophrenics induce unpleasant side effects, any ability of nicotine to attenuate such effects should be reinforcing.

Glynn and Sussman's (1990) findings that 20% of schizophrenics report atten-uation of medication side effects by smoking is consistent with this hypothesis. Most antipsychotic medications block dopamine receptors throughout the brain, including those associated with motivation and reward. Thus, schizophrenics have been hypothesized to smoke in part to overcome dopaminergic blockade and associated medication side effects, including akathisia, drowsiness, dys-tonia, and parkinsonism (Lohr & Flynn, 1992). Observations that nicotine can release dopamine and that smoking appears to attenuate antipsychotic-induced parkinsonism (Goff, Henderson, & Amico, 1992) appear to support this hypoth-esis. Because dopamine release has been proposed to be an important reinforcer of smoking (Clarke, 1990; see Chapter 2), dopamine blockade by neuroleptic medications may make any release of dopamine by nicotine especially reinforc-ing to schizophrenics. Schizophrenics and other individuals characterized by low levels of pleasure (anhedonia) may find smoking more rewarding than do indi-viduals whose pleasure and reward systems function more normally. In addition, the fact that there is a higher prevalence of other drug use (caffeine, cocaine, cannabis, hallucinogens, and inhalants) among schizophrenics (Schneier & Siris, 1987), some of which have little or no effect on dopamine functioning, suggests that a number of other mechanisms also contribute to the high prevalence of smoking in this group.

Psychoticism, Impulsivity, and Unsocialized Disinhibitory Disorders

Reported Reasons for Smoking   Little is known about reported reasons for smoking and psychoticism or P-IUSS. Psychoticism was unrelated to urge to smoke during states of either heightened anger or anxiety (Pritchard & Kay, 1993; Spielberger, 1986). P correlated with only two of the Smoking Motivation Questionnaire's six factors: restful relaxation in men in only one study (Spiel-berger, 1986) and social–sensory motivations in another (Pritchard & Kay, 1993). Although it is reasonable to hypothesize that individuals high in impul-sivity and other components of P-IUSS smoke to reduce their impulsivity (Prit-chard, 1991b), I know of no published assessments of this.

Hypothesized Reasons for the Association of P and Smoking   H. J. Eysenck (1980) found that a significant portion of the genetic basis of smoking could be accounted for by his P factor. Pritchard (1991b) proposed that high-P individuals smoke in part to momentarily elevate functional activity of the ser-otonergic system and thereby control their impulsivity. Thus, he viewed his model and its supportive evidence as consistent with a psychological resource or self-medication model of smoking. He based his model on findings showing that (a) serotonergic activity is linked to P-related behavior in animals and humans, (b) drugs that influence the serotonergic system produce behavioral changes that parallel those of nicotine, (c) nicotine has effects on serotonergic activity, and (d) nicotine reduces P-related behavior.

In addition to the possibilities listed by Pritchard (1991b), it appears very likely that P's correlates (social alienation, impulsivity, low frustration tolerance, cynicism, tough- mindedness, aggressiveness, low agreeableness; low conscientiousness, low academic achievement, and antisocial attitudes and peers) account for a substantial amount of its association with smoking. P may also be associated with greater sensitivity to drugs, a biologically based disposition toward sensation seeking (Zuckerman, 1991), and a need for self-medication due to low positive or high negative affect or cognitive dysfunction (Pritchard, 1991b).

Drug and Alcohol Abuse   G. E. Swan, Cardon, and Carmelli (1994) determined that the best-fitting and parsimonious model of the strong association between smoking, caffeine, and alcohol use was a common pathway model. Their model identified a latent factor referred to as *Polysubstance Use* that was determined entirely by additive genetic sources. Their results suggested that the associations between smoking, caffeine, and alcohol use are genetically mediated by some common biological mechanisms. Tarter and Edwards (1988), like H. J. Eysenck (1980), argued that genetic vulnerability to drug use results from inherited predispositions that, through interaction with the environment, lead to personality and associated behavioral traits. The same personality traits associated with smoking are associated with the use of other drugs (for a review, see Tarter & Edwards, 1988).

It is likely that a number of biological mechanisms and associated genes mediate this Polysubstance Use factor. Phenotypic expressions of these genetic differences may include individual differences in basic biological responses and sensitivity or more complex and indirect psychological mechanisms such as personality, psychopathology, and intelligence. Primary differences across smoking, caffeine, alcohol, and other drug use may be mediated by inherent variation in mesolimbic dopamine sensitivity as the mesolimbic system appears to be involved in many forms of drug reinforcement (Bozarth, 1987). Moreover, differential sensitivity of mesolimbic dopaminergic systems may be related to basic dimensions of personality and psychopathology. For example, schizophrenia appears to be associated with dysfunction of dopaminergic systems. Because P is a personality dimension related to polydrug abuse and may also be related to schizophrenia (H. J. Eysenck, 1992c; see Chapter 4), it may be that this genetically influenced dimension and its associated behavioral correlates (noted earlier) account for a substantial amount of the Polysubstance Use factor.

To the degree that a common Polysubstance Use factor exists and is related to basic drug receptor mechanisms, drug sensitivity, and drug responsivity, magnitude of response to one drug should correlate with magnitude of response to another drug. For example, EEG, hormonal, and subjective response to a challenge dose of nicotine should correlate with the individual's response to caffeine, alcohol, and cocaine. Preliminary findings from my lab show modest correlations between responses to a standard dose of nicotine and a standard dose of caffeine (D. G. Gilbert, Plath, & Hiyane, 1994).

Although it has been suggested (O. F. Pomerleau, Collins, et al., 1993) that both smokers and alcoholics may be abnormally sensitive to nicotine and alcohol, respectively, a recent meta-analysis showed sons of alcoholics to have significantly less sensitivity to alcohol than normal controls (Pollock, 1992). As noted earlier in this chapter, two personality traits strongly associated with smoking, neuroticism and depression are also associated with attentuated response to nicotine (D. G. Gilbert, Meliska, et al., 1994). Thus, it may be that nicotine is associated with less rather than more sensitivity to at least certain of nicotine's effects. To the degree that alcoholics are subsensitive to alcohol and the Polysubstance Use genetic factor mediates both smoking and alcoholism, alcoholics should be less responsive to both alcohol and nicotine.

Socioeconomic Status and Smoking   Education level is the best predictor of smoking status in the United States. Between 1974 and 1985, the prevalence of smoking among college graduates decreased from 28.5% to 18.4%; however, the rate among individuals not completing high school dropped only from 36.3.% to 34.2% (Pierce et al., 1989). Little attention has been given to the mechanisms mediating the greater prevalence of smoking among those low in socioeconomic status. Those higher in socioeconomic status are characterized by long-term net consequences of their actions, whereas those lower in socioeconomic status are more immediate-goal oriented and less prone toward a healthy lifestyle (Adler et al., 1994). In addition, those lower in socioeconomic status are exposed less to job health promotion programs and may receive less antismoking information because they watch fewer television programs and read fewer articles that address the risks of smoking (Ehrich & Emmons, 1994). Finally, individuals lower in socioeconomic status are characterized by more smoking-associated traits; they experience more life stress, are less skilled in coping, and have higher prevalences of psychiatric disorders than higher socioeconomic status individuals (Adler et al., 1994).

SUMMARY AND CONCLUSIONS

There appear to be a number of causal pathways that lead to one's becoming a smoker. Although evidence has indicated that many smokers are motivated in part by a desire to alleviate their primary form(s) of psychological dysfunction, smoking motivations have not been adequately characterized for a number of groups, including individuals high in depression, impulsivity, antisocial behavior, schizophrenic traits, psychoticism, and attentional dysfunction. Smokers with minimal psychopathology are likely to smoke and to have become smokers for different reasons than those predisposed to psychopathology or personality extremes. Such individuals may smoke because of a stressful environment or because of a combination of social and environmental factors such as peer and family modeling. Others may smoke purely as a means of enhancing cognitive, affective, or behavioral performance to levels beyond that possible without the use of nicotine as a pharmacological tool.

Pathways almost certainly include a variety of individual differences mechanisms at different points in the smoker's career. Individual differences in smoking initiation and continuation are related to peer group choice, which is strongly influenced by both genetic and environmental factors (Scarr & McCartney, 1983; see Chapter 4). Individual differences in reward provided by nicotine may be related to fundamental nicotine sensitivity, to reward sensitivity specifically, and to less direct psychological reinforcment, such as concentration enhancement, body weight reduction, and negative affect attenuation. Individuals with significant problems that nicotine helps to self-medicate would be expected to find smoking especially rewarding. Thus, those with attentional, weight, and negative affect problems would be predicted to be more likely to smoke and to find quitting more difficult than those without such problems. Further and more integrated discussions of likely individual differences in causal pathways to smoking initiation, motivation, cessation, and relapse are considered in Chapter 9.

The evidence reviewed here demonstrates that individuals characterized by chronic psychological disorders and those who do not adhere to traditional social values are more likely to smoke than are others. Individuals high in psychopathology and subjective distress are likely to smoke as a form of self-medication for their emotional disorders. Those who are alienated from mainstream social, health, educational, and other future-oriented values are less likely to inhibit their behavior for a number of reasons, including family and peer modeling of smoking, substance use, poor coping skills, and short-term, self-defeating goals and problem solutions.

Evidence reviewed in this chapter has indicated that certain personality traits and psychopathologies constitute important avenues to smoking and relapse for many individuals. There is a clear need for further articulation of the major causal pathways to smoking. With the exception of severe psychopathologies such as those associated with clinical disorders, associations between single personality variables and smoking are modest to weak. However, this does not preclude the possibility that certain combinations of personality characteristics, along with certain environmental and learning histories, do have strong predictive and potential explanatory power. Multiple regression approaches have rarely been used to assess smoking and personality associations. However, such analyses are limited because they can be used with only a limited number of variables and cannot provide information about joint and individual functioning of independent predictiors (Adler et al., 1994). More complex statistical procedures are needed to articulate causal pathways associated with smoking. In addition to causal pathway analysis, tree-structured regression (M. R. Segal & Block, 1989) would be a useful tool to examine combinations of conditions associated with smoking. Tree-structured regression clusters individuals into subgroups and then identifies different paths to an outcome.

Chapter 8

Gender Differences in Tobacco Use and Effects

Questions related to gender differences in smoking are best phrased as "How much?" "When?" "Why?" and "For whom?" The goal of this chapter is to characterize and assess the nature, size, importance, and underlying mechanisms of these differences in smoking and responses to nicotine. With few exceptions, gender differences in smoking-related processes have been inadequately characterized because women have been excluded from many smoking studies.

The reasons for excluding women are generally not stated, but concerns that changes related to menstrual cycle phase might confound, add variance to, or otherwise complicate findings may be important factors, especially in studies involving hormones and other physiological measures. Smoking-influenced dependent variables, including EEG, cortisol, beta-endorphin, and mood are influenced by menstrual cycle phase and oral contraceptive use. Researchers may find themselves in a situation in which they do not assess female smokers because not enough is known about women and smoking, a circular state of affairs that is only recently being challenged by a changing sociopolitical climate.

There is a significant cost in not assessing women as a number of findings have suggested that there are important gender differences in smoking motivations, effects, and relapse patterns. Treatment interventions are likely to be less well suited to women than to men if this historical trend continues. Furthermore, a number of health-related risk factors unique to women need to be examined. For example, smoking combined with oral contraceptive use results in a greatly increased risk for myocardial infarction (Croft & Hannaford, 1989). An under-standing of who smoking oral contraceptive users are and why they choose to both smoke and use oral contraceptives has important health implications. Thus, a purpose of this chapter is not only to characterize gender and menstrual-cycle-phase differences, but also to provide conceptual guidelines that will facilitate quality smoking research with women. This chapter builds on two excellent but brief reviews by Grunberg, Winders, and Wewers (1991) and by C. S. Pomer-leau, Pomerleau, and Garcia (1991).

GENDER DIFFERENCES IN INITIATION AND PREVALENCE OF TOBACCO USE

Smoking Initiation

Gender differences in smoking initiation have changed dramatically in the United States and many westernized countries since the middle of the century. In the United States, approximately 34% of women and 80% of men had tried smoking in 1960 (Hammond & Garfinkel, 1961). By 1980, more women (83%) than men (72%) had experimented with cigarettes (Silverstein, Feld, & Kozlowski, 1980). Incidence of teenage smoking paralleled rates of experimentation (Grunberg et al., 1991). The 1968 rate of U.S. teenage smoking was 30% for boys and 19% for girls, but the 1979 rate had nearly reversed to 19% for boys and 26% for girls (National Institute of Education, 1979).

Prevalence

Cultural Influences   World Health Organization prevalence data tell us that men are more likely to smoke than women and that gender differences are very large in some countries (Crofton, 1990). For example, Hong Kong's rate is 23% for men and 4% for women; India's prevalence is 52% for men and 3% for women, Indonesia's rate is 75% for men and 5% for women, and Japan's rate is 66% for men and 14% for women. In many countries, however, there are minimal gender differences: Canada, men = 31% and women = 28%; New Guinea, men = 85% and women = 80%; United Kingdom, men = 36% and women = 32%; and the United States, men = 28% and women = 23%. Clearly, gender differences in prevalence vary as a function of culture.

Cultures change across time, and so has the prevalence of smoking. Before this century few women smoked in the United States or in Europe. However, the percentage of women smoking increased throughout the century to the point that during the 1980s more young women were smoking than young men (Office on Smoking and Health, 1992; USDHHS, 1988, 1989). Changes in gender roles and other cultural processes were likely contributors to these increases. In ad-dition, advertising directed at women, as well as the introduction of low tar and nicotine cigarettes during the latter part of the century likely contributed to the rise in smoking among women (Grunberg et al., 1991).

Prevalence-Influencing Psychological and Biological Differences   Although smoking prevalence is roughly equal in U.S. men and women, the prevalence of smokeless tobacco (chewing tobacco and snuff) use is much higher in men than in women, as is pipe smoking (USDHHS, 1988). It is not clear whether this male preference for smokeless tobacco is a function of cultural role factors or of gender differences in the method of nicotine delivery. The fact that women report smoking more often for stress reduction and men for stimulation (Best & Hakstian, 1978; Frith, 1971; Spielberger, 1986; Ikard & Tomkins, 1973) suggests that women may be attracted to smoking because it more effectively reduces negative affect than does smokeless tobacco. The phasic boli of smoking-delivered nicotine may be necessary to maximize certain tranquilizing effects of nicotine (Lippiello et al., 1987). The more gradual increase in nicotine arising from smokeless tobacco increases arousal and alertness (see Chapter 5), but may be less effective in relieving certain forms of distress. Smokeless tobacco is also inconvenient and has less socially acceptable aspects (e.g., spitting) that may make women less inclined to use this form of tobacco.

The nature of tobacco products has also changed across time and culture (R. J. Reynolds Co., 1988). On the basis of limited evidence suggesting that women may be especially sensitive to the aversive effects of higher doses of nicotine, the availability of cleaner (filtered) and milder (e.g., lower tar and nicotine) cigarettes may promote smoking among women (Silverstein et al., 1980). Thus, although cultural processes are highly important in determining incidence of tobacco use, changes in products may also play a role in determining gender differences.

REPORTED MOTIVATIONS FOR AND EFFECTS OF SMOKING

The relative importance of various mechanisms underlying reinforcement of smoking may vary as a function of gender. Women as a group generally report that negative affect reduction is their primary smoking motivation, whereas men frequently report that stimulation and other motivations are as important as negative affect reduction (Best & Hakstian, 1978; Frith, 1971; Ikard et al., 1969; Ikard & Tompkins, 1973; Kleinke, Staneski, & Meeker, 1983; Livson & Leino, 1988; McKennell, 1970; O'Connor, 1980; Spielberger, 1986; Zuckerman et al., 1990). The reliability of these findings across studies is impressive, with only a small minority (e.g., G. E. Barnes & Fishlinsky, 1976) finding no gender differences. The size of these differences has ranged from small to moderate. Negative affect smoking among women may result from their being more prone to negative affect (being higher in neuroticism) than are men (H. J. Eysenck & Eysenck, 1985). Consistent with this hypothesis, negative affect smoking correlates with neuroticism (Pritchard & Kay, 1993; Spielberger, 1986). Gender differences in self-reported smoking motivation may also reflect sex role reporting biases. However, evidence reviewed here supports the view that gender differences in reported motivations in part reflect true and functionally important mechanisms of a biological or psychological nature.

SMOKING BEHAVIOR AND NICOTINE INTAKE

Gender Differences in Intake

Why women consume less nicotine per day than men, even after correcting for body weight, is unknown. Women smoke fewer cigarettes than men (Cooreman & Perdrizet, 1980; Russell, Jarvis, Iyer, & Feyerabend, 1980; Srole, 1968), are more likely to smoke low-nicotine cigarettes (Covey, Mushinski, & Wynder, 1983; M. A. H. Russell, Wilson, Taylor, & Baker, 1980; Silverstein et al., 1980), take smaller puffs (Blair et al., 1980), and are less likely to report inhaling (Cooreman & Perdrizet, 1980; Frith, 1971; M. A. H. Russell et al., 1980). If women on the average prefer smaller doses of nicotine per unit body weight, this difference may result from one or more of several basic processes. Women may be more sensitive to nicotine, or men and women may differ in the bioavailability of nicotine disposition kinetics. Alternatively, the relative importance of various psychological, social, or biological processes maintaining smoking may differ. The lesser intake of nicotine among women may reflect lingering cultural inhibitions, self-report and experimental demand effects, or true and preferred intake. Such differences could also result from gender differences in motivations and occasions for smoking. These potential causes of gender differences in nicotine intake are discussed in following sections.

Nonsmoking women (but not men) whose urine was experimentally acidified before they smoked a strong cigarette were more willing to volunteer to smoke additional cigarettes than those whose urine was made alkaline (Silverstein, Kelly, Swan, & Kozlowski, 1982). Because acidified urine facilitates elimination of nicotine from the blood, these gender-specific effects were interpreted as reflecting reduced aversive effects of nicotine caused by reduced blood nicotine concentrations.

Menstrual-Phase-Related Nicotine Intake

Several studies have attempted to determine whether smoking or nicotine intake vary as a function of menstrual cycle phase. Steinberg and Cherek (1989) found that most women puffed more or longer during menses, as compared with other phases. Most of the women in the study by Mello, Mendelson, and Palmieri (1987), however, increased smoking during the premenstrual phase. In contrast to these two studies, the women in C. S. Pomerleau, Garcia, Pomerleau, and Cameron's (1992) investigation tended to consume more nicotine in the mid- to late follicular phase (mid-cycle). The small number of subjects (Ns = from 9 to 24 across the three studies) and great variation in procedures in these studies preclude any clear understanding of potential cycle-phase-dependent nicotine intake.

GENDER DIFFERENCES IN RESPONSE TO SMOKING AND NICOTINE

Nicotine's Subjective Effects

Although numerous studies have shown women to report more negative-affect-reducing effects from smoking than men, few investigations have experimentally verified gender differences in response to smoking, nicotine, or abstinence. Experimental assessments of potential gender differences in affective response to nicotine are reviewed here.

Negative Affect   A small number of studies have reported gender differences in negative affect subsequent to smoking. Perkins, Grobe, Fonte, & Breus, et al. (1992) observed less stress and annoyance and more relaxation among smokers allowed to smoke than among deprived smokers shortly after smoking. This effect disappeared in men shortly after smoking but was sustained in women. Women who consume caffeinated coffee in the morning were more likely than men to report feeling nausea after the first cigarette of the day (Silverstein et al., 1980). However, several studies detected no gender differences in the effects of smoking on anxiety responses to stressful movies (D. G. Gilbert & Hagen, 1985; D. G. Gilbert, Robinson, et al., 1989). Most studies in this area failed to report gender statistics, had small numbers of participants, did not include both genders, or did not find negative-affect-reducing effects in either gender. There is a clear need for large, well-designed studies assessing gender differences in nicotine and negative affect reduction.

Drowsiness and Arousal   D. G. Gilbert, Meliska, et al. (1994) found that overnight-nicotine-deprived female smokers were characterized by more drowsiness than male smokers and than male and female nonsmokers. As nicotine eliminated these differences between female smokers and the other groups, nicotine appeared to have a somewhat stronger stimulant effect in women. Perkins, Grobe, Fonte, & Breus, et al. (1992) found that smoking increased subjective arousal to an equivalent degree in both genders in spite of the fact that it was associated with a more prolonged concomitant decrease in stress and annoyance in women than in men.

Cognitive and Behavioral Effects

Cognition and Perception   Gender differences have been detected in few of the small number of studies assessing gender effects on cognition and perception in humans. A series of studies by Peeke and Peeke (1984) revealed no gender-modulated effects of smoking on memory. Perkins et al. (1994) observed no Gender × Smoking interactions on pain sensitivity, but Epstein et al. (1984) found smoking reduced sensitivity to muscle activity in women but increased sensitivity in men.

Behavioral Effects in Animals   Substantial gender differences in sensitivity to nicotine have been observed in a small number of studies. However, the direction and generalizability of these differences have not been determined. Some studies have found female rodents to be more sensitive behaviorally and physiologically to nicotine (Grunberg, Bowen, & Winders, et al., 1986; Rosecrans, 1971, 1972). In contrast, other studies have shown hormonal and behavioral responses of male rodents to be substantially more sensitive to nicotine than those of female rodents (Fuxe et al., 1990; Marks, Stitzel, & Collins, 1985).

Physiological Sensitivity and Responses to Nicotine

Cardiovascular   Gender differences in heart rate response to quasi-ad-libitum smoking have been observed in some cases (e.g, Peeke & Peeke, 1984; Perkins et al., 1992), but not in studies controlling for nicotine dose (D. G. Gilbert, Meliska, et al., 1994), or in a majority of studies using larger numbers of participants (e.g., D. G. Gilbert, Robinson, et al., 1989). However, studies to date have rarely assessed potential differences as a function of menstrual cycle phase.

Hormonal   No gender differences in beta-endorphin or cortisol responses to nicotine occurred in a study by Meliska and Gilbert (1991) of 8 male and 8 mid-cycle female smokers. Yeh and Barberi (1989) failed to find significant differences in 24-hour urinary-free cortisol in premenopausal smokers and nonsmokers. In contrast, compared with females, male rodents have lower thresholds for hormonal release and larger endocrine responses to nicotine (Fuxe et al., 1990). Any gender differences in hormonal responses to nicotine may be a function of whether women are postmenopausal or premenopausal. Among women, chronic smoking is associated with reduced estrogen concentrations relative to nonsmokers (Barret-Connor, 1990; Cassidenti, Vijod, Vijod, Stanczyk, & Lobo, 1990; MacMahon, Trichopoulos, Cole, & Brown, 1982). In contrast, chronic smoking has been associated with elevated testosterone in men in a majority of studies (Barret-Conner & Khaw, 1987; Dai, Gutai, Kuller, &

Cauley, 1988; Elaiasson, Hagg, Lundblad, Karlsson, & Bucht, 1993), but not in others (Briggs, 1973). It is not clear that these relationships between sex hormones and smoker versus nonsmoker status are causal. For example, male adolescents high in testosterone may be more disposed to take up the smoking habit (Bauman, Foshee, Koch, Haley, & Downton, 1989). Acute smoking appears to have little or no effect on blood testosterone concentrations in men in quiescent situations (Winternitz & Quillen, 1977), but these concentrations were found to increase in a social situation involving smoking (Dotson, Robertson, & Tuchfeld, 1975).

Skin Conductance   In one of the few studies of gender differences in stress reactivity as a function of smoker or nonsmoker status, Knott (1984) found that a small sample of female smokers exhibited larger skin conductance responses to stress than nonsmokers of both genders and than male smokers. However, Knott failed to control for menstrual cycle phase, a variable found to influence skin conductance activity. Martinez-Selva, Gomez-Amor, Olmos, Navairo, and Roman (1987) found attenuated electrodermal reactivity to tones in postovulatory women relative to preovulatory women and to men, but did not assess effects of acute or habitual smoking.

Electrocortical   A small study by D. G. Gilbert, Meliska, et al. (1994) found that nicotine-deprived female smokers were characterized by more drowsiness and slow frequency EEG activity than male smokers and than male and female nonsmokers. As nicotine eliminated these differences between female smokers and other groups, nicotine appeared to have a stronger effect in female than in male smokers. However, in one of the few studies comparing a substantial number of smokers of each gender, D. G. Gilbert (1987) found no male–female differences in EEG response to smoking-delivered nicotine. The failure of the latter study to detect gender differences may be related to the smoking of a single cigarette in a high-stress situation, as opposed to the low-stress, multiple cigarette conditions of the D. G. Gilbert, Meliska, et al. (1994) study. Thus, nothing conclusive can be said about gender differences in electrocortical responses to smoking or nicotine.

Conclusions   Although about half of the studies assessing subjective, behavioral, and physiological responses to smoking and nicotine have reported statistically significant gender effects, the question of whether gender effects are reliable and large enough to be of functional importance cannot be answered because of the very small number of relevant studies.

GENDER AND SMOKING CESSATION

Cessation Rates

Smoking has declined more among men than among women in the United States. Prevalence in U.S. men declined from 50% in 1965 to 28% in 1990, but among women it decreased only from 32 to 23% over the same time (Office on Smoking and Health, 1992). However, smoking cessation rates appear to be higher in women than in men in parts of Asia (Finau, Stanhope, & Prior, 1982; Waldron et al., 1988). Thus, these culture-specific smoking cessation rates suggest that gender and cultural environment interact in promoting or impeding cessation.

Gender and Abstinence Response

Potential gender differences in response to smoking abstinence have received minimal attention. Results of several retrospective studies (Guilford, 1967; Gunn & Shapirio, 1979; S. M. Hall, 1984; Shiffman, 1979) have suggested that the abstinence syndrome is more severe in women than in men and that women have a higher failure rate in abstinence attempts. However, prospective studies assessing gender differences in abstinence response have generally not observed these differences.

Svikis, Hatsukami, Hughes, Carroll, and Pickens (1986) detected no differences between men and women in any of 46 physiological and psychological measures in two small prospective investigations of the first few days of abstinence (Hughes, Hatsukami, Pickens, Krahan, et al., 1984; Hughes & Hatsukami, 1986). However, the power of these investigations to detect differences was very low because of the sample size ($Ns = 11$ men and 9 women and 23 men and 27 women for the two studies, respectively). Furthermore, menstrual-cycle-phase effects were not assessed. Hughes et al. (1991) found no "substantial" gender differences in total withdrawal discomfort. However, this study failed to indicate whether gender differences in specific responses to abstinence occurred. Gunn (1986) assessed subjective cessation responses in 173 women and 112 men and found that neither intensity nor number of symptoms was related to sex. However, he did find that having minimal or mild withdrawal symptoms was predictive of maintaining abstinence in women but not in men. Thus, withdrawal symptoms may be differentially associated by gender with motivation for relapse to smoking. However, this study also failed to report whether the specific abstinence responses differed as a function of gender or menstrual cycle phase.

There are methodological and interpretive problems with studies to date assessing gender differences. First, the fact that men were heavier smokers in most of the studies assessing gender differences presents interpretational problems given that heavier smoking predicts response severity. After controlling for nicotine intake, women may experience more severe abstinence-related symptoms. Also, studies have not assessed whether the specific abstinence responses differed as a function of gender, oral contraceptive use, or menstrual cycle phase.

Menstrual-Cycle-Phase-Dependent Abstinence Effects

Subjective Responses   Several studies have suggested that abstinence symptoms, the affect-modulating effects of nicotine or both, vary as a function of menstrual cycle phase. O'Hara, Portser, and Anderson (1989) found larger increases in subjective withdrawal in the second half of the cycle (Day 15 through onset of menses) as opposed to the first half. Late-cycle but not early-cycle quitters reported more intense withdrawal than men, even though men were heavier smokers. Similarly, Cynthia Pomerleau, Garcia, Pomerleau, and Cameron (1992) found a tendency for more menstrual symptoms in late relative to early-phase abstainers after 12 hours of abstinence. As in O'Hara et al.'s study, abstinence did not lead to increased withdrawal symptoms in the early follicular phase, but did at mid- and late cycle. Craig, Parrott, and Coomber (1992) found that abstinent premenstrual women reported significantly more depression, tiredness, anxiety, and irritability than did mid-cycle women. Mid-cycle women reported only slight changes in feeling state during the 2-day cessation period. Plath (1994) found larger responses to 18-hour abstinence during the first week of oral contraceptive use, compared with the third week. Overall, findings from these investigations provide tentative evidence that quitting smoking early in the menstural cycle may minimize negative abstinence responses and possibly increase the probability of abstinence. Plath's findings, however, suggest that oral contraceptive users may find it easier to give up smoking during the first week than the third. The fact that the follicular phase is characterized by high levels of cortisol but low levels of female hormones (estrogens and progesterone; Gannon, 1985; C. S. Pomerleau et al., 1992) suggests that high levels of cortisol or low levels of female hormones may attenuate smoking-abstinence-associated negative affect.

In two of these studies, correlations between menstrual symptom severity and measures of withdrawal were high, with correlations ranging from .49 to .92 in the O'Hara et al. (1989) study and from .64 to .95 in the C. S. Pomerleau et al. (1992) study. Both menstrual and withdrawal scores were highest during the late luteal phase when abstinent. These high correlations are not surprising given that symptoms of premenstrual distress subsume those of tobacco abstinence: anxiety, irritability, depression, decreased concentration, tension, sleep disturbance, somatic complaints, and weight changes (C. S. Pomerleau et al., 1992). Furthermore, the mood factors associated with menstrual cycle variations correspond closely to those of smoking abstinence. For example, Gallant, Hamilton, Popiel, Morokoff, and Chakraborty (1991) obtained six factors when they assessed moods and symptoms in 30 normal-cycle women and 23 men. These factors were dysphoric moods, well-being, physical symptoms, personal space, food cravings, and depression. Hughes et al. (1991) found four of these six factors in their analysis of changes subsequent to tobacco withdrawal: mood disturbance, somatic complaints, other symptoms (hunger and insomnia), and craving. Hughes et al. did not assess well-being or personal space.

Physiological Responses   Menstrual-cycle-phase-related differences in physiological response to tobacco abstinence have only recently received attention. C. S. Pomerleau et al. (1992) failed to detect Phase × Abstinence interactions for either cortisol or MHPG (a measure of central noradrenergic activity). Plath (1994) found larger systolic blood pressure responses to a standard smoking or nicotine dose during the third week of oral contraceptive use (the week associated with the pill's highest dose of progesterone) than during the first week (the week associated with the pill's lower dose of progesterone). Masson (1995) found that cardiovascular responses to a standard dose of smoke varied as a function of menstrual cycle phase and pill use. Effects of phase on differences in basal physiological activity, responses to stress, and interactions with nicotine and abstinence need to be characterized.

Abstinence and Relapse

Gender and Relapse   Findings that show women attending cessation programs to be more likely than men to relapse (Blair et al., 1980; Eisinger, 1971; Gordon, Kannel, Dawber, & McGee, 1975; Gritz, 1979; Harris, 1983; G. E. Swan, Ward, Jack, & Javitz, 1993) have been interpreted as indicating that women have more difficulty giving up smoking than men. However, this interpretation has been challenged on several bases. For example, these studies did not assess turning to other forms of tobacco (chewing tobacco, cigars, pipe smoking, and snuff), which in the United States are almost exclusively used by men (Grunberg et al., 1991; Jarvis, 1984). More recent evaluations controlling for smokeless tobacco use suggest that men are slightly more likely to successfully quit use of nicotine products permanently than are women (Schoenborn & Boyd, 1989). However, other confounds exist in smoking cessation programs. Men attending such programs are likely to be of different personality and socioeconomic status than are women. For example, high-education and high-status (and more likely male) physicians are much more likely to quit than are lower status (and more likely female) nurses (M. Murray, Swan, & Mattar, 1983; Tagliacozzo & Vaughn, 1982). Even controlling for setting (e.g., a hospital) does not eliminate such confounds. Further sampling biases in gender success may result from the fact that only a very small percentage of smokers quit by attending clinics or programs. Nonetheless, the fact that the percentage of former smokers is higher for men than it is for women in nearly every age group (USDHHS, 1989) is strongly indicative of more success among men than women in giving up smoking permanently.

Gender differences in smoking abstinence response have not been reliably demonstrated. Men reported more withdrawal symptoms than women in a phone survey by Pirie et al., (1991). In a large study by Blake et al. (1989), men differed from women in the smoking cessation strategies they selected. For example, men more often chose to quit entirely, and women preferred to reduce the number of cigarettes they smoked. Marlatt, Curry, and Gordon (1988) performed a longitudinal analysis of unaided smoking cessation and found that men who were light smokers were the most successful quitters. Garvey, Bliss,

Hitchcock, Heinold, and Rosner (1992), however, found no gender differences in a group of 235 smokers they studied for a year after self-initiated smoking cessation.

Evidence has suggested that men and women differ in terms of factors mediating relapse and return to abstinence after smoking lapses. For example, G. G. Swan and Denk (1987) found that increased anger after cessation and daily caffeine intake were associated with faster relapse in men, but not in women. Swan et al. (1993) found heightened systolic blood pressure response to a cognitive challenge stressor to predict relapse in women but not in men. Others (Garvey et al., 1992) have found no gender differences in predictors of smoking relapse.

In summary, it is not clear why women are less likely than men to give up smoking permanently. In the United States, a higher percentage of men than of women have given up smoking. Overall, it appears that women are less successful than men in maintaining long-term cessation in spite of the fact that they are as likely to initiate attempts to quit (Ockene, 1993). Furthermore, studies assessing gender differences in factors facilitating and mediating smoking initiation, cessation, and relapse are needed. Work in this area by Pirie et al. (1991) has indicated that women have greater expectations of weight gain and believe more than men that it would be hard to go out with friends who smoke after quitting. Cultural specificity of some of these factors is suggested by findings that in some cultures cessation rates are higher among women than men (Finau et al., 1982; Waldron et al., 1988). Cultural and workplace factors supporting smoking abstinence are likely to be influential in generating gender differences. For example, with workplace restrictions on smoking and more men than women in the workforce, it is likely that the response cost of smoking is increasing relatively more for men than for women.

Gender Differences in Abstinence-Related Affect   Gender differences in affective response to smoking abstinence have not been adequately assessed. As noted earlier, women tend to report negative affect reduction as their primary motive for smoking, whereas men are more likely to report other motivations. However, studies have not consistently demonstrated a tendency for women to report more negative affect than men subsequent to smoking abstinence (Pirie et al., 1991; see Chapter 6). The failure of studies to date to assess potentially moderating effects of menstrual cycle phase and of gender biases toward certain occupations, personalities, and other subject selection factors may account for this inconsistency.

The fact that some early studies (Orlandi, 1987; Shiffman, 1979) demonstrated that women experience more negative affect subsequent to quitting may reflect differences in the typical characteristics of female smokers relative to male smokers several decades ago. Given that smoking was much less prevalent among women than men in the United States before the 1980s, women who did smoke were more deviant from their population means than men. Female smokers of past decades may have been more neurotic or depression prone than women smokers of more recent times. In contrast, it seems likely that as the incidence of smoking has decreased among men, male smokers have become more deviant than in past years in the United States (see Chapter 7). Complicating this scenario are the studies that show menstrual phase associations with abstinence-related affect (e.g., Craig et al., 1992; O'Hara et al., 1989).

Gender Differences in Abstinence-Related Weight and Appetite
Women, relative to men, generally report being more concerned about cessation-related weight gain (Pirie et al., 1991) and are more likely to report smoking to avoid weight gain (Pirie et al., 1991). Studies have tended to find that women gain more weight than men subsequent to abstinence (Klesges, Meyers, Klesges, & La Vasque, 1989), and nicotine affects body weight and eating more in female than in male rats (Grunberg et al., 1986; Grunberg, Winders, & Popp, 1987). Thus, although gender differences in the desire to avoid weight gain may in part be culturally mediated, women's greater tendency to gain weight may reflect gender-related biological differences in response to nicotine.

Cycle-Phase-Dependent Relapse   The possibility that relapse varies as a function of menstrual cycle phase has received minimal attention in the empirical literature. In a study of 31 normally menstruating women, significantly more (32%) lapsed during the menstrual phase of their cycle than expected by chance (Frye, Ward, Bliss, & Garvey, 1992). Similarly, Craig et al. (1992) found that premenstrual women achieved lower smoking reduction rates than mid-cycle women or male abstainers.

Gender and Response to Nicotine Replacement Therapy   Several studies have suggested that nicotine and other drugs used to assist in smoking cessation may have differential effects in men and women. For example, nicotine gum was found to be more helpful in men than in women in a study by Killen, Fortmann, Newman, and Varady (1990). Clonidine was helpful to women, but not men, in Glassman et al.'s (1988) investigation. C. S. Pomerleau, Garcia, Drewnowski, & Pomerleau, et al. (1991) suggested that drugs with appetite-suppressing effects may be more helpful to women, as women are more likely to be concerned about weight gain.

MECHANISMS UNDERLYING OBSERVED AND POTENTIAL GENDER DIFFERENCES

Menstrual Cycle Phase and Smoking-Related Processes

Even if women do not differ from men in mean frequency and severity of tobacco abstinence symptoms, they may experience menstrual-cycle-phase-dependent effects. As noted earlier, menstrual cycle phase has been reported to correlate with withdrawal symptom severity and with several physiological measures related to the withdrawal process. Noting a striking similarity between symptoms of tobacco withdrawal and symptoms of menstrual distress, O'Hara et al. (1989) found that women in the luteal phase reported more severe tobacco withdrawal symptoms than those quitting earlier in the cycle. Nicotine-induced changes frequently parallel changes associated with the menstual cycle. For example, changes in dominant EEG alpha frequency (Creutzfeldt et al., 1976; B. J. Kaplan, Whitsett, & Robinson, 1990) and EEG photic driving (Vogel, Broverman, & Klaiber, 1971) vary as a function of menstrual cycle phase, as well as in response to acute smoking or nicotine (Pickworth, Herning, & Henningfield, 1988; Vogel, Broverman, & Klaiber, 1977). Menstrual phase influences resting heart rate (B. J. Kaplan, 1990; Stoney, Langer, & Gelling, 1986) and basal body temperature (Hamilton & Gallant, 1988). Smoking abstinence results in similar changes (Fagerstrom, 1978).

Menstrual Disorders and Smoking Status

Sloss and Frerichs (1983) found that women smoking more than a pack of cigarettes per day reported more menstrual problems than light or nonsmokers; Brown, Vessay, and Stratton (1988) reported similar findings. In contrast, Andersch and Milsom (1982) found that smokers reported less severe dysmenorrhea than nonsmokers and suggested that smoking may relieve menstrual discomfort (cited in C. S. Pomerleau et al., 1992).

Oral Contraceptive Use

Menstrual disorders and oral contraceptive use may influence responses to nicotine and to smoking abstinence. Oral contraceptive use and smoking appear to interact synergistically to increase the risk of myocardial infarction (Burkman, 1988). Oral contraceptive users have been found to exhibit larger increases in triglyceride and blood pressure responses during stress than have nonusers and oral-contraceptive-using smokers, whereas acute smoking combined with stress has been found to increase cholesterol and free fatty acid concentrations (Davis & Matthews, 1990). Furthermore, low-dosage estrogen oral contraceptives increase daily catecholamine excretion, especially in individuals who smoke (Blum, Zakarovick, Gelernter, & Blum, 1988). Finally, serum concentrations of cortisol have been found to be higher in oral contraceptive users than in nonusers (Tiller et al., 1988). These oral-contraceptive-modulated effects of stress, smoking, and cortisol concentrations are consistent with the thesis that oral contraceptive use may also influence tobacco withdrawal-related symptoms and processes.

Aging, Menopause and Hormone Replacement Effects

Evidence has suggested that estrogens tend to attenuate stress responses and to enhance feelings of well-being (Lindheim et al., 1992). Thus, one would predict that menopausal and postmenopausal women differ in effects of nicotine and motivations for smoking. Gender differences in smoking and its effects may thus be in part a function of premenopause versus postmenopause and the presence or absence of estrogen replacement therapy in postmenopausal women.

RESEARCH PRIORITIES

Much of the basic research on which treatment interventions are based has used only male smokers; thus, studies focusing on women and gender differences should be given a high priority. Only with additional studies will it be possible to efficiently enhance health care and permanent smoking abstinence in women. Future research should (a) assess gender and individual differences in physiological and psychological responses to short-, intermediate-, and long-term smoking abstinence; (b) test specific hypotheses relating smoking relapse to gender and individual differences in physiological activity under resting and stressful conditions, physiological and subjective responses to nicotine and nicotine withdrawal, precessation habitual nicotine intake, smoking history, and self-report indexes of personality, smoking motivation, and tolerance; and (c) assess menstrual-cycle-phase-related and menopause-related effects associated with each of these processes.

SUMMARY AND CONCLUSIONS

The rather limited data assessing gender differences in smoking and the effects of nicotine suggest that

  1   Permanent quitting is relatively less likely in female than in male smokers in the United States.
  2   Women report smoking more for negative affect reduction and less for stimulation and concentration enhancement.
  3   Stimuli promoting relapse and coping responses used to maintain abstinence may differ with gender.
  4   Culture is an important determinant of gender differences in smoking prevalence.
  5   Menstrual cycle phase may influence withdrawal response to abstinence and cessation success.
  6   Smoking-related gender effects may differ with menopause and age.

A great deal of additional research is required to adequately characterize potential gender-, menstrual-cycle-phase, and menopause-related effects of smoking and nicotine response. Basic research experimental work and studies characterizing natural behavioral patterns and processes are needed.

Chapter 9

A Situation × Trait Adaptive Response Model of Smoking

It has been said that there is nothing as practical as a good theory. This chapter outlines what I believe is a step toward a good and comprehensive theory of smoking behavior. The model is broad enough to include and integrate the wide range of biological, psychological, and environmental factors known to influence smoking. Its goodness may be tested in objective terms, yet it is intended to be open enough to evolve with more precise findings and characterization of its parameters. I call this model the Situation × Trait Adaptive Response (STAR) model. This chapter presents the initial formulation of this biopsychosocial STAR model.

On the basis of evidence reviewed in detail in earlier chapters, the model assumes that smoking and nicotine have multiple reinforcing effects, some more prominent in some individuals than others and at certain times than others. I present the STAR model as follows. First, trait- and situation-specific smoking-related responses are reviewed separately. Although they are important, they are inadequate to fully characterize smoking behavior. Instead, the importance of simultaneously considering situations and traits is demonstrated. The situational and trait variables subsumed by the STAR model are seen in combination to be necessary to adequately characterize smoking prevalence, effects, abstinence effects, and relapse. In addition, a transactional coping view is also needed to fully appreciate smoking motivation and prevalence. The next chapter, *Implications of the STAR Model for Smoking Interventions*, discusses implications of the STAR model for the improvement of smoking cessation programs with high-risk individuals.

Although evidence cited in earlier chapters has indicated that genetic, personality, psychopathology, cultural, and environmental factors all play roles in influencing which, when, where, and why individuals smoke, there is no comprehensive theory or model of how these factors combine to determine smoking in the natural environment. Current knowledge precludes fine-grained definitive articulation of precise interactions of causal influences. However, recent empirical and theoretical advances do indicate that any adequate comprehensive model of smoking must characterize smoking's influences at the biological, psychological, transactional, and social levels and simultaneously model the situation- and personality-trait-specific effects of nicotine.

I expect the STAR model to be of value in understanding what biological, psychological, and life circumstances predispose one individual to decades of heavy smoking, another to never smoke, and a third to smoke just two or three cigarettes per day for years without evidence of addiction. The goal is to outline a working theory that addresses the complexity of smokers and smoking in real-life situations. The model does this by combining the strengths of the behavioral, trait, and biological and pharmacological theories and interventions in an integrated, hierarchical, biopsychosocial systems approach.

The building blocks of the STAR model include (a) the basic psychological and biological effects of nicotine and Nicotine × Situation × Trait effects reviewed in preceding chapters; (b) temperamental traits (e.g., N, E, P, and their facets), (c) long-term cognitive-motivational schema (e.g., identity, long-term goals, and social and emotional competencies and skills), (d) intermediate-term cognitive–motivational schemas (e.g., outcome expectancies concerning smoking cessation and current life concerns and goals); (e) short-term cognitive–motivational–behavioral complexes (e.g., immediately engaged in organized action plans and goals, smoking, planning how to confront one's boss), (f) situational cues and factors related to the individual's organized action patterns, (g) individual differences in sensitivity and biological adaptation to nicotine, and (h) individual differences in conditioning and learning associated with tobacco use.

These eight elemental building blocks are required to provide reasonable predictive and explanatory precision for most forms of multiply determined behavior (McAdams, 1992). McAdams has noted that adequate prediction and description usually requires "judicious and informed selection of many different constructs within the various arenas" (p. 340). He further stated that "if any good lesson is to be drawn from the 'trait versus situation debate' of the 1970s, it is that personality needs to be seen in contextual terms. . . .Context appears to be necessary for accurate prediction, detailed description, and comprehensive understanding" (p. 343). Middle-level, proximal causal processes—such as goals, personal projects, tasks, strategies, and coping skill implementation—are influenced by traits (Little, 1989; McAdams, 1992) but also focus attention on

the environment (Buss & Cantor, 1989). The conclusions of
support the view that middle-level constructs are important contr
range of smoking-related processes. These processes are discus
tegrated systems perspective in this chapter and in Chapter 10.

This chapter summarizes evidence indicating that smokers t   ....pond
to smoking and smoking abstinence in a manner consistent with their temperament and personality. It then refers to evidence reviewed earlier in this book
indicating the situational specificity of many of the effects of smoking and
nicotine. The STAR model is then presented in a hierarchical manner, starting
with a series of propositions and corollaries concerning the basic nature of
nicotine's effects on affect and the reinforcement of tobacco use. Next, relationships among higher order and middle-level constructs are articulated. Finally,
causal pathway models are outlined to summarize processes mediating individual
differences in smoking initiation, reinforcement, and cessation.

TRAIT ADAPTIVE RESPONSES

Evidence has indicated that a significant amount of the variability in response to
smoking and abstinence reflects an individual's typical style of coping with
stress. To the degree that individuals are characterized by personality and other
traits reflecting a tendency to respond to stressors with specific affective and
coping styles, they may be said to exhibit individual trait adaptive responses.
Trait adaptive responses are a function of and part of the major personality
dispositional traits (N, E, and P-IUSS), as well as their component subfactors
(e.g., depression, hostility, anxiety, impulsivity, and tough-mindedness) and
more specific behavioral patterns. Because tobacco abstinence is stressful to
many quitters, one would expect abstinence to induce an individual's typical
coping, affective, and other adaptive responses to stress. Therefore, personality
traits and related trait adapative responses to stress and life in general should
predict abstinence response type, severity, relapse, and endurance to the degree
that tobacco abstinence functions as a generalized stressor. Those traits highest
in an individual's general stress-response habit hierarchy should be those manifested in response to nicotine abstinence and to smoking cues. Thus, the trait
adaptive response model of individual differences in response to cessation predicts that individuals whose dominant response to stress is anger or irritability
will respond to cessation with relatively greater increases in anger and irritability
than in other affective responses (see Figure 9.1). In contrast, a person whose
dominant response to stress is depression is predicted to respond primarily with
depression. Similarly, individuals with attentional problems and those easily
distracted by stress are predicted to experience significant decrements in attention
subsequent to cessation. To the degree that weight gain associated with abstinence is a function of acute distress associated with withdrawal, it is expected
that individuals who respond to stress by eating will gain weight subsequent to
quitting. Finally, all other things being equal, individuals predisposed to alcohol

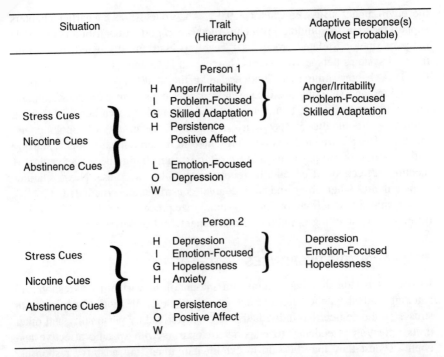

Situation	Trait (Hierarchy)	Adaptive Response(s) (Most Probable)
	Person 1	
Stress Cues Nicotine Cues Abstinence Cues	H Anger/Irritability I Problem-Focused G Skilled Adaptation H Persistence Positive Affect L Emotion-Focused O Depression W	Anger/Irritability Problem-Focused Skilled Adaptation
	Person 2	
Stress Cues Nicotine Cues Abstinence Cues	H Depression I Emotion-Focused G Hopelessness H Anxiety L Persistence O Positive Affect W	Depression Emotion-Focused Hopelessness

Figure 9.1 The trait adaptive response hypothesis predicts that individuals respond to a given situation or state with responses that reflect their general tendency to respond to stress. For example, individuals who habitually are most likely to respond to stress with anger or irritability (such as Person 1, above) are prediced to respond to abstinence-related nicotine and stress cues with anger or irritability. In contrast, individuals, for whom depression and emotion-focused coping are highest in their hierarchy (such as Person 2, above) are expected to experience depression and emotion-focused coping when confronted with stress, nicotine, and abstinence cues.

or drug abuse under stress might be expected to have a higher probability of relapse to these substances while abstaining from cigarettes.

Generally, it is hypothesized that the most important traits moderating nicotine-related adaptive responses are those associated with smoking initiation, prevalence, and relapse (neuroticism, depression, psychoticism, impulsivity, unconventionality, antisocial behavior, and low educational and long-term aspirations, reviewed in Chapter 7). These traits can be viewed as vulnerability traits. The vulnerability is not only to smoking, but to use of other drugs and to suboptimal social and emotional competence (see Chapter 7). Because individuals have a number of different responses to a stressful situation and a hierarchy of different response probabilities in response to stress and nicotine abstinence cues, only the top few most dominant responses are likely to occur (see Figure 9.1).

There is growing support for the trait adaptive response hypothesis. Hughes, Hatsukami, Pickens, and Svikis (1984) observed consistency of tobacco abstinence effects in an experimental design in which periods of smoking and abstinence were alternated in the same smokers. Individuals with a history of depression reported more intense and frequent depressive symptoms subsequent to cessation than did those without such a history (Covey et al., 1990; Glassman, 1993). In a study of affective response to a variety of stressors, D. G. Gilbert, Gilbert & Schultz, et al. (1994) found that emotional responses to each of a variety of stressors (relationship breakup, loss of a loved one, dieting, caffeine abstinence, and alcohol abstinence) correlated highly with affective responses to smoking abstinence. For example, individuals indicating that they experienced large increases in irritability and anxiety subsequent to smoking abstinence also reported large increases in irritability and anxiety after each of the other stressors.

In another line of evidence, breath-hold endurance predicted success in abstaining from smoking (Hajek, Belcher, & Stapleton, 1987), possibly resulting from individual differences in a general willingness to endure discomfort. Hajek (1991) suggested that an unwillingness to endure smoking withdrawal and other forms of discomfort is a reflection of neuroticism. Endurance and tolerance of discomfort may also be influenced by other personality variables, as well as by learning to strive toward long-term goals. Such endurance may account in part for the relationship of successful long-term abstinence with educational achievement and social and emotional skills.

Because the trait portion of most trait adaptive responses reflects genetically and environmentally influenced personality and behavioral patterns (H. J. Eysenck & Eysenck, 1985; see Chapter 7), most trait adaptive responses can be attributed to an interaction of biological and genetic, learning, and environmental factors. Because of the high situational specificity of most behaviors (S. Epstein, 1979) and of many of nicotine's effects (reviewed below), many individual traits can be reliably detected only when conditions are carefully controlled or when samples of the behavior or effect are assessed across a number of settings so that environmental influences can be averaged (S. Epstein, 1979). In a study highlighting the importance of the situation, K. Silverman et al. (1994) demonstrated that the reinforcement value of caffeine was determined by the task (relaxation or vigilance) in which the individual was engaged. Individuals liked caffeine in preference to placebo only when required to perform the vigilance task. When given the opportunity simply to relax, individuals preferred placebo over caffeine. This situational dependency of reinforcing effects is a challenge to models proposing that reinforcement results simply from the direct drug stimulation of mesolimbic reinforcement centers.

SITUATION-DEPENDENT EFFECTS OF NICOTINE AND SMOKING AND ADAPTIVE BEHAVIOR

Adaptive behavior is highly sensitive to situational contingencies and thus is closely related to environmental conditions (S. Epstein, 1979; K. Silverman et al., 1994). Many of the effects of nicotine vary as a function of situational factors and state of the smoker (reviewed in Chapters 5 and 6). Some situations are experienced as highly aversive by almost everyone, yet much, if not most, of the variation in an individual's affect is a function of unique situational cues associated with facilitation or threat to the individual's unique goals (Berscheid, 1982; Mander, 1984). Negative affect occurs subsequent to nicotine abstinence primarily, if not only, when environmental factors are stressful or the individual wants to maintain vigilance and alertness and is not able to do so (see Chapter 5).

Effects of nicotine on a number of electrocortical, physiological, and hormonal measures are situation, state, and dose specific (reviewed in Chapter 6). For example, nicotine typically increases cortical arousal when one is underaroused, but when one is moderately aroused it has minimal or no electrocortical stimulant effects and may in fact reduce cortical and subjective arousal (Church, 1989; J. A. Edwards et al., 1985; H. J. Eysenck, 1980; D. G. Gilbert, Robinson, et al., 1989; Golding & Mangan, 1982; Knott, 1990). Dose, as well as stress, determines cortical response to nicotine. Norton et al. (1991) and Norton and Howard (1988) observed smoking-associated attenuations of cortical event-related potential amplitude in individuals with large nicotine intakes, but amplitude enhancements in low-dose smokers. The low-nicotine group reported increases in subjective arousal subsequent to smoking, whereas high-dose smokers reported decreases in arousal. Ashton et al. (1974) also found high-dose-dependent attenuations of electrocortical activity. Thus, nicotine administration by smoking and other means may allow individuals to achieve a hedonically more desirable level of cortical activation. However, as noted earlier in Chapter 6, several studies have found that smoking increased arousal concomitant with reduction of negative affect. Thus, nicotine has clear CNS stimulant effects in relaxing situations, but it is not clear that it consistently reduces cortical arousal in stressful conditions when negative affect is reduced. Thus, it appears that a simple cortical arousal modulation model is not adequate to account for the situational specificity of nicotine's effects on affective processes.

THE STAR MODEL

Part of the STAR model was introduced in Chapter 5 because such a model is required to account for the situationally dependent affect-modulating effects of smoking and nicotine. The STAR model is based on evidence reviewed in earlier chapters that indicates that tobacco use is reinforced by a number of mechanisms, most of which are situation specific and influenced by and interacting with personality, personality-related goal and behavioral patterns, and trait adaptive responses. This model incorporates the contemporary models of affective processes, individual differences in nicotine sensitivity, personality, and psychopathology reviewed in earlier chapters and synthesizes them into a biopsychosocial model of tobacco use.

STAR Model Basic Mechanisms Mediating Smoking Reinforcement and Affect Modulation

The above-noted findings clearly show that the effects of nicotine on affective and reinforcement mechanisms are mediated in part by situational factors. The effects of nicotine and nicotine abstinence have no direct and invariable affect-modulating and reinforcing effects that generalize across variables of stress, situations, and individuals. Instead, it is hypothesized that nicotine influences information processing that can modulate affect and facilitate both positive and negative reinforcement by a variety of mechanisms. Under certain circumstances nicotine appears to prevent or attenuate negative affect by altering internally driven associative and memory-based processes. In other circumstances, it enhances performance and helps the individual obtain a desired goal state (see Chapter 5). Such performance enhancement promotes positive affect and prevents the negative affect caused by goal frustration. The above evidence suggests the following proposition.

Indirect, Bioinformational Effects

Proposition 1 Most of the affect-modulating and reinforcing effects of nicotine are indirect and are mediated by brain bioinformation-processing mechanisms preceding final emotional output mechanisms (see Figure 9.2 and Chapter 5). Generally, internally driven (e.g., memory, associative, and attention-based) processes are more influenced by nicotine than are externally driven processes resulting from potent (unconditioned and high emotion elicitation potential) external stimuli. Startle and a few other lower order reflexes and responses are exceptions to this proposition (see Chapter 5). Thus, anxiety about tomorrow's job interview may be attenuated by smoking, whereas anxiety during that interview may not be reduced by the identical dose of nicotine if the interviewer provides unequivocal indications that you are doing poorly. Worry about tomorrow is a largely internally driven associative process, whereas unequivocal negative feedback is more externally driven.

Corollaries

1 Nicotine will have minimal effects on affective responses to potent, direct, and proximal stimuli that are of sufficient value to exceed the threshold of the amygdala and other response-side CNS emotional subprocessors.

2 In situations characterized by immediate and clear threat, smoking and nicotine will not attenuate negative affect.

3 In circumstances in which the environment is relatively ambiguous or does not demand immediate coping, cognitive–affective processes are expected to be relatively largely influenced by internal biases, including those produced by nicotine. Thus, affect-related bioinformational stimulus complexes influenced by nicotine include (a) cues of mild to moderate distal or ambiguous threat and

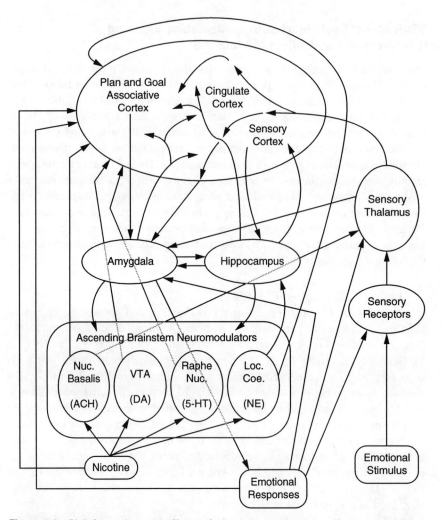

Figure 9.2 Bioinformation and effects of nicotine on cognition, affect, and behavior. The situation- and cue-dependent affect-modulating properties of nicotine suggest that these effects do not reflect direct action on lower, affect-output systems such as the amygdala and hypothalamus but instead bias and prime higher order associative or attentional processes or inhibit certain motor outputs. ACH = acetylcholine; DA = dopamine; 5-HT = serotonin; NE = norepinephrine; NUC = nucleus; VTA = ventral tegmental area; LOC. COE. = locus coeruleus. (Based in part on Derryberry and Tucker, 1992, and LeDoux, 1987. See Chapter 3 for a discussion of the biological bases of emotion and of interconnections of the systems depicted in this figure.)

(b) discrepancies between one's desired and current or anticipated state of performance competence (e.g., ability to sustain attention for a period of time).

Coping and Performance Enhancement   The most frequently proposed alternative to the possibility that nicotine directly modifies affective states is that it does so indirectly by enhancing cognitive functioning and associated task performance (Ashton & Stepney, 1982; Wesnes & Warburton, 1978). The fact that nicotine improves vigilance performance (Wesnes & Warburton, 1978; see Chapter 5) provides support for the enhancement model. The idea that goal attainment results in positive feelings and goal frustration in negative affective states has a long history and much data to support it (Dollard, Doob, Miller, Mowrer, & Sears, 1939; Mander, 1984). On the basis of numerous empirical studies, Gray (1981) equated frustrative nonreward with punishment in his model of the behavioral inhibitory system and introversion. More generally, evidence has suggested that the major personality dimensions are associated with different preferences, motivations, and goals. A consideration of trait-related individual differences in goals, preferences, and reinforcers is likely to be of immense importance when considering interventions to modify smoking and other affect-related behaviors (see Chapter 10).

There is evidence (see Chapter 5) that has suggested that nicotine produces performance enhancement by inherent effects, as well as by alleviating withdrawal symptoms (Wesnes & Warburton, 1978; see Chapter 5). The biological bases of these cognition-enhancing effects of nicotine have received intensive study. The convergence of evidence strongly supports the contention that acetylcholine mediates some of nicotine's attention-enhancing effects (for a review, see Warburton, 1992). However, a number of other neuromodulators, including dopamine, are likely involved in differentially priming nicotine-influenced attentional and motor enhancement (see Chapter 6). ACTH, arginine vasopressin, norepinephrine, and dopamine have tentatively been implicated in the modulation and enhancement of attentional processes (J. R. Cooper et al., 1991) and are elevated by high doses of nicotine (Balfour, 1991a, 1991b).

Dopamine's tendency to facilitate attention to phylogenetically important stimuli and acetylcholine's ability to focus controlled attention (Warburton & Wesnes, 1978; Wise & Bozarth, 1987; see Chapter 6) may combine to facilitate exposure to and active coping with conditioned aversive and threatening situations. Such active coping may not only lead to the extinction of aversive responses to conditioned stimuli, but would also be expected to increase general competence and feelings of self-efficacy and control (Bandura, 1977), all of which should lead to diminished negative affect.

Nicotine-enhanced mesolimbic dopaminergic and central cholinergic activation may contribute to enhanced positive affect and decreased negative affect by influencing tendencies to attend closely to environmental stimuli (see Chapter 6). Enhanced attention to and active interaction with the external environment should also decrease worry and other internal preoccupation with negative mental

SMOKING: INDIVIDUAL DIFFERENCES, PSYCHOPATHOLOGY, AND EMOTION

associations because of limited cognitive capacity. Smoking-cessation-related decrements in dopaminergic and cholinergic systems mediating alertness, concentration, and arousal are predicted to make it difficult for many withdrawing individuals to achieve goals involving sustained vigilance and maximal alertness.

In situations in which the nicotine-deprived smoker is not prompted to perform with sustained high levels of concentration, such as during a relaxing holiday, the individual's decrement in vigilance does not interfere with performance-based goal attainment, and thus increases in negative affect are predicted to be minimal. However, in situations in which the setting demands high levels of alertness and vigilance, transient decrements in arousal resulting from neurobiological adaptation subsequent to quitting would interfere with goal obtainment and result in frustration, irritation, anger, and lessened feelings of self-efficacy that lead in some Situation × Person cases to depression.

The repeatedly demonstrated vigilance-enhancing effects of nicotine are likely to be only one of a number of contributors to nicotine-enhanced performance. Preliminary studies and theories suggest a number of other information-processing mechanisms that are likely to promote feelings of well-being. These information-processing mechanisms are outlined below.

Proposition 2   Nicotine can enhance performance and other forms of goal attainment that facilitate positive affect and prevent goal-frustration-induced negative affect. This performance enhancement is mediated in part by acetylcholine and dopamine and by neuromodulatory hormones including vasopressin, cortisol, and ACTH.

Corollaries

1   Smoking and other forms of nicotine self-administration will increase positive affect and attenuate negative affect in situations in which the smoker is motivated to attain a goal and smoking facilitates goal attainment.

2   Those individuals who obtain large acute performance enhancements from nicotine (e.g., heavy users, neurotics, and those with attention-deficit disorders) will exhibit more frequent and larger performance-related smoking reinforcements and motivations than those who experience smaller effects.

Enhanced Focus on a Primary Task   Attentional reallocation may account for some of nicotine's affect-modulating properties. This model elaborates on the Gilbert and Welser (1989) model and is similar in some respects to that proposed by Steele and Josephs (1988, 1990) to explain alcohol's highly inconsistent effects on anxiety. Steele and Josephs presented evidence supporting the view that alcohol reduces anxiety only in situations that provide distraction from stress-related cues. For example, in a study (Steele & Josephs, 1988) in which subjects waited in preparation for giving a personally stressful speech, individuals in the alcohol-only group experienced the most anxiety, whereas those in the alcohol-plus-distractor-task group experienced the least anxiety. The results of this and related studies (Steele & Josephs, 1990) have supported the view that alcohol reduces negative affect indirectly by reducing the cognitive capacity to allocate attention to multiple sources, as opposed to directly by acting on neurobiological affective centers.

Like alcohol, nicotine can narrow the smoker's focus to the dominant environmental stimulus (Andersson & Hockey, 1977; see Chapter 5). However, nicotine-induced enhancement of focused attention is more adaptive than the use of alcohol because task performance is enhanced by nicotine but reduced by alcohol. Moreover, sensory experiences related to tobacco consumption may combine with nicotine-induced attentional focus by acting as a pleasant distractor. A large percentage of smokers report smoking because they like handling cigarettes, watching smoke, or the sensory experience of smoke in the throat and lungs (M. A. H. Russell, Peto, & Patel, 1974). Nicotine is likely to enhance focus on these dominant, proximal, tobacco-related stimuli to the exclusion of more distal and internally driven information. Experimental studies, though limited in number have supported the view that sensory factors contribute to the negative-affect-alleviating effects of smoking (see Chapter 5). Independent of pharmacological effects, the strong sensory impact associated with tobacco use probably reduces negative affect by providing distraction from negative thoughts and stimulation that relieves boredom and by stimulating sensory and reflex loops that alter central and peripheral physiological activity (Ginzel, 1988; see Chapter 6). This leads to the following proposition.

Proposition 3 In situations in which there are cues of a potential, nonextreme threat, nicotine will reduce anxiety to the degree that the situation also provides moderately distracting, nonthreatening cues onto which nicotine facilitates attentional focus. The potent sensory cues associated with most forms of tobacco use provide such distracting cues.

Corollary Smoking will attenuate anxiety and other forms of information-generated negative affect in a variety of situations, especially those characterized by memory-based associations to ambiguous, low-level distal threats.

Extinction and Habituation Facilitation A number of reports have suggested that smoking- delivered nicotine facilitates habituation of electrocortical and electrodermal measures (L. H. Epstein, Perkins, Jennings, & Pastor, 1990; Friedman et al., 1974; Knott, 1984; Mangan & Golding, 1978). In addition, abstinence from smoking decreased salivary habituation to food cues in a study by L. H. Epstein, Caggiula, Perkins, Mitchell, and Rodefer (1992). Thus, nicotine may reduce negative affect by speeding habituation to conditioned or unconditioned aversive stimuli. Alternatively, nicotine's apparent ability to speed habituation to food stimuli may indirectly attenuate subjective distress by attenuating the approach component of an approach-avoidance conflict in individuals trying to avoid eating and weight gain.

The mechanisms underlying nicotine's effects on extinction have not been determined. Adrenocortical and pituitary hormones have been found to facilitate extinction (H. J. Eysenck & Kelley, 1987). H. J. Eysenck and Kelly (1987) suggested that the effects of vasopressin and certain other pituitary hormones on extinction vary as a function of exposure length because they enhance attention, thereby increasing exposure to the conditioned stimulus. However, cholinergic and dopaminergic mechanisms are clearly involved in some of nicotine's attention-enhancing effects and may be the primary mediators of these effects (Warburton & Walters, 1989; see Chapter 5).

State-dependent learning and extinction may also contribute to nicotine's tendency to speed extinction. Extinction may be speeded to the degree that central and peripheral physiological states associated with nicotine ingestion are similar to those induced by stress and other forms of negative affect. Repeated nicotine-induced, stress-response-like physiological changes may facilitate extinction because such physiological arousal is not followed by aversive response but instead by a state of relaxation (Nesbitt, 1973). Evidence reviewed in the preceding paragraphs suggests the following proposition.

Proposition 4   Nicotine will reduce negative affect elicited by conditioned aversive stimuli by facilitating extinction of conditioned responses in conditions with repeated or protracted conditioned stimulus presentations to which nicotine enhances attention. These attention-promoted, extinction-enhancing effects are in part mediated by nicotine-induced release of several neuromodulators (ACTH, cortisol, vasopressin, dopamine, and acetylcholine).

Corollary   Extinction of conditioned emotional responses will be minimized in situations characterized by very brief stimulus presentations or in which neuromodulator activity is at near maximal levels (as when exposed to intense proximal stressors).

Conflict Reduction by Approach and Engagement   Amsel (1990) has argued that the paradoxical calming and attention-enhancing effects of *d*-amphetamine, methylphenidate, and related stimulants on individuals with attention-deficit hyperactivity disorder is a function of conflict reduction resulting from dopaminergically based enhancement of approach tendencies without any effect on avoidance tendencies. He suggested that those with attention-deficit hyperactivity disorder have not learned to persist and remain in conflict between anticipatory reward-related approach and anticipatory frustration-engendered avoidance tendencies. Thus, he proposed that the raising of the approach but not the avoidance gradient by stimulant medications would be expected to reduce conflict. A number of studies by Robbins (Cador, Robbins, & Everitt, 1989; Robbins, Watson, Gaskin, & Ennis, 1983) have supported the view that amphetamines (but not chlordiazepoxide) increase approach tendencies. Thus, if nicotine also raises the approach but not the avoidance gradient, it would be expected to reduce conflict, conflict-related frustration, and negative affect and to enhance attention. Indeed, the animal literature has supported the view that nicotine enhances approach behavior (Balfour, 1991a, 1991b) but has little effect or possibly reduces avoidance behavior (Hendry & Rosecrans, 1984; Pauly et al., 1992; see Chapter 5). There is a clear need for studies in humans to evaluate the relative effects of nicotine on approach versus avoidance behavior.

The motor model of smoking developed by O'Connor (1989) has much in common with Amsel's (1990) more general approach-enhancement, conflict-reduction model of psychomotor stimulants. O'Connor's model (1989) proposed that

> smoking acts as a behavioral substitute for whatever form of coordinated motor action is necessary to alleviate stress-induced motor conflict. . . . The subjective effects of this may be to introduce a feeling of decisive action where none is possible, or at least a feeling of having achieved more than has actually been done. (p. 157)

Overall, O'Connor's event-related potential studies are consistent with the view that nicotine modulates motor activity. However, currently there appear to be no direct tests of the possibility that nicotine-induced reductions in motor conflict mediate some of its negative-affect-reducing properties. The above evidence suggests the following.

Proposition 5 Nicotine can reduce approach–avoidance-conflict-generated tensions and negative affect by raising the approach gradient and, in some cases, lowering the avoidance gradient. This relative elevation of the approach gradient also minimizes attention to external and internal (memory-associated) cues of punishment and frustrative nonreward and thereby reduces negative-affect-elic-iting associations (see discussion of neuropsychological basis in the lateralized and localized cortical priming section below).

Corollaries

1 Neurotic, introverted, attention-deficit-disordered, schizophrenic, and other individuals characterized by frequent approach–avoidance conflicts (e.g., ambivalence and perceptions of being in a no-win situation) will be especially attracted to smoking and will report conflict reduction as a motivation for smoking.

2 Individuals characterized by low approach tendencies will find smoking a useful self-regulatory resource when they would like to approach a goal but are inhibited by a low approach or high avoidance gradient.

3 Nicotine will attenuate approach–avoidance-conflict-induced negative affect.

Lateralized and Localized Cortical Priming: Neuroinformational Bases of the STAR Model   Striking parallels exist between the effects of nicotine and lateralized CNS affect and behavior-related processes. Thus, nicotine's ability to modulate affect may stem directly or indirectly from its capacity to alter the relative activation and information-processing biases of relatively lateralized CNS neural networks and subprocessors. Evidence has also supported the view that smoking-prevalence-related clinical syndromes (e.g., depression) and personality traits are mediated by relatively lateralized bioinformational systems. Lateralized influences of nicotine are plausible for a number of reasons: (a) Many, if not most, psychoactive substances have lateralized effects; (b) the neurotransmitters that nicotine influences are relatively lateralized; (c) preliminary behavioral and electrocortical evidence supports some lateralization of nicotine's effects; and (d) a lateralized and localized neuropsychological model would account for a number of nicotine's effects parsimoniously, including effects on affect, attention, motivation, and extinction.

Personality, psychopathology, and laterality   A number of observations have suggested that common lateralized mechanisms mediate relationships between smoking, personality, psychopathology, and stress: (a) Like the affect-modulating effects of nicotine, depressed individuals exhibit their dysfunctional attributions primarily when stimuli are ambiguous, distal, and conditioned (Beck, 1991); (b) clinical depression and the induction of depressive affect in nonclinical subjects is associated with an increase in the frontal right- relative to left-hemispheric EEG activation (Davidson, 1993; Chapter 4), whereas smoking-delivered nicotine attenuates this asymmetry (D. G. Gilbert, Gehlbach, et al., 1994; D. G. Gilbert, Meliska, et al., 1994); and (c) the performance-enhancing, frustration-attenuating, and active-approach-promoting effects of nicotine reduce state depression, anxiety, irritation, and impulsive behavior, all of which are related to personality, psychopathology (see Chapter 5), and different lateralized neural network set-points (see Chapter 4).

Evidence of Nicotine's Lateralized Effects   Although it would be inaccurate to imply that one hemisphere or brain region mediates affect or the psychological effects of nicotine, nicotine has been hypothesized to decrease negative affect by increasing the balance of activation in favor of the left relative to the right cerebral hemisphere (D. G. Gilbert & Hagen, 1985; D. G. Gilbert & Welser, 1989). There is reason to believe that nicotine has relatively localized and lateralized CNS effects. Lateralized effects on electrocortical (Elbert & Birbaumer, 1987; D. G. Gilbert, 1985, 1987; D. G. Gilbert, Robinson, et al., 1989; D. G. Gilbert, Gehlbach, et al., 1994; D. G. Gilbert, Meliska, et al., 1994; Norton et al., 1992; Pritchard, 1991a) and electrodermal activity (Boyd & Maltzman, 1984) have been reported. These electrophysiological investigations as well as task-performance studies (reviewed below and in D. G. Gilbert & Welser, 1989) have suggested that during stressful or high-arousal conditions nicotine reduces right-hemisphere processing and activation relatively more than left, whereas during low-stress, relaxing situations, it may activate right-hemisphere processing more than left. In contrast, during highly engaging vigilance tasks smoking appears to activate the left hemisphere more than the right (Hasenfratz & Bättig, 1992). Thus, the lateralized effects of nicotine appear to be situation specific. Nicotine × Situation–Task × Person interactions may account for the modest size of the laterality of EEG effects noted to date. As predicted by the STAR model, nicotine's effects on EEG laterality vary as a function of situation (Gilbert, Robinson, et al., 1989) and neuroticism, extraversion, depression, and type A behavior pattern (H. J. Eysenck & O'Connor, 1979; D. G. Gilbert, 1987; D. G. Gilbert, Gehlbach, et al., 1994; D. G. Gilbert, Meliska, et al., 1994; Golding, 1988). Generally, smoking-sized doses of nicotine appear to facilitate goal achievement and performance and to minimize negative-affect-related electrocortical activity.

Even if the localized and lateralized EEG effects of nicotine prove to be of small magnitude and dependent on situational and dose factors, small information-processing biasing effects may reflect critically important bioinformational processing changes. For example, by means of what is referred to as the butterfly effect (critical differences based on very slight differences in initial conditions), even slight biasing of lateralized and localized neural networks can have very large eventual effects (Lorenz, 1979). Nicotine may be the butterfly of Brain × Situation interactions, producing subtle differences in the balance and activation of various CNS subprocessors and neural networks that, when combined with a complex and ambiguous environment, results in qualitatively different cognitive and affective responses (Pritchard et al., 1993). Behavioral and task-related indexes of lateralized information processes also provide some support for lateralized influences of nicotine.

Limited findings have suggested that during moderately stressful tasks, predominantly left-hemisphere-based performances (e.g., anagram and Stroop word–color tasks) are enhanced by nicotine, whereas right-hemisphere-based processes (e.g., task performance on digit symbol substitution, recall of Bender-gestalt forms, jigsaw puzzle, and facial emotional cue identification) are relatively impaired (D. G. Gilbert & Welser, 1989; see Chapter 5). In contrast to the decrements in right-hemisphere-based performance seen in moderately stressful situations, performance during low-stress tasks has been interpreted as indicating that nicotine enhances relatively right-hemisphere-based performance (see Chapter 5). Although the available evidence has generally supported the view that nicotine has relatively lateralized effects on information processing, the relevant data are very limited. Thus, many additional studies are needed of nicotine's effects on information processing under various task conditions.

Lateralized mechanisms in affect and behavior A convergent body of electrocortical, neuropsychological, pharmacological, psychophysiological, and behavioral data demonstrates that the activation of the right frontal cortex or relative deactivation of the left frontal cortex is associated with the experience of and predisposition to negative affect and avoidance behavior (Davidson, 1984, 1993; Kinsbourne, 1989; see Chapter 3). More generally, the right hemisphere specializes in nonverbal, simultaneous and holistic, and spatial processes, and the left hemisphere is associated with approach behavior, sequential and logical, and verbal information processing (Davidson, 1984, 1993; Kinsbourne, 1989; Tucker & Williamson, 1984). Nicotine's ability to promote approach (Balfour, 1991a, 1991b) and to attenuate avoidance (Pauly et al., 1992) is consistent with its priming left-hemisphere processes while attenuating those of the right frontal cortex. Evidence has suggested that approach and active coping behavior are largely mediated by relatively left-lateralized dopaminergic and cholinergic circuits, whereas withdrawal and phasic arousal are mediated by relatively right-lateralized noradrenergic systems (Kinsbourne, 1989; Tucker & Williamson, 1984).

In addition to acknowledging the left–right laterality differentiation of the cortex, it is essential to distinguish between posterior representational and anterior motor and control systems. The former are primarily located in the parietal cortex, and the latter include the frontal and anterior–temporal cortex (Kinsbourne, 1989; Pribram & McGuinness, 1975). The right posterior cortex mediates a majority of phasic arousal processes (Pribram & McGuiness, 1975) associated with interrupt–withdrawal behavior (Kinsbourne, 1989). In contrast, the left anterior cortex contributes importantly to tonic activation and approach behavior (Davidson, 1993; Kinsbourne, 1989).

Left frontal lateralization of dopaminergic systems suggests that to the degree that dopamine modulates the psychobiological effects of nicotine, alterations of dopaminergic functioning should mimic those of nicotine. Similarities between effects of nicotine and dopamine have been noted by others (see Chapters 2 and 6). In addition, the conclusion that mechanisms mediating nicotine's affect-modulating effects include enhanced vigilance and attentional reallocation in the presence of distal, ambiguous, and low-intensity stress-related cues (see Chapter 5) is similar to Salamone's (1992) observation that the behaviors most easily disrupted by dopamine antagonists and lesions "are highly activated and complex learned instrumental responses that are elicited or supported by mild conditioned stimuli, and maintained for considerable periods of time" (p. 160). These similarities between conditions associated with maximal sensitivity to dopamine activity and maximal nicotinic effects on negative affect suggest that dopamine may mediate these effects of nicotine.

Thus, nicotine-induced reductions of right relative to left-hemisphere activation and associated information processing would be expected to be associated with reductions in physiological and subjective responses to cues associated with stress-related avoidance and right-hemisphere-dominant, negative-affect-related associative networks. Nicotine-induced stimulation of left frontal activation or reduction of right frontal activity during active coping tasks would be expected to reduce negative affect. Enhancement of left relative to right frontal activation would be expected to correlate with enhanced task performance and other forms of active coping, and decreased parietal activation would be expected to result in a general dampening of phasic arousal responses to acute stressors and to the urge to attend to or otherwise react to task-irrelevant stimuli. Decreased right posterior cortical activation and sensitivity by nicotine would decrease interruption sensitivity, distractibility, and arousal to emotion-related stimuli. Decreased interruption and frustration sensitivity should lead to decreased emotional responsivity. Nicotine-enhanced right relative to left parietal activation during low-stimulation vigilance tasks may mediate some of smoking's ability to enhance arousal and sustained vigilance during such conditions.

Consistent with this prediction, simultaneous reductions in right-hemisphere EEG activation and in negative affect have been found while subjects viewed a stressful movie (D. G. Gilbert, Robinson, et al., 1989). Such lateralized effects may result from nicotine's influencing relatively lateralized neurotransmitter systems and thereby priming relatively lateralized affect-specific associative networks (D. G. Gilbert & Hagen, 1985; D. G. Gilbert & Welser, 1989). On the basis of the above evidence, the following proposals are made.

Proposition 6   Nicotine increases left frontal (cholinergic and dopaminergic) activation and thereby enhances controlled processing, approach mechanisms, and left-hemisphere-dominant, positive-affect-related associative networks. Feelings of self-control and well-being are thereby increased, especially in conditions and individuals predisposed to relatively low left-hemisphere activation or relatively high right frontal activation. Relative right-hemisphere activation and negatively valanced associative networks (possibly modulated by serotonin and norepinephrine) are decreased by nicotine during stressful conditions. Such attenuation of right-hemispere activation thereby reduces interruption sensitivity and decreases the probability of irritation- and frustration-induced negative affect.

Corollaries

1   Individuals characterized by decreased left frontal or relatively increased right frontal activation (e.g., depressed, neurotic, and impulsive individuals) will use smoking and other forms of nicotine as a form of self-medication and will experience larger increases in left frontal activation from nicotine than those without such asymmetry.

2   Situations promoting increased right or decreased left frontal activation, as well as those requiring left frontal activation for goal achievement, will elicit smoking urges as a form of self-regulation for goal attainment.

Anterior-Posterior Gradients and General Arousal   *Proposition 7*   Although there frequently appears to be some lateralization of nicotine's influence on cognitive and electrocortical processes, the strongest and most reliable effect is on general arousal functions (see Chapter 6). Knott (1989) found low doses of smoking-delivered nicotine to have relatively greater activating effects on posterior sites, whereas slightly higher doses activated anterior and posterior sites equally, thus, Proposition 7: Low doses of nicotine administered in relaxing situations result in enhanced posterior, especially right posterior, activation and thereby enhanced vigilance. Under such conditions perceptual, rather than overt, motor orientation predominates. This perceptual enhancement will be experienced as a satisfying and tranquil state of alertness if it is consistent with the individual's goals. Such low-dose effects are relatively more mediated by cholinergic and less influenced by more frontal-related dopaminergic activation. Higher (but moderate) smoking-sized doses of nicotine will activate more frontally influenced dopaminergic projections involved in more active motor engagement and active attention. Such frontal dopaminergic activation will be reinforcing if the state facilitates goal achievement and associated cues.

Corollaries

   1   Effects of nicotine on relative activation of various brain sites will be dose and situation dependent.
   2   Effects of nicotine on information processing, motor activity, and subjective state will be highly dose and situation dependent.

   Associative Processes and Memory Indexing   *Proposition 8*   On the basis of the above-reviewed evidence of lateralized effects of nicotine on electrocortical and cognitive measures and on the state-dependent effects of nicotine, it follows that the relatively localized and lateralized effects of nicotine alter the accessibility of hippocampal memory units and bias information in terms of left frontal positive-affect-related associations and schemas and away from right frontal negative-affect- and withdrawal-related schemas. Bioinformational states channel information flow not only by conditioned associative processes, but by lateralized neurotransmitter and neural-network-specific processes. For example, not only does nicotine prime memory cues and schemas by indexing processes similar to the hippocampal memory indexing identified by Teyler and DiScenna (1986), but negative-affect- and avoidance-related information is relatively more encoded in right-hemisphere serotonergic and noradrenergic systems, whereas positive affect and approach-related memory and information processing is more integrated with left-hemisphere dopaminergic neural networks. These lateralized and localized bioinformational networks operate at both limbic and neocortical levels (Derryberry & Tucker, 1992; see Chapter 3).

Corollaries

   1   Changes in brain-state tuning and priming (by means of external situational and perceptual factors and by internal physiological states) can alter the ease or difficulty (probability) of accessing different types of affective information.

2   The effects of nicotine on affective and cognitive processes will be a function of the preexisting state of various CNS bioinformational networks.

Summary of lateralized and localized neuroprocessing model   The propositions listed above and their supportive evidence provide a set of workable hypotheses concerning some of the biological and psychological bases of nicotine's affect-modulating and performance-enhancing effects. Details of the model are certain to be inaccurate in many cases. A number of mechanisms reviewed in Chapter 6 are also likely to contribute to nicotine's reinforcing effects. For example, evidence has suggested that nicotine may in some cases produce muscular relaxation, produce generalized cortical stimulant effects, and provide a number of homeostatic functions both directly and indirectly, such as those posited (in Chapter 6) to be mediated by nicotine-induced elevations of cortisol. The lateralized effects hypothesis is attractive because it suggests a common biological basis for a diverse set of psychological and physiological effects of nicotine. Biological contributions must be supplemented by an understanding of situational and higher order psychological processes if a balanced, integrative, and practically useful modeling of individual differences in smoking is to be obtained. These psychological and environmental dimensions are briefly outlined in the following section.

Abstinence-Related Negative Affect   *Withdrawal in Heavy Smokers*   Although cues related to goal achievement and frustration are major contributors to affective states, such states can also be influenced by physiological conditions that have no direct higher order informational component, yet that bias bioinformational affective networks. For example, physical illnesses frequently cause changes in mood, as do many drugs (Thayer, 1989; see Chapter 3). Rapid drops in bodily nicotine concentrations in very heavy tobacco users may result in such dramatic physiologically induced mood changes, even though evidence reviewed in Chapter 5 has indicated that this is not the case in more average smokers (those who smoke 15–20 cigarettes per day). However, there is no strong evidence to support this possibility, even though it is an assumption that commonly appears in the recent smoking literature.

Thus, the following proposition is highly speculative and might appear contrary to the general rule that negative affect subsequent to nicotine abstinence is conditional on a stressful environment. However, this proposition can be seen as consistent with the STAR model in that the model recognizes large individual differences in biological and psychological dispositions. For an appropriately disposed minority of heavy smokers, it is likely that the physiological nicotine withdrawal state itself produces a bodily state of malaise that is sufficient to elicit various negative affects.

Proposition 9   Heavy smokers (generally those with daily nicotine intakes of 0.4 mg/kg body weight or more) will experience an increased state of negative affect and potentially the onset of a clinical disorder (even in relatively neutral environmental conditions) if their large daily nicotine intake and temperamental traits dispose them toward negative affect or psychopathology.

Corollaries

1   Very heavy smokers who are not disposed toward negative affect (e.g., who are low in neuroticism) will tend not to experience negative affect in response to abstinence in relaxing conditions, whereas those who are predisposed will experience negative affect to the degree of their disposition and in the direction of their disposition (the trait-affective response noted above).

2   Heavy smokers exhibiting large abstinence-related physiological changes will be predisposed to negative affect subsequent to cessation, even in relatively stress-free environments. Highly nicotine-sensitive individuals (O. F. Pomerleau, Collins, et al., 1993) are likely to exhibit such changes.

Personality and Bioinformational Self-Regulatory Systems: Neural Networks and Beyond   Gray's recent work (1981, 1982, 1991) stands out as the pinnacle of current bioinformational models of individual differences in personality and affective processes. Although the term *bioinformational* has received attention in recent models of emotion (e.g., Lang, 1979), it has not systematically been applied to smoking reinforcement and the effects of nicotine (Niaura, Goldstein, & Abrams, 1992). Current bioinformational models of personality (Gale, 1987) and affect (Lang, 1979; Chapter 3) generally recognize the importance of hierarchically arranged, massively parallel, frequently interacting recurrent information processing with different subprocessors operating at different stages and levels of the hierarchy (Gale, 1987). Various biologically based information-processing and information-influencing subsystems have different set-points in different individuals, thus contributing to individual differences in temperament, responsivity, learning, and personality. The biopsychosocial STAR model assumes that nicotine alters numerous mutually influential affect- and reinforcement-related psychological and biological set-points and can promote or otherwise alter a variety of psychological and biological homeostatic processes when used as a self-regulatory tool by the habitual user.

The emotionality characteristic of individuals high in neuroticism is consistent with the hypotheses that such individuals are characterized by relatively weaker self-regulatory (homeostatic) mechanisms and that they have higher emotional set-points or lower thresholds for a variety of affect-related cognitive, affective, and motivational processes. Differences in set-points relevant to neuroticism and psychopathology are generally assumed to be a function of limbic system lability (H. J. Eysenck & Eysenck, 1985; Gale, 1987). However, from a hierarchical systems perspective, a number of higher (e.g., neocortically based)

control systems may be involved in both the instigation of affective and motivational processes (e.g., by the interruption of abstract distal goals) and various
complex learned informational structural inhibitory outputs (e.g., counting to 10
before impulsively responding or by reconceptualizing a stimulus as nonthreatening even though one's conditioned or limbic subsystems are promoting highly
emotive responses). In addition, failure of higher inhibitory informational systems to diminish excessive emotive functions of limbic and other emotional
systems appears to occur when neocortical functioning is physiologically inhibited, as is the case when one uses many drugs or is ill, fatigued, or otherwise
physiologically stressed. Individuals with permanently or frequently compro-
mised higher control functioning, as in the case of those with many brain types
of injuries, demonstrate clearly abnormal personality characteristics (Stuss,
Gow, & Hetherington, 1992).

The individual differences in lability of cognitive–affective structures suggest that the term *affective information-processing states* (AIPS) is a useful
conceptual term for considering relationships between personality, psychopathology, information processing, and affect. AIPS include mood-state-dependent
associations and learning (Blaney, 1986), cognitive-arousal-state-dependent
emotional responses (Zillmann, 1979), and affect-related-physiological biasing
of attentional and general information processing (D. G. Gilbert, 1991). Dissipation of these states across time suggests that individuals differ in their capacity
to rapidly reduce them. Thus, individuals can be viewed as differing in their
time constants for dissipation of different components of AIPS, as well as in
their typical (trait) AIPS for a specific affect.

AIPS influence all stages of information processing: acquisition, storage,
maintenance, selective abstraction, tunnel, polarized thinking, catastrophization
(Beck, 1991), and expression. Individual differences in these states vary as a
function of personality and psychopathology. For example, the fact that extraverts are more sensitive to signs of reward suggests that they have a higher
reward or positive reinforcement set-point or lability and associated neurobiology
(probably residing largely in mesolimbic dopaminergic systems). Differing sensitivities to rewards and punishments, as well as individual differences in AIPS
associated with different affective states are likely to contribute to individual
differences in the development of goals. An understanding of the important, yet
largely neglected, relationships among temperament, goals, environment, and
smoking constitutes much of the remainder of this chapter.

Environmental and Other Situational Factors Promoting Smoking
Family, peer, workplace, and cultural factors are important determinants of
smoking incidence, smoking quit rate, and smoking relapse (Conrad, Flay, &
Hill, 1992; USDHHS, 1988). Modeling, cigarette availability, cost, and smoking
response cost (e.g., workplace and social smoking contingencies), as well as
common genetic factors, appear to mediate such relationships (Carmelli et al.,
1990, 1992; Leventhal, Baker, Brandon, & Fleming , 1989; USDHHS, 1988).

The STAR model views these classical smoking-related situational factors as mediated by individual differences in personality or temperament-influenced goals and preferences. The specifics of these mediating processes are discussed in the following sections.

Temperamental Traits and Long-Term Cognitive–Motivational Schemas: Goals, Social and Emotional Competencies, Expectancies, and Smoking

Current treatment interventions and models of smoking do not adequately attend to the individual smoker's interrelated life goals, expectancies, habits, and temperaments. Instead, most research and intervention efforts have focused relatively exclusively on one or two processes in isolation. For example, intervention techniques either have relied relatively exclusively on cognitive–behavioral techniques developed out of a social learning theory or have used nicotine replacement with minimal or no consideration of how the two interventions might be combined or modified to meet the needs of specific types of smokers so as to promote maximal long-term abstinence. The STAR model of smoking is distinguished by its emphasis on the importance of recognizing the interrelatedness of temperament and personality, personal goals, learning, coping skills, and other middle-level constructs and environmental influences. The model is based on the argument that in addition to the classical conditioning and the deeper core belief networks, an understanding of the individual's temperament, as well as multiple interrelated goals and expectancies of goal achievement or frustration, is necessary to understand why individuals fail to engage in coping skills taught in many traditional smoking cessation programs.

Although the utility of personality traits is supported by empirical evidence showing them to be highly heritable, to differentiate smokers from nonsmokers (see Chapters 5 and 7), and to predict response to abstinence and to nicotine, traditional personality trait measures do not provide the specificity required for high predictability. Social and emotional skills and smoking expectancies appear to contribute to successful long-term abstinence (see Shiffman, 1993b). However, the behavioral and cognitive–behavioral coping skill development procedures used in a vast majority of current smoking-cessation interventions do not address learning, emotional schemas, goals, or temperament that influences motivations to implement such skills (Leventhal et al., 1989), a fact that may in part account for the very modest success of even the best current programs. Neither do the cognitive–behavioral approaches to date address the fact that individual differences in personality and psychopathology are predictive of success in long-term smoking abstinence. Thus, neither of the traditional approaches can be considered integrative or comprehensive enough to account for or lead to highly effective interventions.

The STAR model proposes that an adequate causal understanding of coping skill implementation and successful quitting requires individualized assessments of (a) long- and short-term goals and associated organized action sequences, (b) smoking and coping styles across environments and psychobiological states, (c) temperament and personality traits and dispositions toward psychopathology, (d) nicotine exposure history, and (e) nicotine response profile and sensitivity. Thus, the theory proposes a multimodal–multilevel assessment. Being a biopsychosocial model, it assumes a need to evaluate and intervene with each smoker as an individual with a unique combination of biological, psychological, and social dispositions and risk factors. Being a systems model, it also assumes that each of the three systems (biological, psychological, and social) interacts with the others.

Both temperamental and cognitive traits influence long-term goals (including eventual nonsmoker vs. smoker status) by a number of direct and indirect mechanisms. For example, the sensitivity to punishment characteristic of introverts (Gray, 1981) is likely to lead to a life of caution and to a goal of a healthy lifestyle. In contrast, extraversion, risktaking, and other reward- and sensation-seeking behaviors are likely to make individuals insensitive to cues of potential punishment (e.g., smoking health warnings) and are likely to promote cognitive, social, and behavioral action sequences that reinforce smoking and other risk-taking behavior patterns. The sensation-seeking lifestyle (Zuckerman, 1979)— including smoking, drinking, and a focus on pleasure—is thus likely to be so reinforcing to individuals with a strong genetic disposition toward sensation-seeking that long-term cognitive–motivational schemas include no current plans to quit any of a variety of risky behaviors.

Temperament and personality not only influence behavior by altering rational choices based on preferences and sensitivities to cues of reward and punishment, but also influence the classical and higher order conditioning processes (H. J. Eysenck & Eysenck, 1985). Although smoking cue sensitivity has been found to be predictive of relapse (Niaura, Abrams, Demuth, Pinto, & Monti, 1989), differences in smoking cue reactivity as a function of conditioning-related personality dimensions have not been assessed. Similarly, personality influences on higher order conditioning processes have received little attention in the smoking literature.

Smoking and affect-related schemas result from higher order conditioning and associative processes. Schemas are organized informational, associational networks about one's self and the environment (Mander, 1984). They result from numerous associative processes: conditioning, response consequences, and physiological and state-dependent associations (including sensory–sensory, motor–motor, and sensorimotor connections). In addition, they include higher order associative processes such as organized beliefs, expectancies, and meanings. Schemas tend to act as a unit because one or a few stimuli tend to elicit an organized set of associations and responses. Thus, schemas are helpful in predicting and summarizing responses to various stimulus class sets. Any stimulus of a given class tends to elicit the same response set (e.g., negative affect, smoking expectancies, and eventually lighting up a cigarette). Clinical researchers frequently argue that schemas mediate both adaptive and maladaptive behavior, including psychopathology and substance abuse (Beck, Wright, Newman, & Liese, 1993). The STAR model proposes that emotion-related schemas have tight associative and neurobiological connections with relatively localized and relatively lateralized neurotransmitter and neuromodulatory systems underlying basic emotional systems (see above review and Chapter 3).

Situation × Trait Short-Term Goals: Goal Facilitation, Competence, and Smoking

To the degree that affective states result from facilitated or impeded organized action sequences or goals, affect is a function of goal characteristics, competency in areas facilitating goal attainment, and difficulty achieving the goal. Thus, holding goals and environment constant, highly skilled and otherwise competent individuals should experience more positive affect and less negative affect in situations in which skill is related to positive outcome (goal achievement). In other cases, competence and skill are not related to whether one's goals are achieved. For example, whether one's alma mater wins the football game of the decade may have a great deal to do with one's emotions just after the game and even for days afterward (length of affective response being related to goal importance, among other things). In most cases, immediate goals are not only a function of long-term goals and organized action sequences, but also of expectations.

Whether one achieves the goal of long-term smoking abstinence is a function of each of the influences noted in the preceding paragraph. Whether one uses the coping techniques taught in cessation interventions is a function not only of long-term goals, but of shorter term and immediate environmental contingencies, emotional-state-dependent memory, and one's general hierarchy of short-term and immediate plans and goals. One's long-term goal may be to quit smoking, but recent loss of a loved one, concerns about performing well during final exam week, and any of a myriad of other potentially very important immediate-performance-related plans and goals may temporarily replace long-term, goal-related plans and associated behaviors. Thus, an individual may consciously or unconsciously choose not to implement abstinence-promoting skills or a plan to quit smoking. Such relegation of quitting to a more peripheral position in one's goal hierarchy may explain more of the reason that smokers say they would like to quit but cannot than does physical or psychological addiction. What individuals may be describing when they say they cannot quit is that they observe themselves repeatedly choosing not to quit in the short term, so that in the long term they are hooked and cannot quit. In addition, long-term plans and goals can be overridden by activation of overlearned smoking behavior schemas activated by any of numerous internal or environmental cues, independent of higher level, rational decisions.

Multiple Conscious and Nonconscious Paths to Smoking

Most human behavior is mediated by processes outside of conscious awareness. Such processes are referred to as automatic functions. Automatic functioning is fast, inflexible, and effortless; it lacks control and awareness and is stimulus bound. In contrast, nonautomatic cognitive processing is effortful, flexible, dependent on intention, restricted by limited cognitive capacity, and slow (Posner & Snyder, 1975; Tiffany, 1992). The stereotyped, automatized action sequences of smoking in some individuals has much in common with automatic processing (Tiffany, 1992). Nonautomatic processing is required when individuals attempt to inhibit automatic processing (D. A. Norman & Shallice, 1985). Tiffany proposed that

> [with] a history of repeated practice, the cognitive systems controlling drug procure-
> ment and consumption will become increasingly automatized. That is, drug use in
> the addict should be stereotyped, stimulus bound, effortless, difficult to control, and
> not dependent upon awareness for completion. (p. 132)

Procedures for carrying out these automatized skills are stored as action schemas in long-term memory. The degree to which particular stimulus complexes elicit smoking schemas depends on smoking conditioning history. Urges to smoke arise when smoking action schemas are inhibited by environmental blocks or by nonautomatic cognitive efforts to abstain from smoking. Tiffany argued that most drug use is automatic and that smoking relapse is often absent-minded behavior resulting from activation of smoking schemas without concurrent inhibition by nonautomatic cognitive processes. Thus, individuals who are distracted by cognitively challenging tasks and whose nonautomatic cognitive capacities are reduced (e.g., due to alcohol consumption) and those experiencing negative affect are seen to have fewer non-automatic resources to inhibit smoking action schemas.

Many, if not most, of the causal paths mediating smoking behavior, reinforcement, and relapse occur outside of conscious awareness, yet the effects of such nonconscious processes are eventually manifested in overt behavior and frequently by the conscious experience or urge to smoke and other conflict-related processes. Negative affect management and other forms of smoking as a psychological tool to enhance mood or performance are likely to be highly automatized so that the desire to smoke to obtain such beneficial effects are only consciously recognized when environmental factors have impeded smoking. In some cases, anger and negative affect may arise from the frustration of automatic processing and effort required to inhibit automatic smoking.

In summary, whether one persists in abstaining from smoking and implements one's skills in coping with urges to smoke is related to (a) personal higher order, rational goals; (b) the matrix of environmental cues eliciting short-term cognitive–motivational–behavioral complexes; and, (c) situational cues and factors related to smoking, goal-related, and affective schemas.

CONCLUSION: COMPLEX CAUSAL PATHS TO AND FROM SMOKING

Smoking has multiple causes, and these causes vary across individuals and situations. For example, the existence of very light smokers (chippers) who smoke for years without progressing to heavier smoking presents a challenge to univariate causal models (e.g., pharmacological dependence). The associations of personality and psychopathology with smoking-related processes also require the assessment of individual differences and multiple determination.

The identification of a reasonable number of causal pathways to smoking and abstinence will be an important task of any theoretical and clinically useful theory. Behavior therapy and causal modeling in psychology in general have moved away from simple univariate causal models in recognition of the multiple, interacting determinants of most behaviors (Haynes, 1988). Causal models are important because they in large part determine preintervention assessment and intervention programs. Complex causal models recognize the multiple determinants of behavior and individual differences in causal functions. Such models characterize multiple controlling variables, their causal weights, and additive and interactive influences on behavior. Furthermore, they recognize that causal factors vary across time and types of controlling variables.

The multiple causal pathways and individual differences in these pathways associated with smoking present a challenge to traditional methods of classification and analysis. Traditional behavioral (functional analytic) approaches are very time consuming, whereas traditional diagnostic approaches are cost-efficient but insensitive to the variances in complex causality across individuals (Haynes & O'Brien, 1988). In response to this challenge, Haynes (1988) suggested that progress in behavioral assessment can be made if one assumes that there is a limited set of causal models applicable to a given behavior and if causal markers of these causal processes can be identified. A marker is a relatively easily determined indicator of a more difficult to measure complex causal process.

Evidence has indicated that different smoking-related causal paths are differentiated by individual differences in situations interacting with the multiple traits reviewed in this chapter. The causal paths associated with smoking initiation, maintenance, cessation, and relapse and long-term abstinence appear in many respects to be similar to each other. However, knowledge of these paths is rudimentary. Tasks for scientists include (a) careful characterization of causal paths; (b) characterization of conditional probabilities of each path given personality, psychopathology, gender, age, and other individual differences variables; (c) identification of markers reflective of primary causal paths; and (d) application of individual differences in these paths to prevention efforts, the topic discussed in the next chapter.

Chapter 10

Implications of the STAR Model for Smoking Interventions

A prominent scientist (Saul Shiffman, 1993b) recently concluded that compared with the 1960s and 1970s "research on behavioral approaches to smoking is stagnant . . . [that] few innovative approaches have been introduced over the past decade. . . . [and that] average treatment outcomes have not improved over this period" (p. 718). He proposed that the lack of clinical innovation and at best modestly effective treatments have resulted in part from the near universal use of multicomponent programs, with the outcome that all programs look alike. Furthermore, programs are generally ineffective with the growing percentage of smokers who are disposed to psychopathology, impulsivity, and social alienation (Shiffman, 1993b; see Chapter 7). This lack of treatment efficacy with high-risk groups may largely reflect a failure to develop interventions individualized for specific high-risk smokers. Improvement in abstinence outcomes will require that individualized interventions consider differences in biological, psychological, and social and environmental factors as dominant treatment features. This chapter proposes individualized treatment for smoking based on the empirical and theoretical bases of preceding chapters.

This increased focus on the need for treatment matching for particular smoking subgroups is motivated in part by the high relapse rates in general smoker populations and in particular by the very high rates in special populations that constitute an ever-higher percentage of the smoking population (Coambs et al., 1989). Moreover, empirical evidence has suggested that the relative balance of mechanisms maintaining smoking and promoting relapse vary systematically as a function of individual traits, including one's environment. Special high-risk individuals include those high in characteristics that differentiate smokers from nonsmokers, that is, neuroticism and emotional disorders, impulsivity, and antisocial behavior. The personality-, psychopathology-, and situation-specific mechanisms contributing to low cessation success rates in these groups were addressed in Chapters 7 and 9. Although the need for individualized interventions is increasingly articulated, published intervention approaches to date have not indicated what assessments and interventions should be included in the individualized treatment of smokers.

Current interventions are technique oriented (e.g., coping skills training) and ignore or, at best, do not systematically attend to individual differences (Leventhal et al., 1989). Successful interventions must build on empirically based knowledge of the psychological and biological mechanisms and individual differences mediating smoking and relapse if trial and treatment errors are to be avoided (Leventhal & Cleary, 1980). For example, during the first weeks of smoking abstinence there is a high prevalence of depression and relapse in those with a history of depression (Covey et al., 1990; see Chapter 7). Because depression and other forms of negative affect predict smoking relapse (Shiffman, 1986), depression-prone individuals are likely to benefit from a relatively greater allocation of treatment time devoted to decreasing their depression potential and ameliorating depressive symptomatology. Excessive treatment focus on pathological and affective processes for those with minimal psychopathology, however, wastes time that could more productively be spent on specific coping skills and strategy interventions to maintain abstinence. In short, the allocation of limited resources should be determined by assessment of individual differences, using norm-based syndromal approaches as well as more atomistic and idiographic cognitive–behavioral assessment.

Although there is widespread agreement in theory that smokers should be provided with treatment designed specifically for their individual reasons for smoking, this theory has not been put into practice. Shiffman (1993b) has suggested that successful smoker–treatment matching will require the development of three basic components: (a) a theory of smoker typologies and of a treatment process that dictates client–treatment matching, (b) valid assessment instruments that accurately measure relevant dimensions of individual differences, and (c) treatments that differentially influence different smoker characteristics. These three components are important elements of the individualized approach advocated in this chapter.

ASSESSMENT: AN INDIVIDUALIZED STAR APPROACH

The biopsychosocial STAR model outlined in Chapter 9 implies the need for individualized assessment and intervention based on smoker typologies. The individualized approach recognizes the important guidance provided by nomothetic (norm-based) assessments, including syndromal-based systems such as the *DSM–IV*. Nomothetic approaches allow one to characterize similarities and differences across individuals and thus allow a form of prediction that is not possible without extremely time-consuming idiographic assessment (Haynes, 1988). The individualized (idiographic) cognitive–behavioral assessment and interventions proposed in this chapter are complementary to and operate within the nomothetic systems (Hersen & Bellack, 1988). Information provided by combined nomothetic and idiographic cognitive–behavioral approaches will promote efficient and efficacious smoking interventions.

The STAR model offers a theory of smoker typologies based on nicotine intake and sensitivity, psychopathology, temperament, middle-level traits, and situational factors (reviewed in Chapter 9). The following paragraphs elaborate on the nature and assessment of these STAR-model-derived smoker typologies.

Nicotine Dependence and Sensitivity and Responsivity

Assessment of nicotine intake history, tolerance, dependence, and sensitivity is important to the degree that measures of these constructs predict severity of abstinence response and success in long-term abstinence (USDHHS, 1988; see Chapter 5). Although the convergence of findings have suggested that more heavily dependent and heavier smokers tend to respond better to nicotine replacement therapy (e.g., nicotine gum or patch; Fagerstrom, 1991; M. A. H. Russell, 1994) and may respond differently to other interventions, measures proposed as markers of nicotine dependence have poor predictive validity (Kenford et al., 1994). For example, many studies have failed to find associations between cessation success and pretreatment-proposed dependence markers such as the Fagerstrom Tolerance Questionnaire score, expired air carbon monoxide, baseline blood nicotine and cotinine concentrations, and number of cigarettes smoked per day (Kenford et al., 1994). Furthermore, the various measures of dependence have very low intercorrelations (Heatherton, Kozlowski, Frecker, & Fagerstrom, 1991; Kenford et al., 1994). The STAR model suggests that the failure of these measures reflects a failure to incorporate situational and personality factors into nicotine-dependence constructs. Nonetheless, traditional putative markers of nicotine dependence may be of value when assessing extremely heavy or light smokers and when used in combination with personality and situational variables in an integrated and individualized manner.

Habitual Nicotine Intake and Smoking History Daily nicotine intake and abstinence responses are far more accurately characterized by blood or salivary cotinine concentrations than by self-reported number and type of cigarettes consumed (USDHHS, 1988). Individual differences in daily cigarette consumption and smoking history are poor predictors of abstinence responses and successful long-term abstinence (USDHHS, 1988; see Chapter 5), except in the case of extremely light smoking (Shiffman, 1989). There is a clear need for an accurate, inexpensive, and easy-to-use measure of cotinine (Fagerstrom, 1991) or other indicator of habitual nicotine intake. Cotinine assays are preferable as estimates of daily nicotine intake as this primary metabolite of nicotine has a long half-life that results in much less variability throughout the day than that observed for nicotine. Nicotine's half-life is only about 2 hours, whereas that of cotinine averages about 20 hours (Benowitz, Jacob, Jones, & Rosenbert, 1982). Unfortunately, even though salivary and blood cotinine concentrations are good indicators of nicotine intake during the past 24 hours, the cost and time involved in determining cotinine concentration ($25–$30 per sample) makes the routine and timely use of such assays difficult.

Daily number of cigarettes smoked and cigarette nicotine delivery have very small correlations with cotinine concentrations (Heatherton et al., 1991; USDHHS, 1988) and cannot, therefore, be considered valid indications of other than extreme differences in nicotine intake. Nonetheless, cigarette number and nicotine delivery can provide crude estimates of whether an individual is an extremely light or heavy smoker. Expired breath carbon monoxide may be of some use in highly controlled conditions, but it suffers as a measure of nicotine intake because of its short half-life and reactivity to physical activity level (Kenford et al., 1994; USDHHS, 1988).

Questionnaire-Assessed Smoking Dependence   Psychological dependence on smoking and nicotine is a motivation-related construct for which there is currently no adequately valid measure. The most frequently used instrument designed to assess nicotine tolerance and dependence is the Fagerstrom Tolerance Questionnaire (Fagerstrom, 1978). The weakness of the questionnaire's associations with cessation outcome and other measures (Heatherton et al., 1991) is, in part, a function of its poor internal consistency. It does not reliably assess a single construct (G. E. Swan, Ward, & Jack, 1991). A recent slight revision of the Fagerstrom Tolerance Questionnaire, the Fagerstrom Test for Nicotine Dependence has somewhat improved psychometric properties (Heatherton et al., 1991). Thus, it should be used until better instruments are devised. However, the Fagerstrom Test for Nicotine Dependence should not be viewed as a highly accurate measure of nicotine dependence, tolerance, or intake as it has rather poor predictive ability (Kenford et al., 1994).

A number of studies have found no correlation between Fagerstrom Tolerance Questionnaire score and cardiovascular or other responses to standard challenge doses of nicotine (D. G. Gilbert, Meliska, et al., 1994; D. G. Gilbert & Meliska, 1992; Masson & Gilbert, 1990). Shiffman, Zetttler-Segal, et al. (1992) found that very light smokers were no more sensitive to nicotine (no less tolerant) on a number of physiological measures than were regular smokers. The minority of studies observing correlations of the questionnaire with physiological responses to smoking (Fagerstrom & Schneider, 1989) and with relapse may be explicable in terms of the Fagerstrom Tolerance Questionnaire's correlations with personality and reasons for smoking. The questionnaire correlates significantly with neuroticism (D. G. Gilbert, Meliska, et al., 1994; Masson & Gilbert, 1990) and with reasons for smoking (G. E. Swan et al., 1991). Therefore, causal inferences about the Fagerstrom questionaire's small associations with smoking are ambiguous unless effects of neuroticism and related variables are controlled. *DSM-III-R*-defined dependent smokers have also been found to be higher in neuroticism than smokers not meeting *DSM-III-R* criteria (Breslau, Kilbey, & Andreski, 1993b). Individual differences in the *DSM*-dependence assessed by the Fagerstrom Tolerance Questionnaire, the Fagerstrom Test for Nicotine Dependence, appear in part to reflect general neuroticism.

Factor analysis of the Fagerstrom Test for Nicotine Dependence has shown it to have two factors (Morning Smoking and Cigarette Consumption). In contrast, the Covey, Glassman, and Stetner's (1994) Nicotine Dependence Scale yielded three underlying factors that have yet to be validated. Overall, it is clear that nicotine dependence is a multidimensional construct that is only partly reflected by the Fagerstrom measures. New, more comprehensive and lengthy measures are likely to capture more of this construct. Until more comprehensive and better validated measures are available, it is suggested that cessation interventions use the Nicotine Dependence Scale and Fagerstrom Test for Nicotine Dependence in combination. The STAR model suggests that a multivariate approach including situational, personality, learning, and biological nicotine sensitivity dimensions is required for an adequate characterization of nicotine dependence.

Physical dependence and neuroadaptation may be assessed by physiological, cognitive, and behavioral changes associated with short-term abstinence. Questionnaires proposed as measures of dependence should be validated by associating them with a number of physiological, behavioral, and cessation outcome measures, as well as demonstrating their relationship to and partial independence from personality and reasons-for-smoking constructs. It is difficult to differentiate psychological from pharmacological dependence to nicotine because so many behaviors and psychological processes are associated with smoking (Fagerstrom, 1991). Assessment of physiological and psychological responses to nicotine challenge doses and to 24-hour smoking deprivation may facilitate differentiation of pharmacological from psychological processes.

Nicotine Tolerance and Sensitivity: Responses to Standard Challenge Doses   Individual differences in nicotine sensitivity may be most accurately measured by means of physiological, behavioral, and subjective responses to standardized doses of nicotine. This is most easily assessed with a quantified smoke and nicotine delivery system (D. G. Gilbert, Jensen, & Meliska, 1989; D. G. Gilbert & Meliska, 1992; O. F. Pomerleau, Rose, Pomerleau, & Majchrzak, 1989). Physiological and behavioral measures provide an index of nicotine tolerance and sensitivity independent of self-biases associated with *ad libitum* smoking and self-report questionnaires. Individual differences in sensitivity to the effects of nicotine are likely to be a function of nicotine exposure history, stress, and genetically determined biological differences (Marks, Stitzel, & Collins, 1989; O. F. Pomerleau, Collins, et al., 1993). Responses to standard challenge doses of nicotine may have a unique ability to predict individual differences in smoking abstinence and relapse. Moreover, they may act as markers for important individual differences in biological sensitivity to and effects of nicotine. West and Russell (1988) found a positive correlation between aversive response to smoking and degree of 24-hour withdrawal discomfort. However, this association may simply reflect a tendency of neuroticism to correlate with self-report measures of negative affect. As noted above, most studies assessing responses to quantified doses of tobacco smoke have failed to find a significant association between nicotine-induced physiological changes and the Fagerstrom Tolerance Questionnaire. However, responses to quantified doses of smoke have been found to correlate with neuroticism and depression (D. G. Gilbert, Gehlbach, et al., 1994; D. G. Gilbert, Meliska, et al., 1994; Masson & Gilbert, 1990; see Chapter 7), two factors related to smoking and relapse. The ability of nicotine responses to predict relapse and nicotine abstinence responses is currently under investigation in several laboratories.

Personality, Psychopathology, and Trait Responses

Assessment of typical stress responses, personality traits, and current and lifetime psychopathology contributes to an understanding of smoking-related causal pathways. Individuals high in psychopathology and in personality traits associated with psychopathology are predisposed to smoke, to smoking relapse, and to smoking as a tool to alleviate suboptimal cognitive, arousal, or affective states. For example, a history of depression shows a high association with smoking cessation failure and more intense and frequent depressive symptoms when quitting (Covey et al., 1990). Moreover, depressive affect frequently co-occurs with other negative affects, including anxiety and anger (McNair, Lorr, & Droppleman, 1971). Depression contributes to cessation failure by its associated expectations that important personal goals cannot be achieved (Beck, 1991). In depressed states, individuals give up coping and long-term goal striving, skills required to abstain from smoking. Probable reasons for lower cessation rates in other forms of psychopathology were reviewed in Chapter 7.

Personality and Temperament Assessment   Personality traits and related trait adaptive responses to stress appear to predict abstinence response type, severity, and relapse because tobacco abstinence is a stressor that elicits trait adaptive responses and associated schemas (see Chapter 9). The STAR model hypothesizes that the most important temperament-based traits moderating nicotine-related responses are those associated with smoking initiation, prevalence, and relapse: that is, neuroticism, depression, psychoticism, impulsivity, unconventionality, antisocial behavior, and low educational or long-term aspirations. Determination of temperament-influenced processes underlying an individual's smoking motivation and disposition to relapse should be assessed by empirically validated personality questionnaires that include the major higher order categories (i.e., N, E, P-IUSS, openness–culture–education, agreeableness, and conscientiousness) and the facet factors of these dimensions. Facets of the higher–order categories are required for adequate treatment because specificity is needed to accurately characterize causal paths and therefore to provide individualized (path-specific) interventions. On the basis of its comprehensiveness and extensive validation, NEO–PI–R (Costa & McCrae, 1992c) is recommended to assess the major personality dimensions and their facets.

Assessment of Psychopathology   Clinical, as well as subclinical, psychological syndromes have a significant impact on treatment outcome and should be a part of each treatment assessment. Unlike traditional putative markers of dependence, subclinical and personality trait dispositions, like clinical syndromes, are relatively consistently predictive of smoking, smoking abstinence, relapse, and response to nicotine (H. J. Eysenck, 1986; D. G. Gilbert, Gehlbach, et al. 1994; D. G. Gilbert, Meliska, et al. 1994; M. Martin, 1985; see Chapter 7). A number of venues can accomplish this task. Assessment of current and lifetime clinical *DSM-IV* syndromes can be assessed by the Diagnostic Interview Schedule (Robins, Helzer, Croughan, & Ratcliff, 1981) or other structured clinical interviews for *DSM-IV* Axis I diagnosis (Spitzer, Williams, Gibbon, & First, 1990). The Problem Behavior Inventory (Silverton, 1991) is a *DSM–III–R*-based checklist that may be used to assess current and lifetime clinical syndromes when resources do not allow for structured clinical interview assessments.

Subclinical syndromes should also be assessed, as most forms of psychopathology are better characterized as varying along a continuum than as discrete categories (H. J. Eysenck, 1986; Widiger & Frances, 1994). The Symptom Checklist–90 (Derogatis, 1977) is recommended because of its brevity and psychometric properties. It provides continuous scores on nine clinical syndrome-related dimensions (i.e., somatization, obsessive-compulsive, interpersonal sensitivity, depression, anxiety, hostility, phobic anxiety, paranoid ideation, and psychoticism). Another potentially useful dimensional assessment tool is the Minnesota Multiphasic Personality Inventory, which provides a series of measures of psychopathology. Other, more focal tests that can provide important information include the Beck Depression Inventory (Beck, Ward, Mendelsohn, Mock, & Erbaugh, 1961), the Beck Hopelessness Scale (Beck, Weissman, Lester, & Trexler, 1974), and the Beck Anxiety Inventory (Beck, Epstein, Brown, & Steer, 1988). Measurement of a range of common psychopathological dimensions allows generation of profiles that reflect the individual's state better than a single diagnostic category.

Assessment of Middle-Level Traits

Cognitions, Goals, and Conditioning   Individualized cognitive–behavioral assessment complements the syndromal/*DSM-IV* approach by providing detailed idiographic characterization of cognitions, affect, physiology, and behavior in various settings. These idiographic assessments focus on what are referred to as middle-level traits. That is, behavior can be described in terms of a limited set of proximal causal constructs influenced by a larger set of more distal causal factors, including personality, temperament, and early environment. These middle-level, plastic traits are mediators of relationships between past and current environment, personality, and smoking. Those of particular importance to smoking intervention are discussed below.

Motivation to Quit   Leventhal and Cleary (1980) hypothesized that all effective interventions, regardless of specific technique, must deal with motivation to quit smoking and coping skills to sustain avoidance. Motivation to quit at a particular time varies in nature, as well as in strength. Specifically, smokers vary in the degree to which health concerns, social pressure, and external contingencies create a motivation to quit. Because the smoker's situation constantly changes, motivation to remain abstinent varies across time (Miller & Rollnick, 1991). Motivation to quit can be enhanced and thereby increase abstinence. For example, D. G. Gilbert, Meliska, Welser et al. (1992) found that $400 contingent on a month of verified abstinence led to abstinence in nearly 90% of smokers, but there was a rapid return to smoking in most after termination of the contingency. Halpern and Warner (1993) found that personal concerns about health consequences of smoking and wanting to set a good example for children were motivations for quitting associated with successful cessation. Social pressure and concerns about smoking costs and health effects on others were associated with failure to quit.

Prochaska et al. (1992) recognized motivation for quitting as involving five stages of change: precontemplation, contemplation, preparation, action, and maintenance. Because of its potential lifelong duration, the maintenance phase is more difficult to successfully attain. Prochaska et al. believed that interventions are most effective when the therapist focuses on issues appropriate to the client's stage of change. The 24-item decisional balance measure of the pros and cons of smoking developed by Velicer, DiClemente, Prochaska, and Brandenberg (1985) has proven useful in assessing conflicts in motivations to quit.

Smoking and Abstinence-Related Cognitions   Prospective and cross-sectional studies have found expectancies concerning smoking abstinence and consequences to predict success in maintaining long-term abstinence (Brandon & Baker, 1991; for reviews see Carey, Snel, Carey, & Richards, 1989; Shadel & Mermelstein, 1993). Condiotte and Lichtenstein (1981) found that exsmokers were able to predict whether they would abstain and the situations in which they would relapse. The utility of assessing situations in which individuals believe they will have difficulty maintaining abstinence has implications for more detailed assessment of reasons for high-risk situations and for treatment. Thus, it is recommended that difficulty in resisting smoking in each of the 45 high-risk situations assessed by the Condiotte and Lichtenstein (1981) Confidence Questionnaire be determined and incorporated into smoking cessation interventions.

Corcoran and Rutledge (1989) suggested that the individual differences in perceived alternatives to smoking be assessed. The question may not be whether one can quit, but whether one is motivated to quit. They argued that self-efficacy measures reflect expectancy belief that one will choose to be abstinent after a given period of time rather than the ability to remain abstinent. Given proper incentives, almost all smokers will remain abstinent (D. G. Gilbert, Meliska, Welser et al., 1992).

A number of researchers have emphasized the importance of assessing and treating dysfunctional beliefs about smoking, affect, and behavior (Beck et al., 1993; Marlatt, 1985; Shiffman, Read, Maltese, Rapkin, & Jarvik et al., 1985). Beck et al. (1993) saw addictive beliefs as a cluster of ideas revolving around escape, pleasure seeking, problem solving, and relief. Examples of these dysfunctional beliefs include (a) the belief that one needs to smoke to maintain psychological and emotional balance, (b) the expectation that smoking will improve social and intellectual functioning, and (c) the idea that unless something is done to satisfy the craving or to neutralize the distress, it will continue indefinitely. Dysfunctional beliefs used to justify and entitle one to smoke or use drugs have also been identified (Beck et al., 1993). Functional relationships between smoking-related beliefs, other middle-level traits, and the major personality dimensions need to be characterized for each individual clinically, as well as in nomothetic research.

Smoking Abstinence and Relapse History　Responses to a given situation are generally best predicted by previous responses to similar situations. Thus, the history of previous responses to smoking abstinence and relapse history should be obtained (Hughes & Hatsukami, 1986). Cognitive, affective, and behavioral experiences to previous periods of abstinence require characterization. The intensity and duration of responses, length of abstinence, nature of previous interventions, and abstinence coping efforts should be assessed.

State–Trait Goal Commitment and Conflict Mapping　Assessment of the smoker's hierarchy of short- and long-term goals and their relationship to short-and long-term abstinence plans and goals is an essential but generally ignored element in the understanding of an individual's smoking and relapse. Definitions used by Lazarus (1991) to define goals are useful. A goal hierarchy is an individual's assessment of the relative importance of things as harmful or beneficial. Goal commitment reflects the value attached to a goal, the amount of effort or price one is willing to pay to attain a goal as compared with other goals. Goals are frequently related and sometimes mutually exclusive. Some simultaneously valued goals complement each other, whereas other goals preclude each other. Thus, individuals with important goals with which abstinence interferes (e.g., passing a difficult exam required for success in one's career) will have reduced motivation to maintain abstinence. To the degree that smoking facilitates performance on tasks important to attainment of important goals, abstaining from smoking is expected to produce goal conflict and negative affect. Individuals high in achievement needs would be expected to find it difficult to quit smoking when these goals are threatened by abstinence-related decrements in concentration. Those who value the relaxing and negative-affect-reducing effects of smoking would be expected to be especially disposed to relapse in conditions associated with negative affect. Affective states reflect goal hierarchies (what is important) and progress toward goals (Lazarus, 1991). Generally, individual differences in goals are expected to be related to reasons for smoking, other middle-level factors, and personality.

Novacek and Lazarus (1990) developed a measure of personal commitments that includes a hierarchy of six goal factors: Affiliation, Power–Achievement, Personal Growth, Altruism, Stress Avoidance, and Sensation Seeking. For smoking treatment assessment, it is recommended that this personal commitments measure be used in combination with a parallel measure of commitment to quit smoking. Responses to these personal goal commitment questions can be assessed by interviews. Such interviews should address the degree to which smoking abstinence responses might interfere with current goal commitments. Consistent with the importance of goal assessment, McKeeman and Karoly (1991) found that quitters, in contrast to relapsers and current smokers, reported fewer conflicts between their goal of abstaining from smoking and their eight most important goals.

Cue Reactivity   Reactions to smoking-related stimuli play a role in smoking and relapse to smoking (Niaura, Abrams, Pedraza, Monti, & Rohsenow, 1992; Niaura, Rohsenow, Binkoff, Monti, & Abrams, 1988). Smoking cues, compared with other stimuli, can increase blood pressure and urge to smoke (Niaura, Abrams, et al., 1992; Rickard-Figueroa & Zeichner, 1985). Moreover, relative to nonsmokers and long-term quitters, relapsers have been found to react with more anxiety, less coping skill, greater urges to smoke, and higher heart rates in an interpersonal situation in which a confederate smoked a cigarette (Abrams, Monti, Carey, Pinto, & Jacobus, 1988).

Cue reactivity can be assessed by three methods: in vivo cue exposure, imagery, and questionnaires. In vivo cue exposure has the advantage of precise measurement and control of cognitive, affective, behavioral, and physiological responses to clearly articulated standard cues. Questionnaires cannot articulate with precision either the stimulus or the response to a given situation, but have the advantage of sampling a large number of situations, including ones not easily contrived in a clinic or laboratory. Finally, imagery induction (Tiffany, 1992) allows presentation of a number of smoking stimuli, contextual cues (e.g., affective states), and responses.

Given their ease of administration, it is recommended that individualized cessation programs use a questionnaire of smoking urges. The best current measure may be that developed by Tiffany and Drobes (1991). Because responses to imagery and in vivo cue exposures provide insight into the cues and processes motivating smoking and disposing to relapse (Niaura et al., 1992), such responses should be assessed when possible.

Skill Assessment   Cognitive–behavioral approaches assume that relapse occurs in high-risk situations in those with coping skills deficits (Shiffman et al., 1985). Consistent with these assumptions, relapsers have been found to exhibit fewer and less effective coping responses (Abrams et al., 1988; see Carey et al., 1989). Such coping skills include a variety of cognitive, affective, and interpersonal capacities and can be assessed with verbal reports, questionnaires, self-monitoring, and analogue situations. Shiffman et al. (1985) recommended use of the Coping Response Survey as a self-report and self-monitoring method to assess a range of things smokers might think or d to cope with smoking situations during the early phases of abstinence. Another measure, the Smoking Situational Competency Test (Shiffman et al., 1985), can also be used to assess a smoker's typical responses to high-risk situations. This test gives the (ex)smoker 30 seconds to write down what she or he would say, think, and do to cope with each of 10 high-risk situations. There is a need to characterize the relationship of the Coping Response Survey to personality measures and putative measures of dependence in the general smoking population. In the case of the individual smoker, Coping Response Survey responses should be related to personal goals and goal conflicts as well as to personality traits and smoking motivations and habits.

Smoking and Emotional and Motivational Schema Assessment   A number of dysfunctional thought processes (e.g., arbitrary inferences, selective abstraction, overgeneralizing, absolutistic or all-or-none thinking, and personalization) have been identified (Beck et al., 1993; Ellis, 1985) as contributing to clinical disorders, including depression and anxiety. Beck (1991) has observed that individuals exhibit their dysfunctional thoughts primarily when stimuli are ambiguous and distal, the same conditions in which nicotine decreases negative affect. Cognitive models of clinical disorders attribute a major causal role to negative self-schemas (internal principles that organize responses to certain stimulus classes). Vulnerability schemas are beliefs about the meaning, importance, or consequences of various events in terms of one's goals or self (C. W. Parks & Hollon, 1988). Individuals who are schematic for affiliative issues are thought to become anxious or depressed if they experience frustration in meeting their critical interpersonal goals, whereas those with dysfunctional achievement schemas become anxious or depressed when processing cues suggestive of failed goal attainment in this domain (C. W. Parks & Hollon, 1988). Schemas predisposing one toward psychopathology are best assessed by clinical interviews combined with self-monitoring. These schemas are assessed on an ongoing basis throughout cognitive therapy and are related to goal hierarchies, skills, and cue reactivity.

Situational Assessment Environmental factors promoting smoking and hindering abstinence success include smoking contingencies (smoking response cost), smoking cues, high performance demands, threats to long-term goals, and drugs and alcohol (Shiffman et al., 1985). In conditions without these elements, nicotine abstinence frequently does not significantly increase negative affect (see Chapter 5). Thus, negative affect regulation and goal frustration achievement may explain the relationship of some of these variables to abstinence success. Because affect is highly dependent on goal achievement or facilitation and interference (Lazarus, 1991; see Chapters 3 and 9), an adequate situational assessment includes evaluating the relationship of environmental facilitation and impediment of the individual's long- and short-term goals.

As noted above, exsmokers are able to predict the situations in which they will relapse (Condiotte & Lichtenstein, 1981). A personalized assessment of situational factors predisposing one to smoke should include general measures of high-risk situations (e.g., those assessed by the Condiotte & Lichtenstein Confidence Questionnaire), but also an evaluation of the smoker's interpretation of the environment in terms of smoking risks, short- and long-term personal goals, and conditioned smoking and affect-related responses. Social environment at work and at home can be assessed with the Family Environment Scale (Moos & Moos, 1986) and the Work Environment Scale (Moos, 1986), followed by structured interviews designed to further characterize the smoker's unique environment.

Self-Monitoring Self-monitoring of smoking behavior and associated affect, motivations, and situations is easily accomplished by attaching a wrap sheet to the pack of cigarettes (Shiffman et al., 1985). More recently, self-monitoring has been supplemented by time sampling so that base rates of moods and situations can be controlled in assessing functional relationships between situations, moods, and smoking (Paty & Shiffman, 1991). The value of assessing the base rate of moods is demonstrated when it is realized that although a depressed person may be depressed before smoking most cigarettes, the association is not necessarily causal because the smoker may be depressed most of the time. The conditional probability of smoking when in a given mood or situation must be demonstrated to be greater than the (unconditional) probability of smoking when not in that mood or situation. Thus, it is recommended that, in addition to assessing situations and moods associated with each cigarette, moods and situations be sampled at random throughout the day.

INDIVIDUALIZED MULTIMODAL TREATMENT OF SMOKING (ITS)

It is suggested that the nature and duration of individualized smoking interventions be tailored by the above-reviewed assessments and that interventions address individual vulnerability, dysfunction, and deficit profiles. Teaching assertiveness to individuals high in assertiveness or providing training in relaxation techniques to those with terribly distressed family situations are examples of failures to address primary smoker needs. Such treatment–need incongruency makes the smoking intervention personally irrelevant and unlikely to help one quit. Instead, individuals vulnerable to depression should be given substantial attention to ameliorate and preclude depressive symptomatology. In contrast, achievement-oriented individuals who perceive that they must be at peak cognitive function during the near future to achieve a highly valued goal may benefit by delaying quitting for the current time or by the use of nicotine gum or patch. Those who have completed previous programs may benefit from greater focus on situations they perceive as especially risky, and those with little knowledge of the nature of abstinence responses and general means of coping with smoking urges and stress may benefit from a general, once-over-everything-lightly program in combination with individualized intervention.

Paralleling the general failure of current smoking programs to individualize interventions is an all-too-frequent focus on superficial intellectual learning of how to cope. Programs rarely include interventions based on nonrational and emotional learning and cognitive processes. For example, typically no attention is provided to extinction of craving and reconditioning in the presence of smoking and negative affect cues. The intellectual information-transmitted skill training characteristic of such programs also ignores the importance of repeated practice of skills if they are to be effectively implemented in high-risk situations. As noted by Lichtenstein and Glasgow (1992) "the core assumption of behavioral interventions and relapse prevention is that if participants learn, practice, and use coping skills . . . they will be more successful" (p. 521), yet most relapse prevention programs do not allocate much time to practicing skills. Lichtenstein and Glasgow concluded that the modest success of such groups may be a result of this failure and that more treatment contact over a longer period of time produces better outcome results. Given the health risks associated with smoking and the potential increase in personal well-being associated with more intensive treatments, more intensive interventions may be very cost-effective. Continuing this line of consideration, behavior is influenced by numerous types of learning and psychobiological states, most of which take place outside of conscious awareness (Greenberg & Sarafan, 1988; Posner & Snyder, 1975; Zajonc, 1984; see Chapters 3 and 9). Thus, purely intellectual, didactic teaching of coping does not address the majority of mechanisms that influence urges to smoke and the probability of implementing coping techniques to deal with such urges. When the urge to smoke is strong, a distressing conflict may arise between the conscious executive function's long-term goal of abstinence and felt urges for negative affect reduction by smoking. These urges result from an interaction of environmental situation, physiological state, and relatively automatic overlearned action schemas (Tiffany, 1992; see Chapter 9). Relapses to smoking occur when such automatic, nonconscious schemas are activated and higher cognitive processes do not inhibit schema-based smoking patterns. Given the activation of a smoking action schema, reduced conscious executive functioning due to any of a variety of sources (e.g., alcohol consumption, fatigue, distraction, or negative affect) can result in relapse (Tiffany, 1992).

Given the impossibility of constant maintenance of high levels of abstinence-focused conscious executive functioning, individuals are likely to relapse when willpower is weak. *Willpower* refers to the deliberate conscious effort and skill to inhibit implementation of a behavioral tendency or urge. Thus, work on bottom-up (nonconscious) needs to supplement top-down intellectual approaches. Another reason for bottom-up approaches is that they can deal not only with smoking schemas, but with negative-affect-related schemas as well. Finally, individuals who want to quit are generally consciously ambivalent about quitting as cognitive executive functions not only recognize the importance of long-term goals such as smoking abstinence, but also weigh the importance of current affective state. If the current state includes goals that would be facilitated by smoking, the executive will likely choose to meet these short-term goals at the cost of long-term abstinence goals (see above discussion of goal assessment). Thus, multimodal interventions that include procedures based on conditioning and goal conflicts are needed to supplement linear, executive-directed interventions.

Individualized interventions require a more comprehensive set of procedures than current dominant approaches. Although most current smoking interventions include some training in how to cope with high-risk situations, smoking abstinence response, anxiety, and stress (Lichtenstein & Glasgow, 1992), such generic programs largely focus on a limited number of education-based techniques. A sole focus on the immediate environment ignores broader skills deficits, dispositions, more fundamental cognitive dysfunctions, and nonconscious processes. Furthermore, traditional cognitive–behavioral approaches (Chiauzzi, 1991; Shiffman et al., 1985) tend to address coping with high-risk situations by teaching in a didactic fashion (e.g., problem solving, cognitive coping skills, social skills, and emotional and stress management skills). Techniques include relaxation techniques, behavioral coping responses, cognitive restructuring, imagery, avoidance, escape, physical activity, distraction, and delay. Interventions proposed to supplement these traditional interventions are outlined below. Individualized assessment will dictate which and to what degree the following supplemental interventions are used in individualized multimodel treatment of smoking.

Cognitive–Behavioral Therapy of Psychopathology

Given the strong association between psychopathology and smoking incidence and relapse, it is proposed that individuals assessed as being disposed to psychopathology receive interventions specifically for their psychological problems. Smokers tend to relapse if they experience significant negative affect or other psychological dysfunction after quitting. Cognitive therapy and other cognitive–behavioral approaches are effective interventions for depression and anxiety (Chambless & Gillis, 1993; Hollon, Shelton, & Davis, 1993), so these interventions should facilitate long-term abstinence. Even though cognitive therapy and treatment of dysfunctional cognitive processes have been suggested as a means to diminish craving or relapse episodes (Marlatt, 1985), these treatments for cognitive–affective dispositions to more general clinical syndromes have rarely been implemented or promoted as a means facilitating abstinence.

Life Goal and Lifestyle Modification

In addition to altering core dysfunctional beliefs, many smokers need to change their lifestyle and goals. Shiffman et al. (1985) noted that "a lifestyle that supported smoking is unlikely to support nonsmoking" (p. 513). New ways to manage negative affect and to generate positive affect and pleasure may need to be developed. Ignoring such needs is likely to result in a felt state of dysphoria and deprivation that will promote relapse. Because smokers may frequently be out of touch with their basic needs (Shiffman et al., 1985), interventions should focus on these needs, including long- and short-term goals and satisfactions.

Smoking-Focused Cognitive–Behavioral Interventions

Beck et al. (1993) suggested that the therapeutic application of their model modifies belief systems, allowing the individual to cope with high-risk situations by means other than simple avoidance. As noted above, Marlatt (1985) has elaborated a number of cognitive procedures that can be helpful in coping with risky situations. Some of these techniques are covered briefly in standard cessation programs. Individualization of such techniques may be facilitated by a combination of group and individual discussions plus enactive practice. Such techniques need to be overlearned and conditioned to have a high probability of implementation in risky situations. Repeated exposure to drinking, smoking, and relevant stressful situations while practicing such techniques is recommended.

Interpersonal Support and Treatment

Individuals living with smokers or in situations characterized by high levels of conflict and stress are less likely to remain abstinent. In cases of high relationship conflict, interpersonal skills training combined with cognitive interventions may be best applied by bringing significant others (e.g., spouses or roommates) into sessions focused on reduction of interpersonal problems. More superficial smoking-focused interpersonal interventions have not proved to be an effective means of promoting abstinence (Lichtenstein & Glasgow, 1992).

Cue-Exposure-Based Interventions

Cue exposure techniques may be used to extinguish craving responses (Hodgson & Rankin, 1976; O. F. Pomerleau, 1981). Repeated exposure to smoking stimuli in the absence of smoking should result in extinction of classically conditioned craving responses to such stimuli. Combined cue exposure and cognitive urge control have been suggested as potentially especially effective (Cooney, Baker, & Pomerleau, 1983) but have not been incorporated into standard smoking interventions. Cue exposure when experiencing negative affect may be important as context plays a critical role in determining the generalizability of extinction and learning (Bouton & Swartzentruber, 1991). Bouton and Swartzentruber (1991) concluded that extinction does not erase learning but instead makes behavior sensitive to the context in which it occurs. Memories of conditioning and extinction are retained through extinction and are available for retrieval by conditioned cues. Extinction is observed when the context promotes extinction, but when the context is changed or promotes conditioned performance, conditioned performance is frequently restored (Bouton & Swartzentruber, 1991). Nearly any contextual stimulus can control performance in extinction. Drug state, emotions, and the passage of time can influence extinction by acting as contextual stimuli. The therapist needs to be aware of all contextual stimuli associated with smoking because such cues are especially likely to initiate relapse. Cue exposure in contexts most associated with smoking should facilitate generalizability of extinction.

Cue exposure can also be incorporated into general group interventions designed to provide an overview of information and techniques important to all smokers. For example, discussions could include slide-show exposure, cigarette and pack exposure, videotaped group discussion, and brief self-report assessment. The association of smoking cues with treatment should lead not only to extinction of conditioned craving, but also to conditioning of new abstinence-related coping tendencies.

Smoking cue conditioning is likely to be most effective when it is personality trait and psychopathology specific. For example, introverts and neurotics are highly sensitive to cues associated with punishment, whereas extraverts and sensation seekers appear more sensitive to cues associated with reward (Gray, 1981). Thus, introverted neurotic and depressed individuals may respond best to conditioning associated with fear induction and the relief of anxiety. Emotional confrontation through role playing (Janis & Mann, 1965) in which smokers are required to play the role of a lung cancer patient may be especially effective in such individuals. Rapid-smoking-induced conditioned aversions to smoking (Lichtenstein, 1982) may also be especially helpful to more introverted individuals. Extraverts and sensation seekers would be predicted to respond better to conditioning associated with social or other positive reinforcement. The conditioning model suggests that such procedures would be especially effective if repeated over a number of weeks before quitting.

Attentional and Environmental Cue Control

Given nicotine's tendency to reduce negative affect when negative-affect-related cues are distal and ambiguous suggests several cognitive–affective coping skills that might prove useful in the reduction of negative affect during smoking abstinence. Individuals high in psychopathology and with histories of responding to abstinence with severe negative affect may benefit from intensive cognitive–affective interventions designed to provide a clear, structured, and supportive environment. In addition, cognitive interventions, such as those suggested by Beck et al. (1993), may be especially useful to such individuals when interpreting ambiguous environmental and subjective states. More emotionally stable individuals may benefit from simple environmental manipulations designed to maximize environmental rewards and to minimize stressors by focusing on clearly positively valanced activities and plans.

Arousal Modulation and Concentration Enhancement

Means need to be developed to deal with the lowered arousal and concentration associated with early stages of abstinence. Little research has addressed the effectiveness of such interventions (O'Connor & Stravynski, 1982), but the following possibilities may prove useful. Chewing spicy gum or sucking on candy may be a useful tool to help individuals increase arousal and concentration. Such sensory stimulation would, in addition to providing oral satisfaction, have a strong sensory impact that is likely to stimulate dopaminergic and cholinergic paths and thereby may help overcome abstinence-related deficits in these neuromodulators (see Chapters 6 and 9). In addition, the sugar may provide a form of self-medication by offsetting short-term, stress-induced hypoglycemia or result in higher levels of serotonin that can attenuate negative affect (see Chapter 9). Spicy sugarless gum may provide the needed stimulation for those who want to avoid weight gain.

Increased caffeine intake, sleep, and periods of brief exercise throughout the day might also prove beneficial in maintaining alertness in some individuals. Finally, minimizing tasks that demand high levels of vigilance may be an effective means of maintaining frustration-induced negative moods during the first week of abstinence.

Exercise

Increased exercise may alleviate not only weight control concerns associated with smoking but stress and negative affect and may be viewed as a part of a larger lifestyle change in commitment to health. Thayer, Peters, Takahashi, and Birkhead-Flight (1993) found that exercise produced increased feelings of energy and reduced urge to smoke or snack. Walks approximately doubled the time before smoking the next cigarette in free-smoking conditions. However, a small study by O. F. Pomerleau et al. (1987) found strenuous exercise to have minimal effects on nicotine intake during the 24-hour period after exercise. Thus, it is not clear how effective exercise can be in reducing smoking. Exercise may be most effective as a means of providing distraction and in reducing negative affect. O. F. Pomerleau et al.'s study was not designed to assess this possibility, whereas that of Thayer et al. suggested that exercise can have such effects.

Nicotine Replacement Therapy

Nicotine replacement therapy (nicotine gum and patch) appears to be especially effective in individuals high in neuroticism (negative affect) and in heavy smokers (Russell, 1994). The theoretical basis of nicotine replacement therapy is that nicotine will make it easier for the smoker to cope without cigarettes while learning new nonsmoking coping patterns. Ideally, nicotine replacement therapy should last only as long as necessary to develop new psychological and behavioral patterns while extinguishing old smoking-related patterns. Lifelong nicotine replacement therapy may be beneficial for individuals high in psychopathology and those with cognitive and affective vulnerabilities in that it prevents relapse to smoking. To the degree that nicotine has inherent affect-modulating, cognition-enhancing, or other beneficial effects in highly vulnerable individuals, long-term nicotine replacement therapy may be beneficial not only to help prevent relapse to smoking, but to facilitate psychological functioning more generally. Alternatively, psychotropic medications or psychotherapy may be more appropriate for most individuals as a means of preventing smoking relapse and psychological dysfunction and distress.

Nicotine nasal sprays and relatively *tar*-free *cigarettes* (e.g., Favor (R) and Primier (R)) may be far more effective smoking cessation devices than gum and patch because of the rapid absorption of nicotine and fingertip control of nicotine delivery associated with inhaled nicotine (Leischow, 1994; M. A. H. Russell, 1994; Schneider, 1994). It has been suggested that Primier, the glycerol-based, virtually *tar*-free cigarette briefly manufactured by the R. J. Reynolds Tobacco Company "poses substantially less risk of cancer and chronic obstructive lung disease than conventional cigarettes . . . [and that] it could be particularly valuable for patients with chronic pulmonary disease who continue smoking despite all efforts to persuade them to stop" (Sutherland, Russell, Stapleton, & Feyerabend, 1993, p. 387). Given the health hazards of current cigarettes, the development and wide use of relatively safe cigarettes would save countless lives even if the product had some modest risk ("Nicotine Use," 1991). There is a clear need for an objective and careful cost–benefit analysis of the variety of cigarette substitutes. Rigid adherence to the idea that such products should be discouraged or banned on the grounds that all nicotine use is bad and harmful ignores the fact that current cigarettes are very harmful to health and that a product with less than 10% of the risk of current cigarettes would save many lives and would essentially eliminate problems associated with secondhand smoke. Not to consider such alternatives may be an unintentional crime against the very individuals whom health professionals are trying to help. The development of effective and relatively safe means of delivering nicotine as long-term desirable substitutes for smoking, although highly beneficial from a public health perspective, can predictably be expected to lead to knee jerk rejection by many antismokers. Nonetheless, the continued discussion of less harmful cigarettes and forms of nicotine administration needs to be encouraged given that hundreds of millions of individuals worldwide will continue to smoke well into the 21st century.

Psychotropic Medications

Antidepressants and anxiolytics should be effective in attenuating relapse rates in those disposed to depression and anxiety, respectively. The small number of studies assessing the effectiveness of psychotropic medications for smoking abstinence have provided some (albeit mixed) support for their effectiveness (see Chapter 7). The biopsychosocial STAR model of smoking is open to the use of medications but recognizes the importance of addressing situational, learning, and coping to facilitate long-term abstinence. Furthermore, use of psychotropic medications should be based on an assessment of current psychological state, personality traits, and response to previous quit attempts. The finding that anxiolytics can facilitate abstinence in highly anxious individuals but can actually promote relapse in nonanxious quitters (Cinciripini et al., 1994) is a strong argument for careful assessment of what medications are prescribed and to whom. Such findings suggest that individual differences in personality and psychopathology may be as or more important than degree of nicotine exposure and history.

SUMMARY

The need for innovative individualized (client- and diagnosis-specific) interventions is evident given the ineffectiveness of current programs for the growing percentage of smokers who are high in psychopathology and in personality dispositions not conducive to quitting. Such new individualized interventions need to be based on current psychological and smoking knowledge, measures, and technologies. Temperament- and psychopathology-based assessments and constructs can supplement idiographic, middle-level cognitive and behavioral assessment to point to interventions that are more effective because they are individualized to meet the individual smoker's needs.

Individualized interventions will benefit from incorporation of a combination of more intensive, repetition-based, cue-exposure, cognitive, and behavioral procedures that supplement the purely intellectual knowledge-based interventions so common today. Smoking cessation groups might be made substantially more effective by providing more individualized and intensive treatments along the lines proposed in this chapter. The modest additional cost in time and effort might provide substantial increases in results and could be highly cost-effective in the long run. Individualized and more intensive interventions for smoking could be incorporated into ongoing psychotherapy programs for individuals who suffer from more severe psychopathology. Training of mental health workers in state-of-the-art, individualized biopsychosocial STAR-based interventions may be the most effective manner of addressing the very high incidence of smoking in those high in psychopathology.

The STAR-model-derived interventions outlined in this chapter are meant more as a research and clinical framework than as a complete theory. I am confident that the field will benefit from detailed empirical characterizations and manipulations of basic and clinical processes within the STAR framework. Specific mechanisms and causal paths associated with smoking need further articulation. Markers of individual differences in causal paths are needed to facilitate both clinical and research endeavors. It is a curious fact that there has been far more interest and focus on putative measures of nicotine dependence despite the fact that individual differences in personality and psychopathology have proven to be as good or better predictors of cessation success and abstinence response. Future interventions and research will greatly benefit from a multivariate approach that includes individual differences in personality, psychopathology, and middle-level traits and situations. Gender, ethnicity, culture, and age should also be considered in such multivariate approaches, as well as in fundamental research.

There are few simple answers. Smoking is a function of a multitude of variables. Although almost all smokers smoke to obtain nicotine's effects, it is important to ask what these effects are and when and in whom they occur. Both the causes and effects of nicotine are more complex than envisioned a decade ago. These causes include complex interactions of situation and personal trait profiles across time.

References

Abbott, J., Sutherland, C., & Watt, D. (1987). Cooperative dyadic interactions, perceived control, and task difficulty in Type A and Type B individuals: A comparative study. *Psychophysiology, 24*, 1–13.

Abercrombie, E. A., Keefe, K. A., DiFrischia, D. A., & Zigmond, M. J. (1989). Differential effect of stress on in vivo dopamine release in striatum, nucleus accumbens and medial frontal cortex. *Journal of Neurochemistry, 52*, 1655–1658.

Abrams, D. B., Monti, P. M., Carey, K. B., Pinto, R. P., & Jacobus, S. I. (1988). Reactivity to smoking cues and relapse: Two studies of discriminant validity. *Behaviour Research and Therapy, 26*, 225–233.

Abramson, L. Y., Seligman, M. E. P., & Teasdale, J. D. (1978). Learned helplessness in humans: Critique and reformulation. *Journal of Abnormal Psychology, 87*, 49–74.

Adler, N. E., Boyce, T., Chesney, M. A., Cohen, S., Folkman, S., Kahn, R. L., & Symme, S. L. (1994). Socioeconomic status and health. *American Psychologist, 49*, 15–24.

Aggleton, J. P., & Mishkin, M. (1986). The amygdala: Sensory gateway to the emotions. In R. Plutchik & H. Kellerman (Eds.), *Emotion: Theory, research and experience: Vol.3. Biological foundations of emotion* (pp. 281–299). Orlando, FL: Academic Press.

Ague, C. (1973). Nicotine and smoke: effects upon subjective changes in mood. *Psychopharmacologia, 30*, 323–328.

American Medical News. (1990, Aug. 3). p. 4.

American Psychiatric Association. (1980). *Diagnostic and Statistical manual of mental disorders (3rd ed.)*. Washington, DC: Author.

American Psychiatric Association. (1987). *Diagnostic and statistical manual of mental disorders, (3rd ed., rev.)*. Washington, DC: Author.

American Psychiatric Association. (1994). *Diagnostic and statistical manual of mental disorders. (4th ed.)*. Washington, DC: Author.

Amsel, A. (1990). Arousal, suppression, and persistence: Frustration theory, attention, and its disorders. *Cognition and Emotion, 4,* 239–268.

Anda, R. F., Williamson, D. F., Escobedo, L. G., Mast, E. E., Giovino, G. A., & Remington, P. L. (1990). Depression and the dynamics of smoking. *Journal of the American Medical Association, 264,* 1541–1545.

Andersch, B., & Milsom, I. (1982). An epidemiologic study of young women with dysmenorrhea. *American Journal of Obstetrics and Gynecology, 144,* 655–660.

Andersson, K. (1975). Effects of cigarette smoking on learning and retention. *Psychopharmacologia, 41,* 1–5.

Andersson, K., & Hockey, G. R. (1977). Effects of cigarette smoking on incidental memory. *Psychopharmacology, 52,* 223–226.

Angst, M. S. (1979). Risikofaktoren für starkes Zigaretten–rauchen bei jungen Männern [Risk factors for heavy smoking in young men]. *Journal Suisse de Médecine, 109,* 115–122.

Arci, J. B., & Grunberg, N. E. (1992). A psychophysical task to quantify smoking cessation–induced irritability: The Reactive Irritability Scale (RIS). *Addictive Behaviors, 17,* 587–601.

Armitage, A. K., Hall, G. H., & Morrison, C. F. (1968). Pharmacological basis for the tobacco smoking habit. *Nature, 217,* 331–334.

Armitage, A. K., Hall G. H., & Sellers, C. M. (1969). Effects of nicotine on electrocortical activity and acetylcholine release from the rat cerebral cortex. *British Journal of Pharmacology, 35,* 157–160.

Armstrong–Jones, R. (1927). Tobacco, its use and abuse: From the nervous and mental aspect. *Practitioner, 118,* 6–19.

Arnold, M. B. (1960). *Feelings and emotions.* New York: Academic Press.

Ashton, H., & Golding, J. F. (1989). Smoking: Motivation and models. In T. Ney & A. Gale (Eds.), *Smoking and human behavior* (pp. 21–56). Chichester, England: Wiley.

Ashton, H., Millman, J. E., Rawlins, M. D., Telford, R., & Thompson, J. W. (1978). The use of event related slow potentials of the brain in the analysis of effects of cigarette smoking and nicotine in human. In K. Battig (Ed.), *Behavioural effects of nicotines* (pp. 26–37). Basel, Switzerland: Barger.

Ashton, H., Millman, J. E., Telford, R., & Thompson, J. W. (1974). The effects of caffeine, nitrazepam, and cigarette smoking on the contingent negative variation in man. *Electroencephalography & Clinical Neurophysiology, 37,* 59–71.

Ashton, H., & Stepney, R. (1982). *Smoking: Psychology and pharmacology.* London: Tavistock.

Asterita, M. F. (1985). *The physiology of stress: With special reference to the neuroendocrine system.* New York: Human Sciences Press.

Balfour, D. J. K. (1991a). The influence of stress on psychopharmacological responses to nicotine. *British Journal of Addiction, 86,* 489–493.

Balfour, D. J. K. (1991b). The neurochemical mechanisms underlying nicotine tolerance and dependance. In J. A. Pratt (Ed.), *The biological bases of drug tolerance and dependence* (pp. 121–151). New York: Academic Press.

Balfour, D. J. K., Benwell, M. E. M., & Vale, A. L. (1991). Studies on the role of mesolimbic dopamine in behavioural responses to chronic nicotine. In F. Adlkofer & K. Thurau (Eds.), *Effects of nicotine on biological systems* (pp. 407–416). Basel, Switzerland: Birkhauser Verlag.

Bandura, A. (1977). *Social learning theory*. Englewood Cliffs, NJ: Prentice–Hall.

Barnes, D. M. (1986, June 13). Steroids may influence changes in mood. *Science, 232,* 1344–1345.

Barnes, G.E., & Fishlinsky, M. (1976). Stimulus intensity modulation, smoking and craving for cigarettes. *Addictive Diseases: An International Journal, 2,* 384–479.

Barret–Connor, E. (1990). Smoking and endogenous sex hormones in men and women. In N. Wald & J. Baron (Eds.), *Smoking and hormone related disorders* (pp. 183–196). Oxford, England: Oxford University Press.

Barret–Connor, E., & Khaw, K.–T. (1987). Cigarette smoking and increased endogenous estrogen levels in men. *American Journal of Epidemiology, 126,* 187–192.

Bartol, C. (1975). Extraversion and neuroticism and nicotine, caffeine and drug intake. *Psychological Reports, 36,* 1007–1010.

Bartus, R. T., Dean, R. L., Beer, B., & Lippa, A. S. (1982, July 30). The cholinergic hypothesis of geriatric memory dysfunction. *Science, 217,* 408–417.

Bartussek, D., Diedrich, O., Naumann, E., & Collet, W. (1993). Introversion–extraversion and event–related potential (ERP): A test of J. A. Gray's theory. *Personality and Individual Differences, 14,* 565–574.

Bass, C. (1988). Personality correlates of smoking behavior in men with heart disease. *Personality and Individual Differences, 9,* 397–400.

Bauman, K. E., Foshee, V. A., Koch, G. G., Haley, N. J., & Downton, M. I. (1989). Testosterone and cigarette smoking in early adolescence. *Journal of Behavioral Medicine, 12,* 425–433.

Beck, A. T., Weissman, A., Lester, D., & Trexler, L. (1974). The measurement of pessimism: The hopelessness scale. *Journal of Consulting and Clinical Psychology, 42,* 861–865.

Beck, A. T., Wright, F. D., Newman, C. F., & Liese, B. S. (1993). *Cognitive therapy of substance abuse*. New York: Guilford Press.

Beck, A. T. (1991). Cognitive therapy: A 30–year retrospective. *American Psychologist, 46,* 368–375.

Beck, A. T., Epstein, N., Brown, G., & Steer, R. A. (1988). An inventory for measuring anxiety: Psychometric properties. *Journal of Consulting and Clinical Psychology, 56,* 893–897.

Beck, A. T., Ward, C. H., Mendelsohn, M., Mock, J., & Erbaugh, J. (1961). An inventory for measuring depression. *Archives of General Psychiatry, 4,* 561–571.

Becker, R., & Giacobini, E. (1991). *Cholinergic basis for Alzheimer therapy*. Boston: Birkhauser.

Beckwith, B. E., Lerud, K., Antes, J., & Reynolds, B. W. (1983). Hydrocortisone reduces auditory sensitivity at high tonal frequencies. *Pharmacology, Biochemistry, and Behavior, 19,* 431–433.

Behm, F. M., Levin, E. D., Lee, Y., & Rose, J. E. (1990). Low–nicotine regenerate smoke aerosol reduces desire for cigarettes. *Journal of Substance Abuse, 2,* 237–247.

Behm, F. M., Schur, C., Levin, E. D., Tashkin, D. P., & Rose, J. E. (1993). Clinical evaluation of a citric acid inhaler for smoking cessation. *Drug and Alcohol Dependence, 31,* 131–138.

Bell, R. A., & Daly, J. A. (1985). Some communicator correlates of loneliness. *Southern Speech Communication Journal, 50,* 121–142.

Bell, R., Warburton, D. M., & Brown, K. (1985). Drugs as research tools in psychology: Cholinergic drugs and aggression. *Neuropsychobiology, 14,* 181–192.

Benowitz, N. L., Jacob, III, P., Jones, R. T., & Rosenbert, J. (1982). Interindividual variability in the metabolism and cardiovascular effects of nicotine in man. *Journal of Pharmacology and Experimental Therapeutics, 221,* 368–372.

Benowitz, N. L., Kuyt, F., & Jacob, III, P. (1984). Influence on cardiovascular and hormonal effects of cigarette smoking. *Clinical Pharmacology and Therapeutics, 36,* 74–81.

Benowitz, N. L., Porchet, H., Scheiner, L., & Jacob, P. (1988). Nicotine absorption and cardiovascular effects with smokeless tobacco use: Comparison with cigarettes and nicotine gum. *Clinical Pharmacology and Therapeutics, 44,* 23–28.

Benwell, E. M., & Balfour, D. J. K. (1992). The effects of acute and repeated nicotine treatment on nucleus accumbens dopamine and locomotor activity. *British Journal of Pharmacology, 105,* 849–856.

Benwell, E. M., Balfour, D. K., & Anderson, J. M. (1990). Smoking–associated changes in serotonergic systems of discrete regions of human brain. *Psychopharmacology, 102,* 68–72.

Berenbaum, H., & Fujita, F. (1994). Schizophrenia and personality: Exploring the boundaries and connections between vulnerability and outcome. *Journal of Abnormal Psychology, 103,* 148–158.

Berlyne, D. E. (1971). *Aesthetics and psychobiology.* New York: Appleton.

Bernstein, A. S., Schneider, S. J., Juni, S., & Pope, A. T. (1980). The effect of stimulus significance on the electrodermal response in chronic schizophrenia. *Journal of Abnormal Psychology, 89,* 93–97.

Berscheid, E. (1982). Attraction and emotion in interpersonal relations. In M. S. Clark & S. T. Fiske (Eds.), *Affect and cognition* (pp. 37–54). Hillsdale, NJ: Erlbaum.

Best, J. A., & Hakstian, A. R. (1978). A situation specific model of smoking behavior. *Addictive Behaviors, 3,* 79–82.

Biederman, J., Munir, K., & Knee, D. (1987). Conduct and oppositional disorder in clinically referred children with attention deficit disorder: A controlled family study. *Journal of the American Academy of Child and Adolescent Psychiatry, 26,* 724–727.

Biglan, A., Weissman, W., & Severson, H. (1985). Coping with social influences to smoke. In S. Shiffman & T. A. Wills (Eds.), *Coping and substance abuse* (pp. 95–116). Orlando, FL: Academic Press.

Binnie, A., & Comer, K. (1978). The effects of cigarette smoking on the contingent negative variation (CNV) and eye movement. In R. Thornton (Ed.), *Smoking behaviour: Physiological and psychological influences* (pp. 69–75). Edinburgh, Scotland: Churchill Livingstone

Blair, A., Blair, S. N., Howe, H. G., Pate, R. R., Rosenberg, M., Parker, G. M., & Pickle, L. W. (1980). Physical, psychological, and sociodemographic differences among smokers, exsmokers, and nonsmokers in a working population. *Preventive Medicine, 90,* 747–759.

Blake, S. M., Klepp, K.–I., Pechacek, T. F., Folsom, A. R., Lluepker, R. V., Jacobs, D. R., & Mittelmark, M. B. (1989). Differences in smoking cessation strategies between men and women. *Addictive Behaviors, 14,* 409–418.

Blaney, P. H. (1986). Affect and memory: A review. *Psychological Bulletin, 99,* 229–246.

Blum, M., Zacharovick, D., Gelernter, I., & Blum, I. (1988). Influence of oral contraceptive treatment on blood pressure and 24–hour urinary catecholamine excretion in smoking as compared with non–smoking women. *Advances in Contraception, 4,* 143–149.

Bohus, B., DeKloet, E. R., & Veldhuis, H. D. (1982). Adrenal steroids and behavioral adaptation: Relationship to brain corticoid receptors. In D. Ganten & D. Pfaff (Eds.), *Current topics in neuroendocrinology* (pp. 107–148). New York: Springer–Verlag.

Born, J., Hitzler, V., Pietrowsky, R., Pauschinger, P., & Fehm, H.L. (1988). Influences of cortisol on auditory evoked potentials (AEPs) and mood in humans. *Neuropsychobiology, 20,* 145–151.

Born, J., Kern, W., Fehm–Wolfsdorf, G., & Fehm, H. L. (1987). Cortisol effects on attentional processes in man as indicated by event–related potentials. *Psychophysiology, 24,* 286–292.

Borod, J. C. (1992). Interhemispheric and intrahemispheric control of emotion: A focus on unilateral brain damage. *Journal of Consulting and Clinical Psychology, 60,* 339–348.

Bouton, M. E., & Swartzentruber, D. (1991). Sources of relapse after extinction in Pavlovian and instrumental learning. *Clinical Psychology Review, 11,* 123–140.

Bower, G. H. (1981). Mood and memory. *American Psychologist, 36,* 129–148.

Boyd, G. M., & Maltzman, I. (1984). Effects of cigarette smoking on bilateral skin conductance. *Psychophysiology, 21,* 334–341.

Bozarth, M. A. (1987). Ventral tegmental reward system. In L. Oreland & J. Engel (Eds.), *Brain reward systems and abuse* (pp. 1–17). New York: Raven Press.

Bozarth, M. A. (1990). Drug addiction as a psychobiological process. In D. M. Warburton (Ed.), *Addiction controversies* (pp. 112–134). London: Harwood Academic.

Bozarth, M. A. (1991). The mesolimbic dopamine system as a model reward system. In P. Willner & J. Scheel–Kruger (Eds.), *The mesolimbic dopamine system: From motivation to action* (pp. 301–330). Chichester, England: Wiley.

Brackenridge, C. J., & Bloch, S. (1972). Smoking in medical students. *Journal of Psychosomatic Research, 16,* 35–40.

Brandon, T. H., & Baker, T. B. (1991). The Smoking Consequences Questionnaire: The subjective expected utility of smoking in college students. *Psychological Assessment, 3,* 484–491.

Brantmark, B., Ohlin, P., & Westling, H. (1973). Nicotine containing chewing gum as an anti–smoking aid. *Psychopharmacologia, 31,* 191–200.

Breslau, N., Kilbey, M. M., & Andreski, P. (1991). Nicotine dependence, major depression, and anxiety in young adults. *Archives of General Psychiatry, 48,* 1069–1074.

Breslau, N., Kilbey, M. M., & Andreski, P. (1992). Nicotine withdrawal symptoms and psychiatric disorders: Findings from an epidemiologic study of young adults. *American Journal of Psychiatry, 149,* 464–469.

Breslau, N., Kilbey, M. M., & Andreski, P. (1993a). Nicotine dependence and major depression: New evidence from a prospective investigation. *Archives of General Psychiatry, 50,* 31–35.

Breslau, N., Kilbey, M. M., & Andreski, P. (1993b). Vulnerability to psychopathology in nicotine–dependent smokers: An epidemiologic study of young adults. *American Journal of Psychiatry, 150,* 941–946.

Breslau, N., Kilbey, M. M., & Andreski, P. (in press). DSM–III–R nicotine dependence in young adults: Prevalence, correlates, and associated psychiatric disorders. *Addiction.*

Briggs, M. H. (1973). Cigarette smoking and infertility in men. *The Medical Journal of Australia, 1,* 616–617.

Brook, J. S., Gordon, A. S., & Brook, D. W. (1987). Fathers and daughters: Their relationship and personality characteristics associated with the daughter's smoking behavior. *Journal of Genetic Psychology, 148,* 31–44.

Brook, J. S., Whiteman, M., & Gordon, A. S. (1981). Maternal and personality determinants of adolescent smoking behavior. *The Journal of Genetic Psychology, 139,* 185–193.

Brook, J. S., Whiteman, M., Gordon, A. S., & Brook, D. W. (1983). Fathers and sons: Their relationship and personality characteristics associated with the son's smoking behavior. *Journal of Genetic Psychology, 142,* 271–281.

Brown, S., Vessay, M., & Stratton, I. (1988). The influence of method of contraception and cigarette smoking on menstrual patterns. *British Journal of Obstetrics & Gynaecology, 95,* 905–910.

Buchsbaum, M. S., Wu, J., Haier, R., Hazlett, E., Bull, R., Katz, M., Sokolska, K. M., Lagunas–Solar, M., & Langer, D. (1987). Positron emission tomography assessment of effects of benzodiazepines on regional glucose metabolic rate in patients with anxiety disorder. *Life Sciences, 40,* 2393–2400.

Buck, R. (1984). *The communication of emotion.* New York: Guilford Press.

Buck, R. (1991). Temperament, social skills, and the communication of emotion: A developmental–interactionist view. In D. G. Gilbert & J. J. Connolly (Eds.), *Personality, social skills, and psychopathology: An individual differences approach* (pp. 85–105). New York: Plenum Press.

Bukstein, O. G., Brent, D. A., & Kaminer, Y. (1989). Comorbidity of substance abuse and other psychiatric disorders in adolescents. *American Journal of Psychiatry, 146,* 1131–1141.

Burkman, R. T. (1988). Obesity, stress and smoking: Their role as cardiovascular risk factors in women. *American Journal of Obstetrics and Gynecology, 158,* 1592–1597.

Buss, D. M., & Cantor, N. (1989). Introduction. In D. M. Buss & N. Cantor (Eds.), *Personality psychology: Recent trends and emerging directions* (pp. 1–12). New York: Springer–Verlag.

Cabanac, M. (1971, September 17). Physiological role of pleasure. *Science, 173,* 1103–1107.

Cador, M., Robbins, T. W., & Everitt, B. J. (1989). Involvement of the amygdala in stimulus–reward associations: Interaction with the ventral striatum. *Neuroscience, 30,* 77–86.

Calabresi, P., Lacey, M. G., & North, R. A. (1989). Nicotinic excitation of rat ventral tegmental neurones in vitro studied by intracellular recording. *British Journal of Pharmacology, 98,* 135–140.

Candor, M., Robbins, T. W., Everitt, B. J., Simon, H., Le Moal, M., & Stinus, L. (1991). Limbic–striatal interactions in reward–related processes: Modulation by the dopaminergic system. In P. Willner & J. Scheel–Kruger (Eds.), *The mesolimbic dopamine system: From motivation to action* (pp. 225–250). Chichester, England: Wiley.

Carey, G., & DiLalla, D. L. (1994). Personality and psychopathology: Genetic perspectives. *Journal of Abnormal Psychology, 103,* 32–43.

Carey, M. P., Kalra, D. L., Carey, K. B., Halperin, S., & Richards, C. S. (1993). Stress and unaided smoking cessation: A prospective investigation. *Journal of Consulting and Clinical Psychology, 61,* 831–838.

Carey, M. P., Snel, D. L., Carey, K. B., & Richards, C. S. (1989). Self–initiated smoking cessation: A review of the empirical literature from a stress and coping perspective. *Cognitive Therapy and Research, 13,* 323–341.

Carillo–de–le–Pena, M. T., & Barratt, E. S. (1993). Impulsivity and ERP augmenting/
reducing. *Personality and Individual Differences, 15,* 25–32.

Carmelli, D., Swan, G. E., Robinette, D., & Fabsitz, R. R. (1990). Heritability of
substance use in the NAS–NRTC Twin Registry. *Acta Geneticae Medicae et Gemel-
lologiae (Roma), 39,* 91–98.

Carmelli, D., Swan, G. E., Robinette, D., & Fabsitz, R. R. (1992). Genetic influence
on smoking—A study of male twins. *New England Journal of Medicine, 327,* 829–
833.

Carment, D. W., & Miles, C. G. (1971). Persuasiveness and persuasibility as related to
intelligence and extraversion. In H. J. Eysenck (Ed.), *Readings in extraversion–introversion: Vol. 2. Fields of application* (pp. 140–149). New York: Wiley–Intersci-
ence.

Carpenter, W. T., & Gruen, P. H. (1982). Cortisol's effects on human mental functioning. *Journal of Clinical Psychopharmacology, 2,* 91–101.

Cassidenti, D. L., Vijod, A. G., Vijod, M. A., Stanczyk, F. Z., & Lobo, R. A. (1990).
Short–term effects of smoking on the pharmacokinetic profiles of micronized estradiol
in postmenopausal women. *American Journal of Obstetrics and Gynecology, 163,*
1953–1960.

Cederlof, R., Friberg, L., & Lundman, T. (1977). The interactions of smoking, environment and heredity and their implications for disease etiology. *Acta Medica Scandinavia*
(Suppl. 612).

Cegala, D. J., Savage, G. T., Brunner, C. C., & Conrad, A. B. (1982). An elaboration
of the meaning of interaction involvement: Toward the development of a theoretical
concept. *Communication Monographs, 49,* 229–248.

Cetta, M. F. (1977). The effects of cigarette smoking upon variation in anxious, aggressive, and pleasant mood states. *Dissertation Abstracts International, 38* (01), 349B.
(University Microfilms No. 77/4269)

Chait, L. D., & Griffiths, R. R. (1984). Effects of methadone on human cigarette smoking
and subjective ratings. *Journal of Pharmacology and Experimental Therapeutics, 229,*
636–640.

Chambless, D. L., & Gillis, M. M. (1993). Cognitive therapy of anxiety disorders.
Journal of Consulting and Clinical Psychology, 61, 248–260.

Charlton, A. (1984). Smoking and weight control in teenagers. *Public Health (London),
98,* 277–281.

Chassin, L., Presson, C. C., & Sherman, S. J. (1989). "Constructive" vs. "destructive"
deviance in adolescent health–related behaviors. *Journal of Youth and Adolescence,
18,* 245–262.

Chassin, L., Presson, C. C., Sherman, S. J., Corty, E., & Olshavsky, R. W. (1984).
Predicting the onset of cigarette smoking in adolescents: A longitudinal study. *Journal
of Applied Social Psychology, 14,* 224–243.

Cherek, D. R. (1981). Effects of smoking different doses of nicotine on human aggressive
behavior. *Psychopharmacology, 75,* 339–345.

Cherek, D. R. (1984). Effects of cigarette smoking on human aggressive behavior. In K.
J. Flannelly, R. J. Blanchard, & D. C. Blanchard (Eds.), *Biological perspectives on
aggression* (pp. 333–344). New York: A. R. Liss.

Cherek, D. R., Bennett, R. H., & Grabowski, J. (1991). Human aggressive responding
during acute tobacco abstinence: Effects of nicotine and placebo gum. *Psychopharmacology, 104,* 317–322.

Cherek, D. R., Smith, J. D., Lane, J. D., & Brauchi, J. T. (1982). Effects of cigarettes on saliva cortisol levels. *Clinical Pharmacology and Therapeutics, 32*, 765–768.

Cherry, N., & Kiernan, K. (1976). Personality scores and smoking behavior: A longitudinal study. *British Journal of Preventive and Social Medicine, 30*, 123–131.

Chiauzzi, E. (1991). *Preventing relapse in the addictions: A biopsychosocial approach.* New York: Pergamon Press.

Church, R. E. (1989). Smoking and the human EEG. In T. Ney & A. Gale (Eds.), *Smoking and human behavior* (pp. 115–140). Chichester, England: Wiley.

Cinciripini, P. M., Benedict, C. F., Van Vunakis, H., Mace, R. M., & Nezami, E. (1989). The effects of smoking on mood, cardiovascular and adrenergic reactivity of heavy and light smokers in a nonstressful environment. *Biological Psychology, 29*, 273–289.

Cinciripini, P. M., Lapitsky, L., Seay, S., Wallfisch, A., Meyer, W. J., & Van Vunakis, H. (1994). *A placebo controlled evaluation of the effects of buspirone on smoking cessation: Differences between high and low anxiety smokers.* Manuscript submitted for publication.

Claridge, G. (1986). Eysenck's contribution to the psychology of personality. In S. Modgil & C. Modgil (Eds.), *Hans Eysenck: Consensus and controversy* (pp. 73–85). Philadelphia: Falmer Press.

Claridge, G. (1987). Psychoticism and arousal. In J. Strelau & H. J. Eysenck (Eds.), *Personality dimensions and arousal* (pp. 133–150). New York: Plenum.

Clark, M. S. G., & Rand, M. J. (1968). Effect of tobacco smoke on the knee–jerk reflex in man. *European Journal of Pharmacology, 3*, 294–302.

Clarke, P. B. S. (1990). The central pharmacology of nicotine: Electrophysiological approaches. In S. Wonnacott, M. A. H. Russell, & I. P. Stolerman (Eds.), *Nicotine psychopharmacology: Molecular, cellular, and behavioural aspects* (pp. 158–193). Oxford, England: Oxford University Press.

Clarke, P. B. S., & Fibiger, H. C. (1987). Apparent absence of nicotine–induced conditioned place preference in rats. *Psychopharmacology, 92*, 84–88.

Clarke, P. B. S., Fu, S. D., Jakubovic, A., & Fibiger, H. C. (1988). Evidence that mesolimbic dopaminergic activation underlies the locomotor stimulant action of nicotine in rats. *Journal of Pharmacology and Experimental Therapeutics, 246*, 701–708.

Clavel, F., Benhamou, S., & Flamant, R. (1987). Nicotine dependence and secondary effects of smoking cessation. *Journal of Behavioral Medicine, 10*, 555–558.

Cleghorn, R. A. (1951). Adrenal cortical insufficiency: Psychological and neurological observations. *Canadian Medical Association Journal, 65*, 449–454.

Cloninger, C. R. (1987). A systematic method for clinical description and classification of personality variants. *Archives of General Psychiatry, 44*, 573–588.

Cloninger, C. R., & Gottesman, I. I. (1987). Genetic and environmental factors in antisocial behavior. In S. A. Mednick, T. E. Moffitt, & S. A. Stack (Eds.), *The causes of crime: New biological approaches* (pp. 92–109). Cambridge, England: Cambridge University Press.

Coambs, R. B., Kozlowski, L. T., & Ferrence, R. G. (1989). The future of tobacco use and smoking research. In T. Ney & A. Gale (Eds.), *Smoking and human behavior* (pp. 337–348). Chichester, England: Wiley.

Coan, R. (1973). Personality variables associated with cigarette smoking. *Journal of Personality and Social Psychology, 26*, 86–104.

Coburn, K. L., Ashford, J. W., & Fuster, J. M. (1990). Visual response latencies in temporal lobe structures as a function of stimulus information load. *Behavioral Neuroscience, 104*, 62–73.

Coccaro, E. F., Astill, J. L., Szeeley, P. J., & Malkowicz, D. E. (1990). Serotonin in personality disorder. *Psychiatric Annals, 20,* 587–592.

Cohen, S., & Lichenstein, E. (1990). Perceived stress, quitting smoking, and smoking relapse. *Health Psychology, 9,* 466–478.

Cohen, S., Schwartz, J. E., Bromet, E. J., & Parkinson, D. K. (1991). Mental health, stress and poor health behaviors in two community samples. *Preventative Medicine, 20,* 306–315.

Collins, A. C. (1990). An analysis of the addiction liability of nicotine. In C. K. Erickson, M. Javors, & W. W. Morgan (Eds.), *Addiction potential of abused drugs and drug classes* (pp. 83–101). New York: Haworth Press.

Colrain, I. M., Mangan, G. L., Pellett, O. L., & Bates, T. C. (1992). Effects of post–learning smoking on memory consolidation. *Psychopharmacology, 108,* 448–451.

Condiotte, M. M., & Lichtenstein, E. (1981). Self–efficacy and relapse in smoking cessation programs. *Journal of Consulting and Clinical Psychology, 49,* 648–658.

Connolly, J. J. (1991). Longitudinal studies of personality, psychopathology, and social behavior. In D. G. Gilbert & J. J. Connolly (Eds.), *Personality, social skills, and psychopathology: An individual differences approach* (pp. 19–47). New York: Plenum Press.

Conrad, K. M., Flay, B. R., & Hill, D. (1992). Why children start smoking cigarettes: Predictors of onset. *British Journal of Addiction, 87,* 1711–1724.

Cooney, N. L., Baker, L, & Pomerleau, O. F. (1983). Cue exposure for relapse prevention in alcohol treatment. In R. J. McMahon & K. D. Craig, (Eds.), *Advances in clinical behavior therapy* (pp.194–210). New York: Brunner/Mazel.

Cooper, C., & McConville, C. (1993). Affect intensity: Factor or artifact? *Personality and Individual Differences, 14,* 135–143.

Cooper, J., & Scalise, C. J. (1974). Dissonance produced by deviations from lifestyles: The interaction of Jungian typology and conformity. *Journal of Personality and Social Psychology, 29,* 566–671.

Cooper, J. R., Bloom, F. E., & Roth, R. H. (1991). *The biochemical basis of neuro-pharmacology (6th ed.)* New York: Oxford University Press.

Cooper, P. J., & Bowskill, R. (1986). Dysphoric mood and overeating. *British Journal of Clinical Psychology, 25,* 155–156.

Cooreman, J., & Perdrizet, S. (1980). Smoking in teenagers: Some psychological aspects. *Adolescence, 25,* 581–588.

Corcoran, K. J., & Rutledge, M. W. (1989). Efficacy expectation changes as a function of hypothetical incentives in smokers. *Psychology of Addictive Behaviors, 3,* 22–28.

Corrigall, W. A. (1991). Understanding brain mechanisms in nicotine reinforcement. *British Journal of Addiction, 86,* 507–510.

Corrigall, W. A., & Coen, S. M. (1991). Opiate antagonists reduce cocaine but not nicotine self–administration *Psychopharmacology, 101,* 167–170.

Corrigall, W. A., Franklin, K. B. J., Coen, K. M., & Clarke, P. B. S. (1992). The mesolimbic dopaminergic system is implicated in the reinforcing effects of nicotine. *Psychopharmacology, 107,* 285–289.

Corrigall, W. A., Herling, S., & Coen, S. M. (1988). Evidence for opioid mechanisms in the behavioral effects of nicotine. *Psychopharmacology, 96,* 29–35.

Costa, P. T., & McCrae, R. R. (1980). Influence of extraversion and neuroticism on subjective well–being: Happy and unhappy people. *Journal of Personality and Social Psychology, 38,* 668–678.

Costa, P. T., & McCrae, R. R. (1992a). Four ways five factors are basic. *Personality and Individual Differences, 13,* 653–665.

Costa, P. T., & McCrae, R. R. (1992b). Reply to Eysenck. *Personality and Individual Differences, 13,* 861–865.

Costa, P. T., & McCrae, R. R. (1992c). Revised NEO Personality Inventory (NEO–PI–R) and NEO Five–Factor Inventory (NEO–FFI) professional manual. Odessa, FL: *Psychological Assessment Resources.*

Costa, P. T., McCrae, R. R., & Dye, D. A. (1992). Facet scales for agreeableness and conscientiousness: A revision of the NEO Personality Inventory. *Personality and Individual Differences, 12,* 887–898.

Covey, L. S., Glassman, A. H., & Stetner, F. (1990). Depression and depressive symptoms in smoking cessation. *Comprehensive Psychiatry, 31,* 350–354.

Covey, L. S., Glassman, A. H., & Stetner, F. (1994). The Nicotine Dependence Scale: A measure based on psychiatric criteria. *Annals of Behavioral Medicine, 16S,* 60.

Covey, L. S., Mushinski, M. H., & Wynder, E. L. (1983). Smoking habits in hospitalized population: 1970–1980. *American Journal of Public Health, 73,* 1293–1297.

Covey, L. S., & Tam, D. (1990). Depressive mood, the single–parent home, and adolescent cigarette smoking. *American Journal of Public Health, 80,* 1330–1333.

Craig, D., Parrott, A., & Coomber, J. (1992). Smoking cessation in women: Effects of the menstrual cycle. *International Journal of the Addictions, 27*(6), 697–706.

Creutzfeld, O.D., Arnold, P.–M., Becker, D., Langenstein, S., Tirsch, W., Wilhelm, H., & Wuttke, W. (1976). EEG changes during spontaneous and controlled menstrual cycles and their correlation with psychological performance. *Electroencephalography & Clinical Neurophysiology, 40,* 113–131.

Croft, P., & Hannaford, P. C. (1989). Risk factors for acute myocardial infarction in women: Evidence from the Royal College of Practitioners' oral contraception study. *British Medical Journal, 298,* 165–168.

Crofton, J. (1990). Tobacco and the Third World. *Thorax, 45,* 164–169.

Dabbs, J. M., & Hopper, C. (1990). Cortisol, arousal, and personality in two groups of normal men. *Personality and Individual Differences, 11,* 931–935.

Dai, W. S., Gutai, J. P., Kuller, L. H., & Cauley, J. A. (1988). Cigarette smoking and serum sex hormones in men. *American Journal of Epidemiology, 128,* 796–805.

Dalgleish, T., & Watts, F. N. (1990). Biases of attention and memory in disorders of anxiety and depression. *Clinical Psychology Review, 10,* 589–604.

Davidson, R. J. (1984). Hemispheric asymmetry and emotion. In K. R. Scherer & P. Ekman (Eds.), *Approaches to emotion* (pp. 39–57). Hillsdale, NJ: Erlbaum.

Davidson, R. J. (1993). Cerebral asymmetry and emotion: Conceptual and methodological conundrums. *Cognition and Emotion, 7,* 115–138.

Davidson, R. J., Ekman, P., Saron, C. D., Senulis, J. A., & Friesen, W. V. (1990). Approach–withdrawal and cerebral asymmetry: Emotional expression and brain physiology: I. *Journal of Personality and Social Psychology, 58,* 330–341.

Davis, M., Hitchcock, J. M., & Rosen, J. B. (1987). Anxiety and the amygdala: Pharmacological and anatomical analysis of the fear–potentiated startle paradigm. In G. Bower (Ed.), *The psychology of learning and motivation* (pp. 263–305). New York: Academic Press.

Davis, M. C., & Matthews, K. A. (1990). Cigarette smoking and oral contraceptive use influence women's lipid, lipoprotein, and cardiovascular responses during stress. *Health Psychology, 9,* 717–736.

DeGrandpre, R. J., Bickel, W. K., Hughes, J. R., & Higgins, S. T. (1992). Behavioral economics of drug self–administration: III. A reanalysis of the nicotine regulation hypothesis. *Psychopharmacology, 108,* 1–10.

Dengerink, H. A., Lindgren, F. L., & Axelsson, A. (1992). The interaction of smoking and noise on temporary threshold shifts. *Acta Otolaryngologica, 112,* 932–938.

Derogatis, L. R. (1977). *SCL–90 administration, scoring and procedures manual–1.* Baltimore: Johns Hopkins University Press.

Derryberry, D., & Tucker, D. M. (1992). Neural mechanisms of emotion. *Journal of Consulting and Clinical Psychology, 60,* 329–338.

DeWied, D. (1980). Peptides and adaptive behaviour. In D. DeWied & P.A. Van Keep (Eds.), *Hormones and the brain* (pp. 103–113). Lancaster, England: MTP Press.

Diaz, A., & Pickering, A. D. (1993). The relationship between Gray's and Eysenck's personality spaces. *Personality and Individual Differences, 15,* 297–305.

Diener, E., & Emmons, R. A. (1985). The independence of positive and negative affect. *Journal of Personality and Social Psychology, 47,* 1105–1117.

Diener, E., & Iran–Nejad, A. (1986). The relationship in experience between different types of affect. *Journal of Personality and Social Psychology, 50,* 1131–1138.

Digman, J. M. (1990). Personality structure: Emergence of the five–factor model. *Annual Review of Psychology, 41,* 417–440.

Dobbs, S. D., Strickler, D. P., & Maxwell, W. E. (1981). The effects of stress and relaxation in the presence of stress on urinary pH and smoking behavior. *Addictive Behaviors, 6,* 345–353.

Dollard, J., Doob, L. W., Miller, N. E., Mowrer, O. H., & Sears, R. R. (1939). *Frustration and aggression.* New Haven, CT: Yale University Press.

Dollard, J., & Miller, N. E. (1950). *Personality and psychotherapy: An analysis in terms of learning, thinking, and culture.* New York: McGraw–Hill.

Domino, E. F. (1967). Electroencephalographic and behavioral arousal effects of small doses of nicotine. A neuropsychopharmacological study. In *Annals of the New York Academy of Sciences,* (pp. 142, 216–244).

Domino, E. F. (1973). Neuropsychopharmacology of nicotine and tobacco smoking. In W. L. Dunn, Jr. (Ed.), *Smoking behavior: Motives and incentives* (pp. 5–31). Washington, DC: V. H. Winston.

Dorsey, J. L. (1936). Control of the tobacco habit. *Annals of Internal Medicine, 4,* 628–631.

Dotson, L. E., Robertson, L. S., & Tuchfeld, B. (1975). Plasma alcohol, smoking, hormone concentrations and self–reported aggression: A study in a drinking situation. *Journal of Studies on Alcohol, 36,* 578–586.

Dunne, M. P., MacDonald, D., & Hartley, L. R. (1986). The effects of nicotine upon memory and problem solving performance. *Physiology and Behavior, 37,* 849–854.

Dworkin, S. I., Broadbent, J., Guarino, R., & Robinson, J. H. (1991). Environmental determinants of the relative reinforcing efficacy of nicotine. *Society of Neuroscience Abstracts, 17,* 425.

Easterbrook, J. A. (1959). The effect of emotion on cue utilization and the organization of behavior. *Psychological Review, 66,* 183–201.

Eaven, P. C. (1989). Adolescent smoking, toughmindedness, and attitudes to authority. *Australian Psychologist, 24,* 27–35.

Eaves, L. J., & Eysenck, H. J. (1980). The inheritance of smoking: Evidence from twin studies. In H. J. Eysenck (Ed.). The causes and effects of smoking (pp. 140–157). London: Maurice Temple Smith.

Eaves, L. J., Eysenck, H. J., & Martin, N. (1989). Genes, culture and personality. New York: Academic Press.

Edwards, J. A., Wesnes, K., Warburton, D. M., & Gale, A. (1985). Evidence of more rapid stimulus evaluation following cigarette smoking. Addictive Behaviors, 10, 113–126.

Edwards, G., Arif, A., & Hodgson, R. (1981). Nomenclature and classification of drug– and alcohol–related problems: A WHO memorandum. Bulletin of the World Health Organization, 59, 225–242.

Edwards, N. B., Simmons, R. C., Rosenthal, T. L., Hoon, P. W., & Downs, J. M. (1988). Doxepin in the treatment of nicotine withdrawal. Psychosomatics, 29, 203–206.

Ehrich, B., & Emmons, K. (1994). Addressing the needs of smokers in the 1990s. The Behavior Therapist, 17 (16), June, 119–122.

Eisinger, R. A. (1971). Psychosocial predictors of smoking recidivism. Journal of Health and Social Behavior, 12, 355–362.

Ekman, P., & Friesen, W. V. (1975). Unmasking the face. Englewood Cliffs, NJ: Prentice Hall.

Ekman, P., Levenson, R. W., & Friesen, W. V. (1983, Sept 16). Autonomic nervous system activity distinguishes among emotions. Science, 221, 1208–1210.

Elaiasson, M., Hagg, E., Lundblad, D., Karlsson, R., & Bucht, E. (1993). Influence of smoking and snuff use on electrolytes, adrenal and calcium regulating hormones. Acta Endocrinologica, 128, 35–40.

Elbert, T., & Birbaumer, N. (1987). Hemispheric differences in relation to smoking. In A. Glass (Ed.), Individual differences in hemispheric specialization (pp. 195–206). Tübingen, W. Germany: Butterworth.

Ellis, A. (1985). Cognition and affect in emotional disturbance. American Psychologist, 40, 471–472.

Emley, G. S., & Hutchinson, R. R. (1972). Basis of behavioral influence of chlorpromazine. Life Sciences, 11, 43–47.

Engberg, G. (1989). Nicotine induced excitation on locus coeruleus neurons mediated via release of excitatory amino acids. Life Sciences, 44, 1535–1540.

Epstein, L. H., Caggiula, A. R., Perkins, K. A., Mitchell, S. L., & Rodefer, J. S. (1992). Abstinence from smoking decreases habituation to food cues. Physiology and Behavior, 52, 641–646.

Epstein, L., & Collins, F. (1977). The measurement of situational influence of smoking. Addictive Behaviors, 2, 47–54.

Epstein, L. H., Dickson, B. E., McKenzie, S., & Russell, P. O. (1984). The effects of smoking on perception of muscle tension. Psychopharmacology, 83, 107–113.

Epstein, L. H., Perkins, K. A., Jennings, J. R., & Pastor, S. (1990). Effects of smoking context on habituation to repeated cognitive task. Psychopharmacology, 100, 366–371.

Epstein, S. (1979). The stability of behavior I: On predicting most of the people much of the time. Journal of Personality and Social Psychology, 37, 1097–1126.

Epstein, S. (1983). Aggregation and beyond: Some basic issues on the prediction of behavior. Journal of Personality, 51, 360–391

Erdmann, G. (1983). Autonomic drugs as tools in differential psychopharmacology. In W. Janke (Ed.), *Response variability to psychotropic drugs* (pp. 275–292). New York: Pergamon Press.

Erdmann, G., & Janke, W. (1978). Interaction between physiological and cognitive determinants of emotions: Experimental studies on Schachter's theory of emotions. *Biological Psychology, 6*, 61–74.

Etscorn, F. (1980). Sucrose aversions in mice as a result of injected nicotine or passive tobacco smoke inhalation. *Bulletin of the Psychonomic Society, 15*, 54–56.

Eysenck, H. J. (1965). *Smoking, health, and personality.* London: Pergamon Press.

Eysenck, H. J. (1967). *The biological basis of personality.* Springfield, IL: Charles C Thomas.

Eysenck, H. J. (1973). Personality and the maintenance of the smoking habit. In W. L. Dunn (Ed.), *Smoking behavior: Motives and incentives* (pp. 113–146). Washington, DC: V.H. Winston.

Eysenck, H. J. (1975). The measurement of emotion: Psychological parameters and methods. In L. Levi (Ed.) *Emotions: Their parameters and measurements* (pp. 439–467).

Eysenck, H. J. (1977). *Crime and personality* (2nd ed.). London: Routledge & Kegan Paul.

Eysenck, H. J. (1979). The conditioning model of neurosis. *The Behavioral and Brain Sciences, 2*, 459–482.

Eysenck, H. J. (1980). *The causes and effects of smoking.* London: Maurice Temple Smith.

Eysenck, H. J. (1986). A critique of contemporary classification and diagnosis. In T. Millon & G. Klerman (Eds.), *Contemporary directions in psychopathology* (pp. 73–98). New York: Guilford Press.

Eysenck, H. J. (1991). Dimensions of personality: 16, 5, or 3?—Criteria for a taxonomic paradigm. *Personality and Individual Differences, 12*, 773–790.

Eysenck, H. J. (1992a). The definition and measurement of psychoticism. *Personality and Individual Differences, 13*, 757–785.

Eysenck, H. J. (1992b). Four ways five factors are not basic. *Personality and Individual Differences, 13*, 667–673.

Eysenck, H. J. (1992c). A reply to Costa and McCrae. P or A and C—The role of theory. *Personality and Individual Differences, 13*, 867–868.

Eysenck, H.J., & Eysenck, M. W. (1985). *Personality and individual differences: A natural sciences approach.* New York: Plenum.

Eysenck, H. J., & Eysenck, S. B. G. (1976). *Psychoticism as a dimension of personality.* New York: Crane, Russak.

Eysenck, H. J., & Kelley, M. J. (1987). The interaction of neurohormones with Pavlovian A and Pavlovian B conditioning in the causation of neurosis, extinction, and incubation of anxiety. In G. Davey (Ed.), *Cognitive processes and Pavlovian conditioning in humans* (pp. 251–286). Chichester, England: Wiley.

Eysenck, H. J., & O'Connor, K. (1979). Smoking arousal and personality. In A. Remond & C. Izard (Eds.), *Electrophysiological effects of nicotine* (pp. 147–157). Amsterdam: Elsevier/North Holland.

Eysenck, H. J., & Wakefield, J. A. (1981). Psychological factors as predictors of marital satisfaction. *Advances in Behavior Research and Therapy, 3*, 151–192.

Eysenck, H. J., & Wilson, G. (1979). *The psychology of sex.* London: Dent.

Eysenck, M. W. (1987). Trait theories of anxiety. In J. Strelau & H. J. Eysenck (Eds.), *Personality and dimensions of arousal* (pp. 79–97). New York: Plenum Press.

Fabricant, N. D., & Rose, I. W. (1951). Effects of smoking cigarettes on the flicker fusion threshold of normal persons. *Eye Ear Mouth, 31,* 541–543.

Fada, F., Argiolas, A., Melis, M.R., Tissari, A. H., Onali, P.C., & Gessa, G. L. (1978). Stress–induced increase in 3,4–dihydroxyphenylacetic acid (DOPAC) levels in the cerebral cortex and in nucleus accumbens: Reversal by diazepam. *Life Science, 23,* 2219–2224.

Fagerstrom, K. O. (1978). Measuring degree of physical dependence to tobacco smoking with reference to individualization of treatment. *Addictive Behaviors, 3,* 235–241.

Fagerstrom, K. O. (1991). Towards better diagnoses and more individual treatment of tobacco dependence. *British Journal of Addiction, 86,* 543–547.

Fagerstrom, K. O. (1994). Combined use of nicotine replacement products. *Health Values, 18,* 15–20.

Fagerstrom, K., & Gotestam, K. G. (1977). Increase of muscle tonus after tobacco smoking. *Addictive Behaviors, 2,* 203–206.

Fagerstrom, K. O., & Schneider, N. (1989). A review of the Fagerstrom tolerance questionnaire. *Journal of Behavioral Medicine, 12,* 159–182.

Farley, C. J. (1994). The butt stops here. *Time,* April 18, 58–64.

Fehm–Wolfsdorf, G., & Nagel, D. (1993). Stress–induced cortisol secretion elevates acoustic threshold. *Journal of Psychophysiology, 7,* 134–135.

Feldman, W., Hodgson, C., & Corber, S. (1985). Relationship between higher prevalence of smoking and weight concern amongst adolescent girls. *Canadian Journal of Public Health, 76,* 205–206.

Fernstrom, J. D., & Wurtman, R. J. (1971, December 3). Brain serotonin content: Increase following ingestion of carbohydrate diet. *Science, 174,* 1023–1025.

Ferster, C. B. (1970). Comments on paper by Hunt and Matarazzo. In W. A. Hunt (Ed.), *Learning mechanisms in smoking* (pp. 91–102). Chicago: Aldine.

Fertig, J. B., Pomerleau, O. F., & Sanders, B. (1986). Nicotine–produced antinociception in minimally deprived smokers and ex–smokers. *Addictive Behaviors, 11,* 239–248.

File, S. E., Vellucci, S. V., & Wendlandt, S. (1979). Corticosterone—an anxiogenic or anxiolytic agent? *Journal of Pharmacy and Pharmacology, 31,* 300–305.

Finau, S. A., Stanhope, J. M., & Prior, I. A. (1982). Kava, alcohol and tobacco consumption among Tongans with urbanization. *Social Science Medicine, 16,* 35–41.

Finck, A. D. (1989). Opiate receptors and endogenous opioid peptides. *Current Opinion in Anaesthesiology, 2,* 428–433.

Fleming, S. E., & Lombardo, T. W. (1987). Effects of cigarette smoking on phobic anxiety. *Addictive Behaviors, 12,* 195–198.

Fletcher, C., & Doll, R. (1969). A survey of doctors' attitudes to smoking. *British Journal of Preventive and Social Medicine, 23,* 145–153.

Floderus, B. (1974). *Psychosocial factors in relation to coronary heart disease and associated risk factors. Nordisk Hygienisk Tidskrift.* (Suppl. 6).

Forsman, L. (1980). Habitual catecholamine excretion and its relation to habitual distress. *Biological Psychology, 11,* 83–97.

Fox, N. A. (1991). If it's not left, it's right. *American Psychologist, 46,* 863–872.

Frankenhaeuser, M., Myrsten, A., Post, B., & Johansson, G. (1971). Behavioural and physiological effects of cigarette smoking in a monotonous situation. *Psychopharmacologia, 22*, 1–7.

Franks, P., Harp, J., & Bell, B. (1989). Randomized, controlled trial of clonidine for smoking cessation in a primary care setting. *Journal of the American Medical Association, 262*, 3011–3013.

Frearson, W., Barrett, P., & Eysenck, H. J. (1988). Intelligence, reaction time, and the effects of smoking. *Personality and Individual Differences, 9*, 497–517.

Fridlund, J. A., & Izard, C. E. (1983). Electromyographic studies of facial expressions of emotions and patterns of emotions. In J. T. Cacioppo & R. E. Petty (Eds., *Social psychophysiology: A sourcebook* (pp. 243–286). New York: Guilford Press.

Friedman, J., Horvath, T., & Meares, R. (1974). Tobacco smoking and a "stimulus barrier". *Nature, 248*, 455–456.

Frith, C. D. (1971). Smoking behaviour and its relation to the smoker's immediate experience. *British Journal of Social and Clinical Psychology, 10*, 73–78.

Frye, C. A., Ward, K. D., Bliss, R. E., & Garvey, A. J. (1992, March). Influence of the menstrual cycle on smoking relapse and withdrawal symptoms. *Proceedings of the Thirteenth Annual Scientific Sessions of the Society of Behavioral Medicine*, (p. 107) Rockville, MD: Society of Behavioral Medicine.

Fudala, P. J., & Iwamoto, E. T. (1986). Further studies on nicotine–induced conditioned place preference in the rat. *Pharmacology, Biochemistry, and Behavior, 25*, 1041–1049.

Fudula, P. J., Teoh, K. W., & Iwamoto, E. T. (1985). Pharmacologic characterization of nicotine–induced conditioned place preference. *Pharmacology, Biochemistry, and Behavior, 22*, 237–241.

Fuller, R. G. C., & Forrest, D. W. (1977). Cigarette smoking under relaxation and stress. *Irish Journal of Psychology, 3*, 165–180.

Fuxe, K., Agnati, L. F., Jansson, A., von Euler, G., Tanganelli, S., Andersson, K., & Eneroth, P. (1990). Regulation of endocrine function by the nicotinic cholinergic receptor. In G. Bock & J. Marsh (Eds.), *The biology of nicotine dependence* (pp. 113–130). Chichester, England: Wiley.

Gainotti, G., Caltagirone, C., & Zoccolotti, P. (1993). Left/right and cortical/subcortical dichotomies in the neuropsychological study of human emotions. *Cognition and Emotion, 7*, 71–93.

Gale, A. (1983). Electroencephalographic studies of extraversion–introversion: A case study in the psychophysiology of individual differences. *Personality and Individual Differences, 4*, 371–380.

Gale, A. (1987). Arousal, control, energetics and values: An attempt at review and appraisal. In J. Strelau & H. J. Eysenck (Eds.), *Personality dimensions and arousal* (pp. 287–316). New York: Plenum Press.

Gallant, S. J., Hamilton, J. A., Popiel, D. A., Morokoff, P. J., & Chakraborty, P. K. (1991). Daily moods and symptoms: Effects of awareness of study focus, gender, menstrual–cycle phase, and day of the week. *Health Psychology, 10*, 180–189.

Gallup Poll National Survey [on–line database] (1990).

Gannon, L. (1985). *Menstrual disorders and menopause: An integration of biological, psychological, and cultural research.* New York: Praeger.

Garvey, A. J., Bliss, R. E., Hitchcock, J. L., Heinold, J. W., & Rosner, B. (1992). Predictors of smoking relapse among self–quitters: A report from the normative aging study. *Addictive Behaviors, 17*, 367–377.

Geist, C. R., & Herrmann, S. M. (1990). A comparison of the psychological characteristics of smokers, ex–smokers, and nonsmokers. *Journal of Clinical Psychology, 46,* 102–105.

Gerner, R. H., & Wilkins, J. N. (1983). CSF cortisol in patients with depression, mania or anorexia nervosa and in normal subjects. *American Journal of Psychiatry, 140,* 92–94.

Gilbert, B. O. (1991). Physiological and nonverbal correlates of extraversion, neuroticism, and psychoticism during active and passive coping. *Personality and Individual Differences, 12,* 1325–1331.

Gilbert, B. O., & Gilbert, D. G. (1991). Electrodermal responses to movie–induced stress as a function of EPI and MMPI scale scores. *Journal of Social Behavior and Personality, 6,* 903–914.

Gilbert, D. G. (1979). Paradoxical tranquilizing and emotion–reducing effects of nicotine. *Psychological Bulletin, 86,* 643–661.

Gilbert, D. G. (1980). Introversion and self–reported reason for and times of urge for smoking. *Addictive Behaviors, 5,* 97–99.

Gilbert, D. G. (1985, March). *Nicotine's effects on lateralized EEG and emotion.* Paper presented at the Sixth Annual Meeting of the Society of Behavioral Medicine, New Orleans, LA.

Gilbert, D. G. (1987). Effects of smoking and nicotine on EEG lateralization as a function of personality. *Personality and Individual Differences, 8,* 933–941.

Gilbert, D. G. (1988). EEG and personality differences between smokers and nonsmokers. *Personality and Individual Differences, 9,* 659–665.

Gilbert, D. G. (1991). A Personality × Personality × Setting biosocial model of interpersonal affect and communication. In D. G. Gilbert & J. J. Connolly (Eds.), *Personality, social skills, and psychopathology: An individual differences approach* (pp. 107–135). New York: Plenum.

Gilbert, D. G., Gehlbach, B., Estes, S. L., Rabinovich, N., & Detwiler, F. R. J. (1994, October). *Effects of smoking deprivation and a quantified dose of tobacco smoke on EEG power and lateralization as a function of depression and habitual nicotine intake.* Paper presented at the Thirty–Fourth Annual Meeting of the Society for Psychophysiological Research, Atlanta, GA.

Gilbert, D. G., Gilbert, B. O., & Schultz, V. (1994). *Commonalities in response to abstinence from smoking, alcohol, caffeine, food, and to relationship breakup and bereavement.* Manuscript submitted for publication.

Gilbert, D. G., & Hagen, R. L. (1980). The effects of nicotine and extraversion on self–report, skin conductance, electromyographic, and heart responses to emotional stimuli. *Addictive Behaviors, 5,* 247–257.

Gilbert, D. G., & Hagen, R. L. (1985). Electrodermal responses to movie stressors: Nicotine × Extraversion interactions. *Personality and Individual Differences, 6,* 573–578.

Gilbert, D. G., Hagen, R. L., & D'Agostino, J. (1986). The effects of cigarette smoking on human sexual potency. *Addictive Behaviors, 11,* 431–434.

Gilbert, D. G., Jensen, R. A., & Meliska, C. J. (1989). A system for administering quantified doses of tobacco smoke to human subjects: Plasma nicotine and filter pad validation. *Pharmacology, Biochemistry, and Behavior, 31,* 905–908.

Gilbert, D. G., & Meliska, C. J. (1992). Individual differences in reliability of electroencephalogram, cortisol, beta–endorphin, heart rate, and subjective responses to smoking multiple cigarettes via a quantified smoke delivery system. In P. M. Lippiello,

A. C. Collins, J. A. Gray, & J. H. Robinson (Eds.), *The biology of nicotine: Current research issues* (pp. 141–155). New York: Raven Press.

Gilbert, D. G., Meliska, C. J., Welser, R., & Estes, S. L. (1994). Depression, personality, and gender influence EEG, cortisol, beta–endorphin, heart rate, and subjective responses to smoking multiple cigarettes. *Personality and Individual Differences, 16,* 247–264.

Gilbert, D. G., Meliska, C. J., Welser, R., Scott, S., Jensen, R. A., & Meliska, J. (1992, March). *Individual differences in the effects of smoking cessation on EEG, mood and vigilance.* Paper presented at the Thirteenth Annual Meeting of the Society of Behavioral Medicine, New York.

Gilbert, D. G., Meliska, C. J., Williams, C., & Jensen, R. A. (1992). Subjective correlates of smoking–induced elevations of plasma beta–endorphin and cortisol. *Psychopharmacology, 106,* 275–281.

Gilbert, D. G., Robinson, J. H., Chamberlin, C. L., & Spielberger, C. D. (1989). Effects of smoking/nicotine on anxiety, heart rate, and lateralization of EEG during a stressful movie. *Psychophysiology, 26,* 311–320.

Gilbert, D. G., & Spielberger, C. D. (1987). Effects of smoking on heart rate, anxiety, and feelings of success during social interaction. *Journal of Behavioral Medicine, 10,* 629–638.

Gilbert, D. G., & Welser, R. (1989). Emotion, anxiety and smoking. In T. Ney & A. Gale (Eds), *Smoking and human behavior* (pp. 171–196). Chichester, England: Wiley.

Gilligan, S. G., & Bower, G. H. (1984). Cognitive consequences of emotional arousal. In C. E. Izard, J. Kagan, & R. B. Zajonc (Eds.), *Emotions, cognition, and behavior (pp. 547–588).* New York: Cambridge University Press.

Ginzel, K. H. (1988). The lungs as sites of origin of nicotine–induced skeletomotor relaxation and behavioral and electrocortical arousal in the cat. In M. J. Rand & K. Thurau (Eds.), *The pharmacology of nicotine* (pp. 269–292). Washington, DC: IRL Press.

Glaser, G. H., Kornfield, D. S., & Knight, R. P., Jr. (1955). Intravenous hydrocortisone, corticotropin and the electroencephalogram. *AMA Archives of Neurology and Psychiatry, 73,* 338–344.

Glassman, A. H. (1993). Cigarette smoking: Implications for psychiatric illness. *American Journal of Psychiatry, 150*(86), 507–510.

Glassman, A. H., Helzer, J. E., Covey, L. S., Cottler, L. B., Stetner, F., Tipp, J. E., & Johnson, M. (1990). Smoking, smoking cessation, and major depression. *Journal of the American Medical Association, 264,* 1546–1549.

Glassman, A. H., Jackson, W. K., Walsh, B. T., Roose, S. P., & Rosenfeld, B. (1984). Cigarette craving, smoking withdrawal and clonidine. *Science, 226,* 864–867.

Glassman, A. H., Steiner, F., Walsh, B. T., Raizman, P. S., Fleiss, J. L., Cooper, T. B., & Covery, L. S. (1988). Heavy smokers, smoking cessation, and clonidine. *Journal of the American Medical Association, 259,* 2863–2866.

Glauser, S. C., Glauser, E. M., Reidenberg, M. M., Rusy, B. R., & Tallarida, R. J. (1970). Metabolic changes associated with the cessation of cigarette smoking. *Archives of Environmental Health, 20,* 377–381.

Glynn, S. H., & Sussman, S. (1990). Why patients smoke [letter]. *Hospital and Community Psychiatry, 41,* 1027.

Goff, D. C., Henderson, D. C., & Amico, E. (1992). Cigarette smoking in schizophrenia: Relationship to psychopathology and medication side effects. *American Journal of Psychiatry, 149,* 1189–1194.

Goldberg, L. R. (1993). The structure of phenotypic personality traits. *American Psychologist, 48,* 26–34.

Goldberg, S. R., Spealman, R. D., & Goldberg, D. M. (1981, October 30). Persistent behavior at high rates maintained by intravenous self–administration of nicotine. *Science, 214,* 573–575.

Golding, J. F. (1988). Effects of cigarette smoking on resting EEG, visual evoked potential and photic driving. *Pharmacology, Biochemistry, and Behavior, 29,* 23–32.

Golding, J. F., Harpur, T., & Brent–Smith, H. (1983). Personality, drinking and drug–taking correlates of cigarette smoking. *Personality and Individual Differences, 6,* 703–706.

Golding, J., & Mangan, G. L. (1982). Arousing and de-arousing effects of cigarette smoking under conditions of stress and mild sensory isolation. *Psychophysiology, 19,* 449–456.

Goldstein, L., Beck, R. A., & Mundschenk, D. L. (1967). Effects of nicotine upon cortical and subcortical electrical activity of the rabbit brain: Quantitative analysis. In H. B. Murphree & C. C. Pfeiffer (Eds.), *Annals of the New York Academy of Sciences, Vol. 142* (pp. 170–180). New York: New York Academy of Sciences.

Gopalaswamy, A. K., & Morgan, R. (1986). Smoking in chronic schizophrenia [letter]. *British Journal of Psychiatry, 149,* 523.

Gordon, T., Kannel, W. B., Dawber, T. R., & McGee, D. (1975). Changes associated with quitting cigarette smoking: The Framingham study. *American Heart Journal, 90,* 322–328.

Gorelick, D. A., Rose, J., & Jarvik, M. E. (1989). Effects of naloxone on cigarette smoking. *Journal of Substance Abuse, 1,* 153–159.

Gorenstein, E. E., & Newman, J. P. (1980). Disinhibitory psychopathology: A new perspective and a model for research. *Psychological Review, 87,* 301–315.

Gottesman, I. I. (1991). *Schizophrenia genesis: The origins of madness.* New York: W. H. Freeman.

Gottlieb, A. M., Killen, J. D., Marlatt, G. A., & Taylor, C. B. (1987). Psychological and pharmacological influences in cigarette smoking withdrawal: Effects of nicotine gum and expectancy on smoking withdrawal symptoms and relapse. *Journal of Consulting and Clinical Psychology, 55,* 606–608.

Gray, J. A. (1981). A critique of Eysenck's theory of personality. In H. J. Eysenck (Ed.), *A model for personality* (pp. 246–276). New York: Springer.

Gray, J. A. (1982). *The neuropsychology of anxiety.* New York: Oxford University Press.

Gray, J. A. (1990). Brain systems that mediate both emotion and cognition. *Cognition and Emotion, 4,* 269–288.

Gray, J. A. (1991). The neuropsychology of schizophrenia. *Brain and Brain Sciences, 14,* 1–20.

Graziano, W. G., Rahe, D. F., & Feldesman, A. B. (1985). Extraversion, social cognition, and the salience of aversiveness in social encounters. *Journal of Personality and Social Psychology, 49,* 971–980.

Greenberg, L. S., & Sarafan, J. D. (1988). *Emotion in psychotherapy: Emotion, cognition and the process of change.* New York: Guilford.

Grenhoff, J., Aston–Jones, G., & Svensson, T. H. (1986). *Acta Physiologica Scandinavica, 128,* 351–358.

Gritz, E. R. (1979). Women and smoking: A realistic appraisal. In J. L. Schwartz (Ed.), *Progress in smoking cessation: Proceedings of the International Conference on Smoking Cessation* (pp. 119–141). New York: American Cancer Society.

Gross, J., & Stitzer, M. L. (1989). Nicotine replacement: ten–week effects on tobacco withdrawal symptoms. *Psychopharmacology, 98,* 334–341.

Grunberg, N. E. (1982). The effects of nicotine and cigarette smoking on food consumption and taste preferences. *Addictive Behaviors, 7,* 317–331.

Grunberg, N. E. (1985). Nicotine, cigarette smoking, and body weight. *British Journal of Addiction, 80,* 369–377.

Grunberg, N. E., Bowen, D. J., & Winders, S. E. (1986). Effects of nicotine on body weight and food consumption in female rats. *Psychopharmacology, 90,* 101–105.

Grunberg, N. E., & Raygada, M. (1991). Effects of nicotine on insulin: Actions and implications. In F. Adlkofer & K. Thurau (Eds.), *Effects of nicotine on biological systems* (pp. 131–142). Basel, Switzerland: Birkhauser Verlag.

Grunberg, N. E., Winders, S. E., & Popp, K. A. (1987). Sex differences in nicotine's effects on consummatory behavior and body weight in rats. *Psychopharmacology, 91,* 221–225.

Grunberg, N. E., Winders, S. E., & Wewers, M. E. (1991). Gender differences in tobacco use. *Health Psychology, 10,* 143–153.

Guha, D., & Pradhan, S. N. (1976). Effects of nicotine on EEG and evoked potentials and their interactions with autonomic drugs. *Neuropharmacology, 15,* 225–232.

Guilford, J. S. (1966). *Factors related to successful abstinence from smoking: Final report.* Washington, DC: U. S. Public Health Service, Division of Chronic Diseases, Bureau of State Services.

Guilford, J. S. (1967). Sex differences between successful and unsuccessful abstainers from smoking. In S. V. Zagona (Ed.), *Studies and issues in smoking behavior* (pp. 95–102). Tucson: University of Arizona Press.

Gunn, R. C. (1986). Reactions to withdrawal symptoms and success on smoking cessation clinics. *Addictive Behaviors, 11,* 49–53.

Gunn, R. C., & Shapiro, A. (1979). Life stress, weight gain and resuming smoking after success in a cessation clinic. *Psychological Reports, 57,* 1035–1039.

Gupta, A. K., Sethi, B. B., & Gupta, S. C. (1976). EPI and 16PF observations in smokers. *Indian Journal of Psychiatry, 18,* 252–259.

Gupta, U. (1984). Phenobarbitone and the relationship between extraversion and reinforcement in verbal operant conditioning. *British Journal of Psychology, 75,* 499–506.

Gur, R. C., Packer, I., Hungerbuhler, J., Reivich, M., Obrist,W., Amarnek, W., & Sackeim, H. (1980, March 14). Differences in the distribution of gray and white matter in human cerebral hemispheres. *Science, 207,* 1226–1228.

Gurling, H. M. D., Grant, S., & Dangl, J. (1985). The genetic and cultural transmission of alcohol use, alcoholism, cigarette smoking and coffee drinking: A review and an example using a log–linear cultural transmission model. *British Journal of Addition, 80,* 269–279.

Gynther, L., Hewitt, J. K., Heath, A. C., & Eaves, L. (1993, July). Genetic and environmental influences on smoking and motives for smoking. In *Proceedings of the Twenty–third Annual Meeting of the Behavior Genetics Association* (p. 27). Sydney, New South Wales, Australia: BGA.

Haertzen, C. A., & Hickey, J. E. (1987). Addiction research center inventory: measurement of euphoria and other drug effects. in M. A. Bozarth (ed.). methods of assessing the reinforcing properties of abused drugs (pp. 489–524). New York: Springer–Verlag.

Hajek, P. (1991). Individual differences in difficulty quitting smoking. *British Journal of Addiction, 86,* 555–558.

Hajek, P., Belcher, M., & Stapleton, J. (1987). Breath holding endurance as a predictor of success in smoking cessation. *Addictive Behaviors, 12,* 285–288.

Hale, F., Margen, S., & Rabak, D. (1982). Postprandial hypoglycemia and "psychological" symptoms. *Biological Psychiatry, 17,* 125–131.

Hall, G. H., & Morrison, C. F. (1973). New evidence for a relationship between tobacco smoking, nicotine dependence and stress. *Nature, 243,* 199–210.

Hall, S. M. (1984). The abstinence phobias: Links between substance abuse and anxiety. *International Journal of Addiction, 19,* 613–631.

Hall, S. M., Bachman, J. S., Henderson, J., Barstow, R., & Jones, R. T. (1983). Smoking cessation in patients with cardiopulmonary disease: An initial study. *Addictive Behaviors, 8,* 33–42.

Hall, S. M., Ginsberg, D., & Jones, R. T. (1986). Smoking cessation and weight gain. *Journal of Consulting and Clinical Psychology, 54,* 342–346.

Hall, S. M., Havassey, B. E., & Wasserman, D. A. (1990). Commitment to abstinence and acute stress in relapse to alcohol, opiates, and nicotine. *Journal of Consulting and Clinical Psychology, 58,* 175–181.

Hall, S. M., McGee, R., Tunstall, C., Duffy, J., & Benowitz, N. (1989). Changes in food intake and activity after quitting smoking. *Journal of Consulting and Clinical Psychology, 57,* 81–86.

Hall, S. M., Munoz, R. F., & Reus, V. I. (1991). Depression and smoking treatment: A clinical trial of an affect regulation treatment. In *Problems of drug dependence 1991: Proceedings of the 53rd Annual Scientific Meeting,* (pp. 326), The Committee on Problems of Drug Dependence, Inc. Rockville, MD: National Institute on Drug Abuse.

Hall, S. M., Munoz, R. F., Reus, V. I., & Sees, K. L. (1993). Nicotine, negative affect, and depression. *Journal of Consulting and Clinical Psychology, 61,* 761–767.

Halpen, D. L., Blake, R., & Hillenbrand, J. (1986). Psychophysics of a chilling sound. *Perception and Psychophysics, 39,* 77–80.

Halpern, M. T., & Warner, K. E. (1993). Motivations for smoking cessation: A comparison of successful quitters and failures. Journal of Substance Abuse, 5, 247–256.

Hamilton, J. A. & Gallant, S. A. (1988). Premenstrual symptom changes and plasma beta–endorphin/beta–lipotropin throughout the menstrual cycle. *Psychoneuroendocrinology, 13,* 505–514.

Hammond, G., & Garfinkel, L. (1961). Smoking habits of men and women. *Journal of the National Cancer Institute, 27,* 419–442.

Hannah, M. C., Hopper, J. L., & Mathews, J. D. (1985). Twin concordance for a binary trait, II: Nested analysis of ever–smoking and ex–smoking traits and unnested analysis of a "committed smoking" trait. *American Journal of Human Genetics, 37,* 153–165.

Harding, W. M., Zinberg, N. E., Stelmack, S. M., & Barry, A. (1980). Formerly–addicted–now–controlled opiate users. *The International Journal of the Addictions, 15,* 47–60.

Harpur, T. J., Hare, R. D., & Hakstian, A. R. (1989). Two–factor conceptualization of psychopathy: Construct validity and assessment implications. Psychological Assessment: *A Journal of Consulting and Clinical Psychology, 1,* 6–17.

Harris, J. E. (1983). Cigarette smoking among successive birth cohorts of men and women in the United States during 1900–1980. *Journal of the National Cancer Institute, 71,* 473–479.

Hartsough, C. S., & Lambert, N. M. (1987). Pattern and progression of drug use among hyperactives and controls: A prospective short–term longitudinal study. *Journal of Child Psychology, 28,* 543–553.

Hasenfratz, M., & Bättig, K. (1992). Action profiles of smoking and caffeine: Stroop effect, EEG, and peripheral physiology. *Pharmacology, Biochemistry, and Behavior, 42,* 155–161.

Hasenfratz, M., & Bättig, K. (1993). Psychophysiological interactions between smoking and stress coping? *Psychopharmacology, 113,* 37–44.

Hasenfratz, M., Michel, C., Nil, R., & Bättig, K. (1989). Can smoking increase attention in rapid information processing during noise? Electrocortical, physiological and behavioral effects. *Psychopharmacology, 98,* 75–80.

Hatch, J. P., Bierner, S. M., Fisher, J. G. (1983). The effects of smoking and cigarette nicotine content on smokers' preparation and performance of a psychosocially stressful task. *Journal of Behavioral Medicine, 6,* 207–216.

Hatsukami, D. K., Dahlgren, L., Zimmerman, R., & Hughes, J. R. (1988). Symptoms of tobacco withdrawal from total cigarette cessation versus partial cigarette reduction. *Psychopharmacology, 94,* 242–247.

Hatsukami, D. K., Gust, S. W., & Keenan, R. M. (1987). Physiologic and subjective changes from smokeless tobacco withdrawal. *Clinical Pharmacology and Therapeutics, 41,* 103–107.

Hatsukami, D. K., Huber, M., Callies, A., & Skoog, K. (1993). Physical dependence on nicotine gum: effect of duration of use. *Psychopharmacology, 111,* 449–456.

Hatsukami, D. K., Hughes, J. R., & Pickens, R. (1984). Tobacco withdrawal symptoms: An experimental analysis. *Psychopharmacology, 84,* 231–236.

Hatsukami, D. K., Skoog, K., Huber, M., & Hughes, J. R. (1991). Signs and symptoms of nicotine gum abstinence. *Psychopharmacology, 104,* 496–504.

Haynes, S. N. (1988). Causal models and the assessment–treatment relationship in behavior therapy. *Journal of Psychopathology and Behavioral Assessment, 10,* 171–183.

Haynes, S. N., & O'Brien, W. H. (1988). The Gordion knot of DSM–III–R use: Integrating principles of behavior classification and complex causal models. *Behavioral Assessment, 10,* 95–105.

Heath, A. C., Cloninger, C. R., & Martin, N. G. (1994). Testing a model for the genetic structure of personality: A comparison of the personality systems of Cloninger and Eysenck. *Journal of Personality and Social Psychology, 66,* 762–775.

Heath, A. C., & Madden, P. A. F. (1993, November). *Personality correlates of smoking behavior: A genetic perspective.* Paper presented at the American Society of Addiction Medicine, Nicotine Dependence Conference. Atlanta, GA.

Heath, A. C., & Madden, P. A. F. (in press). Genetic influence on smoking behavior. In J. R. Turner, L. R. Cardon, & J. K Hewitt (Eds), *Behavior genetic applications in behavioral medicine research.* New York: Plenum.

Heath, R. G. (1954). Definition of the septal region. In R. G. Heath & Tulane University Department of Psychiatry and Neurology (Eds.), *Studies in schizophrenia* (pp. 3–5). Cambridge, MA: Harvard University Press.

Heath, R. G. (1964). Developments toward new physiologic treatments in psychiatry. *Journal of Neuropsychiatry, 5,* 318–331.

Heath, R. G. (1986). The neural substrate for emotion. In R. Plutchik & H. Kellerman (Eds.), *Emotion theory, research, and experience* (pp. 3–35). Orlando, FL: Academic Press.

Heatherton, T. F., Kozlowski, L. T., Frecker, R. C., & Fagerstrom, K. O. (1991). The Fagerstrom Test for Nicotine Dependence: A revision of the Fagerstrom Tolerance Questionnaire. *British Journal of Addiction, 86,* 1119–1127.

Heilman, K. M., Schwartz, H. D., & Watson, R. T. (1978). Hypoarousal in patients with neglect and emotional indifference. *Neurology, 28,* 229–232.

Heimstra, N. W. (1973). The effects of smoking on mood change. In W. L. Dunn (Ed.), *Smoking behavior: Motives and incentives* (pp. 197–207). Washington, DC: V.H. Winston.

Heimstra, N. W., Bancroft, N. R., & DeKock, A. R. (1967). Effects of smoking upon sustained performance in a simulated driving task. In H. B. Murphree (Ed.) *Annals of the New York Academy of Sciences,* (Vol. 143, pp. 295–307). New York: New York Academy of Sciences.

Heishman, S. J., Snyder, F. R., & Henningfield, J. E. (1990). Effects of repeated nicotine administration. In L. Harris (Ed.), *Problems of drug dependence 1990: Proceedings of the 52nd Annual Meeting of the Committee on Problems of Drug Dependence* (NIDA Research Monograph 105, pp. 314–315). Rockville, MD: National Institute of Drug Abuse.

Hendrick, C., & Brown, S. R. (1971). Introversion, extraversion, and interpersonal attraction. *Journal of Personality and Social Psychology, 20,* 31–36.

Hendrickson, D. E., & Hendrickson, A. A. (1980). The biological basis of individual differences in intelligence. *Personality and Individual Differences, 1,* 3–34.

Hendry, J. S., & Rosecrans, J. A. (1982). Effects of nicotine on conditioned and unconditioned behavior in experimental animals. *Pharmacology and Therapeutics, 17,* 431–454.

Hendry, J. S., & Rosecrans, J. A. (1984). Effects of nicotine on conditioned and unconditioned behaviors in experimental animals. In D. J. K. Balfour (Ed.), *International encyclopedia of pharmacology and therapeutics: section 114,* Nicotine and the tobacco smoking habit (pp. 75–99). Oxford, England: Pergamon Press.

Henkin, R. I. (1970). The effects of corticosteroids and ACTH on sensory system. In D. DeWied & J. A. W. M. Weijnen (Eds.), *Pituitary, adrenal and the brain: Vol. 32. Progress in brain research* (pp. 279–294). Amsterdam: Elsevier.

Henningfield, J. E. (1984). Pharmacological basis and treatment of cigarette smoking. *Journal of Clinical Psychiatry, 45,* 24–34.

Henningfield, J. E., Clayton, R., & Pollin, W. (1990). Involvement of tobacco in alcoholism and illicit drug use. *British Journal of Addiction, 85,* 279–292.

Henningfield, J. E., & Goldberg, S. R. (1983). Control of behavior by intravenous nicotine injections in human subjects. *Pharmacology, Biochemistry, and Behavior, 19,* 1021–1026.

Henningfield, J. E., & Griffiths, R. R. (1981). Cigarette smoking and subjective response: Effects of d–amphetamine. *Clinical Pharmacology and Therapeutics, 30,* 497–505.

Henningfield, J. E., & Jasinski, D. R. (1988). Pharmacological basis for nicotine replacement. In O. F. Pomerleau, C. S. Pomerleau, K. O. Fagerstrom, J. E. Henningfield, & J. R. Hughes (Eds.), *Nicotine replacement: A critical evaluation* (pp. 35–61). New York: Alan R. Liss.

Henningfield, J. E., & Keenan, R. M. (1993). Nicotine delivery kinetics and abuse liability. *Journal of Consulting and Clinical Psychology, 61,* 743–750.

Henningfield, J. E., Lucas, S. E., & Bigelow, G. E. (1986). Human studies of drugs as reinforcers. In S. R. Goldberg & I. P. Stolerman (Eds.), *Behavioral analysis of drug dependence* (69–122). Orlando, FL: Academic Press.

Henningfield, J. E., Miyasato, K., & Jasinski, D. R. (1985). Abuse liability and pharmacodynamic characteristics of intravenous and inhaled nicotine. *The Journal of Pharmacology and Experimental Therapeutics, 234*, 1–12.

Henriques, J. B., & Davidson, R. J. (1991). Left frontal hypoactivation in depression. *Journal of Abnormal Psychology, 100*, 535–545.

Henry, J. P. (1986). Neuroendocrine patterns of emotional response. In R. Plutchik & H. Kellerman (Eds.), *Emotion: Theory, research, and experience* (pp. 37–60). Orlando, FL: Academic Press.

Herman, B. H., & Panksepp, J. (1978). Effects of morphine and naloxone on separation distress and approach attachment: Evidence for opiate mediation of social affect. *Pharmacology, Biochemistry, and Behavior, 9*, 213–220.

Herman, B. H., & Panksepp, J. (1981, March 16). Ascending endorphin inhibition of distress vocalization. *Science, 211*, 1060–1062.

Herman, C. P., & Polivy, J. (1975). Anxiety, restraint, and eating behavior. *Journal of Abnormal Psychology, 84*, 666–672.

Hernandez, S. K., & Mauger, P. A. (1980). Assertiveness, aggressiveness and Eysenck's personality variables. *Personality and Individual Differences, 1*, 143–149.

Hersen, M., & Bellack, A. S. (1988). DSM–III and behavioral assessment. In A. S. Bellack & M. Hersen (Eds.), *Behavioral assessment: A practical handbook* (3rd ed., pp. 67–84). New York: Pergamon Press.

Hertz, B. F. (1978). The effects of cigarette smoking on perception of nonverbal communications (Doctoral dissertation,) *Dissertation Abstracts International, 9*, 2501B–2502B.

Hickey, R. J., & Harner, E. B. (1973). Ethological and biochemical interactions and their relationships to smoking. In W. L. Dunn (Ed.), *Smoking behavior: Motives and incentives* (pp. 267–282). Washington, DC: V. H. Winston.

Himadi, W. G., Arkowitz, H., Hinton, R., & Perl, J. (1980). Minimal dating and its relationship to other social problems and general adjustment. *Behavior Therapy, 11*, 345–352.

Himmelsback, C. K. (1943). Morphine, with reference to physical dependence. *Federation Proceedings, 2*, 201–203.

Hindmarch, I., Kerr, J. S., & Sherwood, N. (1990). Effects of nicotine gum on psychomotor performance in smokers and non–smokers. *Psychopharmacology, 100*, 535–541.

Hodgson, R. J., & Rankin, H. (1976). Modification of excessive drinking by cue exposure. *Behaviour Research and Therapy, 14*, 305–307.

Hofstetter, A., Schutz, Y., Jequier, E., & Wahren, J. (1986). Increased 24–hour energy expenditure in cigarette smokers. *New England Journal of Medicine, 314*, 79–82.

Hokanson, J. E., & Rupert, M. P. (1991). Interpersonal factors in depression. In D. G. Gilbert & J. J. Connolly (Eds.), *Personality, social skills, and psychopathology* (pp. 157–184). New York: Plenum.

Hollingworth, H. L. (1939, October 27). Chewing as a technique for relaxation. *Science, 90*, 385–387.

Hollon, S. D., Shelton, R. C., & Davis, D. D. (1993). Cognitive therapy for depression: Conceptual issues and clincal efficacy. *Journal of Consulting and Clinical Psychology, 61*, 248–260

Horn, D. H., & Waingrow, S. (1966). Some dimensions of a model from smoking behavior change. *American Journal of Public Health, 56,* 21–26.

Horney, K. (1945). *Our inner conflicts: A constructive theory of neurosis.* New York: Norton.

Houston, J. P., Schneider, N. G., & Jarvik, M. E. (1978). Effects of smoking on free recall and organization. *American Journal of Psychiatry, 135,* 220–222.

Hubert, W., & de Jong–Meyer, R. (1992). Saliva cortisol response to unpleasant film stimuli differ between high and low trait anxious subjects. *Neuropsychobiology, 25,* 115–120.

Hughes, J. R. (1986). Genetics of smoking: A brief review. *Behavior Therapy, 17,* 335–345.

Hughes, J. R. (1987). Craving as a dependent variable. *British Journal of Addiction, 82,* 38.

Hughes, J. R. (1991). Distinguishing withdrawal relief and direct effects of smoking. *Psychopharmacology, 104,* 409–410.

Hughes, J. R. (1992). Tobacco withdrawal in self–quitters. *Journal of Consulting and Clinical Psychology, 60,* 689–697.

Hughes, J. R., Gulliver, S. B., Amori, G., Mireault, G. C., & Fenwick, J. F. (1989). Effects of instructions and nicotine on smoking cessation, withdrawal symptoms and self–administration of nicotine gum. *Psychopharmacology, 99,* 486–491.

Hughes, J. R., Gust, S. W., Skoog, K., Keenan, R. M., & Fenwick, J. W. (1991). Symptoms of tobacco withdrawal: A replication and extension. *Archives of General Psychiatry, 48,* 52–59.

Hughes, J. R., & Hatsukami, D. K. (1986). Signs and symptoms of tobacco withdrawal. *Archives of General Psychiatry, 43,* 289–294.

Hughes, J. R., Hatsukami, D. K., Mitchell, J. E., & Dahlgren, L. A. (1986). Prevalence of smoking among psychiatric outpatients. *American Journal of Psychiatry, 143,* 993–997.

Hughes, J. R., Hatsukami, D. K., Pickens, R. W., & Svikis, D. S. (1984). Consistency of the tobacco withdrawal syndrome. *Addictive Behaviors, 9,* 409–412.

Hughes, J. R., Hatsukami, D. K., & Skoog, K. P. (1986). Physical dependence on nicotine in gum. A placebo substitution trial. *Journal of the American Medical Association, 255,* 3277–3279.

Hughes, J. R., Hatsukami, D. K., Pickens, R. W., Krahn, D., Malin, S., & Luknic, A. (1984). Effect of nicotine on the tobacco withdrawal syndrome. *Psychopharmacology, 83,* 82–87.

Hughes, J. R., Higgins, S. T., & Hatsukami, D. (1990). Effects of abstinence from tobacco: A critical review. In L. T. Kozlowski, H. M. Annis, H. D. Cappell, F. B. Glaser, M. S. Goodstadt, Y. Israel, H. Kalant, E. M. Sellers, & E. R. Vingilis (Eds.), *Research advances in alcohol and drug problems* (Vol. 10, pp. 317–398). New York: Plenum.

Hughes, J. R., Pickens, R. W., Spring, W., & Keenan, R. M. (1985). Instructions control whether nicotine will serve as a reinforcer. *The Journal of Pharmacology and Experimental Therapeutics, 235,* 106–112.

Hughes, J. R., Strickler, G., King, D., Higgins, S. T., Fenwick, J. W., Gulliver, S. B., & Mireault, G. (1989). Smoking history, instructions and the effects of nicotine: Two pilot studies. *Pharmacology, Biochemistry, and Behavior, 34,* 149–155.

Hunt, W. A., Barnett, L. W., & Branch, L. G. (1971). Relapse rates in addiction programs. *Journal of Clinical Psychology, 27,* 455–456.

Hutchinson, R. R., & Emley, G. B. (1973). Effects of nicotine on avoidance, conditioned suppression and aggression response measures in animals and man. In W. L. Dunn (Ed.), *Smoking behavior: Motives and incentives* (pp. 171–196). Washington, DC: V. H. Winston.

Ikard, F. F., Green, D., & Horn, D. (1969). A scale to differentiate between types of smoking as related to the management of affect. *International Journal of Addictions, 4,* 649–659.

Ikard, F. F., & Tompkins, S. (1973). The experience of affect as a determinant of smoking behavior: A series of validity studies. *Journal of Abnormal Psychology, 81,* 172–181.

Imperato, A., Mulas, A., & Di Chiara, G. (1986). Nicotine preferentially stimulates dopamine release in the limbic system of freely moving rats. *European Journal of Pharmacology, 132,* 337–338.

Imperato, A., Puglisi–Allegra, S., Casolini, P., Zocchi, A., & Angelucci, L. (1989). Stress–induced enhancement of dopamine and acetylcholine release in limbic structure, role of cortisone, *European Journal of Pharmacology, 165,* 337–339.

Infante, D. A. (1987). Aggressiveness. In J. C. McCroskey & J. A. Daly (Eds.), *Personality and interpersonal communication.* (pp. 157–192). Beverly Hills, CA: Sage.

Istvan, J., & Matarazzo, J. D. (1984). Tobacco, alcohol, and caffeine use: A review of their interrelationships. *Psychological Bulletin, 95,* 301–326.

Iwamoto, E. T. (1989). Antinociception after nicotine administration into the mesopontine tegmentum of rats: Evidence for muscarinic actions. *Journal of Pharmacology and Experimental Therapeutics, 251,* 412–421.

Iwamoto, E. T. (1990). Nicotine conditions place preferences after intracerebral administration in rats. *Psychopharmacology, 100,* 251–257.

Izard, C. (1971). *The face of emotion.* New York: Appleton–Century–Crofts.

Izard, C. E. (1990). Facial expressions and the regulation of emotions. *Journal of Personality and Social Psychology, 58,* 487–498.

Izard, C. E. (1992). Basic emotions, relations among emotions, and emotion–cognition relations. *Psychological Review, 99,* 561–565.

Jacobs, M. A., Anderson, L. S., Champagne, E., Karush, N., Richman, S. J., & Knapp, P. H. (1966). Orality, impulsivity and cigarette smoking in men: Further findings in support of a theory. *Journal of Nervous and Mental Disease, 143,* 207–219.

Jacobs, M. A., Knapp, P. H., Anderson, L. S., Karush, N., Meissner, R., & Richman, S. J. (1965). Relationship of oral frustration factors with heavy cigarette smoking in males. *Journal of Nervous and Mental Disease, 141,* 161–171.

Jacobs, M. A., & Spilken, A. Z. (1971). Personality patterns associated with heavy cigarette smoking in male college students. *Journal of Consulting and Clinical Psychology, 37,* 428–432.

Jaffe, J. H. (1990). Tobacco smoking and nicotine dependence. In S. Wonnacott, M. A. H. Russell, & I. P. Stolerman (Eds.), *Nicotine psychopharmacology* (pp. 1–37). New York: Oxford University Press.

James, W. & Lange, C. G. (1922). *The emotions.* Baltimore: Williams & Wilkins. (Original works published 1884 & 1885)

Jamison, R. N. (1979). Cigarette smoking and personality in male and female adolescents. *Psychological Reports, 44,* 842.

Janis, I. L., & Mann, L. (1965). Effectiveness of emotional role–playing in modifying smoking habits and attitudes. *Journal of Experimental Research in Personality, 1,* 84–90.

Jardine, R., Martin, N. G., & Henderson, A. S. (1984). Genetic covariation between neuroticism and the symptoms of anxiety and depression. *Genetic Epidemiology, 1,* 89–107.

Jarvik, M. E. (1973). Further observations on nicotine as the reinforcing agent in smoking. In W. L. Dunn (Ed.), *Smoking behavior: Motives and incentives* (pp. 33–49). Washington, DC: V. H. Winston.

Jarvik, M. E., Caskey, N. H., Rose, J. E., Herskovic, J. E., & Sadeghpour, M. (1989). Anxiolytic effects of smoking associated with four stressors. *Addictive Behaviors, 14,* 379–386.

Jarvik, M. E., Saniga, S. S., Herskovic, J. E., Weiner, H., & Oisboid, D. (1989). Potentiation of cigarette craving and satisfaction by two types of meals. *Addictive Behaviors, 14,* 35–41.

Jarvis, M. (1984). Gender and smoking: Do women really find it harder to give up? *British Journal of Addiction, 79,* 383–387.

Jarvis, M. J., Raw, M., Russell, M. A. H., & Feyerabend, C. (1982). Randomized controlled trial of nicotine chewing–gum. *British Medical Journal, 285,* 537–540.

Jasinski, D. R., Johnson, R. E., & Henningfield, J. E. (1984). Abuse liability assessment in human subjects. *Trends in Pharmacological Science, 5,* 196–200.

Jensen, R. A., Gilbert, D. G., Meliska, C. J., Landrum, T. A., & Szary, A. B. (1990). Characterization of a dose–response curve for nicotine–induced conditioned taste aversion in rats: Relationship to elevation of plasma B–endorphin concentration. *Behavioral and Neural Biology, 53,* 428–440.

Jiang, T.–Y. E. (1988). Effects of cigarette smoking on match–to–sample reaction time and accuracy. *Dissertation Abstracts International, 49*(11), 5056B.

Joffe, R., Lowe, M. R., & Fisher, E. B. (1981). A validity test of the reasons for smoking scale. *Addictive Behaviors, 6,* 41–45.

Johnston, L. M. (1942). Tobacco smoking and nicotine. *Lancet, 2,* 742.

Jones, G. M. M., Sahakian, B. J., Levy, R., Warburton, D. M., & Gray, J. A. (1992). Effects of acute subcutaneous nicotine on attention, information processing and short–term memory in Alzheimer's disease. *Psychopharmacology, 108,* 485–494.

Jones, R. T. (1980). Human effects: An overview. In R. C. Peterson (Ed.), *Marijuana research findings: 1980* (pp. 54–80). Washington, DC: National Institute on Drug Abuse.

Jones, R. T. (1984). The pharmacology of cocaine. In J. Grabowski (Ed.), *Cocaine: Pharmacology, effects, and treatment of abuse* (pp. 34–53). Washington, DC: National Institute on Drug Abuse.

Jorenby, D. E., Steinpreis, R. E., Sherman, J. E., & Baker, T. B. (1990). Aversion instead of preference learning indicated by nicotine place conditioning in rats. *Psychopharmacology, 101,* 533–538.

Jubis, R. M. (1986). Effects of alcohol and nicotine on free recall of relevant cues. *Perceptual and Motor Skills, 62,* 363–369.

Kalant, H. (1977). Comparative aspects of tolerance to, and dependence on, alcohol, barbiturates, and opiates. In M. M. Gross (Ed.), *Alcohol intoxication and withdrawal III* (pp. 169–186). New York, NY: Plenum Press.

Kalant, H. (1978). Behavioral criteria for tolerance and physical dependence. In J. Fishman (Ed.), *The bases of addiction*, (pp. 199–220). Berlin, W. Germany: Dahlem Konferenzen.

Kandel, D. B., & Davies, M. (1986). Adult sequelae of adolescent depressive symptoms. *Archives of General Psychiatry, 43,* 255–262.

Kanekar, S., & Dolke, A. M. (1970). Smoking, extraversion, and neuroticism. *Psychological Reports, 26,* 384.

Kaplan, B. J., Whitsett, S. F., & Robinson, J. W. (1990). Menstrual cycle phase is a potential confound in psychophysiology research. *Psychophysiology, 27,* 445–450.

Kaplan, H. S. (1987). *Sexual aversion, sexual phobias, and panic disorder.* New York: Brunner/Mazel.

Kaprio, J., Hammer, N., Koskenvuo, M., Floderns–Myrhed, B., Langinvainia, H., & Sarna, S. (1982). Cigarette smoking and alcohol use in Finland and Sweden: A cross–national twin study. *International Journal of Epidemiology, 11,* 378–386.

Karras, A., & Kane, J. M. (1980). Naloxone reduces cigarette smoking. *Life Sciences, 27,* 1541–1545.

Kassel, J. D., Shiffman, S., Gnys, M., Paty, J., & Zettler–Segal, M.(1994). Psychosocial and personality differences in chippers and regular smokers. *Addictive Behaviors, 19,* 565–575.

Kawamura, H., & Domino, E. F. (1969). Differential actions of m and n cholinergic agonists on the brainstem activating system. *International Journal of Neuropharmacology, 8,* 105–115.

Kellam, S. G., Ensminger, M. E., & Simon, M. B. (1980). Mental health in first grade and teenage drug, alcohol, and cigarette use. *Drug and Alcohol Dependence, 5,* 273–304.

Kendler, K. S., Neale, M. C., Kessler, R. C., Heath, A. C., & Eaves, L. J. (1992a). The genetic epidemiology of phobias in women: The interrelationship of agoraphobia, social phobia, situational phobia, and simple phobia. *Archives of General Psychiatry, 49,* 273–281.

Kendler, K. S., Neale, M. C., Kessler, R. C., Heath, A. C., & Eaves, L. J. (1992b). Major depression and generalized anxiety disorder: Same genes, (partly) different environments? *Archives of General Psychiatry, 49,* 716–722.

Kendler, K. S., Neale, M. C., MacLean, C. J., Heath, A. C., Eaves, L. J., & Kessler, R. C. (1993). Smoking and major depression: A causal analysis. *Archives of General Psychiatry, 50,* 36–43.

Kenford, S. L., Fiore, M. C., Jorenby, D. E., Smith, S. S., Wetter, D., & Baker, T. B. (1994). Predicting smoking cessation: Who will quit with and without the nicotine patch. *Journal of the American Medical Association, 271,* 589–594.

Kentridge, R. W., & Aggleton, J. P. (1990). Emotion: Sensory representation, reinforcement, and the temporal lobe. *Cognition and Emotion, 4,* 191–208.

Kerr, J. S., Sherwood, N., & Hindmarch, I. (1991). Separate and combined effects of the social drugs on psychomotor performance. *Psychopharmacology, 104,* 113–119.

Khantzian, E. J., & Treece, C. J. (1977). Psychodynamic aspects of drug dependence: An overview. In J. D. Blaine & D. A. Julius (Eds.), *Psychodynamics of drug dependence* (Research Monograph No. 12, pp. 11–25). Rockville, MD: National Institute on Drug Abuse.

Killen, J. D., Fortmann, S. P., Newman, B., & Varady, A. (1990). Evaluation of a treatment approach combining nicotine gum with self–guided behavioral treatments for smoking relapse prevention. *Journal of Consulting and Clinical Psychology, 58,* 85–92.

Kinnunen, T., Doherty, K., Militello, F. S., & Garvey, A. J. (1994). Quitting smoking and feeling blue: Nicotine replacement as an aid for the depressed [Summary]. *Annals of Behavioral Medicine, 16,* S068.

Kinsbourne, M. (1989). A model of adaptive behavior related to cerebral participation in emotional control. In G. Gainotti & C. Caltagirone (Eds.), *Emotions and the dual brain* (pp. 248–260). New York: Springer–Verlag.

Kirschbaum, C., Wust, S., & Strasburger, C. J. (1992). "Normal" cigarette smoking increases free cortisol in habitual smokers. *Life Sciences, 50,* 435–442.

Kleinke, C. L., Staneski, R. A., & Meeker, F. B. (1983). Attributions for smoking behavior: Comparing smokers with nonsmokers and predicting smokers' cigarette consumption. *Journal of Research in Personality, 17,* 242–255.

Klesges, R. C., & Klesges, L. M. (1988). Cigarette smoking as a dietary strategy in a university population. *International Journal of Eating Disorders, 7,* 413–417.

Klesges, R. C., Meyers, A. W., Klesges, L. M., & La Vasque, M. E. (1989). Smoking, body weight, and their effects on smoking behavior: *A comprehensive review of the literature. Psychological Bulletin, 106,* 204–230.

Klesges, R. C., & Shumaker, S. A. (1992). Understanding the relations between smoking and body weight and their importance to smoking cessation and relapse. *Health Psychology, 11*(Suppl.), 1–3.

Kline, P. (1972). *Fact and fantasy in Freudian theory.* London: Methuen.

Kline, P., & Barrett, P. (1983). The factors in personality questionnaires among normal subjects. *Advances in Behaviour Research and Therapy, 5,* 141–202.

Knott, V. J. (1979). Personality, arousal and individual differences in cigarette smoking. *Psychological Reports, 45,* 423–428.

Knott, V. J. (1984). Electrodermal activity during aversive stimulation: Sex differences in smokers and non–smokers. *Addictive Behaviors, 9,* 195–199.

Knott, V. J. (1989). Brain event–related potentials (ERPs) in smoking performance research. In T. Ney & A. Gale (Eds.), *Smoking and human behavior* (93–114). Chichester, England: Wiley.

Knott, V. J. (1990). Effects of cigarette smoking on subjective and brain evoked responses to electrical pain stimulation. *Pharmacology, Biochemistry, and Behavior, 35,* 341–346.

Knott, V. J., & de Lugt, D. (1991). Subjective and brain–evoked responses to electrical pain stimulation: Effects of cigarette smoking and warning condition. *Pharmacology, Biochemistry, and Behavior, 39,* 889–893.

Kohn, P. M., & Annis, H. M. (1977). Drug use and four kinds of novelty–seeking. *British Journal of Addiction, 72,* 135–141.

Koopmans, J. R., Boomsma, D. I., van Doornen, L. J. P., & Orlebeke, J. F. (1993, July). Alcohol use, smoking and personality in adolescent twins. In *Proceedings of the Twenty–third Annual Meeting of the Behavior Genetics Association* (p. 34). Sydney, New South Wales, Australia: BGA.

Korbacher, C., Arndt, R., Maier, C., & Fehm–Wolfsdorf, G. (1993). Influence of cortisol level on the perception of temperature and pain. *Journal of Psychophysiology, 7,* 158–159.

Kozlowski, L. T., & Herman, C. P. (1984). The interaction of psychosocial and biological determinants of tobacco use: More on the boundary model. *Journal of Applied Social Psychology, 14,* 244–256.

Kozlowski, L. T., & Wilkinson, D. A. (1987). Comments on Kozlowski and Wilkinson's "Use and misuse of the concept of craving by alcohol, tobacco and drug researchers": A reply from the authors. *British Journal of Addiction, 82,* 489–492.

Kozlowski, L. T, Wilkinson, D. A., Skinner, W., Kent, C., Franklin, T., & Pope, M. (1989). Comparing tobacco cigarette dependency with other drug dependencies: Greater or equal "difficulty quitting" and "urges to use" but less pleasure from cigarettes. *Journal of the American Medical Association, 261,* 898–901.

Kumar, R., Pratt, J. A., & Stolerman, I. P. (1983). Characteristics of conditioned taste aversion produced by nicotine in rats. *British Journal of Pharmacology, 79,* 245–253.

Kunzendorf, R., & Wigner, L. (1985). Smoking and memory, state–specific effects. *Perceptual and Motor Skills, 61,* 158.

Lane, J. D., & Rose, J. E. (1994, April). *Effect of caffeine on heart rate and blood pressure responses to cigarette smoking.* Paper presented at the fifteenth annual meeting of The Society of Behavioral Medicine, Boston.

Lang, P. J. (1968). Fear reduction and fear behavior: Problems in treating a construct. In J. M. Schlien (Ed.), *Research in psychotherapy* (Vol. 3, pp. 90–102). Washington, DC: American Psychological Association.

Lang, P. J. (1979). A bio–informational theory of emotional imagery. *Psychophysiology, 16,* 495–512.

Lanzetta, J. T., & McHugo, G. J. (1989). Facial expressive and psychophysiological correlates of emotion. In G. Gainotti & C. Caltagirone (Eds.), *Emotions and the dual brain* (pp. 91–118). New York: Springer–Verlag.

Larsen, R. J., & Ketelaar, T. (1991). Personality and susceptibility to positive and negative emotional states. *Journal of Personality and Social Psychology, 61,* 132–140.

Larson, P. S., Finnegan, J. K., & Haag, H. B. (1950). Observations on the effects of cigarette smoking on the fusion frequency of flicker. *Journal of Clinical Investigation, 29,* 483–485.

Lawrence, P. S., Amodei, N., & Murray, A. L. (1982). *Withdrawal symptoms associated with smoking cessation.* Paper presented at the 21st Convention of the Association for Advancement of Behavior Therapy, Los Angeles.

Lazarus, R. S. (1991). *Emotion and adaptation.* New York: Oxford University Press.

LeDoux, J. E. (1987). Emotion. In F. Plum (Ed.), *Handbook of physiology: Vol. V. Higher functions of the brain: Part I* (pp. 419–459). Bethesda, MD: American Physiological Society.

LeDoux, J. E. (1989). Cognitive–emotional interactions in the brain. *Cognition and Emotion, 3,* 267–289.

LeHouezec, J., Halliday, R., Benowitz, N. L., Callaway, E., Naylor, H., & Herzig, K. (1994). A low dose of subcutaneous nicotine improves information processing in non–smokers. *Psychopharmacology, 114,* 628–634.

Lee, E. H. Y. (1985). Effects of nicotine on exploratory behavior in rats: Correlation with regional brain monoamine levels. *Behavioural Brain Research, 17,* 59–66.

Lee, B. L., Jacob III, P., Jarvik, M. E., & Benowitz, N. L. (1989). Food and nicotine metabolism. *Pharmacology, Biochemistry, and Behavior, 33,* 621–625.

Leischow, S. J. (1994). The nicotine vaporizer. *Health Values, 18,* 4–9.

Leischow, S. J., & Stitzer, M. L. (1991). Effects of smoking cessation on caloric intake and weight gain in an inpatient unit. *Psychopharmacology, 104,* 522–526.

Leon, G. R., Kolotkin, R., & Korgeski, G. (1979). MacAndrew Addiction Scale and other MMPI characteristics associated with obesity, anorexia and smoking behavior. *Addictive Behaviors, 4,* 401–407.

Lerner, J. V. & Vicary, J. R. (1984). Difficult temperament and drug use: Analyses from the New York Longitudinal Study. *Journal of Drug Education, 14,* 1–7.

Levenson, R. W., Carstensen, L. L., Friesen, W. V., & Ekman, P. (1991). Emotion, physiology, and expression in old age. *Psychology and Aging, 6,* 28–35.

Levenson, R. W., Ekman, P., & Friesen, W. V. (1990). Voluntary facial expression generates emotion–specific nervous system activity. *Psychophysiology, 27,* 363–384.

Leventhal, H., & Avis, N. (1976). Pleasure, addiction, and habit: Factors in verbal report or factors in smoking behavior? *Journal of Abnormal Psychology, 85,* 478–488.

Leventhal, H., Baker, T., Brandon, T., & Fleming, R. (1989). Intervening and preventing smoking. In T. Ney & A. Gale (Eds.), *Smoking and human behavior* (pp. 313–336). Chichester, England: Wiley.

Leventhal, H., & Cleary, P. D. (1980). The smoking problem: A review of the research and theory in behavioral risk modification. *Psychological Bulletin, 88,* 370–405.

Levin, E. D., Briggs, S. J., Christopher, N. C., & Rose, J. E. (1993). Sertraline attenuates hyperphagia in rats following nicotine withdrawal. *Pharmacology, Biochemistry, and Behavior, 44,* 51–61.

Levin, E. D., Rose, J. E., Behm, F., & Caskey, N. H. (1991). The effects of smoking–related sensory cues on psychological stress. *Pharmacology, Biochemistry, and Behavior, 39,* 265–268.

Levine, R. L., & Lombardo, T. W. (1985, March). Smoking affects perception of EMG in facial muscles associated with mood. Paper presented at the Annual Meeting of the Society of Behavioral Medicine, New Orleans, LA.

Levy, J. (1990, February). Discussant comments. In W. Heller & R. J. Davidson (Chairs), *The neuropsychology of mood.* Symposium conducted at the International Neuropsychological Society, Orlando, Fl.

Lewinsohn, P. M., Steinmetz, J. L., Larson, D. W., & Franklin, J. (1981). Depression–related cognitions: Antecedent or consequence? *Journal of Abnormal Psychology, 90,* 213–219.

Lichtenstein, E. (1982). The smoking problem: A behavioral perspective. *Journal of Consulting and Clinical Psychology, 50,* 804–819.

Lichtenstein, E., Antonuccio, D. O., & Rainwater, G. (1977, April). *Unkicking the habit: The resumption of cigarette smoking.* Paper presented at the annual meeting of the Western Psychologicl Association, Seattle, WA.

Lichtenstein, E., & Glasgow, R. E. (1992). Smoking cessation: What have we learned over the past decade? *Journal of Consulting and Clinical Psychology, 60,* 518–527.

Lickey, M. E., & Gordon, B. (1991). *Medicine and mental illness.* New York: W. H. Freeman.

Lindheim, S. R., Legro, R. S., Bernstein, L., Stanczyk, F. Z., Vijod, M. A., Presser, S. C., & Lobo, R. A. (1992). Behavioral stress responses in premenopausal and postmenopausal women and the effects of estrogen. *American Journal of Obstetrics and Gynecology, 167,* 1831–1836.

Lippiello, P. M., Sears, S. B., & Fernandes, K. G. (1987). Kinetics and mechanism of L–[3H] nicotine binding to putative high affinity receptor sites in rat brain. *Molecular Pharmacology, 31,* 392–400.

Lishman, W. A. (1972). Selective factors in memory: Part 1. Age, sex, and personality attributes. *Psychological Medicine, 2,* 121–138.

Little, B. R. (1989). Personal project analysis: Trivial pursuits, magnificent obsessions, and the search for coherence. In D. M. Buss & N Cantor (Eds.), *Personality psychology: Recent trends and emerging directions* (pp. 15–31). New York: Springer–Verlag.

Livson, N., & Leino, E. V. (1988). Cigarette smoking motives: Factorial structure and gender differences in a longitudinal study. *The International Journal of the Addictions*, *23*, 535–544.

Loehlin, J. C. (1992). *Genes and environment in personality development.* Newbury Park, CA: Sage.

Lohr, J. B., & Flynn, K. (1992). Smoking and schizophrenia. *Schizophrenia Research*, *8*, 93–102.

Lolas, F. (1987). Hemispheric asymmetry of slow brain potentials in relation to neuroticism. *Personality and Individual Differences, 8*, 969–971.

Lombardo, T. W., & Epstein, L. H. (1986). The nicotine paradox: Effects of smoking on autonomic discrimination. *Addictive Behaviors, 11*, 341–344.

London, E. D., Connolly, R. J., Szikszay, M., & Wamsley, J. K. (1985). Distribution of cerebral metabolic effects of nicotine in the rat. *European Journal of Pharmacology*, *110*, 391–392.

London, E. D., Weissman, A. D., Fanelli, R. J., Wilkerson, G., Broussolle, E. P., & Jaffe, J. H. (1986). Mapping the cerebral distributions of action of euphoriant drugs. *Clinical Neuropharmacology*, 9 (Suppl. 4), 208–210.

Lorenz, E. N. (1979, December). *Predictability: Does the flap of a butterfly's wings in Brazil set off a tornado in Texas?* Paper presented at the annual meeting of the American Association for the Advancement of Science, Washington, DC.

Lyon, R. J., Tong, J. E., Leigh, G., & Clare, G. (1975). The influence of alcohol and tobacco on the components of choice reaction time. *Journal of Studies on Alcohol, 36*, 587–596.

Lytton, H. (1980). *Parent–child interaction: The socialization process observed in twin and single families.* New York: Plenum.

Lyvers, M., Boyd, G., & Maltzman, I. (1987). Smoking, personality, and imagery preference in relation to spontaneous bilateral electrodermal activity. *Pavlovian Journal of Biological Science, 22*, 7–15.

MacLean, P. D. (1990). *The triune brain in evolution: Role in paleocerebral functions.* New York: Plenum Press.

MacMahon, B., Trichopoulos, D., Cole, P., & Brown, J. (1982). Cigarette smoking and urinary estrogens. *New England Journal of Medicine, 307*, 1062–1065.

Madden, P. A., Heath, A. C., Bucholz, K. K., Dinwiddie, S. H., Dunne, M. P., & Martin, N. G. (1993, July). Novelty seeking and the genetic determinants of smoking initiation and problems related to alcohol use in female twins. In *Proceedings of the Twenty–third Annual Meeting of the Behavior Genetics Association* (p. 37). Sydney, New South Wales, Australia: BGA.

Majewska, M. D., Harrison, N. L., Schwartz, R. D., Barker, J. L., & Paul, S. M. (1986, May 23). Steroid hormone metabolites are barbiturate–like modulators of the GABA receptor. *Science, 232*, 1004–1007.

Mandler, G. (1984). *Mind and body: Psychology of emotion and stress.* New York: Norton.

Mandler, G., & Kremen, I. (1960). Autonomic feedback: A correlational study [Erratum]. *Journal of Personality, 28*, 545.

Mandler, G., Mandler, J. M., Kremen, I., & Sholiton, R. T. (1961). The response to threat: Relations among verbal and physiological indices. *Psychological Monographs: General and Applied, 75*(9, Whole No. 513).

Mangan, G. L. (1983). The effects of cigarette smoking on verbal learning and retention. *Journal of General Psychology, 108*, 203–210.

Mangan, G. L., & Golding, J. (1978). An enhancement model of smoking maintenance. In R. E. Thorton (Ed.), *Smoking behaviour: Physiological and psychological influences* (pp. 87–114). Edinburgh, Scotland: Churchill Livingstone.

Maranon, G. (1924). Contribution a l'etude de l'action emotive de l'adrenaline[contribution of the study of adrenaline on emotions]. *Revue Francaise d'Endocrinologie, 2,* 300–325.

Markel, N. N., Phillis, J. A., Vargas, R., & Harvard, K. (1972). Personality traits associated with voice types. *Journal of Psycholinguistic Research, 1,* 249–255.

Marks, M. J., Stitzel, J. A., & Collins, A. C. (1989). Genetic influences on nicotine responses. *Pharmacology, Biochemistry, and Behavior, 33,* 667–668.

Marlatt, G. A. (1985). Cognitive assessment and intervention procedures for relapse prevention. In G. A. Marlatt & J. R. Gordon (Eds.), *Relapse prevention* (pp. 201–279). New York: Guilford Press.

Marlatt, G. A., Curry, S., & Gordon, J. R. (1988). A longitudinal analysis of unaided smoking cessation. *Journal of Consulting and Clinical Psychology, 56,* 715–720.

Marlatt, G. A., & Gordon, J. R.. (1980). Determinants of relapse: Implications for the maintenance of behavior change. In P. O. Davidson & S. M. Davidson (Eds.), *Behavioral medicine: Changing health lifestyles* (pp. 410–452). New York: Brunner/Mazel.

Marmot, M. G., Smith, G. D., Stansfeld, S., Patel, C., North, F., Head, J., Whilte, I., Brunner, E., & Feeney, A. (1991). Health inequalities among British civil servants: The Whitehall II study. *Lancet, 337,* 1387–1393.

Marshall, G. D., & Zimbardo, P. G. (1979). Affective consequences of inadequately explained physiological arousal. *Journal of Personality and Social Psychology, 37,* 953–969.

Martin, M. (1985). Neuroticism as predisposition toward depression: A cognitive mechanism. *Personality and Individual Differences, 6,* 353–365.

Martin, N., & Jardine, R. (1986). Eysenck's contributions to behaviour genetics. In S. Modgil & C. Modgil (Eds.), *Hans Eysenck: Consensus and controversy* (pp. 13–47). Philadelphia: Falmer.

Martinez–Selva, J. M., Gomez–Amor, J., Olmos, E., Navarro, N., & Roman, F. (1987). Sex and menstrual cycle differences in habituation and spontaneous recovery of the electrodermal orienting reaction. *Personality and Individual Differences, 8,* 211–217.

Martinot, J.–L., Hardy, P., Feline, A., Huret, J.–D., Mazoyer, B., Attar–Levy, D., Pappata, S., & Syrota, A. (1990). Left prefrontal glucose hypometabolism in the depressed state: A confirmation. *American Journal of Psychiatry, 147,* 1313–1317.

Maslach, C. (1979). Negative emotional biasing of unexplained arousal. *Journal of Personality and Social Psychology, 37,* 970–988.

Mason, S. T. (1984). *Catecholamines and behavior.* Cambridge, England: Cambridge University Press.

Masson, C. L. (1995). Cardiovascular responses to a quantified dose of nicotine in oral contraceptive users and non–users. Unpublished doctoral dissertation, Southern Illinois University, Carbondale.

Masson, C. L., & Gilbert, D. G. (1990). Cardiovascular responses to a quantified dose of nicotine as a function of personality and nicotine tolerance. *Journal of Behavioral Medicine, 13,* 505–521.

Masterson, F., & O'Shea, B. (1984). Smoking and malignancy in schizophrenia. *British Journal of Psychiatry, 145,* 429–432.

Matarazzo, J. D., & Saslow, G. (1960). Psychological and related characteristics of smokers and non–smokers. *Psychological Bulletin, 57,* 493–513.

McAdams, D. P. (1992). The five–factor model in personality: A critical appraisal. *Journal of Personality, 60,* 329–361.

McColloch, M., & Gilbert, B. O. (1991). The development and maintenance of aggressive behavioral patterns. In D. G. Gilbert & J. J. Connolly (Eds.), *Personality, social skills, and psychopathology: An individual differences approach* (pp. 185–210). New York: Plenum Press.

McCormick, W. J. (1935). The role of the glycemic response to nicotine. *American Journal of Hygiene, 22,* 214–220.

McCrae, R. R., Costa, P. T., & Bosse, R. (1978). Anxiety, extraversion, and smoking. *British Journal of Social and Clinical Psychology, 17,* 269–273.

McFall, R. M. (1970). Parameters of self–monitoring. In R. B. Stuart (Ed.), *Behavioral self–management: Strategies, techniques, and outcome* (pp. 196–214.) New York: Brunner/Mazel.

McGee, L., & Newcomb, M. D. (1992). General deviance syndrome: Expanded hierarchical evaluations at four ages from early adolescence to adulthood. *Journal of Consulting and Clinical Psychology, 60,* 766–776.

McGue, M., Bacon, S., & Lykken, D. T. (1993). Personality stability and change in early adulthood: A behavioral genetic analysis. *Developmental Psychology, 29,* 96–109.

McKearney, J. W. (1968, June 14). Maintenance of responding under a fixed–interval schedule of electric shock presentation. *Science, 160,* 1249–1251.

McKeeman, D., & Karoly, P. (1991). Interpersonal and intrapsychic goal–related conflict reported by cigarette smokers, quitters, and relapsers. *Addictive Behaviors, 16,* 543–548.

McKenna, R. J. (1972). Some effects of anxiety level and food cues on the eating behavior of obese and normal subjects: A comparison of the Schachterian and psychosomatic conceptions. *Journal of Personality and Social Psychology, 22,* 311–319.

McKennell, A. C. (1970). Smoking motivation factors. *British Journal of Social and Clinical Psychology, 9,* 8–22.

McManus, I. C., & Weeks, S. J. (1982). Smoking, personality and reasons for smoking. *Psychological Medicine, 12,* 349–356.

McNair, D. M., Lorr, M., & Droppleman, L. F. (1971). *Manual for the Profile of Mood States.* San Diego, CA: Educational & Industrial Testing Service.

McNeill, A. D., Jarvis, M., & West, R. (1987). Subjective effects of cigarette smoking in adolescents. *Psychopharmacology, 92,* 115–117.

Meehl, P. E. (1989). Schizotaxia revisited. *Archives of General Psychiatry, 46,* 935–944.

Meehl, P. E. (1990). Toward an integrated theory of schizotaxia, schizotypy, and schizophrenia. *Journal of Personality Disorders, 4,* 1–99.

Meliska, C. J., & Gilbert, D. G. (1991). Hormonal and subjective effects of cigarette smoking in males and females. *Pharmacology, Biochemistry, and Behavior, 40,* 229–235.

Mello, N. K., Mendelson, J. H., & Palmieri, S. L. (1987). Cigarette smoking by women: Interactions with alcohol use. *Psychopharmacology, 93,* 8–15.

Mendenhall, W. L. (1925). A study of tobacco smoking. *American Journal of Physiology, 72,* 549–557.

Mereu, G., Yoon, K.–W. P., Boi, V., Gessa, G. L., Naes, L. & Westfall, T. C. (1987). Preferential stimulation of ventral tegmental area dopaminergic neurons by nicotine. *European Journal of Pharmacology, 141,* 395–399.

Messer, S. C., Morris, T. L., & Gross, A. M. (1990). Hypoglycemia and psychopathology: A methodological review. *Clinical Psychology Review, 10,* 631–648.

Meyer, R. E. (1986). How to understand the relationship between psychopathology and addictive disorders: Another example of the chicken and the egg. In R. E. Meyer (Ed.), *Psychopathology and addictive disorders* (pp. 3–16). New York: Guilford Press.

Milgrom–Friedman, J., Penman, R., & Meares, R. A. (1983). Preliminary study of pain perception and tobacco smoking. *Clinical and Experimental Pharmacology and Physiology, 10,* 161–169.

Miller, W. R., & Rollnick, S. (1991). Motivational interviewing. New York: Guilford Press.

Mitchell, S. N., Smith, K. M., Joseph, M. H., & Gray, J. A. (1992). Acute and chronic effects of nicotine on catecholamine synthesis and release in the rat central nervous system. In P. M. Lippiello, A. C. Collins, J. A. Gray, & J. H. Robinson (Eds.), *The biology of nicotine: Current research issues* (pp. 97–119). New York: Raven Press.

Moos, R. H . (1986). *Work Environment Scale Manual (2nd ed.).* Palo Alto, CA: Consulting Psychologist Press.

Moos, R. H ., & Moos, B. (1986). *Family Environment Scale Manual (2nd ed.).* Palo Alto, CA: Consulting Psychologist Press.

Mogenson, G. J. (1987). Limbic–motor integration. In A. N. Epstein & A. R. Morrison (Eds.), *Progress in psychobiology and physiological psychology* (Vol. 12, pp. 117–170). Orlando, FL: Academic Press.

Morley, J. E., Levine, A. S., & Rowland, N. E. (1983). Stress induced eating. *Life Sciences, 32,* 2169–2182.

Morris, D. (1977). *Manwatching.* London: Jonathan Cape.

Morris, P. H., & Gale, A. (1993). Effects of situational demands on the direction of electrodermal activation during smoking. *Addictive Behaviors, 18,* 35–40.

Morrison, J. (1980). Adult psychiatric disorders in parents of hyperactive children. *American Journal of Psychiatry, 137,* 825–827.

Morse, W. H., Mead, R. N., & Kelleher, R. T. (1967, July 14). Modulation of elicited behavior by a fixed–interval schedule of electric shock presentation. *Science, 157,* 215–217.

Mueser, K., Waller, D., Levander, S., & Schalling, D. (1984). Smoking and pain—A method of limits and sensory decision theory analysis. *Scandinavian Journal of Psychology, 25,* 289–296.

Muller, M. M. (1992). Do smokers differ from nonsmokers in anger and anger coping? The investigation of a more specific trait in the search for a "smoker's personality." *Personality and Individual Differences, 13,* 281–285.

Munck, A., Guyre, P. M., & Holbrook, N. K. (1984). Physiological functions of glucocorticoids in stress and their relation to pharmacological actions. *Endocrine Reviews, 5,* 25–44.

Murphree, H. B. (1979). EEG effects in humans of nicotine, tobacco smoking, withdrawal from smoking and possible surrogates. In A. Redmond & C. Izard (Eds.), *Electrophysiological effects of nicotine* (pp. 227–243). New York, NY: Elsevier/North-Holland Biomedical Press.

Murray, A. L., & Lawrence, P. S. (1984). Sequelae to smoking cessation: A review. *Clinical Psychology Review, 4,* 143–157.

Murray, M., Swan, A. V., & Mattar, N. (1983). The task of nursing and risk of smoking. *Journal of Advanced Nursing, 8,* 131–138.

Myrsten, A.–L., Andersson, K., Frankenhaeuser, M., & Elgerot, A. (1975). Immediate effects of cigarette smoking as related to different smoking habits. *Perceptual and Motor Skills, 40,* 515–523.

Myrsten, A.–L., Post, B., Frankenhaeuser, M., & Johansson, G. (1972). Changes in behavioral and physiological activation induced by cigarette smoking in habitual smokers. *Psychopharmacologia, 27,* 305–312.

Nash, M. R., Hulsey, T. L., Sexton, M. C., Harralson, T. L., & Lambert, W. (1993). Long–term sequelae of childhood sexual abuse: Perceived family environment, psychopathology, and dissociation. *Journal of Consulting and Clinical Psychology, 61,* 276–283.

National Institute of Education. (1979). *Teenage smoking: Immediate and long–term patterns* (prepared by D. Green). Washington, DC: U.S. Department of Health, Education, and Welfare.

Nauta, W. J. H. (1971). The problem of the frontal lobe: A reinterpretation. *Journal of Psychiatric Research, 8,* 167–187.

Naveteur, J., & Baque, E. F. (1987). Individual differences in electrodermal activity as a function of subjects' anxiety. *Personality and Individual Differences, 8,* 615–626.

Neetz, R. A. (1979). *The effect of smoking deprivation on psychomotor performance, mood, and task perception of female smokers. Dissertation Abstracts International, 40*(06), 2879. (University Microfilms No).

Nelson, J. M., & Goldstein, L. (1972). Improvement of performance on an attention task with chronic nicotine treatment in rats. *Psychopharmacology, 26,* 347–360.

Nelson, J. M., & Goldstein, L. (1973). Chronic nicotine treatments in rats: 1. Acquisition and performance of an attention task. *Research Communications in Chemical and Pathological Pharmacology, 5,* 681–693.

Nemeth–Coslett, R., & Griffiths, R. R. (1986). Naloxone does not affect cigarette smoking. *Psychopharmacology, 89,* 261–264.

Nemeth–Coslett, R., & Henningfield, J. E. (1986). Effects of nicotine chewing gum on cigarette smoking and subjective and physiologic effects. *Clinical Pharmacology and Therapeutics, 39,* 625–630.

Nesbitt, P. D. (1969). Smoking, physiological arousal, and emotional response. *Dissertation Abstracts International, 31*(04), 4395B. University Microfilms No. 70/18836.

Nesbitt, P. D. (1973). Smoking, physiological arousal, and emotional response. *Journal of Personality and Social Psychology, 25,* 137–144.

Netter, P. (1985). Biochemical differences as related to differences in trait anxiety and neuroticism [Poster session abstract]. *Personality and Individual Differences, 6,* XII.

Newhouse, P. A., Sunderland, T., Narang, P. K., Mellow, A. M., Fertig, J. B., Lawlor, B. A., & Murphy, D. L. (1990). Neuroendocrine, physiologic, and behavioral responses following intravenous nicotine in nonsmoking health volunteers and in patients with Alzheimer's disease. *Psychoneuroendocrinology, 15,* 471–484.

Newman, J. P., Widom, C. S., & Nathan, S. (1985). Passive avoidance in syndromes of disinhibition: Psychopathy and extraversion. *Journal of Personality and Social Psychology, 48,* 1316–1327.

Niaura, R., Abrams, D., Demuth, B., Pinto, R., & Monti, P. (1989). Responses to smoking–related stimuli and early relapse to smoking. *Addictive Behaviors, 14,* 419–428.

Niaura, R., Abrams, D. B., Pedraza, M., Monti, P., & Rohsenow, D. J. (1992). Smoker's reactions to interpersonal interaction and presentation of smoking cues. *Addictive Behaviors, 17,* 557–566.

Niaura, R., Goldstein, M., & Abrams, D. (1992). A bioinformational systems perspective on tobacco dependence. *British Journal of Addiction, 86,* 593–597.

Niaura, R. S., Rohsenow, D. J., Binkoff, J. A., Monti, P. M., & Abrams, D. B. (1988). Relevance of cue reactivity to understanding alcohol and smoking relapse. *Journal of Abnormal Psychology, 97,* 133–152.

Nicotine use after the year 2000 [Editorial]. (1991). *The Lancet, 337,* 1191–1192.

Nil, R., & Battig, K. (1989). Smoking behavior: A multivariate process. In T. Ney & A. Gale (Eds.), *Smoking and human behavior* (pp. 199–221). Chichester, England: John Wiley.

Norman, D. A., & Shallice, T. (1985). Attention to action: Willed and automatic control of behavior. In R. J. Davidson, G. E. Schwartz, & D. Shapiro (Eds.), *Consciousness and self–regulation: Vol. 4. Advances in research and theory* (pp. 2–18). New York: Plenum Press.

Norman, R. M. G., & Waston, L. D. (1976). Extraversion and reactions to cognitive inconsistency. *Journal of Research in Personality, 10,* 446–456.

Norton, R., Brown, K., & Howard, R. (1992). Smoking, nicotine dose and the lateralisation of electrocortical activity. *Psychopharmacology, 108,* 473–479.

Norton, R., & Howard, R. (1988). Smoking, mood and the contingent variation (CNV) in a go–no go avoidance task. *Journal of Psychophysiology, 2,* 109–118.

Norton, R., Howard, R., & Brown, K. (1991). Nicotine dose–dependent effects of smoking on P300 and mood. *Medical Science Research, 19,* 355–356.

Novacek, J., & Lazarus, R. S. (1990). The structure of personal commitments. *Journal of Personality, 58,* 693–715.

Noyes, R. (1991). Treatments of choice for anxiety disorders. In W. Coryell & G. Winokur (Eds.), *The clinical management of anxiety disorders* (pp. 140–153). New York: Oxford University Press.

Obrist, P. (1981). *Cardiovascular psychophysiology: A perspective.* New York: Plenum.

Ochoa, E. I. M., Li, L., & McNeamee, M. G. (1992). Desensitization of central cholinergic mechanisms and neuroadaptation to nicotine. *Molecular Neurobiology, 4,* 251–287.

Ockene, J. K. (1993). Smoking among women across the life span: Prevalence interventions, and implications for cessation research. *Annals of Behavioral Medicine, 15,* 135–148.

O'Connor, K. (1980). Individual differences in situational preference amongst smokers. *Personality and Individual Differences, 1,* 249–257.

O'Connor, K. (1989). Individual differences and motor systems in smoker motivation. In T. Ney & A. Gale (Eds.), *Smoking and human behavior* (pp. 141–170). Chichester, England: Wiley.

O'Connor, K. (1982). Individual differences in the effect of smoking on the frontal–central distribution of the CNV: Some observations on smokers' control of attentional behaviour. *Personality and Individual Differences, 3,* 271–285.

O'Connor, K. P., & Stravynski, A. (1982). Evaluation of a smoking typology by use of a specific behavioural substitution method of self–control. *Behaviour Research and Therapy, 20,* 279–288.

O'Farrell, T. J, Connors, G. J., & Upper, D. (1983). Addictive behaviors among hospitalized schizophrenic patients. *Addictive Behaviors, 8,* 329–333.

Office on Smoking & Health, National Center for Chronic Disease Prevention and Health Promotion, Division of Health Interview Statistics. (1992). Cigarette smoking among adults–United States, 1990. *Morbidity and Mortality Weekly Report, 41,* 354–362.

O'Hara, P., Portser, S. A., & Anderson, B. P. (1989). The influence of menstrual cycle changes on the tobacco withdrawal syndrome in women. *Addictive Behaviors, 14,* 595–600.

O'Keefe, J., & Nadel, L. (1978). *The hippocampus as a cognitive map.* Oxford, England: Clarendon Press.

Olds, J., & Milner, P. (1954). Positive reinforcement produced by electrical stimulation of septal area and other regions of rat brain. *Journal of Comparative and Physiological Psychology, 47,* 419–427.

Olds, J., & Olds, M. (1965). Drives, rewards and the brain. In F. Barron (Ed.), *New directions in psychology.*(Vol. 2). New York: Holt, Rinehart & Winston.

Oliveto, A. H., Hughes, J. R., Terry, S. Y., Bickel, W. K., Higgins, S. T., Pepper, S. L., & Fenwick, J. W. (1992). Effects of caffeine on tobacco withdrawal. *Clinical Pharmacology and Therapeutics, 50,* 157–164.

Olton, D. S., Becker, J. T., & Handelmann, G. E. (1979). Hippocampus, space, and memory. *Behavioral and Brain Sciences, 5,* 407–422.

O'Neill, S. T., & Parrott, A. C. (1992). Stress and arousal in sedative and stimulant cigarette smokers. *Psychopharmacology, 107,* 442–446.

Orlandi, M. A. (1987). Gender differences in smoking cessation. *Women Health, 11,* 237–251.

Palmer, R. F., & Berens, A. (1983). Double blind study of the effects of naloxone on the pleasure of cigarette smoking [abstract]. *Federation Proceedings, 42,* 654.

Panksepp, J. (1986). The anatomy of emotions. In R. Plutchik & H. Kellerman (Eds.), *Emotion theory, research, and experience* (pp. 91–124). Orlando, FL: Academic Press.

Panksepp, J. (1990). Gray zones at the emotion/cognition interface: A commentary. *Cognition and Emotion, 4,* 289–302.

Panksepp, J. (1992). A critical role for "affective neuroscience" in resolving what is basic about basic emotions. *Psychological Review, 99,* 554–560.

Parks, C. W., & Hollon, S. D. (1988). Cognitive assessment. In A. S. Bellack & M. Hersen (Eds.), *Behavioral assessment: A practical handbook* (3rd ed., pp. 161–212). New York: Pergamon Press.

Parks, K. R. (1984). Smoking and the Eysenck personality dimensions: An interactive model. *Psychological Medicine, 14,* 825–834.

Parks, R. W., Becker, R. E., Rippey, R. F., Gilbert, D. G., Matthews, J. R., Kabatay, E., Young, C. S., Vohs, C., Danz, Keim, P., Collins, G. T., Zigler, S. S., & Urycki, P. G. (1994). *Increased regional cerebral glucose metabolism and semantic memory performance in Alzheimer's disease: A double blind transdermal nicotine PET study.* Manuscript submitted for publication.

Parrott, A. C., & Craig, D. (1992). Cigarette smoking and nicotine gum (0, 2 and 4 mg): Effects upon four visual attention tasks. *Neuropsychobiology, 25,* 34–43.

Parrott, A. C., & Winder, G. (1989). Nicotine chewing gum (2 mg, 4 mg) and cigarette smoking: Comparative effects upon vigilance and heart rate. *Psychopharmacology, 97,* 257–261.

Patton, D., Barnes, G. E., & Murray, R. P. (1993). Personality characteristics of smokers and ex–smokers. *Personality and Individual Differences, 15,* 653–664.

Paty, J. A., & Shiffman, S. (1991, March). Stimulus antecedents of smoking in chippers and regular smokers. In S. Shiffman (Chair), *Chippers: Studies of non–dependent cigarette smokers.* Symposium conducted at the annual meeting of the Society of Behavioral Medicine, Washington, DC.

Pauly, J. R., Grun, E. U., & Collins, A. C. (1992). Glucocorticoid regulation of sensitivity to nicotine. In P. M. Lippiello, A. C. Collins, & J. A. Gray (Eds.), *The biology of nicotine: Current research issues* (pp. 121–155). New York: Raven Press.

Pauly, J. R., Ullman, E. A., & Collins, A. C. (1988). Adrenocortical hormone regulation of nicotine sensitivity in mice. *Physiology and Behavior, 44,* 109–116.

Pederson, N. (1981). Twin similarity for usage of common drugs. In L. Gedda, P. Parisi, & W. E. Nance (Eds.), Twin research: 3. Proceedings of the Third International Congress on Twin Studies: Part C. *Epidemiological and clinical studies* (pp. 53–59). New York: Alan Liss.

Peeke , S. C., & Peeke, H. V. S. (1984). Attention, memory, and cigarette smoking. *Psychopharmacology, 84,* 205–216.

Peele, S. (1985). *The meaning of addiction: Compulsive experience and its interpretation.* Lexington, MA: Lexington Books.

Peele, S. (1988). A moral vision of addiction: How people's values determine whether they become and remain addicts. In S. Peele (Ed.), *Visions of addiction: Major contemporary perspectives on addiction and alcoholism* (pp. 201–233). Lexington, MA: Lexington Books.

Perez–Stable, E. J., Marin, G., Marin, B. V., & Katz, M. H. (1990). Depressive symptoms and cigarette smoking among Latinos in San Francisco. *American Journal of Public Health, 80,* 1500–1502.

Perkins, K. A. (1992). Effects of tobacco smoking on caloric intake. *British Journal of Addiction, 87,* 193–205.

Perkins, K. A., Epstein, L. H., Marks, B. L., Stiller, R. L., & Jacob, R. G. (1989). The effect of nicotine on energy expenditure during light physical activity. *The New England Journal of Medicine, 320,* 898–903.

Perkins, K. A., Epstein, L. H., Sexton, J. E., Solberg–Kassel, R., Stiller, R. L., & Jacob, R. G. (1992). Effects of nicotine on hunger and eating in male and female smokers. *Psychopharmacology, 106,* 53–59.

Perkins, K. A., Epstein, L. H., Stiller, R. L., Fernstrom, M. H., Sexton, J. E., & Jacob, R. G. (1990). Perception and hedonics of sweet and fat taste in smokers and nonsmokers following nicotine intake. *Psychopharmacology, Biochemistry, and Behavior, 35,* 671–676.

Perkins, K. A., & Grobe, J. E. (1992). Increased desire to smoke during acute stress. *British Journal of Addiction, 87,* 231–234.

Perkins, K. A., Grobe, J. E., Epstein, L. H., Caggiula, A. R., & Stiller, R. L. (1992). Effects of nicotine on subjective arousal may be dependent on baseline subjective state. *Journal of Substance Abuse, 4,* 131–141.

Perkins, K. A., Grobe, J. E., Epstein, L. H., Caggiula, A. R., Stiller, R. L., & Jacob, R. G. (1993). Chronic and acute tolerance to subjective effects of nicotine. *Pharmacology, Biochemistry, and Behavior, 45,* 375–381.

Perkins, K. A., Grobe, J. E., Fonte, C. F., & Breus, M. (1992). "Paradoxical" effects of smoking on subjective stress versus cardiovascular arousal in males and females. *Pharmacology, Biochemistry, and Behavior, 42,* 301–311.

Perkins, K. A., Grobe, J. E., Fonte, C. F., Goettler, J., Caggiula, A. R., Reynolds, W. A., Stiller, R. L., Scierka, A., & Jacob, R. G. (in press). Chronic and acute tolerance to subjective, behavioral, and cardiovascular effects of nicotine in humans. *Journal of Pharmacology and Experimental Therapeutics.*

Perkins, K. A., Grobe, J. E., Stiller, R. L., Scierka, A., Goettler, J., Reynolds, W., & Jennings, J. R. (1994). Effects of nicotine on thermal pain detection in humans. *Experimental and Clinical Psychopharmacology, 2,* 95–106.

Perkins, K. A., Sexton, J. E., Stiller, R. L., Fonte, C., DiMarco, A., Goettler, J., & Scierka, A. (1994). Subjective and cardiovascular responses to nicotine combined with caffeine during rest and casual activity. *Psychopharmacology, 113,* 438–444.

Perlick, D. A. (1977). *The withdrawal syndrome: Nicotine addiction and the effects of stopping smoking in heavy and light smokers. Dissertation Abstracts International, 38*(01), 409B. University Microfilms No. 77/4833.

Peters, R., & McGee, R. (1982). Cigarette smoking and state–dependent memory. *Psychopharmacology, 76,* 232–235.

Petrie, R. X. A., & Dreary, I. J. (1989). Smoking and human information processing. *Psychopharmacology, 99,* 393–396.

Pfaff, D. W., Silva, M. T., & Weiss, J. M. (1971, April 23). Telemetered recording of hormone effects on hippocampal neurons. *Science, 172,* 394–5.

Phillips, A. G., Pfaus, J. G., & Blaha, C. D. (1991). Dopamine and motivated behavior: Insights provided by in vivo analyses. In P. Willner & J. Scheel–Kruger (Eds.), *The mesolimbic dopamine system: From motivation to action* (pp. 199–224). Chichester, England: Wiley.

Pickworth, W. B., Herning, R. I., & Henningfield, J. E. (1988). Mecamylamine reduces some EEG effects of nicotine chewing gum in humans. *Pharmacology, Biochemistry, and Behavior, 30,* 149–153.

Pierce, J. P., Fiore, M. C., Novotny, T. E., Hatziandreu, E. J., & Davis, R. M. (1989). Trends in cigarette smoking in the United States: Educational differences are increasing. *Journal of the American Medical Association, 261,* 56–60.

Pirie, P. L., Murray, D. M., & Luepker, R. V. (1991). Gender differences in cigarette smoking and quitting in a cohort of young adults. *American Journal of Public Health, 81,* 324–327.

Plath, L. C. (1994). *Effects of oral contraceptive week (high versus low progesterone dose) on cardiovascular and mood responses to smoking deprivation and to a quantified dose of nicotine.* Unpublished master's thesis, Southern Illinois University, Carbondale.

Plomin, R., & DeFries, J. C. (1980). Genetics and intelligence: Recent data. *Intelligence, 4,* 15–24.

Plomin, R., Scheier, M. F., Bergeman, C. S., Pedersen, N. L., Nesselroade, J. R., & McClearn, G. E. (1992). Optimism, pessimism and mental health: A twin/adoption analysis. *Personality and Individual Differences, 13,* 921–930.

Plutchik, R. (1962). *The emotions: Facts, theories, and a new model.* New York: Random House.

Plutchik, R. (1970). Emotions, evolution, and adaptive processes. In M. B. Arnold (Ed.), *Feelings and emotions,* (pp. 3–24). New York: Academic Press.

Pohl, R., Yeragani, V. K., Balon, R., Lycaki, H., & McBride, R. (1992). Smoking in patients with panic disorder. *Psychiatry Research, 43,* 253–262.

Pollock, V. E. (1992). Meta–analysis of subjective sensitivity to alcohol in sons of alcoholics. *American Journal of Psychiatry*, *149*, 1534–1538.

Pomerleau, C. S., Garcia, A. W., Drewnowski, A., & Pomerleau, O. F. (1991). Sweet taste preference in women smokers: Comparison with nonsmokers and effects of menstrual phase and nicotine abstinence. *Pharmacology, Biochemistry, and Behavior*, *41*, 995–999.

Pomerleau, C. S., Garcia, A. W., Pomerleau, O. F., & Cameron, O. G. (1992). The effects of menstrual phase and nicotine abstinence on nicotine intake and on biochemical and subjective measures in women smokers: A preliminary report. *Psychoneuroendocrinology*, *17*, 627–638.

Pomerleau, C. S., & Pomerleau, O. F. (1987). The effects of a psychological stressor on cigarette smoking and on subsequent behavioral and physiological responses. *Psychophysiology*, *24*, 278–285.

Pomerleau, C. S., & Pomerleau, O. F. (1992). Euphoriant effect of nicotine in smokers. *Psychopharmacology*, *108*, 460–465.

Pomerleau, C. S., Pomerleau, O. F., & Garcia, A. W. (1991). Biobehavioral research on nicotine use in women. *British Journal of Addiction*, *86*, 527–531.

Pomerleau, O. F. (1981). Underlying mechanisms in substance abuse: Examples from research on smoking. *Addictive Behaviors*, *6*, 187–196.

Pomerleau, O. F., Adkins, D., & Pertschuk, M. (1978). Predictors of outcome and recidivism in smoking cessation treatment. *Addictive Behaviors*, *3*, 65–70.

Pomerleau, O. F., Collins, A. C., Shiffman, S., & Pomerleau, C. S. (1993). Why some people smoke and others do not: New perspectives. *Journal of Consulting and Clinical Psychology*, *61*, 723–731.

Pomerleau, O. F., Fertig, J. R., & Shanhan, S. O. (1983). Nicotine dependence in cigarette smoking: An empirically based, multivariate model. *Pharmacology, Biochemistry, and Behavior*, *19*, 291–299.

Pomerleau, O. F., & Pomerleau, C. S. (1984). Neuroregulators and the reinforcement of smoking: Towards a biobehavioral explanation. *Neuroscience and Biobehavioral Reviews*, *3*, 503–513.

Pomerleau, O. F., & Pomerleau, C. S. (1989). A biobehavioral perspective on smoking. In T. Ney & A. Gale (Eds.), *Smoking and human behavior* (pp. 69–90). Chichester, England: Wiley.

Pomerleau, O. F., & Pomerleau, C. S. (1990). Behavioural studies in humans: anxiety, stress, and smoking. In G. Bock & J. Marsh (Eds.), *The biology of nicotine dependence* (pp. 225–239). Chichester, England: Wiley.

Pomerleau, O. F., Pomerleau, C. S., Morrell, E. M., & Lowenbergh, J. M. (1991). Effects of fluoxetine on weight gain and food intake in smokers who reduce nicotine intake. *Psychoneuroendocrinology*, *16*, 433–440.

Pomerleau, O. F., Rose, J. E., Pomerleau, C. S., & Majchrzak, M .J. (1989). A noninvasive method for delivering controlled doses of nicotine via cigarette smoke. *Behavior Research Methods, Instruments, & Computers*, *21*, 598–602.

Pomerleau, O. F., & Rosecrans, J. (1989). Neuroregulatory effects of nicotine. *Psychoneuroendocrinology*, *14*, 407–423.

Pomerleau, O. F., Scherzer, H. H., Grunberg, N. E., Pomerleau, C. S., Judge, J., Fertig, J. B., & Burleson, J. (1987). The effects of acute exercise on subsequent cigarette smoking. *Journal of Behavioral Medicine*, *10*, 117–127.

Pomerleau, O. F., Turk, D. C., & Fertig, J. B. (1984). The effects of cigarette smoking on pain and anxiety. *Addictive Behaviors, 9,* 265–271.

Posner, M. I., & Snyder, C. R. R. (1975). Attention and cognitive control. In R. L. Solso (Ed.), *Information processing and cognition: The Loyola Symposium* (pp. 55–85). New York: Wiley.

Post, R. M., Gold, P., Rubinow, D. R., Ballenger, J. C., Bunney, Jr., W. E., & Goodwin, F. K. (1982). Peptides in the cerebrospinal fluid of neuropsychiatric patients: An approach to central nervous system peptide function. *Life Science, 31,* 1–15.

Powell, G. E., Stewart, R. A., & Grylls, D. G. (1979). The personality of young smokers. *British Journal of Addiction, 74,* 311–315.

Pribram, K. H., & McGuiness, D. (1975). Arousal, activation, and effort in the control of attention. *Psychological Review, 82,* 116–149.

Price, J. L., & Amaral, D. G. (1981). An autoradiographic study of the projections of the central nucleus of the monkey amygdala. *Journal of Neuroscience, 1,* 1242–1259.

Pritchard, W. S. (1991a). Electroencephalographic effects of cigarette smoking. *Psychopharmacology, 104,* 485–490.

Pritchard, W. S. (1991b). The link between smoking and P: A serotonergic hypothesis. *Personality and Individual Differences, 12,* 1187–1204.

Pritchard, W. S., & Duke, D. W. (1992). Modulation of EEG dimensional complexity by smoking. *Journal of Psychophysiology, 6,* 1–10.

Pritchard, W. S., Gilbert, D. G., & Duke, D. W. (1993). Flexible effects of quantified cigarette–smoke delivery on EEG dimensional complexity. *Psychopharmacology, 113,* 95–102.

Pritchard, W. S., & Kay, D. L. C. (1993). Personality and smoking motivation of U. S. smokers as measured by the state–trait personality inventory, the Eysenck Personality Questionnaire, and Spielberger's Smoking Motivation Questionnaire. *Personality and Individual Differences, 14,* 629–637.

Pritchard, W. S., Robinson, J. H., & Guy, T. D. (1992). Enhancement of continuous performance task reaction time by smoking in non–deprived smokers. *Psychopharmacology, 108,* 437–442.

Prochaska, J. O., DiClemente, C. C., & Norcross, J. C. (1992). In search of how people change: Applications to addictive behaviors. *American Psychologist, 47,* 1102–1114.

Prochazka, A. V., Petty, T. L., Nett, L., Silvers, G. W., Sachs, D. P. L., Rennard, S. I., Daughton, D. M., Grimm, R. H., & Heim, C. (1992). Transdermal clonidine reduced some withdrawal symptoms but did not increase smoking cessation. *Archives of Internal Medicine, 152,* 2065–2069.

Provost, S. C., & Woodward, R. (1991). Effects of nicotine gum on repeated administration of the Stroop test. *Psychopharmacology, 104,* 536–540.

Puddey, I. B., Vandongen, R., Berlen, L. J., & English, D. (1984). Haemodynamic and neuroendocrine consequences of stopping smoking: A controlled study. *Clinical and Experimental Pharmacology and Physiology, 11,* 423–426.

Puddey, I. B., Vandongen, R., Beilin, L. J., English, D. R., & Ukich, A. W. (1985). The effect of stopping smoking on blood pressure—A controlled trial. *Journal of Chronic Diseases, 38,* 483–493.

Pulvirenti, L., Swerdlow, N. R., Huber, C. B., & Koob, G. F. (1991). The role of limbic–accumbens–pallidal circuitry in the activating and reinforcing properties of psychostimulant drugs. In P. Willner & J. Scheel–Kruger (Eds.), *The mesolimbic dopamine system: From motivation to action* (pp. 131–140). Chichester, England: Wiley.

Rachman, S. (1977). The conditioning theory of fear–acquisition: A critical examination. *Behaviour Research and Therapy, 15,* 375–387.

Rae, G. (1975). Extraversion, neuroticism and cigarette smoking. *British Journal of Social and Clinical Psychology, 14,* 429–430.

Raine, A., Venables, P. H., & Williams, M. (1990). Relationships between central and autonomic measures of arousal at age 15 years and criminality at 24 years. *Archives of General Psychiatry, 47,* 1003–1007.

Rausch, J. L., Nichinson, B., Lamke, C., & Matloff, J. (1990). Influence of negative affect on smoking cessation treatment outcome: A pilot study. *British Journal of Addiction, 85,* 929–933.

Reasor, B. A., Reynolds, M. L., Ferris, R. P. (1988). Sensory assessment of tobacco smoke. *Recent Advances in Tobacco Science, 14,* 3–48.

Reavill, C., & Stolerman, I. P. (1990). Locomotor activity in rats after administration of nicotine agonists locally. *British Journal of Pharmacology, 99,* 273–278.

Reiman, E. M., Raiche, M. E., Robins, E., Botler, F. K., Herscovitch, P., Fox, P., & Perlmutter, J. (1986). The application of positron emission tomography to the study of panic disorder. *American Journal of Psychiatry, 143,* 469–477.

Reisenzein, R. (1983). The Schachter theory of emotion: Two decades later. *Psychological Bulletin, 94,* 239–264.

Rickard–Figueroa, K., & Zeichner, A. (1985). Assessment of smoking urge and its concomitants under and environmental smoking cue manipulation. *Addictive Behaviors, 10,* 249–256.

R. J. Reynolds Tobacco Company. (1988). *Chemical and biological studies on new cigarette prototypes that heat instead of burn tobacco.* Winston–Salem, NC: Author.

Robbins, T. W., Watson, B. A., Gaskin, M., & Ennis, C. (1983). Contrasting interactions of pipradrol, d–amphetamine, cocaine, cocaine analogues, apomorphine, and other drugs with conditioned reinforcement. *Psychopharmacology (Berlin), 80,* 113–119.

Robins, L. N., Helzer, J. E., Hesselbrock, M., & Wish, E. (1980). Vietnam veterans three years after Vietnam: How our study changed our view of heroin. In L. Brill & C. Winick (Eds.), *The yearbook of substance use and abuse* (Vol. 2, pp 213–230). New York: Human Sciences Press.

Robins, L. N., Helzer, J. E., Croughan, J., & Ratcliff, K. S. (1981). National Institute of Mental Health Diagnostic Interview Schedule: Its history, characteristics, and validity. *Archives of General Psychiatry, 38,* 381–389.

Robinson, J. H., & Pritchard, W. S. (1992). The role of nicotine in tobacco use. *Psychopharmacology, 108,* 397–407.

Robinson, T. N., Killen, J. D., Taylor, C. B., Telch, M. J., Bryson, S. W., Saylor, K. E., Maron, D. J., Maccoby, N., & Farquhar, J. W. (1987). Perspectives on adolescent substance use: A defined population study. *Journal of the American Medical Association, 258,* 2072–2076.

Rodin, J. (1987). Weight change following smoking cessation: The role of food intake and exercise. *Addictive Behaviors, 12,* 303–317.

Roessler, R. (1973). Personality, psychophysiology, and performance. *Psychophysiology, 10,* 315–327.

Rolls, E. T. (1990). A theory of emotion, and its application to understanding the neural basis of emotion. *Cognition and Emotion, 4,* 161–190.

Rose, J. E. (1986). Cigarette smoking blocks, caffeine-induced arousal. *Alcohol and Drug Research, 7,* 49–55.

Rose, J. E. (1988). The role of upper airway stimulation in smoking. In O. F. Pomerleau & C. S. Pomerleau (Eds.), *Nicotine replacement: A critical evaluation* (pp. 96–106). New York: Alan R. Liss.

Rose, J. E., Ananda, S., & Jarvik, M. E. (1983). Cigarette smoking during anxiety–provoking and monotonous tasks. *Addictive Behaviors, 8,* 353–359.

Rose, J. E., & Behm, F. M. (1987). Refined cigarette smoke as a means to reduce nicotine intake. *Pharmacology Biochemistry, and Behavior, 28,* 305–310.

Rose, J. E., & Behm, F. M. (1991). Psycholophysiological interactions between caffeine and nicotine. *Pharmacology, Biochemistry & Behavior, 38,* 333–337.

Rose, J. E., Tashkin, D. P., Ertle, A., Zinser, M. C., & Lafer, R. (1985). Sensory blockade of smoking satisfaction. *Pharmacology, Biochemistry, and Behavior, 23,* 289–293.

Rosecrans, J. (1971). Effect of nicotine on behavioral arousal and brain 5–hydroxytryptamine function in female rats selected for differences in activity. *European Journal of Pharmacology, 14,* 29–37.

Rosecrans, J. (1972). Brain area nicotine levels in male and female rats with different levels of spontaneous activity. *Neuropharmacology, 11,* 863–870.

Rosecrans, J., & Karan, L. D. (1993). Neurobehavioral mechanisms of nicotine action: Role in the initiation and maintenance of tobacco dependence. *Journal of Substance Abuse Treatment, 10,* 161–170.

Royce, J. R., & Powell, S. (1983). *Theory of personality and individual differences: Factors, systems, and processes.* Englewood Cliffs, NJ: Prentice–Hall.

Rubin, R. P., & Warner, W. (1975). Nicotine–induced stimulation of steroidogenesis in adrenocortical cells of the cat. *British Journal of Pharmacology, 53,* 357–362.

Russell, B. (1927/1961). *An outline of philosophy.* Cleveland, OH: World Publishing.

Russell, M. A. H. (1994, April). Future of nicotine replacement. In E. D. Glover (Chair), *Evaluating the newest approaches to nicotine withdrawal therapy (nicotine oral inhaler, nicotine nasal spray, combination therapy)* (p. 35). Symposium conducted at the Fifteenth Annual Meeting of The Society of Behavioral Medicine, Boston.

Russell, M. A. H., Jarvis, M. J., Jones, G., & Feyerabend, C. (1990). Non–smokers show acute tolerance to subcutaneous nicotine. *Psychopharmacology, 102,* 56–58.

Russell, M. A. H., Peto, J., & Patel, U.A. (1974). The classification of smoking by factorial structure of motives. *The Journal of the Royal Statistical Society, Series A (General), 137*(3), 313–346.

Russell, M. A. H., Wilson, C., Taylor, C., & Baker, C. (1980). Smoking habits of men and women. *British Medical Journal, 281,* 17–20.

Rusted, J. M., & Eaton–Williams, P. (1991). Distinguishing between attentional and amnestic effects in information processing: The separate and combined effects of scopolamine and nicotine on verbal free recall. *Psychopharmacology, 104,* 363–366.

Rustin, R. M., Kittel, T., Dramaix, M., Kornitzer, M., & de Backer, G. (1978). Smoking habits and psycho–socio–biological factors. *Journal of Psychosomatic Research, 22,* 89–99.

Sahakian, B., Jones, G., Levy, R., Gray, J. Warburton, D. M. (1989). The effects of nicotine on attention, information processing, and short–term memory in patients with dementia of the Alzheimer type. *British Journal of Psychiatry, 154,* 797–800.

Sahley, T. L., & Berntson, G. G. (1979). Antinociceptive effects of central and systemic administrations of nicotine in the rat. *Psychopharmacology, 65,* 279–283.

Salamone, J. D. (1991). Behavioral pharmacology of dopamine systems: A new synthesis. Principles of operation. In P. Willner & J. Scheel–Kruger (Eds.), *The mesolimbic dopamine system: From motivation to action* (pp. 599–613). Chichester, England: Wiley.

Salamone, J. D. (1992). Complex motor and sensorimoter functions of striatal and accumbens dopamine: Involvement in instrumental behavior processes. *Psychopharmacology, 107,* 160–174.

Saper, C. B. (1987). Diffuse cortical projection systems: Anatomical organization and role in cortical function. In F. Plum (Ed.), *Handbook of physiology: Sec. 1. The nervous system: Vol. 5. Higher functions of the brain* (Pt. 1, pp. 169–210). Bethesda, MD: American Physiological Society.

Scarr, S., & McCartney, K. (1983). How people make their own environments: A theory of genotype → environment effects. *Child Development, 54,* 424–435.

Schachter, S. (1971). *Emotion, obesity and crime.* New York: Academic Press.

Schachter, S. (1973). Nesbitt's paradox. In W. L. Dunn (Ed.), *Smoking behavior: Motives and incentives* (pp. 147–155). Washington, DC: V.H. Winston.

Schachter, S. (1978). Pharmacological and psychological determinants of smoking. *Annals of Internal Medicine, 88,* 104–114.

Schachter, S. (1979). Regulation, withdrawal, and nicotine addiction. In N. A. Krasnegor (Ed.), *Cigarette smoking as a dependence process* (pp. 123–133). Rockville, Maryland: National Institute on Drug Abuse.

Schachter, S. B. (1982). Recidivism and self–cure of smoking and obesity. *American Psychologist, 37,* 436–444.

Schachter, S., Silverstein, B., & Perlick, D. (1977). Psychological and pharmacological explanations of smoking under stress. *Journal of Experimental Psychology: General, 106,* 31–40.

Schachter, S., & Singer, J. E. (1962). Cognitive, social, and physiological determinants of emotional state. *Psychological Review, 69,* 379–399.

Schechter, M. D., & Rand, M. J. (1974). Effects of acute deprivation of smoking on aggression and hostility. *Psychopharmacologia, 35,* 19–28.

Scheel–Kruger, J., & Willner, P. (1991). The mesolimbic system: Principles of operation. In P. Willner & J. Scheel–Kruger (Eds.), *The mesolimbic dopamine system: From motivation to action* (pp. 559–597). Chichester, England: Wiley.

Scheibel, A. B. (1990). Dendritic correlates of higher cognitive function. In A. B. Scheibel & A. F. Wechsler (Eds.), *Neurobiology of higher cognitive function* (pp. 239–270). New York: Guilford Press.

Scherwitz, L., & Rugulies, R. (1992). Life–style and hostility. In H. S. Friedman (Ed.), *Hostility coping and health* (pp. 77–98). Washington DC: American Psychological Association.

Schneider, N. G. (1978). The effects of nicotine on learning and short–term memory (Doctoral dissertation, University of California, Los Angeles, 1979). *Dissertation Abstracts International, 39*(10), B.

Schneider, N. G., & Houston, J. P. (1970). Smoking and anxiety. *Psychological Reports, 26,* 941.

Schneider, N. G. (1994). Nicotine nasal spray. *Health Values, 18,* 10–14.

Schneider, N. G., & Jarvik, M. E. (1985). Nicotine gum vs. placebo gum: Comparisons of withdrawal symptoms and success rates. In J. Grabowski & S. M. Hall (Eds.), *Pharmacological adjuncts in smoking cessation (NIDA Research Monograph 53,* pp. 83–101). Rockville, MD: National Institute on Drug Abuse.

Schneier, F. R., & Siris, S. G. (1987). A review of psychoactive substance use and abuse in schizophrenia: Patterns of drug choice. *The Journal of Nervous and Mental Disease, 175,* 641–652.

Schoenborn, C., & Boyd, G. (1989). *Smoking and other tobacco use.* United States, 1987. Hyattville, Md: U.S. Depart. of Health and Human Services,, Public Health Service.

Schori, T. R., & Jones, B. W. (1974). Smoking and multiple–task performance. *Virginia Journal of Science, 25,* 147–151.

Schubert, D. S. P. (1965). Arousal seeking as a central factor in tobacco smoking among college students. *International Journal of Social Psychiatry, 11,* 221–225.

Schultze, M. J. (1982). Paradoxical aspects of cigarette smoking: physiological arousal, affect, and individual differences in body cue utilization (Doctoral dissertation, Clark University, 1982). *Dissertation Abstracts International, 42*(11), B.

Schuman, M., Gitlin, M. J., & Fairbanks, L. (1987). Sweets, chocolate, and atypical depressive traits. *The Journal of Nervous and Mental Disease, 175,* 491–495.

Seevers, M. H. (1968). Psychopharmacological elements of drug dependence. *Journal of the American Medical Association, 206,* 1263–1266.

Segal, B. S., Huba, G. J., & Singer, J. F. (1980). *Drugs, daydreaming, and personality: A study of college youth.* Hillsdale, NJ: Erlbaum.

Segal, M. R., & Block, D. A. (1989). A comparison of estimated proportional hazards models and regression trees. *Statistics in Medicine, 8,* 539–550.

Seligman, M., & Hager, J. (1972). *Biological boundaries of learning.* New York: Appleton–Century–Crofts.

Seltzer, C., & Oechsli, F. (1985). Psychosocial characteristics of adolescent smokers before they started smoking: Evidence of self–selection: A prospective study. *Journal of Chronic Diseases, 38,* 17–26.

Sem–Jacobsen, C. W. (1968). *Depth-electrographic stimulation of the human brain and behavior.* Springfield, IL: Thomas.

Seyler, L. E., Pomerleau, O. F., Fertig, J., Hunt, D., & Parker, K. (1986). Pituitary hormone response to cigarette smoking. *Pharmacology, Biochemistry, and Behavior, 24,* 159–162.

Shadel, W. G., & Mermelstein, R. J. (1993). Cigarette smoking under stress: The role of coping expectancies among smokers in a clinic–based smoking cessation program. *Health Psychology, 12,* 443–450.

Shapiro, E. (1994). Tobacco executives tell panel nicotine is not addiction. *The Wall Street Journal* (p. 4), April 15.

Sherwood, N., Kerr, J. S., & Hindmarch, I. (1990). No differences in the psychomotor response of heavy, light and non–smokers to the acute administration of nicotine. *Medical Science Research, 18,* 839–840.

Sherwood, N., Kerr, J. S., & Hindmarch, I. (1991). Effects of nicotine on short–term memory. In F. Adlkofer & K. Thurau (Eds.), *Effects of nicotine on biological systems* (pp. 531–535). Basel, Switzerland: Birkhauser Verlag.

Sherwood, N., Kerr, J. S., & Hindmarch, I. (1992). Psychomotor performance in smokers following single and repeated doses of nicotine gum. *Psychopharmacology, 108,* 432–436.

Shiffman, S. (1979). The tobacco withdrawal syndrome. In N. A. Krasnegor (Ed.), *Cigarette smoking as a dependence process* (NIDA Research Monograph 23, pp. 153–184). Rockville, MD: *Public Health Service.*

Shiffman, S. (1982). Relapse following smoking cessation: A situational analysis. *Journal of Consulting and Clinical Psychology, 50,* 71–86.

Shiffman, S. A (1986). Cluster analytic classification of smoking relapse episodes. *Addictive Behaviors, 11,* 295–307.

Shiffman, S. (1989). Tobacco "chippers": individual differences in tobacco dependence. *Psychopharmacology, 97,* 535–538.

Shiffman, S. (1991, March). *Chippers: Characteristics of non–dependent cigarette smokers.* Symposium conducted at the annual meeting of the Society of Behavioral Medicine, Washington, DC.

Shiffman, S. (1993a). Assessing smoking patterns and motives. *Journal of Consulting and Clinical Psychology, 61,* 732–742.

Shiffman, S. (1993b). Smoking cessation treatment: Any progress? *Journal of Consulting and Clinical Psychology, 61,* 718–722.

Shiffman, S., Fischer, L. B., Zettler–Segal, M., & Benowitz, N. L. (1990). Nicotine exposure among nondependent smokers. *Archives of General Psychiatry, 47,* 333–336.

Shiffman, S., & Jarvik, M. E. (1984). Cigarette smoking, physiological arousal, and emotional response: Nesbitt's paradox re–examined. *Addictive Behaviors, 9,* 95–98.

Shiffman, S., Paty, J., Kassel, J., & Gnys, M. (1993). *Smoking typology profiles of chippers and regular smokers.* Unpublished manuscript, University of Pittsburgh.

Shiffman, S., & Prange, M. (1988). Self–reported and self–monitored smoking patterns. *Addictive Behaviors, 13,* 201–204.

Shiffman, S., Read, L., Maltese, J., Rapkin, D., & Jarvik, M. E. (1985). Preventing relapse in ex–smokers: A self–management approach. In G. A. Marlatt & J. R. Gordon (Eds.), *Relapse prevention: Maintenance strategies in the treatment of addictive behaviors* (pp. 472–520). New York: Guilford Press.

Shiffman, S., Reynolds, W. A., Maurer, A., & Quick, D. (1992, March). *An experimental test of Horn's Reasons for Smoking Scale.* Poster presented at the 13th annual meeting of the Society of Behavioral Medicine, New York, NY.

Shiffman, S., & Wills, T. A. (Eds.). (1985). *Coping and substance use.* New York: Academic Press.

Shiffman, S., Zettler–Segal, M., Kassel, J., Paty, J., Benowitz, N. E., & O'Brien, G. (1992). Nicotine elimination and tolerance in non–dependent cigarette smokers. *Psychopharmacology, 109,* 449–456.

Shimohama, S., Taniguchi, T., Fujiwara, M., & Kameyama, M. (1985). Biochemical characterization of the nicotineic cholinergic receptors in human brain: Binding of (–)[3H]nicotine. *Journal of Neurochemistry, 45,* 604–610.

Shoaib, M., Stolerman, I. P., & Kumar, R. C. (1994). Nicotine–induced place preferences following prior nicotine exposure in rats. *Psychopharmacology, 113,* 445–452.

Sieber, M. F., & Angst, J. (1990). Alcohol, tobacco and cannabis: 12–year longitudinal associations with antecedent social context and personality. *Drug and Alcohol Dependence, 25,* 281–292.

Silverman, A. P. (1971). Behaviour of rats given a "smoking dose" of nicotine. *Animal Behaviour, 19,* 67–74.

Silverman, K., Mumford, G. K., & Griffiths, R. R. (1994). Enhancing caffeine reinforcement by behavioral requirements following drug ingestion. *Psychopharmacology, 114,* 424–432.

Silverstein, B. (1982). Cigarette smoking, nicotine addiction, and relaxation. *Journal of Personality and Social Psychology, 42,* 946–950.

Silverstein, B., Feld, S., & Kozlowski, L. T. (1980). The availability of low–nicotine cigarettes as a cause of cigarette smoking among teenage females. *Journal of Health and Social Behavior, 21,* 383–388.

Silverstein, B., Kelly, E., Swan, J., & Kozlowski, L. T. (1982). Physiological predisposition toward becoming a cigarette smoker: Experimental evidence for a sex difference. *Addictive Behaviors, 7,* 83–86.

Silverton, L. (1991). *The Problem Behavior Inventory.* Los Angeles: Western Psychological Services.

Singer, M. T. (1974). Presidential address—Engagement–involvement: A central phenomenon in psychophysiological research. *Psychosomatic Medicine, 36,* 1–17.

Sipprelle, R. C., Ascough, J. C., Detrio, D. M., & Horst, P. A. (1977). Neuroticism, extroversion, and response to stress. *Behavior Research and Therapy, 15,* 411–418.

Sloss, E. M., & Frerichs, R. R. (1983). Smoking and menstrual disorders. *International Journal of Epidemiology, 12,* 107–109.

Smith, B. D., Wilson, R. J., & Jones, B. E. (1983). Extraversion and multiple levels of caffeine–induced arousal: Effects of overhabituation and dishabituation. *Psychophysiology, 20,* 29–34.

Smith, G. M. (1970). Personality and smoking: A review of the empirical literature. In W. A. Hunt (Ed.), *Learning mechanisms in smoking* (pp. 42–61). Chicago: Aldine.

Smith, P., & Lombardo, T. (1986, November). *Effect of abstinence from smoking on motor activity.* Paper presented at the Annual Meeting of the Association for the Advancement of Behavior Therapy, Chicago.

Smith, D. L., Tong, J. E., & Leigh, G. (1977). Combined effects of tobacco and caffeine on the components of choice reaction time, heart rate, and hand steadiness. *Perceptual and Motor Skills, 45,* 635–639.

Snyder, F. R., & Henningfield, J. E. (1989). Effects of nicotine administration following 12 h of tobacco deprivation: Assessment on computerized performance tasks. *Psychopharmacology, 97,* 17–22.

Snyder, S. H. (1973). Amphetamine psychosis: A "model" schizophrenia mediated by catecholamines. *American Journal of Psychiatry, 130,* 60–61.

Snyder, S., & Pitts, W. M., Jr. (1984). Electroencephalograpy of DSM–III borderline personality disorder. *Acta Psychiatrica Scandinavica, 69,* 129–134.

Solomon, R., & Corbit, J. (1973). An opponent–process theory of motivation: II. Cigarette addiction. *Journal of Abnormal Psychology, 81,* 158–171.

Solomon, R. L., & Corbit, J. D. (1974). An opponent–process theory of motivation: I. Temporal dynamics of affect. *Psychological Review, 81,* 119–145.

Spielberger, C. D. (1986). Psychological determinants of smoking behavior. In R.D. Tollison (Ed.), *Smoking and society: Toward a more balanced assessment* (pp. 89–134). Lexington, MA: D.C. Heath.

Spielberger, C. D., & Jacobs, G. A. (1982). Personality and smoking behavior. *Journal of Personality Assessment, 46,* 396–403.

Spielberger, C. D., Jacobs, G. A., Crane, R. S., & Russell, S. F. (1983). On the relation between family smoking habits and the smoking behavior of college students. *International Review of Applied Psychology, 32,* 53–69.

Spitzer, R. L., Williams, J. B. W., Gibbon, M., & First, M. D. (1990). *Structured clinical interview for DSM–III–R: Patient edition* (SCID–P, Version 1.0). Washington, DC: American Psychiatric Press.

Spring, B., Chiodo, J., & Bowen, D. J. (1987). Carbohydrates, tryptophan, and behavior: A methodological review. *Psychological Bulletin, 102,* 234–256.

Spring, B., Chiodo, J., Harden, M., Bourgeois, M. J., Mason, J. D., & Lutherer, L. (1989). Psychobiological effects of carbohydrates. *Journal of Clinical Psychiatry, 50(5, Suppl.),* 27–34.

Spring, B., Pingitore, R., Kessler, K., Mahableshwarker, A., Bruckner, E., Kohlbeck, & Braun, J. (1993). Fluoxetine prevents withdrawal dysphoria but not anticipatory anxiety about quitting smoking. *Annals of Behavioral Medicine, 15,* 129.

Spring, B., Wurtman, J., Gleason, R., Wurtman, R., & Kessler, K. (1991). Weight gain and withdrawal symptoms after smoking cessation: A preventive intervention using d–fenfluramine. *Health Psychology, 10,* 216–223.

Srivastava, E. D., Russell, M. A. H., Feyerabend, C., Masterson, J. G., & Rhodes, J. (1991). Sensitivity and tolerance to nicotine in smokers and nonsmokers. *Psychopharmacology, 105,* 63–68.

Srole, L. (1968). Social and psychological factors in smoking behavior: The Midtown Manhattan Study. *Bulletin of the New York Academy of Medicine, 44,* 1502–1513.

Staats, A. W., & Eifert, G. H. (1990). The paradigmatic behaviorism theory of emotions: Basis for unification. *Clinical Psychology Review, 10,* 539–566.

Stanaway, R. G., & Watson, D. W. (1981). Smoking and personality: A factorial study. *British Journal of Clinical Psychology, 20,* 213–214.

Starkman, M. N., Schteingart, D. E., & Schork, M. A. (1986). Cushing's syndrome after treatment: Changes in cortisol and ACTH levels, and amelioration of the depressive syndrome. *Psychiatry Research, 19,* 177–188.

Starr, C. (1969, Sept 19). Social benefits versus technological risk. *Science, 165,* 1232–1238.

Steele, C. M., & Josephs, R. A. (1988). Drinking your troubles away: II. An attention-allocation model of alcohol's effects on psychological stress. *Journal of Abnormal Psychology, 97,* 196–205.

Steele, C. M., & Josephs, R. A. (1990). Alcohol myopia: Its prized and dangerous effects. *American Psychologist, 45,* 921–933.

Stefanis, C. N., & Kokkevi, A. (1986). Depression and drug use. *Psychopathology, 19* (Suppl 2), 124–131.

Stein, J. A., Newcomb, M. D., & Bentler, P. M. (1987). Personality and drug use: Reciprocal effects across four years. *Personality and Individual Differences, 8,* 419–430.

Steinberg, J. L., & Cherek, D. R.. (1989). Menstrual cycle and smoking behavior. *Addictive Behaviors, 14,* 173–179.

Stemmler, G., & Meinhardt, E. (1990). Personality, situation and physiological arousability. *Personality and Individual Differences, 11,* 293–308.

Stepney, R. (1980). Cigars and Sigmund. *World Medicine, 15,* 71–72.

Stepney, R. (1982). Human smoking behavior and the development of dependence on tobacco smoking. *Pharmacology and Therapeutics, 15,* 183–206.

Sternberg, R. J., & Gardner, M. K. (1982). A componential interpretation of the general factor in human intelligence. In H. J. Eysenck (Ed.), *A model for intelligence* (pp. 231–254). New York: Springer–Verlag.

Stitzer, M. L., & Gross, J. (1988). Smoking relapse: The role of pharmacological and behavioral factors. In O. F. Pomerleau & C. S. Pomerleau (Eds.), *Nicotine replacement: A critical evaluation* (pp. 163–184). New York: Alan Liss.

Stolerman, I. P. (1990). Behavioural pharmacology of nicotine in animals. In S. Wonnacott, M. A. H. Russell, & I. P. Stolerman (Eds.), *Nicotine psychopharmacology: Molecular, cellular, and behavioural aspects* (pp. 278–306). Oxford, England: Oxford University Press.

Stolerman, I. P. (1991). Behavioural pharmacology of nicotine: Multiple mechanisms. *British Journal of Addiction, 86,* 533–536.

Stoney, C. M., Langer, A. W., & Gelling, P. D. (1986). The effects of menstrual cycle phase on cardiovascular and pulmonary responses to behavioral and exercise stress. *Psychophysiology, 23,* 393–402.

Strelau, J., & Eysenck, H. J. (Eds.). (1987). *Personality dimensions and arousal.* New York: Plenum.

Stuss, D. T., Gow, C. A., & Hetherington, C. R. (1992). "No longer Gage": Frontal lobe dysfunction and emotional changes. *Journal of Consulting and Clinical Psychology, 60,* 349–359.

Suedfeld, P., & Best, J. A. (1977). Satiation and sensory deprivation combined in smoking therapy: Some case studies and unexpected side effects. *International Journal of the Addictions, 12,* 337–359.

Suedfeld, P., & Ikard, F. F. (1974). Use of sensory deprivation in facilitating the reduction of cigarette smoking. *Journal of Consulting and Clinical Psychology, 42,* 888–895.

Sult, S. C., & Moss, R. A. (1986). The effects of cigarette smoking on the perception of electrical stimulation and cold pressor pain. *Addictive Behaviors, 11,* 447–451.

Surawy, C., & Cox, T. (1987). Smoking under natural conditions: A diary study. *Personality and Individual Differences, 8,* 33–41.

Sutherland, G., Russell, M. A. H., Stapleton, J. A., & Feyerabend, C. (1993). Glycerol particle cigarettes: A less harmful option for chronic smokers. *Thorax, 48,* 385–387.

Sutton, S. R. (1991). Great expectations: Some suggestions for applying the balanced placebo design to nicotine and smoking. *British Journal of Addiction, 86,* 659–662.

Svikis, D. S., Hatsukami, D. K., Hughes, J. R., Carroll, K. M., & Pickens, R. W. (1986). Sex differences in tobacco withdrawal syndrome. *Addictive Behaviors, 11,* 459–462.

Swan, G. E., Cardon, L. R., & Carmelli, D. (1994). The consumption of tobacco, alcohol, and caffeine in male twins: A multivariate genetic analysis. *Annals of Behavioral Medicine, 16,* S069.

Swan, G. E., Ward, M. M., & Jack, L. (1991, March). *The Fagerstrom Tolerance Questionnaire: A psychometric analysis.* Paper presented at the annual meeting of the Society of Behavioral Medicine, Washington, DC.

Swan, G. E., Ward, M. M., Jack, L. M., & Javitz, H. S. (1993). Cardiovascular reactivity as a predictors of relapse in male and female smokers. *Health Psychology, 12*, 451–458.

Swan, G. E., & Denk, C. E. (1987). Dynamic models for the maintenance of smoking cessation: Event history analysis of late relapse. *Journal of Behavioral Medicine, 10*, 527–553.

Swerdlow, N. R., & Koob, G. F. (1987). Dopamine, schizophrenia, mania, and depression: Toward a unified hypothesis of cortico–striato–pallido–thalamic function. *Behavioral and Brain Sciences, 10*, 197–245.

Tagliacozzo, R., & Vaughn, S. (1982). Stress and smoking in hospital nurses. *American Journal of Public Health, 72*, 441–448.

Tarter, R. E., & Edwards, K. L. (1988). Vulnerability to alcohol and drug abuse: A behavior–genetic view. In S. Peele (Ed.), *Visions of addiction: Major contemporary perspectives on addiction and alcoholism* (pp. 67–83). Lexington, MA: D.C. Heath.

Tate, J. C., & Stanton, A. L. (1990). Assessment of the validity of the Reasons for Smoking Scale. *Addictive Behaviors, 15*, 129–135.

Tellegen, A., & Waller, N. G. (in press). Exploring personality through test constructions: Development of the Multidimensional Personality Questionnaire. In S. R. Briggs & J. M. Checks (Eds.), *Personality measures: Development and evaluation* (Vol. 1). Greenwich, CT: JAI Press.

Teyler, T. J., & DiScenna, P. (1986). The hippocampal memory indexing theory. *Behavioral Neuroscience, 100*, 147–154.

Thayer, R. E. (1989). *The biopsychology of mood and arousal.* New York: Oxford University Press.

Thayer, R. E., Peters, D. P.. III, Takahashi, P. J., & Birkhead–Flight, A. M. (1993). Mood and behavior (smoking and sugar snacking) following moderate exercise: A partial test of self–regulation theory. *Personality and Individual Differences, 14*, 97–104.

Thierry, A. M., Tassin, J. P., Blanc, G., & Glowinski, J. (1976). Selective activation of mesocortical dopaminergic system by stress. *Nature, 263*, 242–244.

Thomas, C. B. (1960). Characteristics of smokers compared with nonsmokers in a population of healthy, young adults, including observations on family history, blood pressure, heart rate, body weight, cholesterol and certain psychological traits. *Annals of Internal Medicine, 53*, 697.

Thomas, C. B. (1973). The relationship of smoking and habits of nervous tension. In W. L. Dunn (Ed.), *Smoking behavior: Motives and incentives* (pp. 157–169). Washington, DC: V. H. Winston.

Thompson, R. F. (1985). *The brain: An introduction to neuroscience.* New York: W. H. Freeman.

Thorne, A. (1987). The press of personality: A study of conversations between introverts and extraverts. *Journal of Personality and Social Psychology, 53*, 718–726.

Thorpe, S. J., Rolls, E. T., & Maddison, S. (1983). The orbitofrontal cortex: Neuronal activity in the behaving monkey. *Experimental Brain Research, 49*, 93–115.

Tiffany, S. T. (1992). A critique of contemporary urge and craving research: Methodological, psychometric and theoretical issues. *Advances in Behaviour Research and Therapy, 14*, 123–139.

Tiffany, S. T., & Drobes, D. J. (1991). The development and initial validation of a questionnaire on smoking urges. *British Journal of Addiction, 86*, 1467–1476.

Tiller, J. W. G., Maguire, K. P., Schweitzer, I., Biddle, N., Campbell, D. G., Outch, K., & Davies, B. M. (1988). The dexamethasone suppression test: A study in normal population. *Psychoneuroendocrinology, 13,* 377–384.

Tilley, S. (1987). Alcohol, other drugs and tobacco use and anxiolytic effectiveness: A comparison of anxious patients and psychiatric nurses. *British Journal of Psychiatry, 151,* 389–392.

Toan, I. L., & Schultz, W. (1985). Responses of rat pallidum cells to cortex stimulation and effects of altered dopaminergic activity. *Neuroscience, 15,* 683–694.

Tomarken, A., Davidson, R. J., Wheeler, R. E., & Doss, R. C. (1992). Individual differences in anterior brain asymmetry and fundamental dimensions of emotion. *Journal of Personality and Social Psychology, 62,* 676–687.

Tomkins, S. S. (1962). *Affect, imagery, consciousness: Vol. 1. The positive affects.* New York: Springer.

Tomkins, S. S. (1966). Psychological model of smoking behavior. *American Journal of Public Health, 56*(suppl.), 17–20.

Tomkins, S. S. (1968). A modified model of smoking behavior. In E. F. Borgatta & R. Evans (Eds.), *Smoking, health and behavior* (pp. 165–186). Chicago: Aldine.

Tomkins, S. S. (1981). The role of facial response in the experience of emotion: A reply to Tourangeau and Ellsworth. *Journal of Personality and Social Psychology, 40,* 355–357.

Tong, J. E., Knott, V. J., McGraw, D. J., & Leigh, G. (1974). Alcohol, visual discrimination and heart rate. *Quarterly Journal of Studies of Alcohol, 35,* 1003–1022.

Transdermal Nicotine Study Group (1991). Transermal nicotine for smoking cessation: Six month results from two multicenter controlled clinical trials. *JAMA, 266,* 3133–3138.

Tucker, D. M. (1991). Developing emotions and cortical networks. In M. Gunnar & C. Nelson (Eds.), *Minnesota Symposium on child psychology: Vol. 24. Developmental behavioral neuroscience* (pp. 74–128). Hillsdale, NJ: Erlbaum.

Tucker, D. M., & Williamson, P. A. (1984). Asymmetric neural control systems in human self–regulation. *Psychological Review, 91,* 185–215.

Uhl, G. R., Persico, A. M., & Smith, S. S. (1992). Current excitement with D2 dopamine receptor gene alleles in substance abuse. *Archives of General Psychiatry, 49,* 157–160.

U.S. Department of Health and Human Services. (1988). *The health consequences of smoking: Nicotine addiction. A report from the U. S. Surgeon General.* Washington, DC: U. S. Government Printing Office.

U.S. Department of Health and Human Services. (1989). *Reducing the health consequences of smoking: 25 years of progress. A report from the U.S. Surgeon General, Office of Smoking and Health* (DHHS Publication No. [CDC] 89–8411). Washington, DC: U.S. Government Printing Office.

U. S. Public Health Service. (1964). *Smoking and health: Report of the Advisory Committee to the Surgeon General of the Public Health Service* (PHS Publication No. 1103). U. S. Department of Health Education and Welfare, Public Health Service, Centers for Disease Control. Washington, DC: U.S. Government Printing Office.

Valenstein, E. S. (1973). *Brain control: A critical examination of brain stimulation and psychosurgery.* New York: Wiley.

Vandenberg, S. G., Singer, S. M., & Pauls, D. L. (1986). *The heredity of behavior disorders in adults and children.* New York: Plenum.

Velicer, W. F., DiClemente, C. C., Prochaska, J. O., & Brandenburg, N. (1985). A decisional balance measure for predicting smoking cessation. *Journal of Personality and Social Psychology, 48,* 1279–1289.

Vogel, W., Broverman, D. M., & Klaiber, E. L. (1971, April 23). EEG responses in regularly menstruating women and in amenorrheic women treated with ovarian hormones. *Science, 172,* 388–391.

Vogel, W., Broverman, D., & Klaiber, E. L. (1977). Electroencephalographic responses to photic stimulations in habitual smokers and nonsmokers. *Journal of Comparative and Physiological Psychology, 91,* 418–422.

von Knorring, L., & Oreland, L. (1985). Personality traits and platelet monamine oxidase in tobacco smokers. *Psychological Medicine, 15,* 327–334.

Waal–Manning, H. J., & de Hammel, F. A. (1978). Smoking habit and psychometric scores: A community study. *New Zealand Medical Journal, 88,* 188–191.

Waldron, I., Bratelli, G., Carriker, C., Sung, W.–C., Vogeli, C., & Waldman, E. (1988). Gender differences in tobacco use in Asia, Africa, and Latin America. *Social Science Medicine, 27,* 1269–1275.

Waller, D., & Levander, S. (1980). Smoking and vigilance: the effects of tobacco on CFF as related to personality and smoking habits. *Psychopharmacology, 70,* 131–136.

Waller, D., Schalling, D., Levander, S., & Erdman, G. (1983). Smoking, pain tolerance, and physiological activation. *Psychopharmacology,79,* 193–198.

Wang, M. Q., Fitzhugh, E. C., Westerfield, R. C., & Eddy, J. M. (1994). Predicting smoking status by symptoms of depression for U. S. adolescents. *Psychological Reports, 75* 911–914.

Warburton, D. M. (1988). The puzzle of nicotine use. In M. Lader (Ed.), *The psychopharmacology of addiction* (pp. 27–49). Oxford, England: Oxford University Press.

Warburton, D. M. (1989). Is nicotine use an addiction? *The Psychologist: Bulletin of the British Psychological Society, 4,* 166–170.

Warburton, D. M. (1990). Heroin, cocaine and now nicotine. In D. M. Warburton (Ed.), *Addiction controversies* (pp. 21–35). London: Harwood Academic Publishers.

Warburton, D. M. (1992). Nicotine as a cognitive enhancer. *Progress in Neuro–Psychopharmacology and Biological Psychiatry, 16,* 181–191.

Warburton, D. M., Revell, A., & Walters, A. C. (1988). In M. J. Rand & K. Thurau (Eds.), *The pharmacology of nicotine* (pp. 359–373). Oxford, England: IRL Press.

Warburton, D. M., Rusted, J. M., & Fowler, J. (1992). Comparison of the attentional and consolidation hypotheses for the facilitation of memory by nicotine. *Psychopharmacology, 108,* 443–447.

Warburton, D. M., Rusted, J. M., & Muller, C. (1992). Patterns of facilitation of memory by nicotine. *Behavioural Pharmacology, 3,* 375–378.

Warburton, D. M., & Walters, A. C. (1989). Attentional processing. In T. Ney & A. Gale (Eds.), *Smoking and human behavior* (pp. 223–237). New York: Wiley.

Warburton, D. M., & Wesnes, K. (1978). Individual differences in smoking and attentional performance. In R. E. Thornton (Ed.), *Smoking behaviour: Physiological and psychological influences* (pp. 19–43). Edinburgh, Scotland: Churchill Livingstone.

Warburton, D. M., Wesnes, K., & Revell, A. (1983). Personality factors in self–medication by smoking. In W. Janke (Ed.), Response variability to psychotropic drugs (pp. 167–184). New York: Pergamon Press.

Warburton, D. M., Wesnes, K., Shergold, K., & James, M. (1986). Facilitation of learning and state dependence with nicotine. *Psychopharmacology, 89,* 55–59.

Ward, M. M., Swan, G. E., & Jack, L. M. (1994). Subjective complaints after smoking cessation: Transient vs. offset effects. *Annals of Behavioral Medicine, 16,* S043.

Ward, N. G., & Doerr, H. O. (1986). Skin conductance: A potentially sensitive and specific marker for depression. *The Journal of Nervous and Mental Disease, 174,* 553–559.

Warwick, K. M., & Eysenck, H. J. (1963). The effects of smoking on CFF threshold. *Life Sciences, 4,* 219–225.

Waters, W. E. (1971). Smoking and neuroticism. *British Journal of Preventive and Social Medicine, 25,* 162–164.

Watson, D., Clark, L. A., & Harkness, A. (1994). Structures of personality and their relevance to the study of psychopathology. *Journal of Abnormal Psychology, 97,* 346–353.

Watson, D., & Tellegen, A. (1985). Toward a consensual structure of mood. *Psychological Bulletin, 98,* 219–235.

Webster, D. D. (1964). The dynamic quantification of spasticity with automated integrals of passive motion resistance. *Clinical Pharmacology and Therapeutics, 5,* 900–908.

Wenusch, A., & Schöller, R. (1936). Mber den Einfluss des Rauchens auf die Reizschwelle des Drucksinnes [Concerning the influence of smoking on the threshold of stimulation of the sense of pressure]. *Medizinische Klinik, 32,* 356–358.

Wesnes, K., & Warburton, D. M. (1978). The effects of cigarette smoking and nicotine tablets upon human attention. In R. E. Thornton (Ed.), *Smoking behaviour: Physiological and psychological influences* (pp. 131–147). Edinburgh, Scotland: Churchill Livingstone.

Wesnes, K., & Warburton, D. M. (1983). Smoking, nicotine and human performance. *Pharmacology and Therapeutics, 21,* 189–208.

Wesnes, K., & Warburton, D. M. (1984). Effects of scopolamine and nicotine on human rapid information processing performance. *Psychopharmacology, 82,* 147–150.

Wesnes, K., Warburton, D. M., & Matz, B. (1983). Effects of nicotine on stimulus sensitivity and response bias in a visual vigilance task. *Neuropsychobiology, 9,* 41–44.

West, R., & Grunberg, N. E. (1991). Editorial: Implications of tobacco use as an addiction. *British Journal of Addiction, 86,* 485–488.

West, R. J., & Hack, S. (1991). Effects of cigarettes on memory search and subjective ratings. *Pharmacology, Biochemistry, and Behavior, 38,* 281–286.

West, R. J., Hajek, P., & Belcher, M. (1987). Time course of cigarette withdrawal symptoms during four weeks of treatment with nicotine chewing gum. *Addictive Behaviors, 12,* 199–203.

West, R., Hajek, P., & McNeill, A. (1991). Effect of buspirone on cigarette withdrawal symptoms and short–term abstinence rates in a smokers clinic. *Psychopharmacology, 104,* 91–96.

West, R. J., & Jarvis, M. J. (1986). Effects of nicotine on finger tapping rate in non–smokers. *Pharmacology, Biochemistry, and Behavior, 25,* 727–731.

West, R. J., Jarvis, M. J., Russell, M. A. H., Carruthers, M. E., & Feyerabend, C. (1984). Effect of nicotine replacement on the cigarette withdrawal syndrome. *British Journal of Addiction, 79,* 215–219.

West, R. J., & Russell, M. A. H. (1985). Pre–abstinence smoke intake and smoking motivation as predictors of severity of cigarette withdrawal symptoms. *Psychopharmacology, 87,* 334–336.

West, R. J., & Russell, M. A. H. (1987). Cardiovascular and subjective effects of smoking before and after 24 hr of abstinence from cigarettes. *Psychopharmacology, 92*, 118–121.

West, R. J., & Russell, M. A. H. (1988). Loss of acute nicotine tolerance and severity of cigarette withdrawal. *Psychopharmacology, 94*, 563–565.

West, R. J., Russell, M. A. H., Jarvis, M. J., & Feyerabend, C. (1984). Does switching to an ultra–low nicotine cigarette induce nicotine withdrawal effects? *Psychopharmacology, 84*, 120–123.

West, R. J., Russell, M. A. H., Jarvis, M. J., Pizzey, T., & Kadam, B. (1984). Urinary adrenaline concentrations during 10 days of smoking abstinence. *Psychopharmacology, 84*, 141–142.

Weybrew, B. B., & Stark, J. E. (1967). *Psychological and physiological changes associated with deprivation from smoking* (U.S. Naval Submarine Medical Center, Report No. 490). Washington, DC: U.S. Navy.

White, P. O. (1981). Some major components in general intelligence. In H. J. Eysenck (Ed.), *A model for intelligence* (pp. 44–90). New York: Springer–Verlag.

Widiger, T. A., & Frances, A. J. (1994). Toward a dimension model of the personality disorders. In P. T. Costa & T. A. Widiger (Eds.), *Personality disorders and the five–factor model of personality* (pp. 19–39). Washington, DC: American Psychological Association.

Wijatkowski, S., Forgays, D. G., Wrzesniewski, K., & Gorski, T. (1990). Smoking behavior and personality characteristics in Polish adolescents. *The International Journal of the Addictions, 25*, 363–373.

Williams, D. G. (1979). Different cigarette-smoker classification factors and subjective state in acute abstinence. *Psychopharmacology, 64*, 231–235.

Williams, D. G. (1980). Effects of cigarette smoking on immediate memory and performance in different kinds of smokers. *British Journal of Psychology, 71*, 83–90.

Williams, D. G., Tata, P. R., & Miskella, J. (1984). Different "types" of cigarette smokers received similar effects from smoking. *Addictive Behaviors, 9*, 207–210.

Williams, S. G., Hudson, A., & Redd, C. (1982). Cigarette smoking, manifest anxiety and somatic symptoms. *Addictive Behaviors, 7*, 427–428.

Williamson, D. F., Madans, J., Anda, R. F., Kleinman, J. C., Giovino, G. A., & Byers. (1991). Smoking cessation and severity of weight gain in a national cohort. *New England Journal of Medicine, 324*, 739–745.

Wills, T. A. (1985). Stress, coping, and tobacco and alcohol use in early adolescence. In S. Shiffman & T. A. Wills (Eds.), *Coping and substance use* (pp. 67–94). Orlando, FL: Academic Press.

Willner, P. (1985). *Depression: A psychobiological synthesis.* New York: Wiley.

Willner, P., & Scheel–Kruger, J. (Eds.), (1991). *The mesolimbic dopamine system: From motivation to action.* New York: Wiley.

Wilson, D. J., & Doolabh, A. (1992). Reliability, factorial validity and equivalence of several forms of the Eysenck Personality Inventory/Questionnaire in Zimbabwe. *Personality and Individual Differences, 13*, 637–643.

Winternitz, J. N., & Quillen, D. (1977). Acute hormonal responses to cigarette smoking. *Journal of Clinical Pharmacology, 17*, 389–397.

Wise, R. A. (1988). The neurobiology of craving: Implications for the understanding and treatment of addiction. *Journal of Abnormal Psychology, 97*, 118–132.

Wise, R. A. (1989). The brain and reward. In J. M. Liebman & S. J. Cooper (Eds.), *The neuropharmacological basis of reward* (pp. 377–424). Oxford, England: Oxford University Press.

Wise, R. A., & Bozarth, M. A. (1987). A psychomotor stimulant theory of addiction. *Psychological Review, 94*, 469–492.

Witt, E. M., Kaelin, J. A., & Stoner, S. B. (1988). Smoking behavior and anger. *Psychological Reports, 63*, 117–118.

Wolkowitz, O. M., Breier, A., Doran, A., Rubinow, D., Berrettini,W., Coppola, R., Gold, P., & Pickar, D. (1988). Prednisone–induced behavioral and biological changes in medically healthy volunteers. *Psychopharmacology Bulletin, 24*, 492–494.

Wolkowitz, O. M., Reus, V. I., Weingartner, H., Thompson, K., Brier, A., Doran, A., Rubinow, D., & Pickar, D. (1990). Cognitive effects of corticosteroids. *American Journal of Psychiatry, 147*, 1297–1303.

Woodson, P. P., Buzzi, R., Nil, R., & Battig, K. (1986). Effects of smoking on vegetative reactivity to noise in women. *Psychophysiology, 23*, 272–282.

Wurtman, R. J., & Wurtman, J. J. (1983). Nutrients, neurotransmitters, and the control of food intake. *Psychiatric Annals,* 13, 854–857.

Yeh, J., & Barbieri, R. L. (1989). Twenty–four–hour urinary–free cortisol in premenopausal cigarette smokers and nonsmokers. *Fertility and Sterility, 52*, 1067–1069.

Young, E. A., Haskett, R. F., Murphy–Weinberg, V., Watson, S. J., & Akil, H. (1991). Loss of glucocorticoid fast feedback in depression. *Archives of General Psychiatry, 48*, 693–699.

Young, P. T. (1975). *Understanding your feelings and emotions.* Englewood Cliffs, NJ: Prentice–Hall.

Zacny, J. P., & De Wit, H. (1990). Effects of 24–hour fast on cigarette smoking in humans. *British Journal of Addiction, 85*, 555–560.

Zajonc, R. B. (1984). On the primacy of affect. *American Psychologist, 39*, 117–123.

Zeidenberg, P., Jaffe, J. H., Kanzler, M., Levitt, M. D., Langone, J. J., & Van Vunakis, H. (1977). Nicotine: Cotinine levels in blood during cessation of smoking. *Comprehensive Psychiatry, 18*, 93–101.

Zelman, D. C., Brandon, T. H., Jorenby, D. E., & Baker, T. B. (1992). Measures of affect and nicotine dependence predict differential response to smoking cessation treatments. *Journal of Consulting and Clinical Psychology, 60*, 943–952.88

Zillmann, D. (1979). *Hostility and aggression.* Hillsdale, NJ: Erlbaum.

Zuckerman, M. (1979). *Sensation seeking: Beyond the optimal level of arousal.* Hillsdale, NJ: Erlbaum.

Zuckerman, M. (1990). Still another failure of arousal theory: A critique of "Personality, situation and physiolgical arousability" by G. Gtemmler and E. Meinhardt. *Personality and Individual Differences, 11*, 309–312.

Zuckerman, M. (1991). *Psychobiology of personality.* New York: Cambridge University Press.

Zuckerman, M. (1992). What is a basic factor and which factors are basic? Turtles all the way down. *Personality and Individual Differences, 13*, 675–681.

Zuckerman, M., Ball, S., & Black, J. (1990). Influences of sensation seeking, gender, risk appraisal, and situational motivation on smoking. *Addictive Behaviors, 15*, 209–220.

Zuckerman, M., Kuhlman, D. M., & Camac, C. (1988). What lies beyond E and N? Factor analyses of scales believed to measure basic dimensions of personality. *Journal of Personality and Social Psychology, 54,* 96–107.

Zuckerman, M., Kuhlman, D., M., Thornquist, M., & Kiers, H. (1991). Five (or three) robust questionnaire scale factors of personality without culture. *Personality and Individual Differences, 12,* 929–941.

Index